D0900886

PETER GRILL
AND THE PHILOSOPHER'S TIME

Story & Art by
DAISUKE HIYAMA

06

CONTENTS

Previously, on *Peter Grill*...

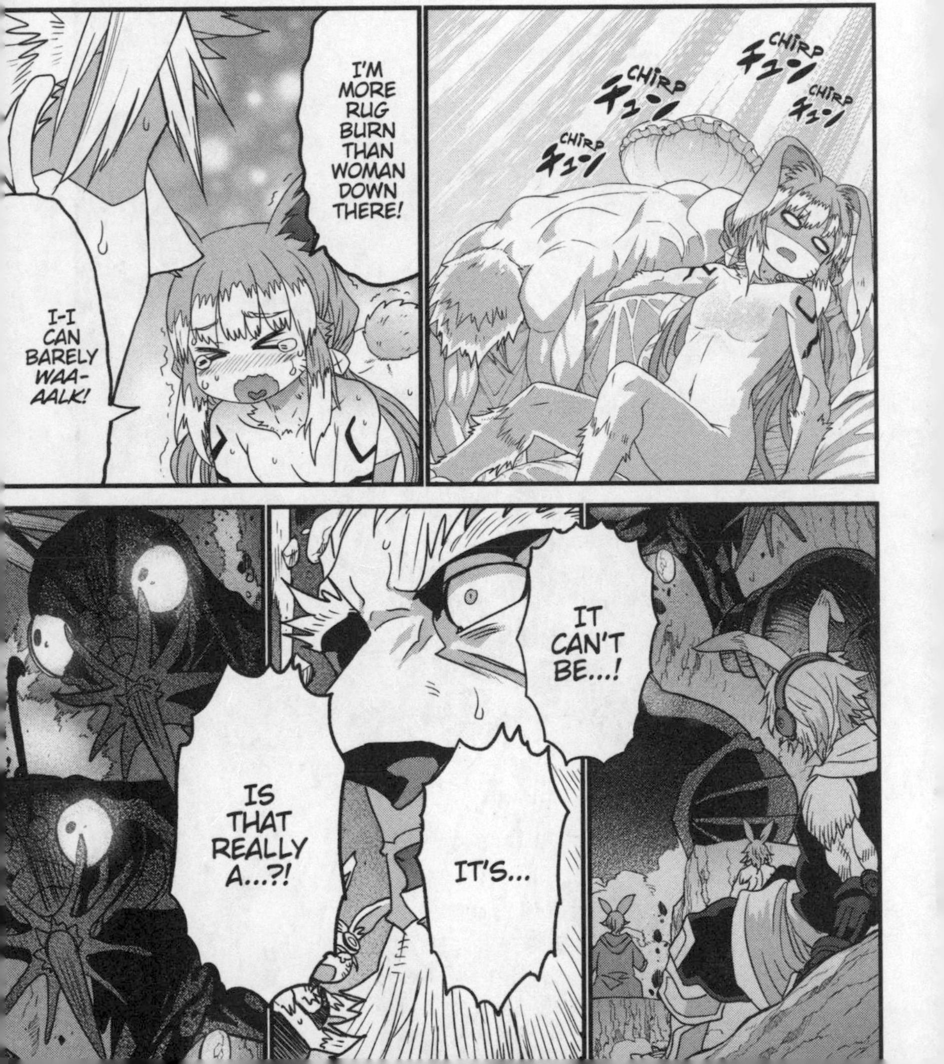
CHIRP
CHIRP
CHIRP
CHIRP
I'M MORE RUG BURN THAN WOMAN DOWN THERE!
I-I CAN BARELY WAA-AALK!
IT CAN'T BE...!
IT'S...
IS THAT REALLY A...?!

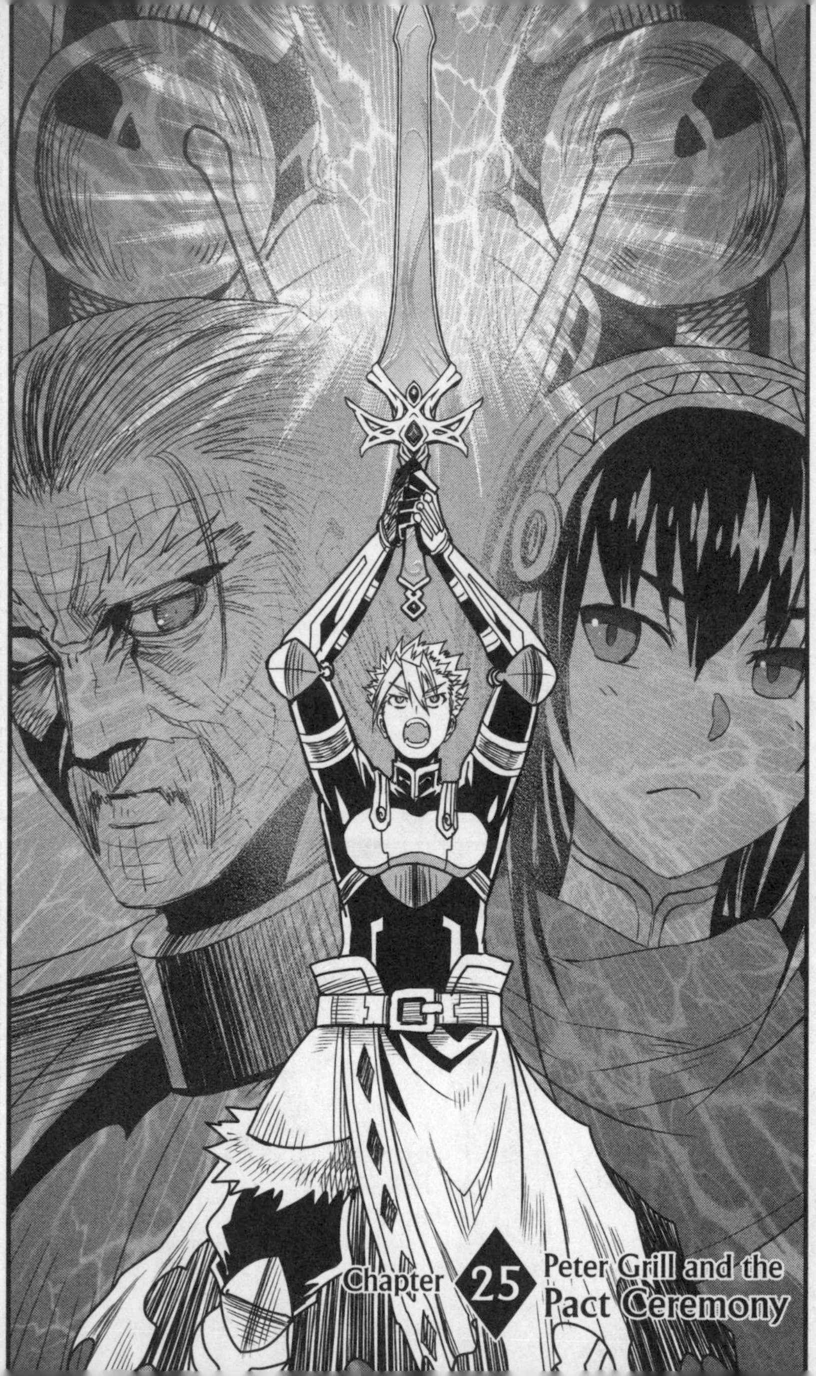
Chapter 25 Peter Grill and the Pact Ceremony

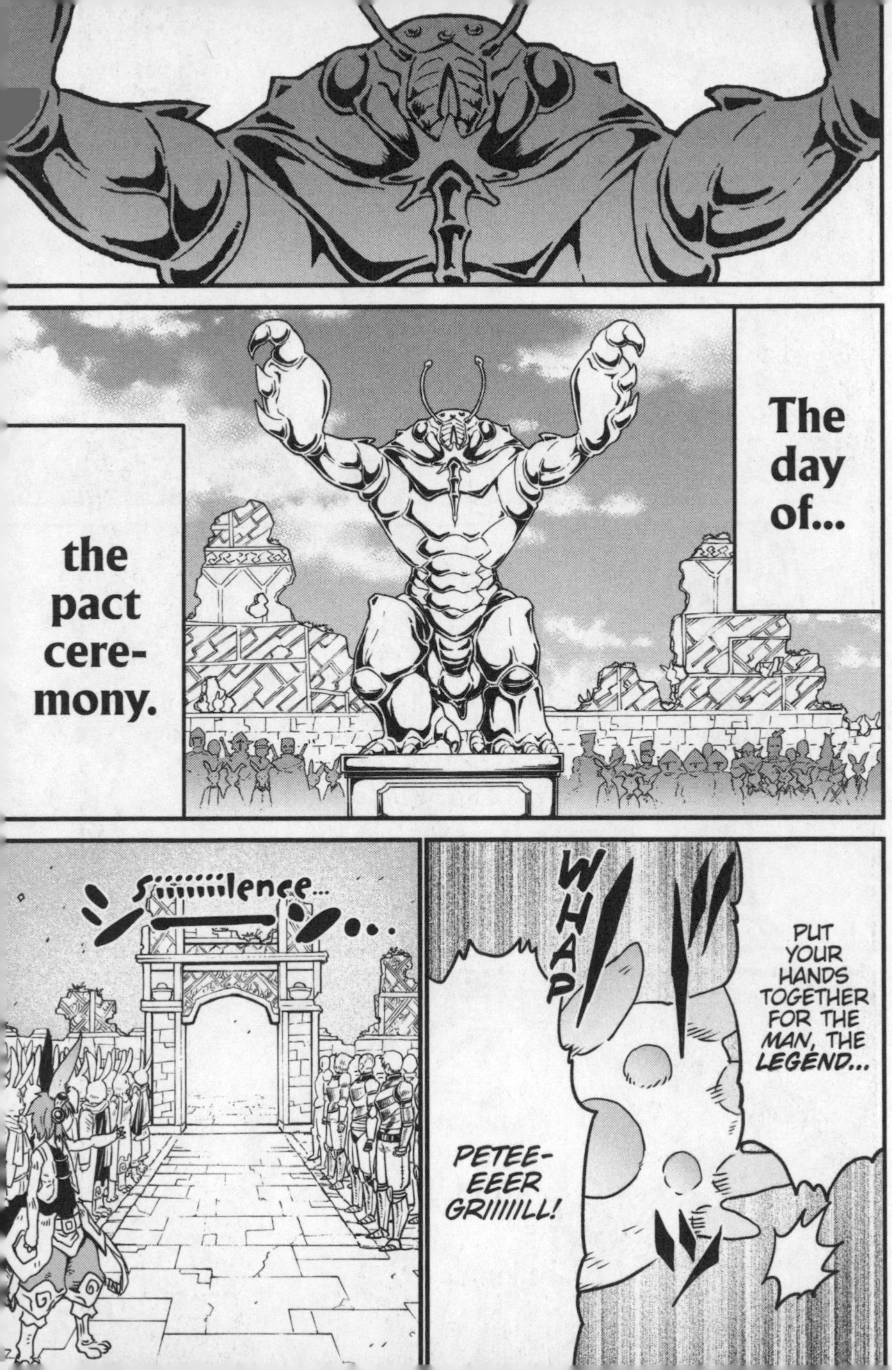

The day of...
the pact ceremony.
WHAP
PUT YOUR HANDS TOGETHER FOR THE MAN, THE LEGEND...
PETEE-EEER GRIIIIILL!
Siiiiiiilence...

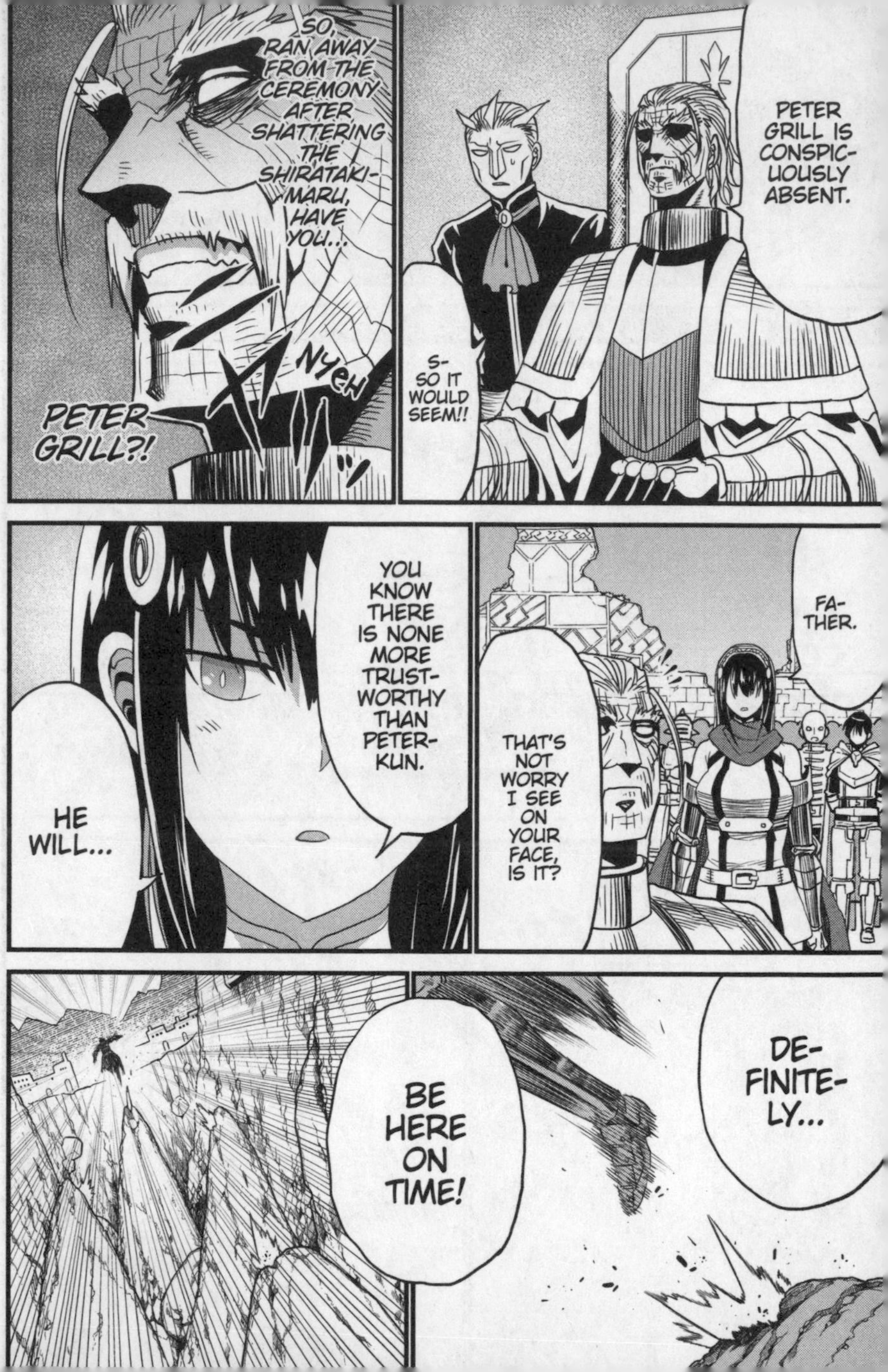
PETER GRILL IS CONSPICUOUSLY ABSENT.
S-SO IT WOULD SEEM!!
SO, RAN AWAY FROM THE CEREMONY AFTER SHATTERING THE SHIRATAKI-MARU, HAVE YOU...
NYEH
PETER GRILL?!
FATHER.
THAT'S NOT WORRY I SEE ON YOUR FACE, IS IT?
YOU KNOW THERE IS NONE MORE TRUSTWORTHY THAN PETER-KUN.
HE WILL...
DEFINITELY...
BE HERE ON TIME!

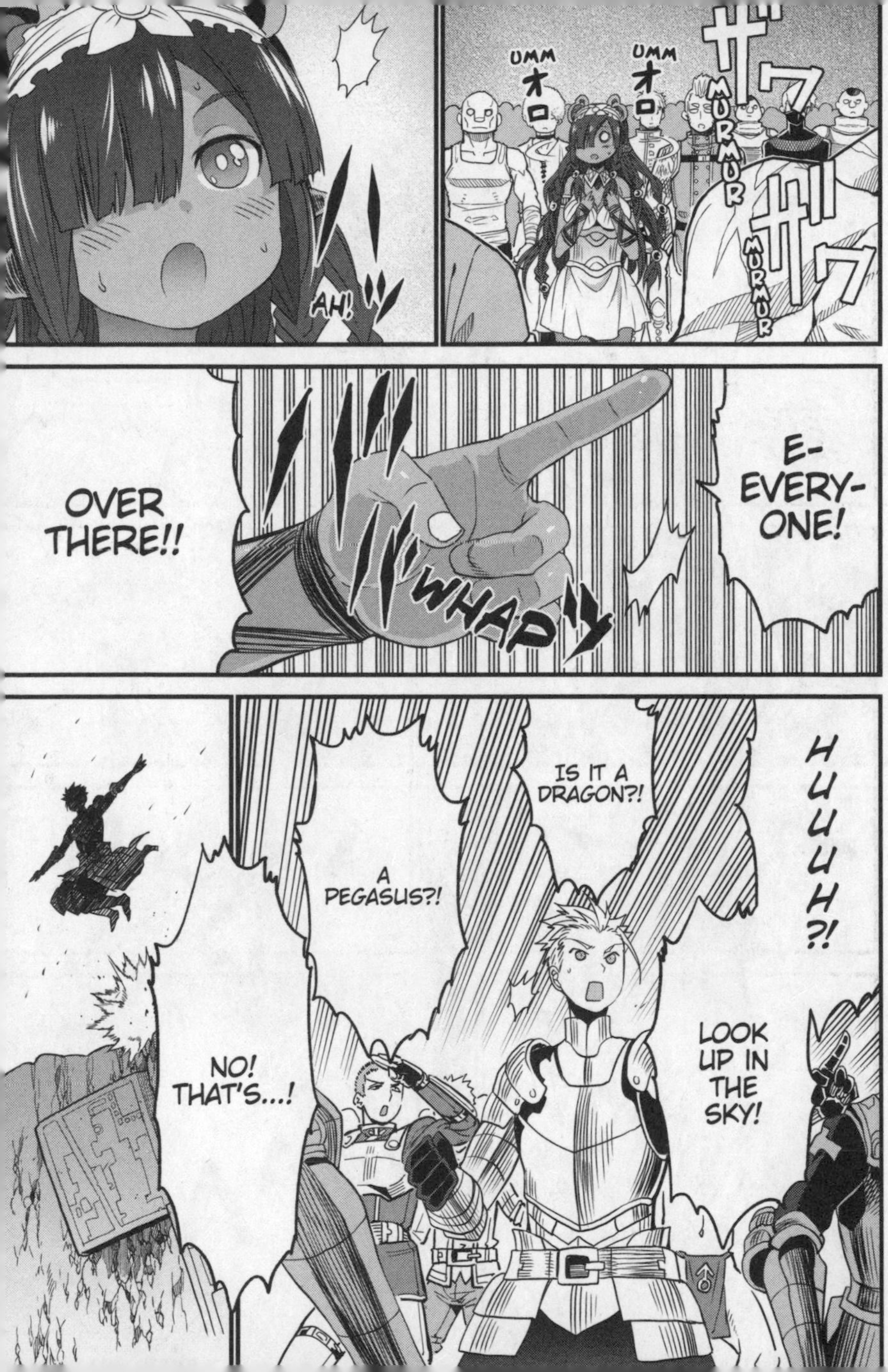
ザワ
MURMUR
ザワ
MURMUR
UMM
オロ
UMM
オロ
AH!
E-EVERYONE!
WHAP
OVER THERE!!
HUUUH?!
IS IT A DRAGON?!
LOOK UP IN THE SKY!
A PEGASUS?!
NO! THAT'S...!

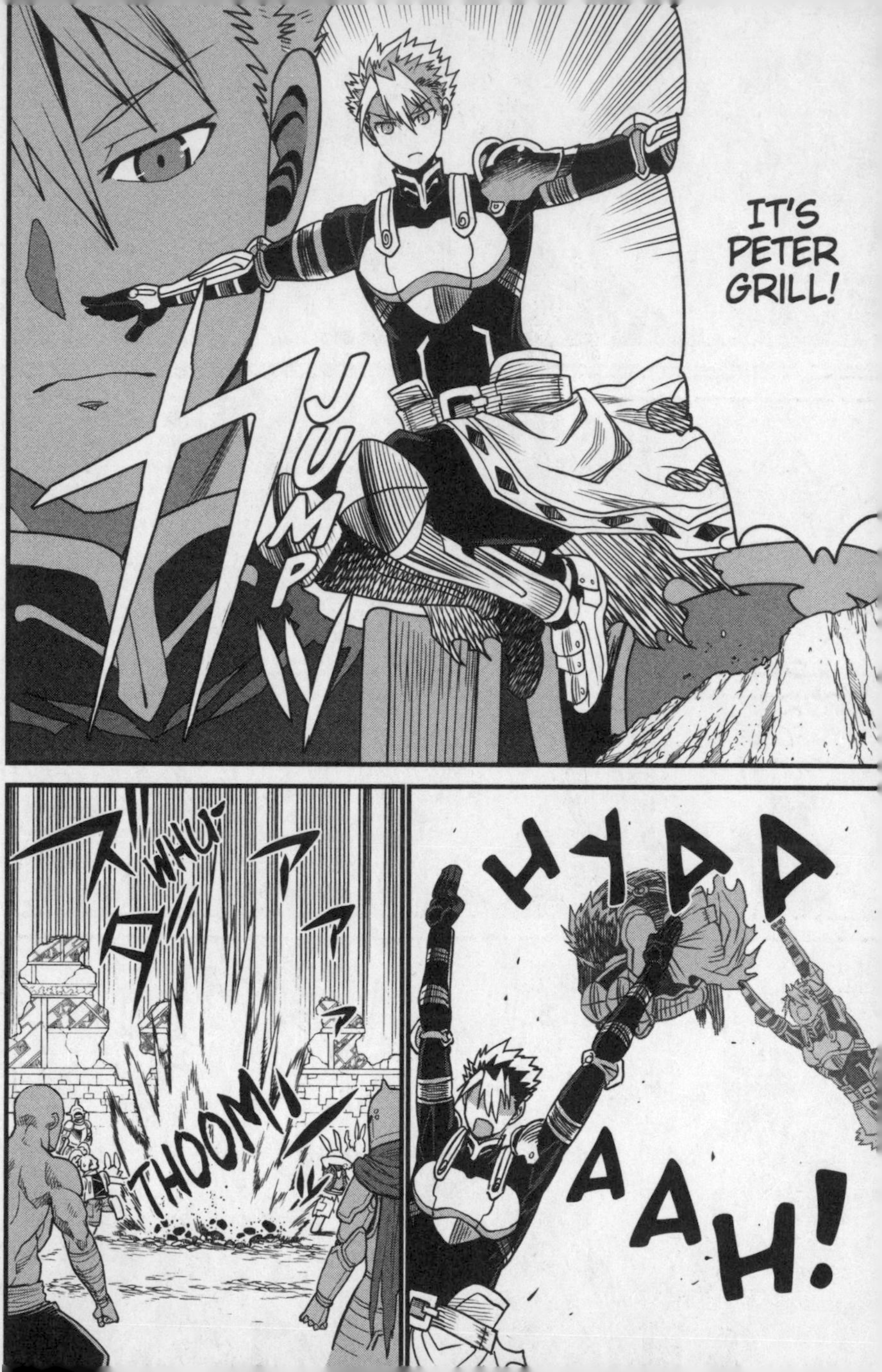
IT'S PETER GRILL!
JUMP
HYAAAAH!
WHU-
THOOM!

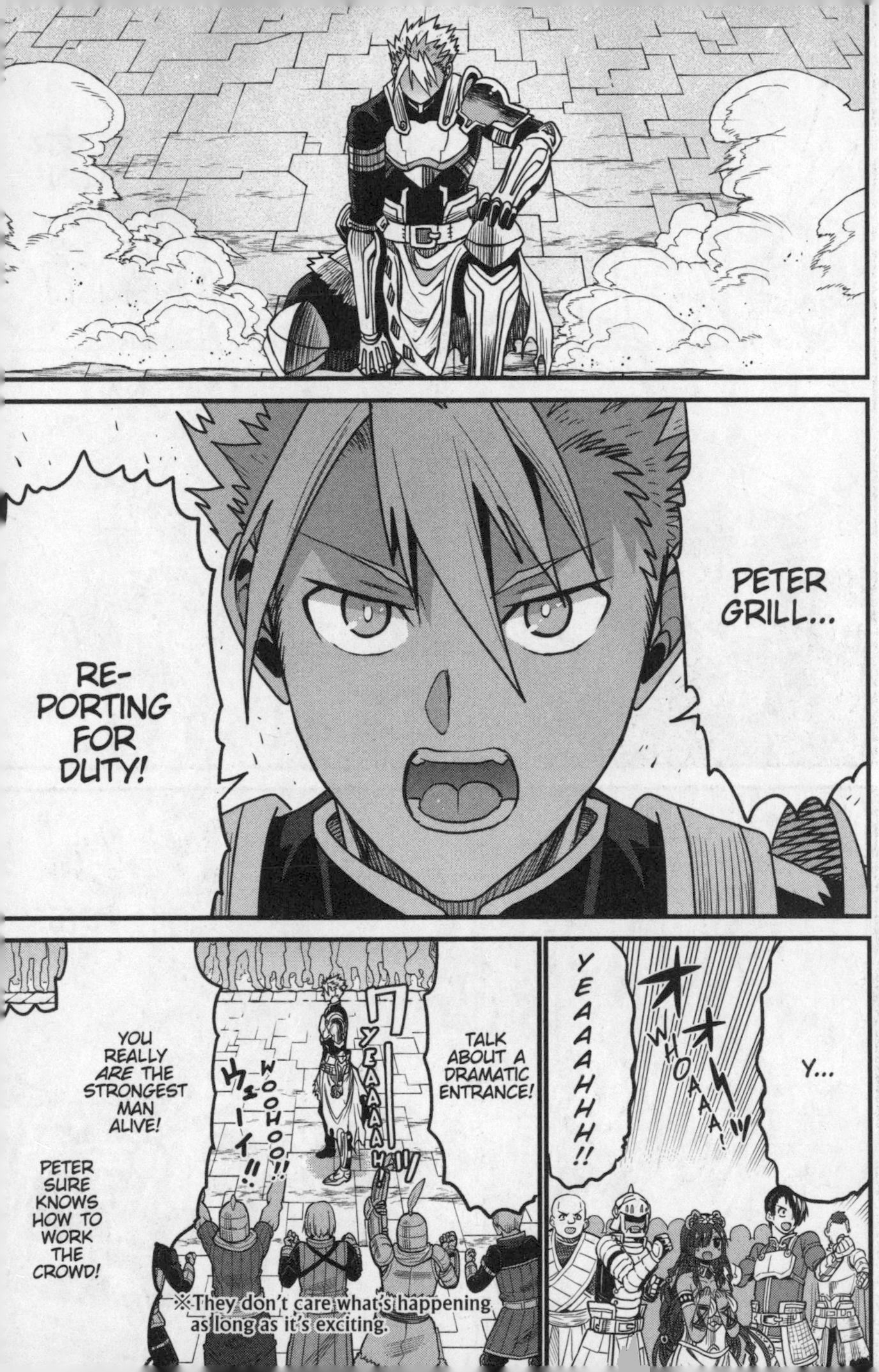
PETER GRILL...
RE-PORTING FOR DUTY!
Y...
YEAAAAHHH!!
WHOAAA!!
TALK ABOUT A DRAMATIC ENTRANCE!
YEAAAAHH!!
WOOHOO!!
YOU REALLY ARE THE STRONGEST MAN ALIVE!
PETER SURE KNOWS HOW TO WORK THE CROWD!
※They don't care what's happening as long as it's exciting.

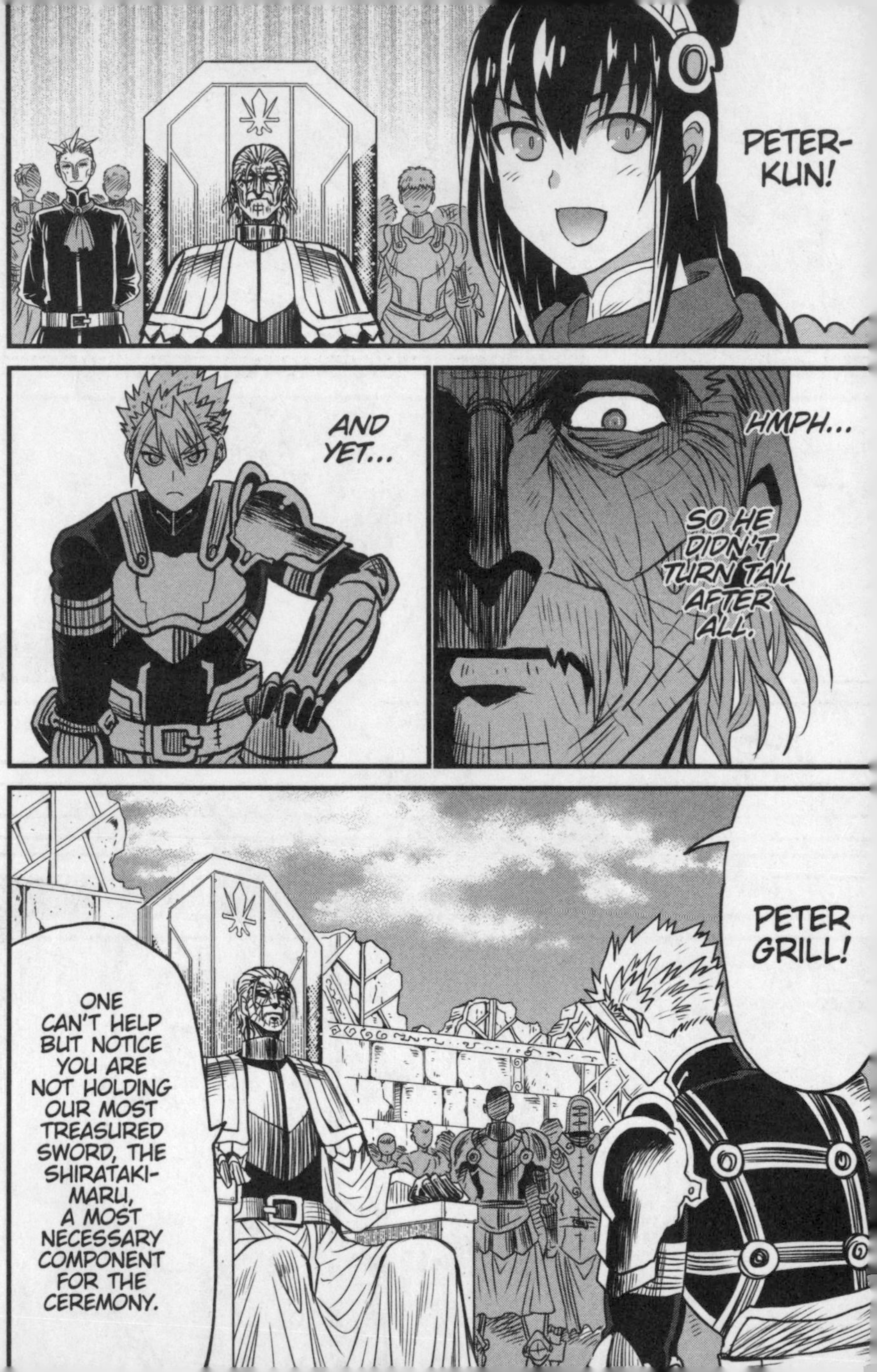
PETER-KUN!
HMPH...
SO HE DIDN'T TURN TAIL AFTER ALL.
AND YET...
PETER GRILL!
ONE CAN'T HELP BUT NOTICE YOU ARE NOT HOLDING OUR MOST TREASURED SWORD, THE SHIRATAKI-MARU, A MOST NECESSARY COMPONENT FOR THE CEREMONY.

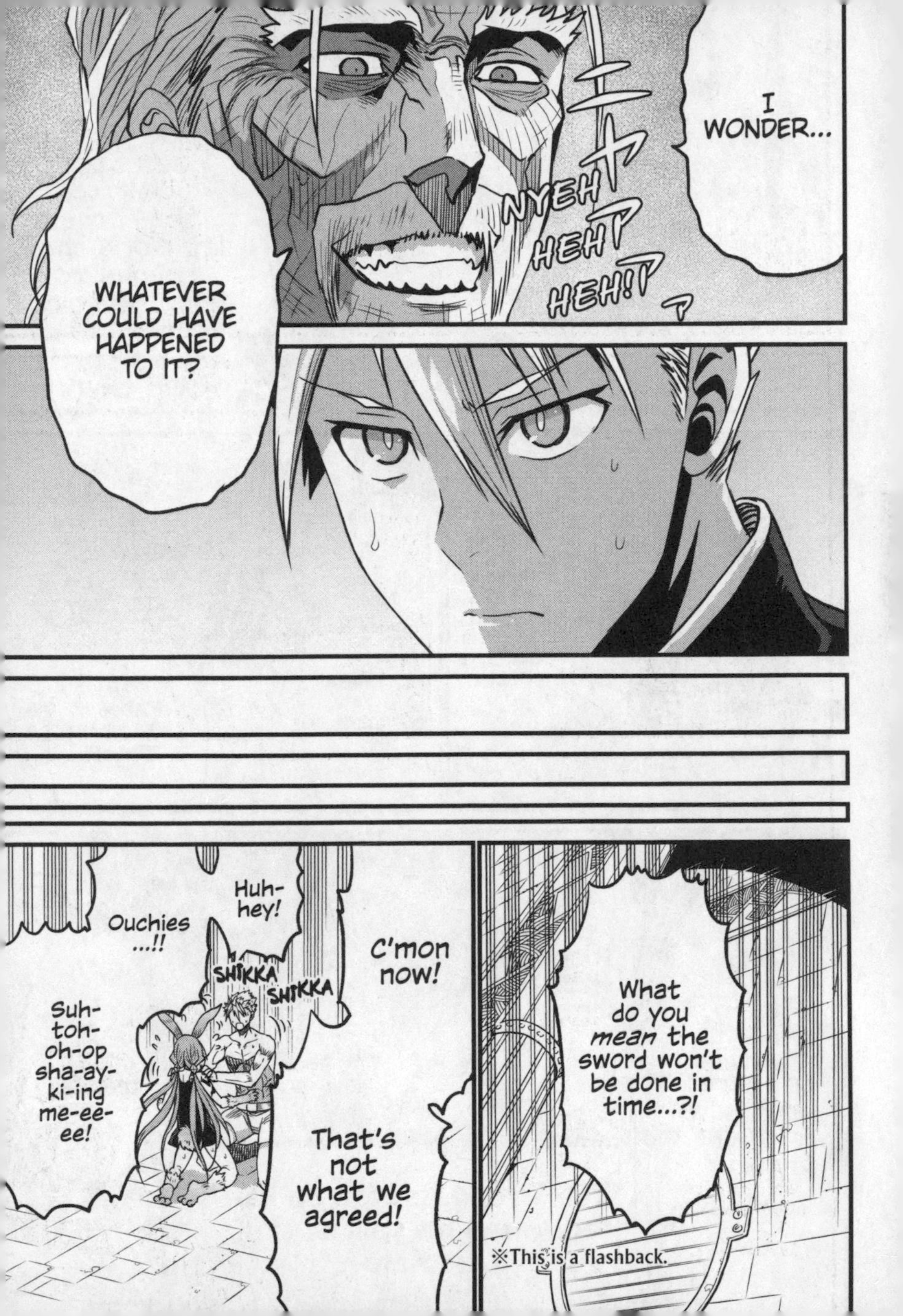
I WONDER...
NYEH HEH HEH!
WHATEVER COULD HAVE HAPPENED TO IT?
What do you *mean* the sword won't be done in time...?!
※This is a flashback.
C'mon now!
That's not what we agreed!
Huh-hey!
Ouchies ...!!
SHIKKA SHIKKA
Suh-toh-oh-op sha-ay-ki-ing me-ee-ee!

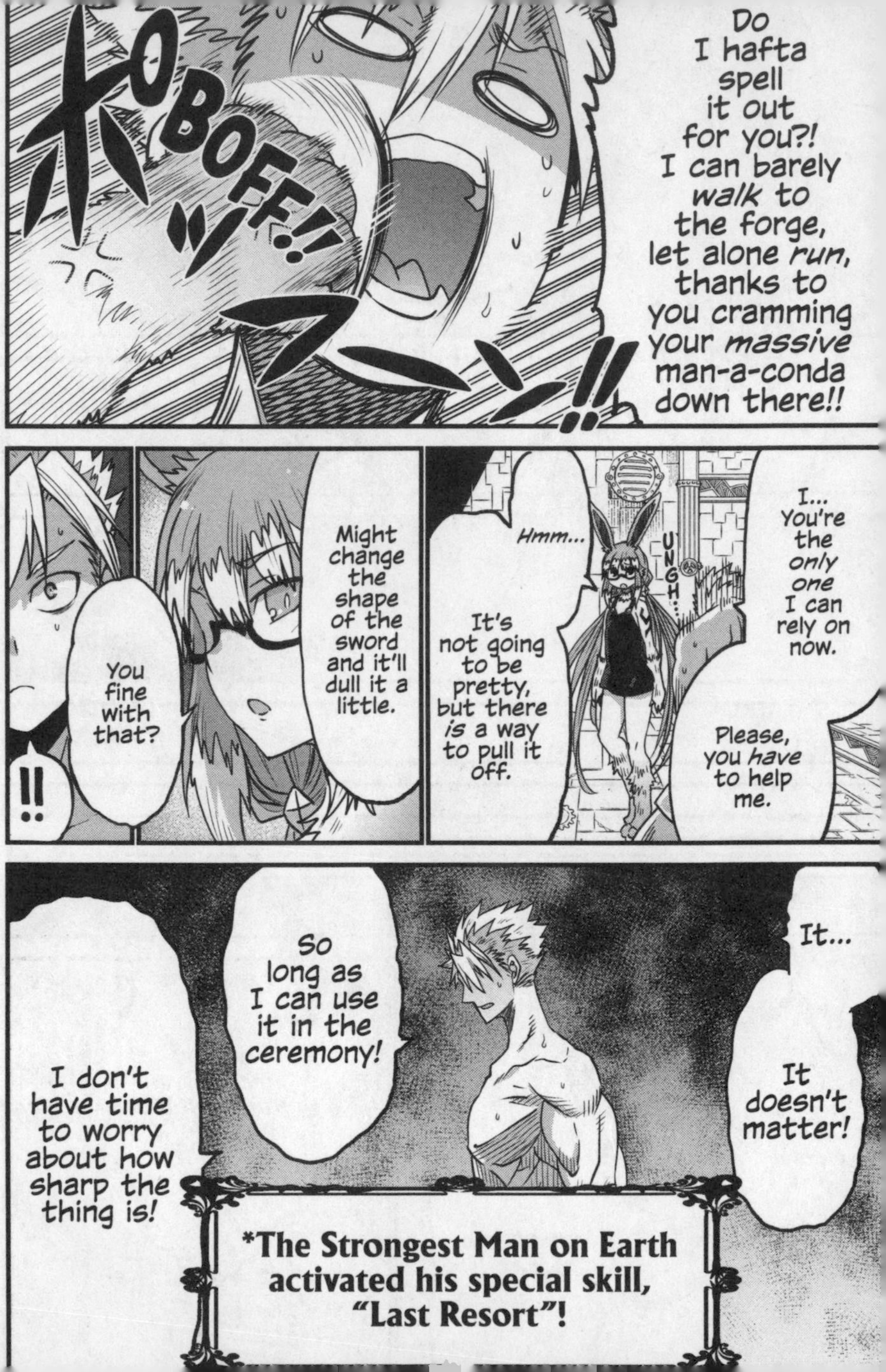
Do I hafta spell it out for you?! I can barely *walk* to the forge, let alone *run*, thanks to you cramming your *massive* man-a-conda down there!!
BOFF!!
I... You're the *only one* I can rely on now.
Please, you *have* to help me.
UNGH...
Hmm...
It's not going to be pretty, but there *is* a way to pull it off.
Might change the shape of the sword and it'll dull it a little.
You fine with that?
!!
It...
It doesn't matter!
So long as I can use it in the ceremony!
I don't have time to worry about how sharp the thing is!
*The Strongest Man on Earth activated his special skill, "Last Resort"!

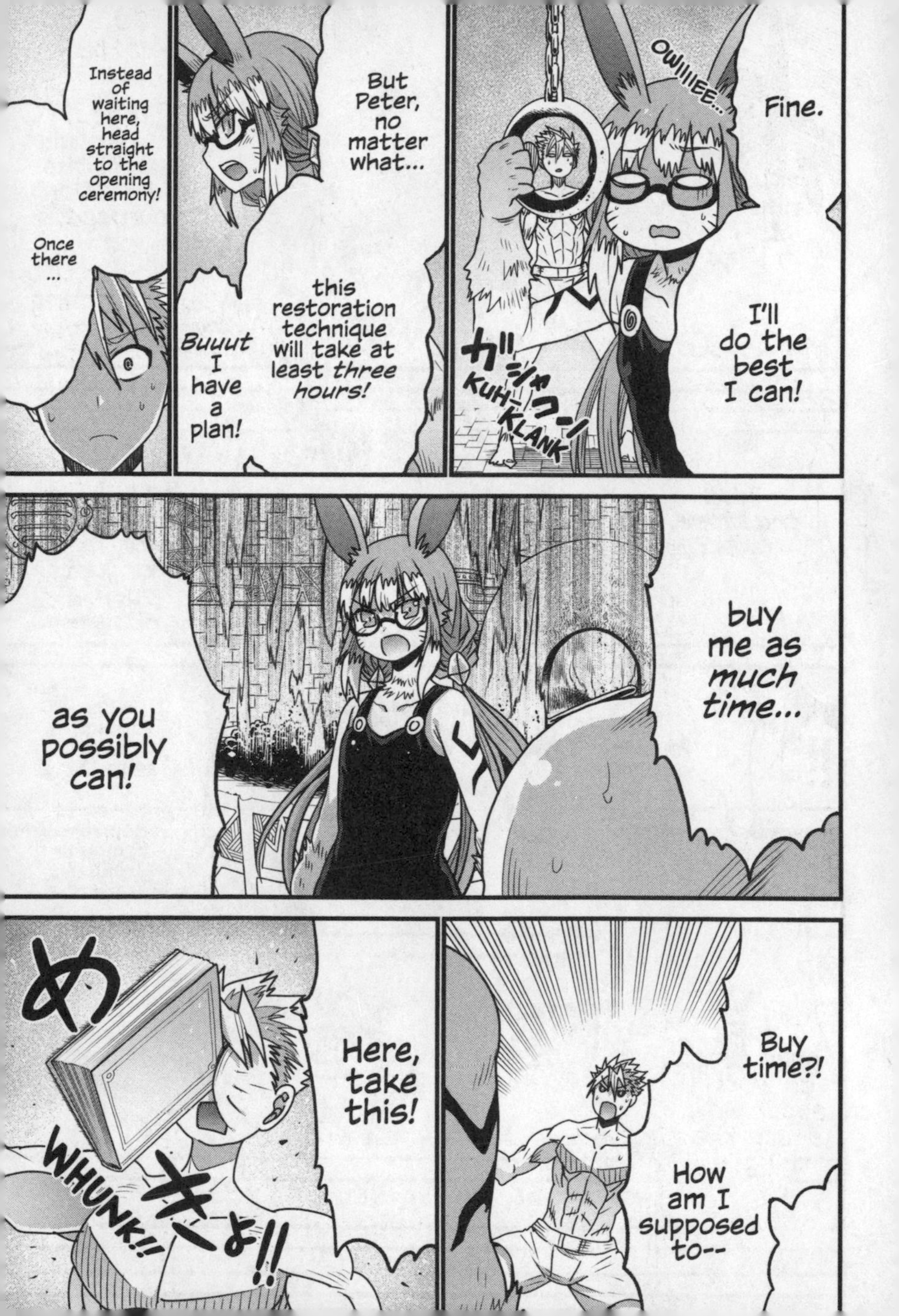
OWIIIIEE...
Fine.
I'll do the best I can!
ガシャコーン
KUH-KLANK
But Peter, no matter what...
this restoration technique will take at least *three hours!*
Buuut I have a plan!
Instead of waiting here, head straight to the opening ceremony!
Once there ...
buy me as *much time...*
as you possibly can!
Buy time?!
How am I supposed to--
Here, take this!
めきょ!!
WHUNK!!!

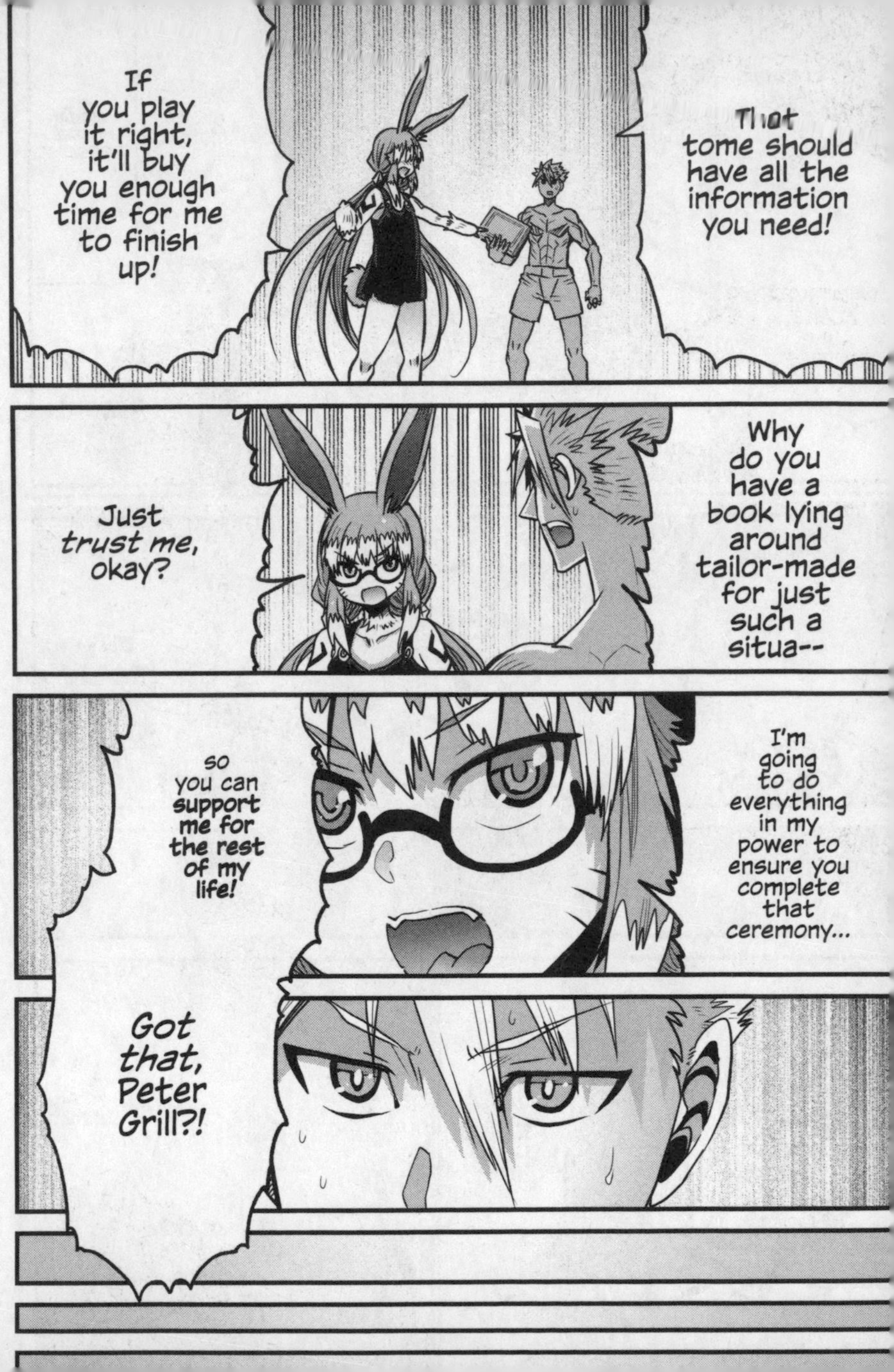
That tome should have all the information you need!
If you play it right, it'll buy you enough time for me to finish up!
Why do you have a book lying around tailor-made for just such a situa--
Just *trust me*, okay?
I'm going to do everything in my power to ensure you complete that ceremony...
so you can support me for the rest of my life!
Got that, Peter Grill?!

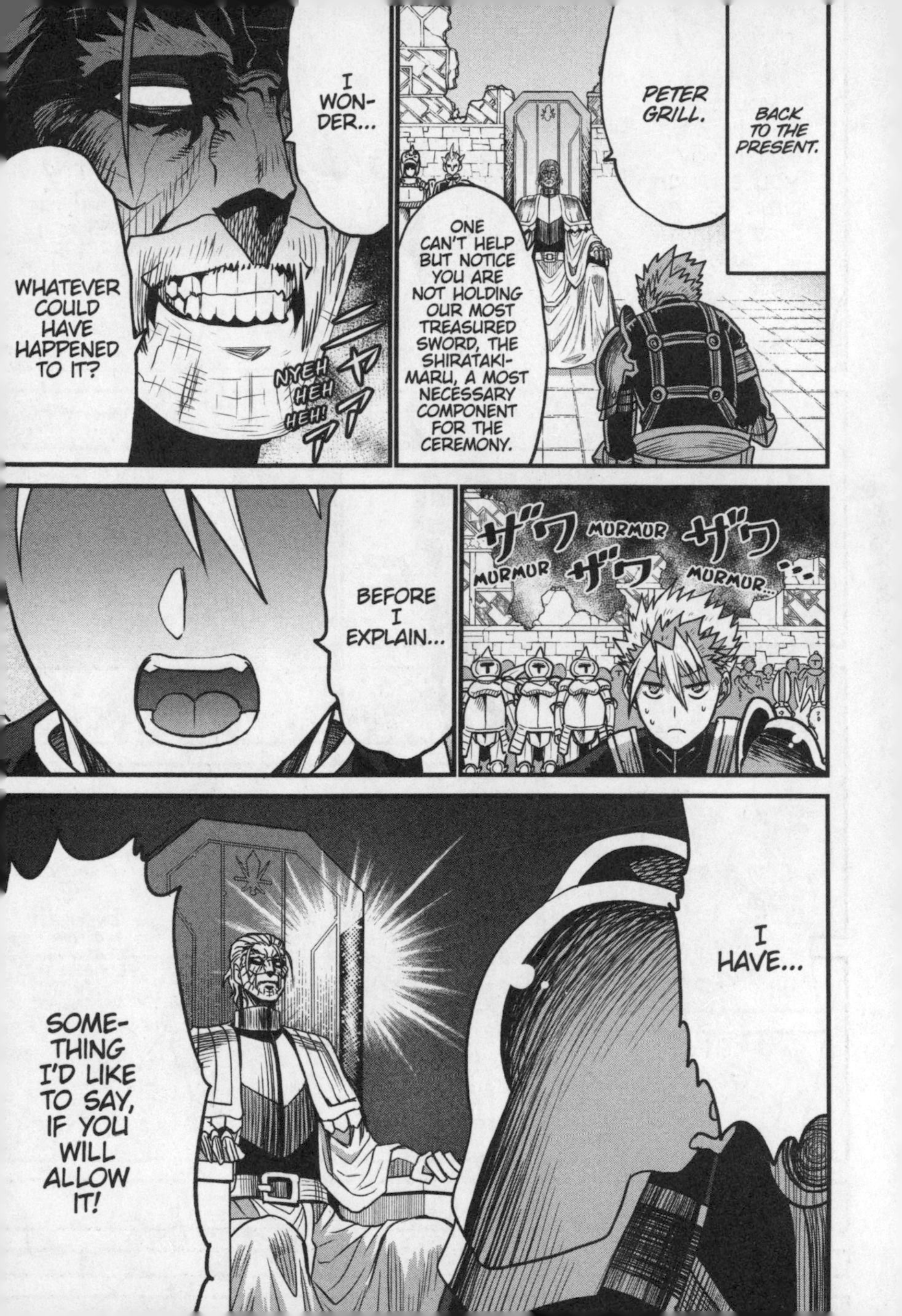
BACK TO THE PRESENT.
PETER GRILL.
ONE CAN'T HELP BUT NOTICE YOU ARE NOT HOLDING OUR MOST TREASURED SWORD, THE SHIRATAKI-MARU, A MOST NECESSARY COMPONENT FOR THE CEREMONY.
I WON-DER...
WHATEVER COULD HAVE HAPPENED TO IT?
NYEH HEH HEH!
ザワ MURMUR ザワ
MURMUR ザワ
MURMUR...
BEFORE I EXPLAIN...
I HAVE...
SOME-THING I'D LIKE TO SAY, IF YOU WILL ALLOW IT!

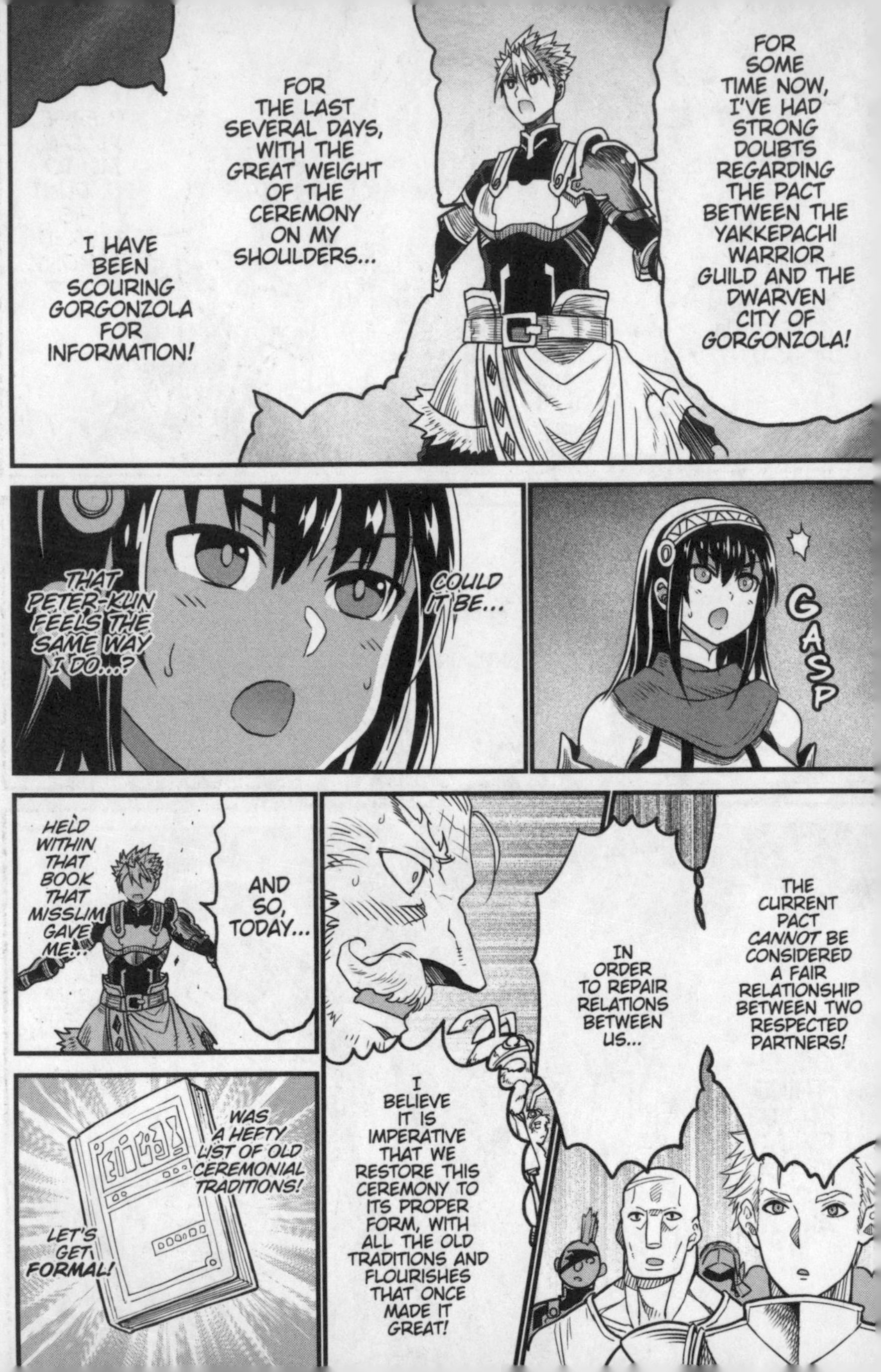
FOR SOME TIME NOW, I'VE HAD STRONG DOUBTS REGARDING THE PACT BETWEEN THE YAKKEPACHI WARRIOR GUILD AND THE DWARVEN CITY OF GORGONZOLA!
FOR THE LAST SEVERAL DAYS, WITH THE GREAT WEIGHT OF THE CEREMONY ON MY SHOULDERS...
I HAVE BEEN SCOURING GORGONZOLA FOR INFORMATION!
GASP
COULD IT BE...
THAT PETER-KUN FEELS THE SAME WAY I DO...?
THE CURRENT PACT CANNOT BE CONSIDERED A FAIR RELATIONSHIP BETWEEN TWO RESPECTED PARTNERS!
IN ORDER TO REPAIR RELATIONS BETWEEN US...
I BELIEVE IT IS IMPERATIVE THAT WE RESTORE THIS CEREMONY TO ITS PROPER FORM, WITH ALL THE OLD TRADITIONS AND FLOURISHES THAT ONCE MADE IT GREAT!
AND SO, TODAY...
HELD WITHIN THAT BOOK THAT MISSLIM GAVE ME...
WAS A HEFTY LIST OF OLD CEREMONIAL TRADITIONS!
LET'S GET FORMAL!

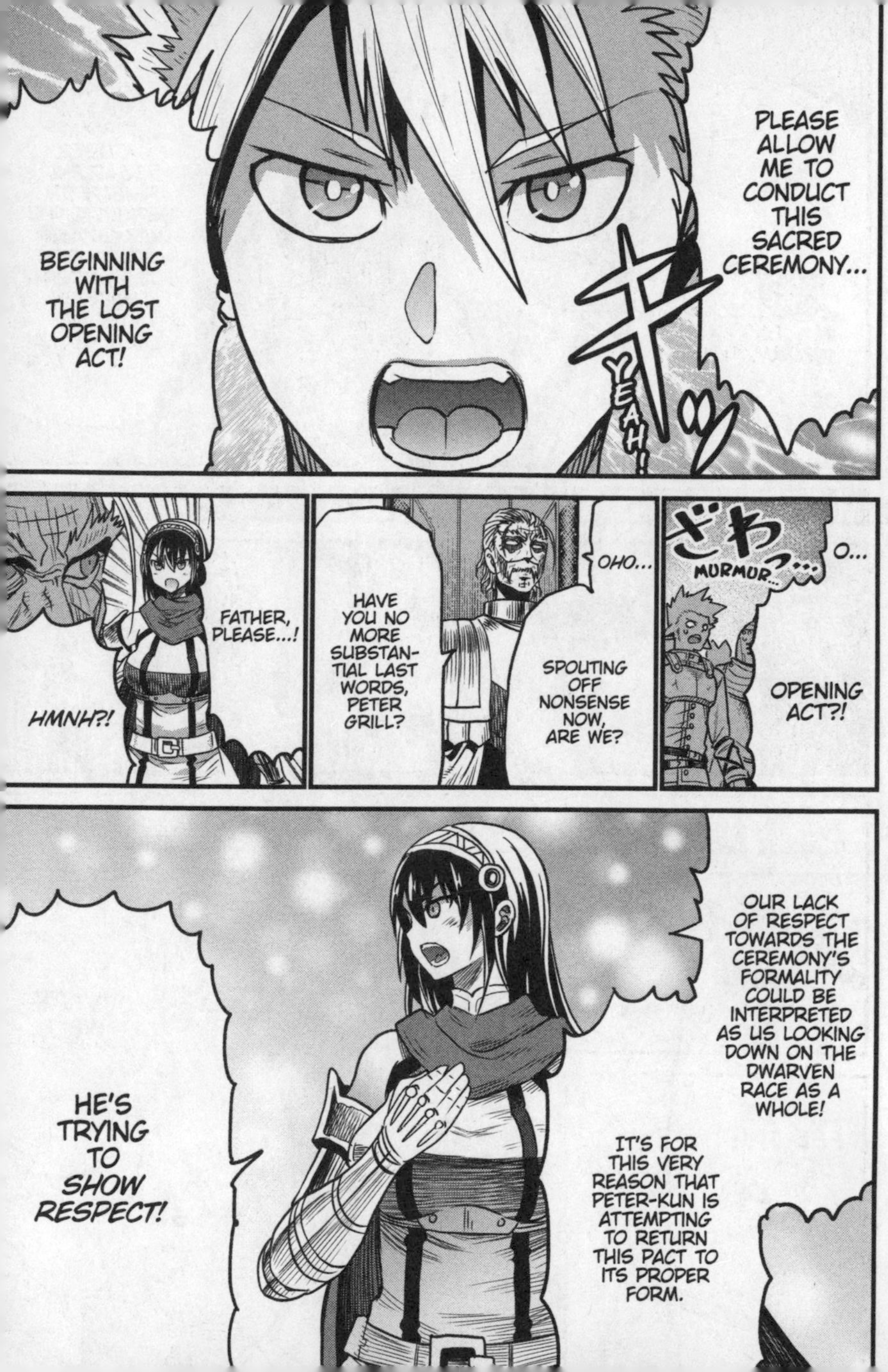
PLEASE ALLOW ME TO CONDUCT THIS SACRED CEREMONY...
YEAH!
BEGINNING WITH THE LOST OPENING ACT!
ざわ
MURMUR...
O...
OPENING ACT?!
OHO...
SPOUTING OFF NONSENSE NOW, ARE WE?
HAVE YOU NO MORE SUBSTANTIAL LAST WORDS, PETER GRILL?
FATHER, PLEASE...!
HMNH?!
OUR LACK OF RESPECT TOWARDS THE CEREMONY'S FORMALITY COULD BE INTERPRETED AS US LOOKING DOWN ON THE DWARVEN RACE AS A WHOLE!
IT'S FOR THIS VERY REASON THAT PETER-KUN IS ATTEMPTING TO RETURN THIS PACT TO ITS PROPER FORM.
HE'S TRYING TO SHOW RESPECT!

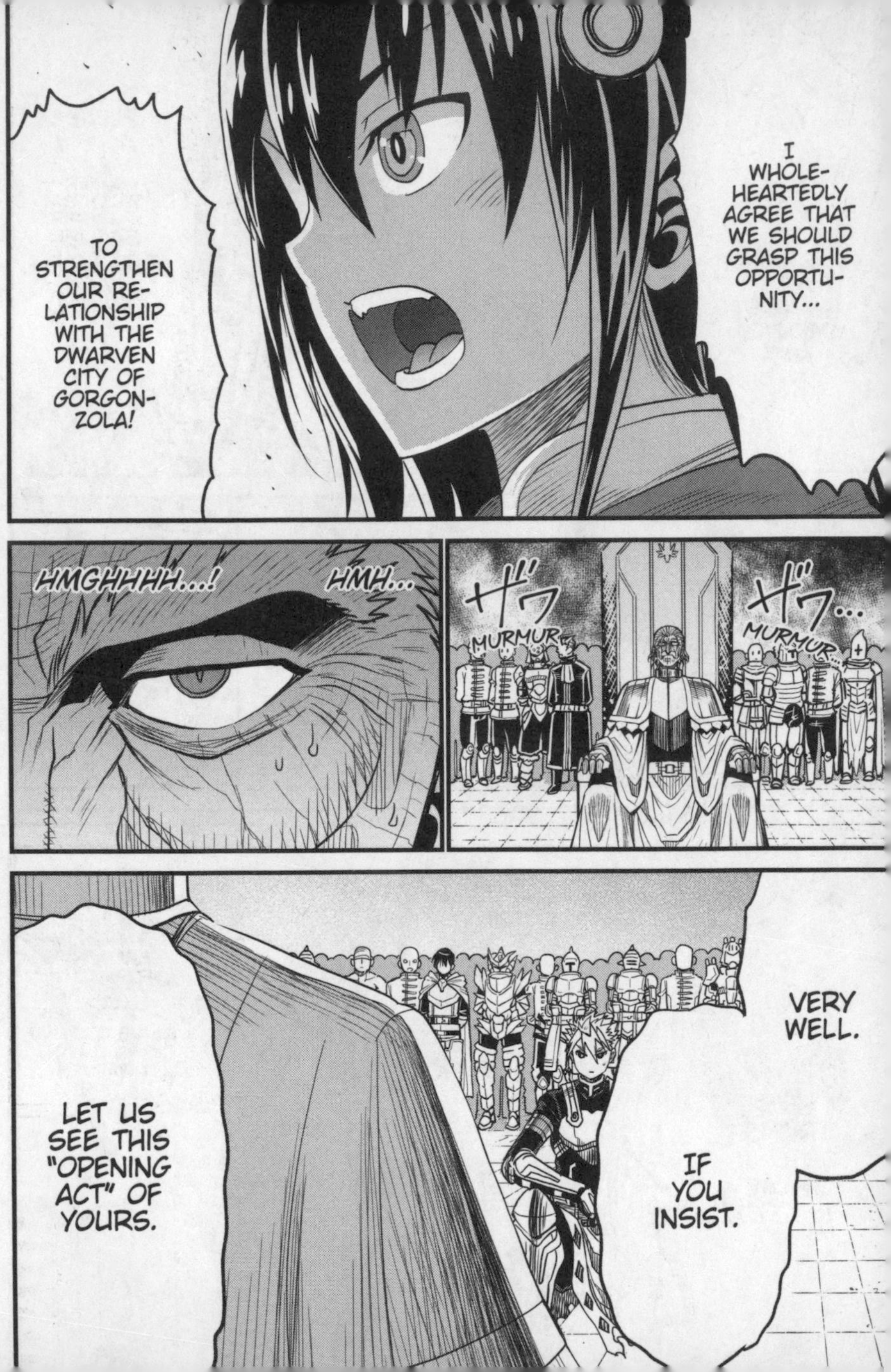
I WHOLEHEARTEDLY AGREE THAT WE SHOULD GRASP THIS OPPORTUNITY...
TO STRENGTHEN OUR RELATIONSHIP WITH THE DWARVEN CITY OF GORGONZOLA!
ザワ...
MURMUR...
ザワ
MURMUR
HMH...
HMGHHHH...!
VERY WELL.
IF YOU INSIST.
LET US SEE THIS "OPENING ACT" OF YOURS.

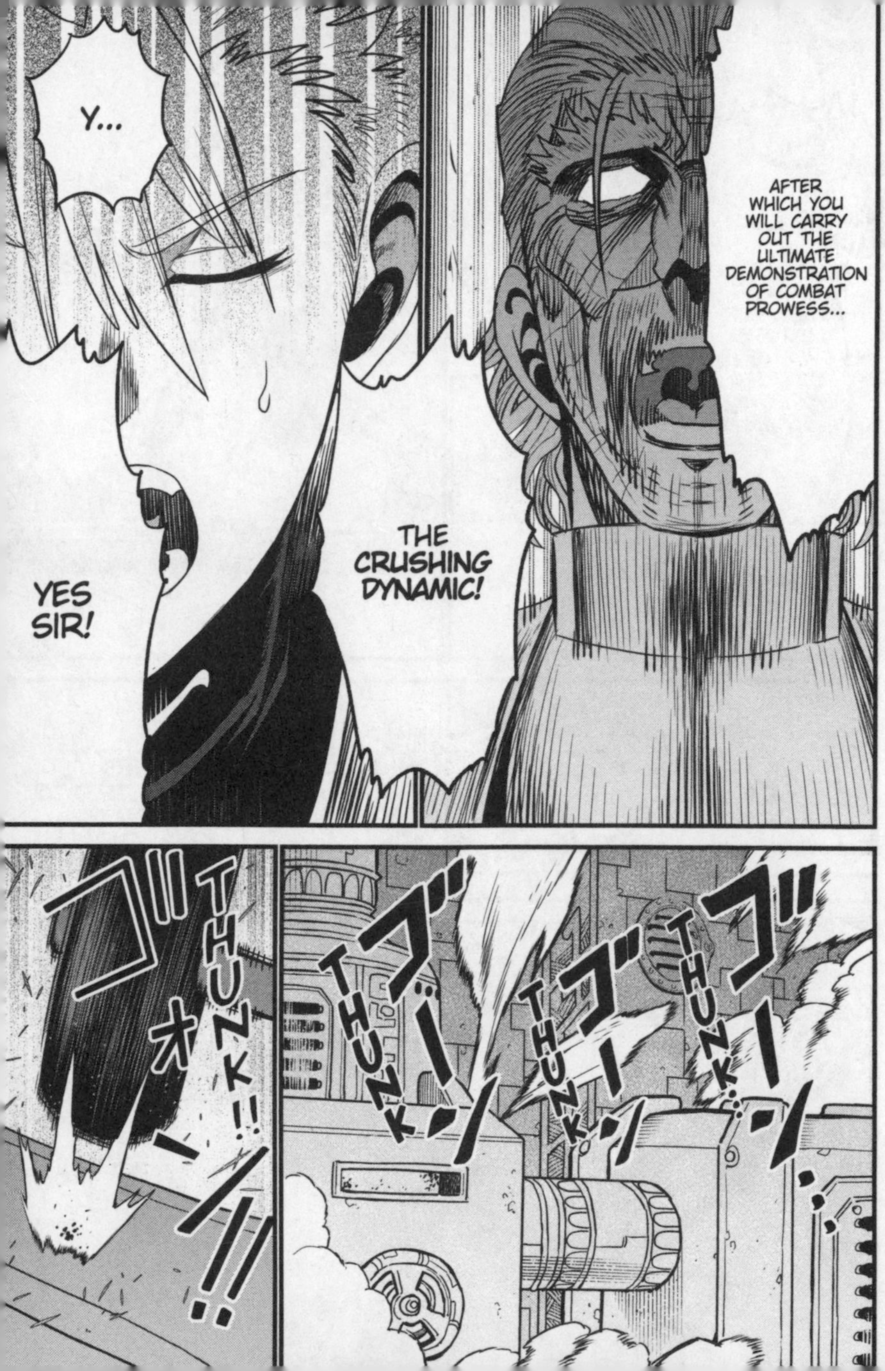
AFTER WHICH YOU WILL CARRY OUT THE ULTIMATE DEMONSTRATION OF COMBAT PROWESS...
THE CRUSHING DYNAMIC!
Y...
YES SIR!
THUNK
THUNK
THUNK
THUNK!!

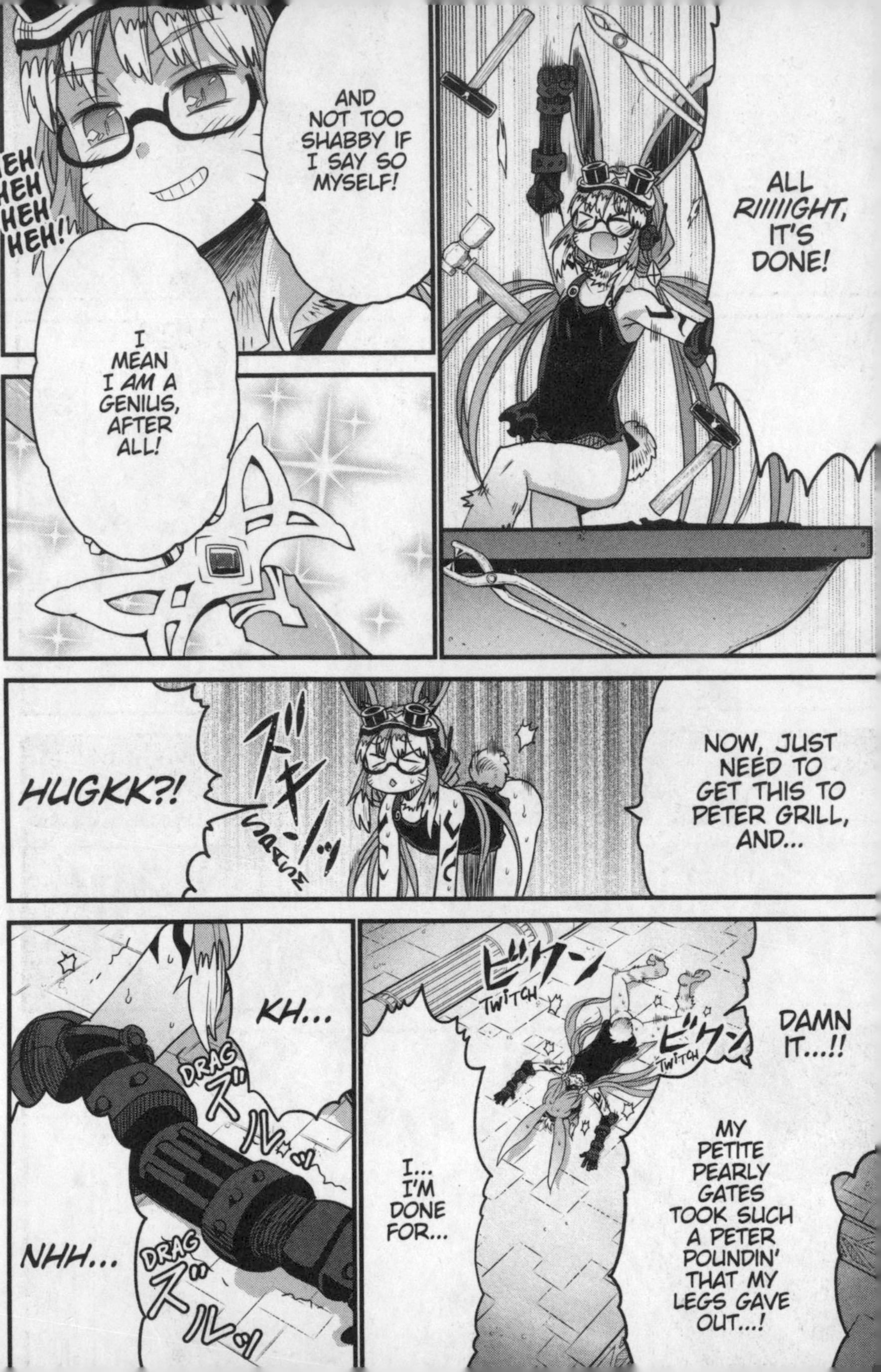
ALL RIIIIIGHT, IT'S DONE!
AND NOT TOO SHABBY IF I SAY SO MYSELF!
HEH HEH HEH HEH!!
I MEAN I AM A GENIUS, AFTER ALL!
NOW, JUST NEED TO GET THIS TO PETER GRILL, AND...
HUGKK?!
DAMN IT...!!
TWITCH
TWITCH
MY PETITE PEARLY GATES TOOK SUCH A PETER POUNDIN' THAT MY LEGS GAVE OUT...!
I... I'M DONE FOR...
KH...
DRAG
NHH...
DRAG

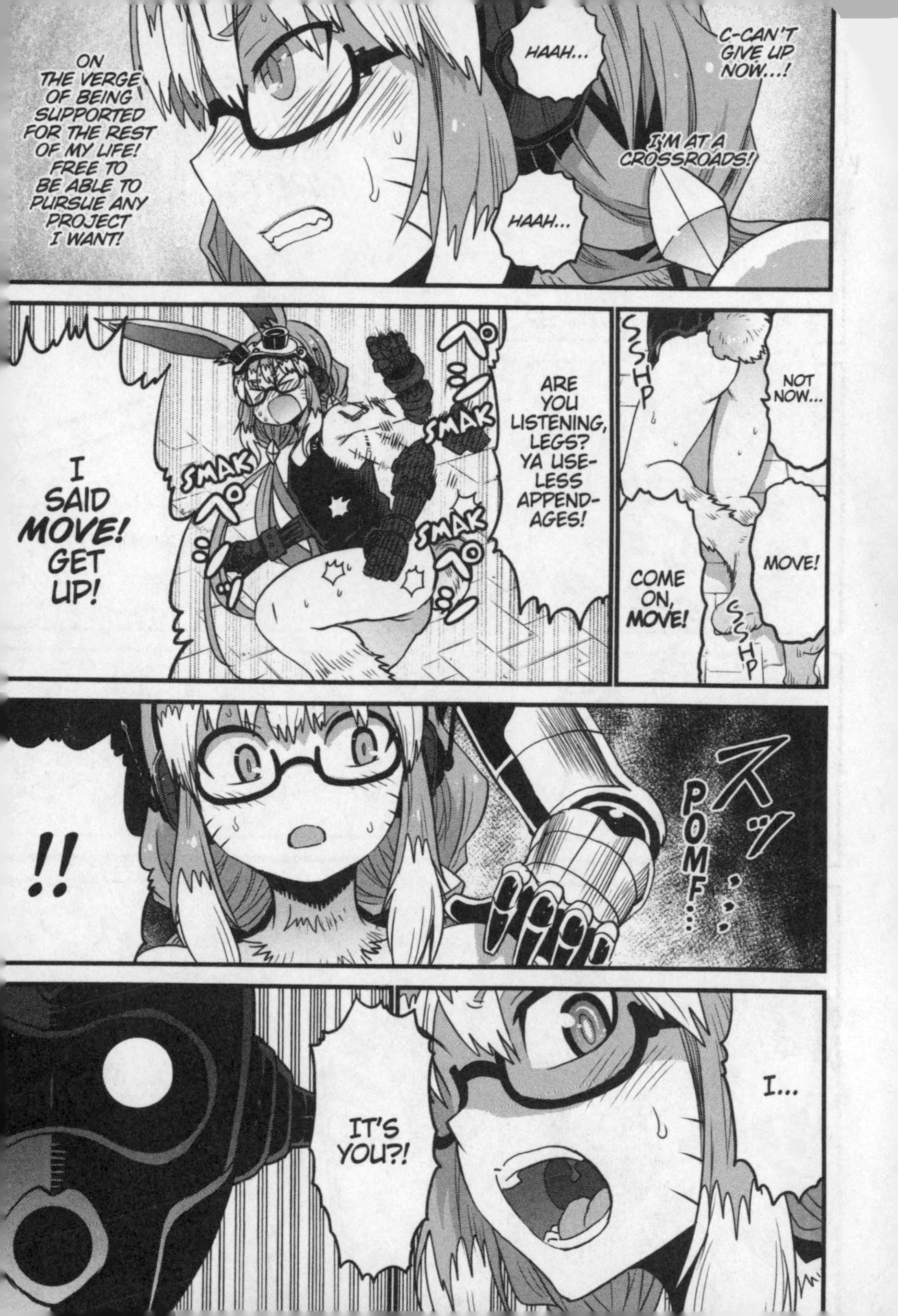
C-CAN'T GIVE UP NOW...!
HAAH...
I'M AT A CROSSROADS!
HAAH...
ON THE VERGE OF BEING SUPPORTED FOR THE REST OF MY LIFE! FREE TO BE ABLE TO PURSUE ANY PROJECT I WANT!
SSHP
NOT NOW...
MOVE!
COME ON, MOVE!
SSHP
ARE YOU LISTENING, LEGS? YA USELESS APPENDAGES!
SMAK
SMAK
SMAK
I SAID MOVE! GET UP!
スッ
POMF...
!!
I...
IT'S YOU?!

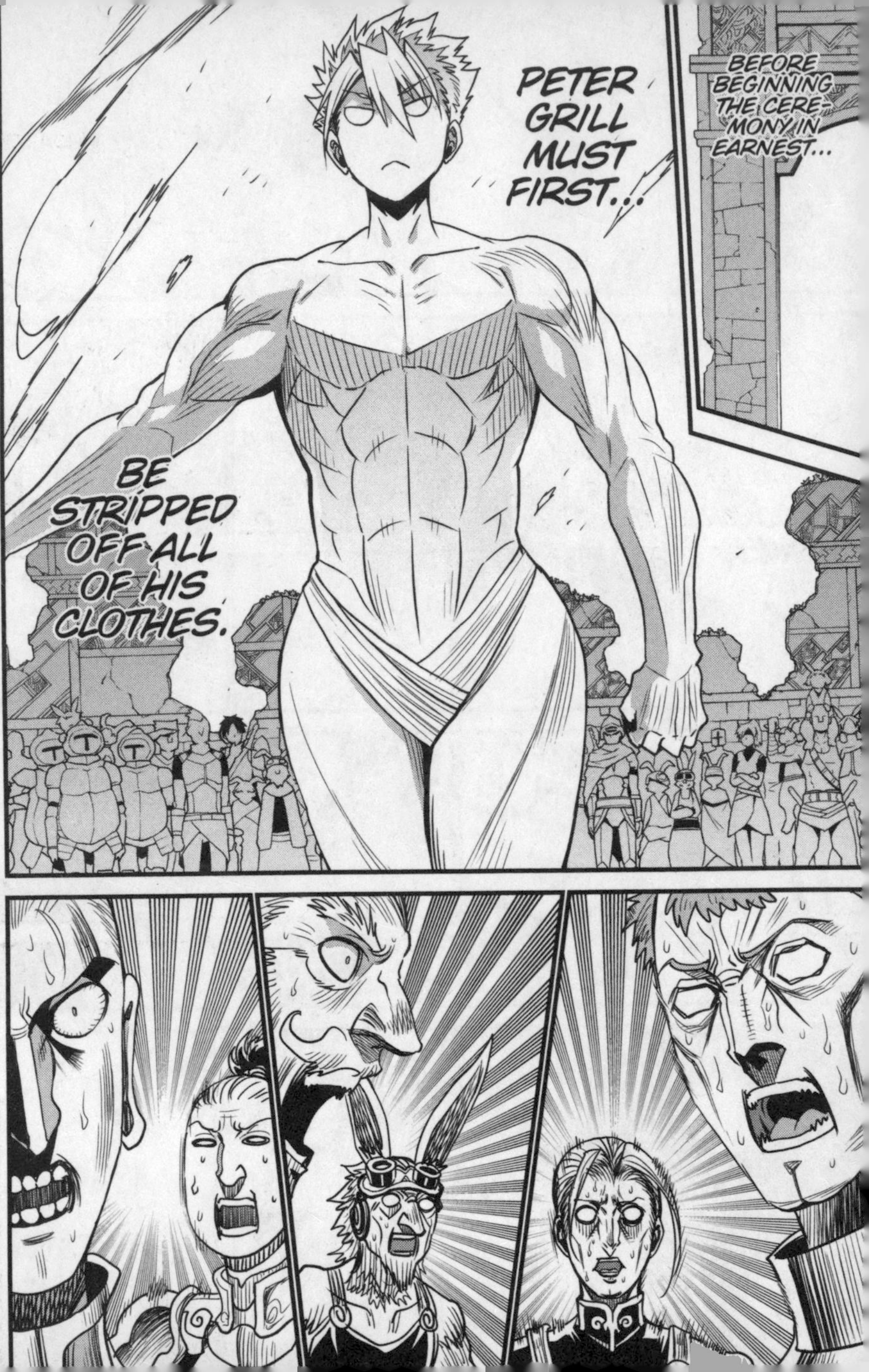
BEFORE BEGINNING THE CERE-MONY IN EARNEST...
PETER GRILL MUST FIRST...
BE STRIPPED OFF ALL OF HIS CLOTHES.

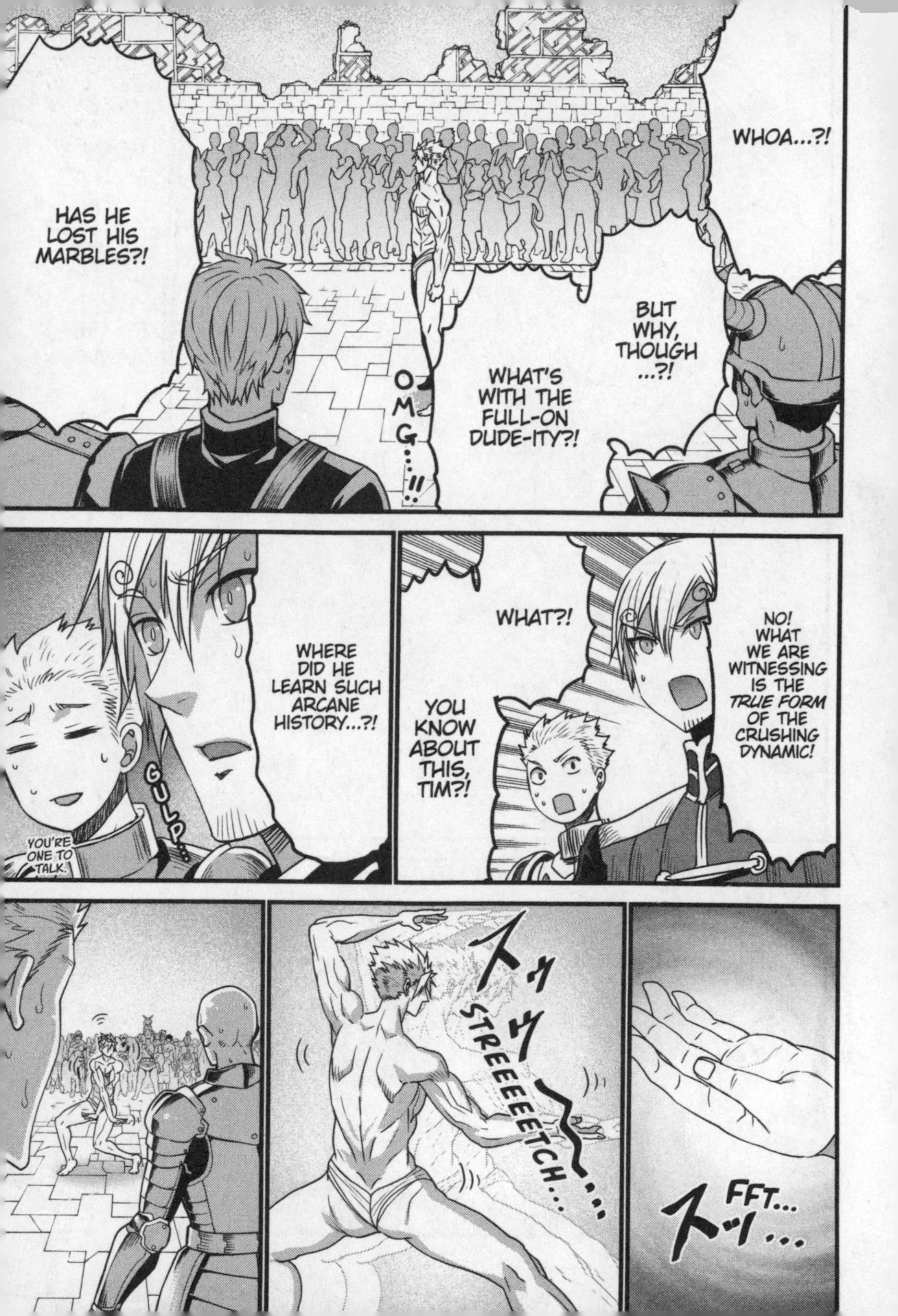

WHOA...?!
BUT WHY, THOUGH...?!
WHAT'S WITH THE FULL-ON DUDE-ITY?!
OMG...!!
HAS HE LOST HIS MARBLES?!
NO! WHAT WE ARE WITNESSING IS THE *TRUE FORM* OF THE CRUSHING DYNAMIC!
WHAT?!
YOU KNOW ABOUT THIS, TIM?!
WHERE DID HE LEARN SUCH ARCANE HISTORY...?!
GULP...
YOU'RE ONE TO TALK.
FFT...
STREEEEEETCH...

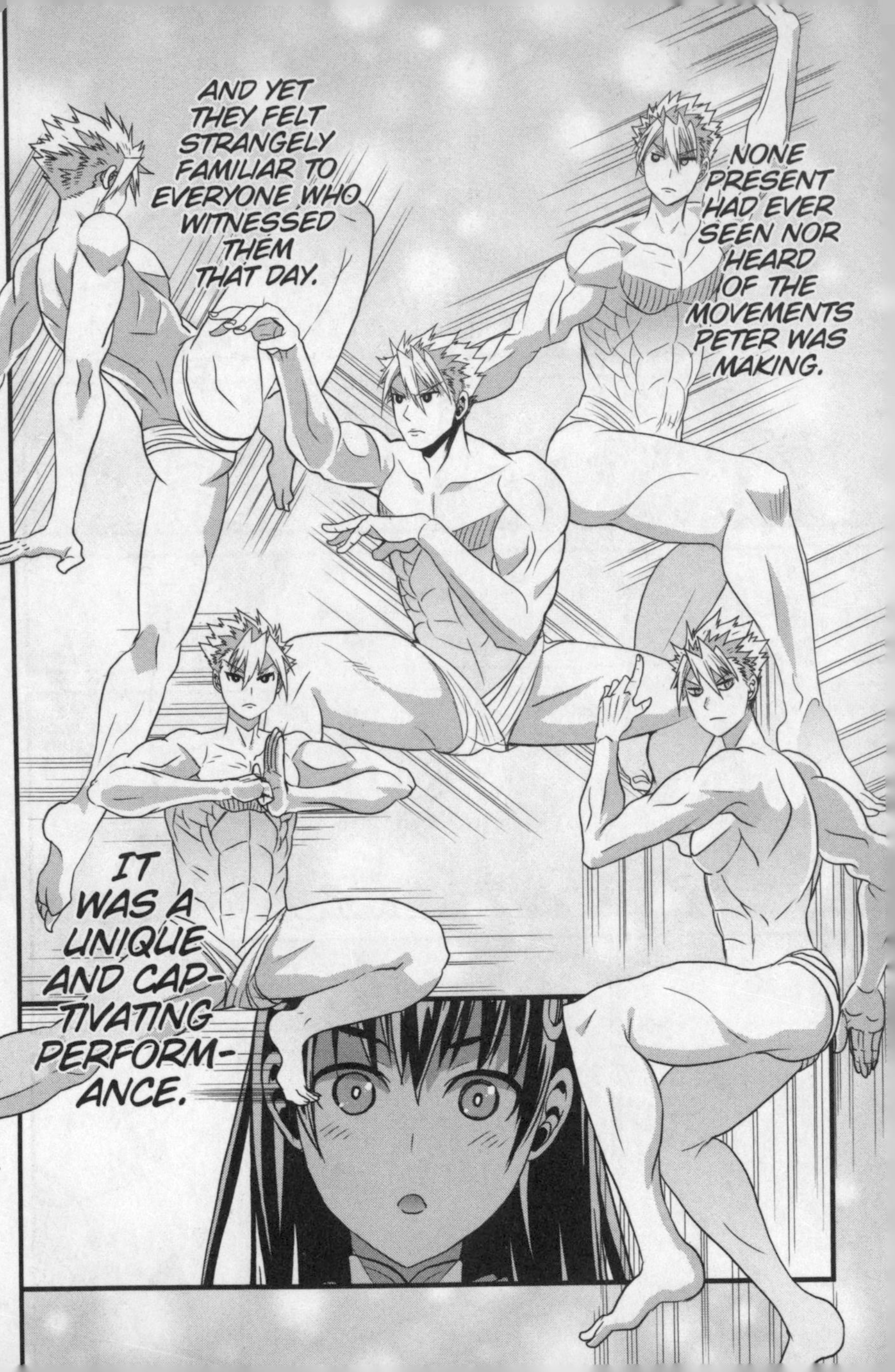
NONE PRESENT HAD EVER SEEN NOR HEARD OF THE MOVEMENTS PETER WAS MAKING.
AND YET THEY FELT STRANGELY FAMILIAR TO EVERYONE WHO WITNESSED THEM THAT DAY.
IT WAS A UNIQUE AND CAPTIVATING PERFORMANCE.

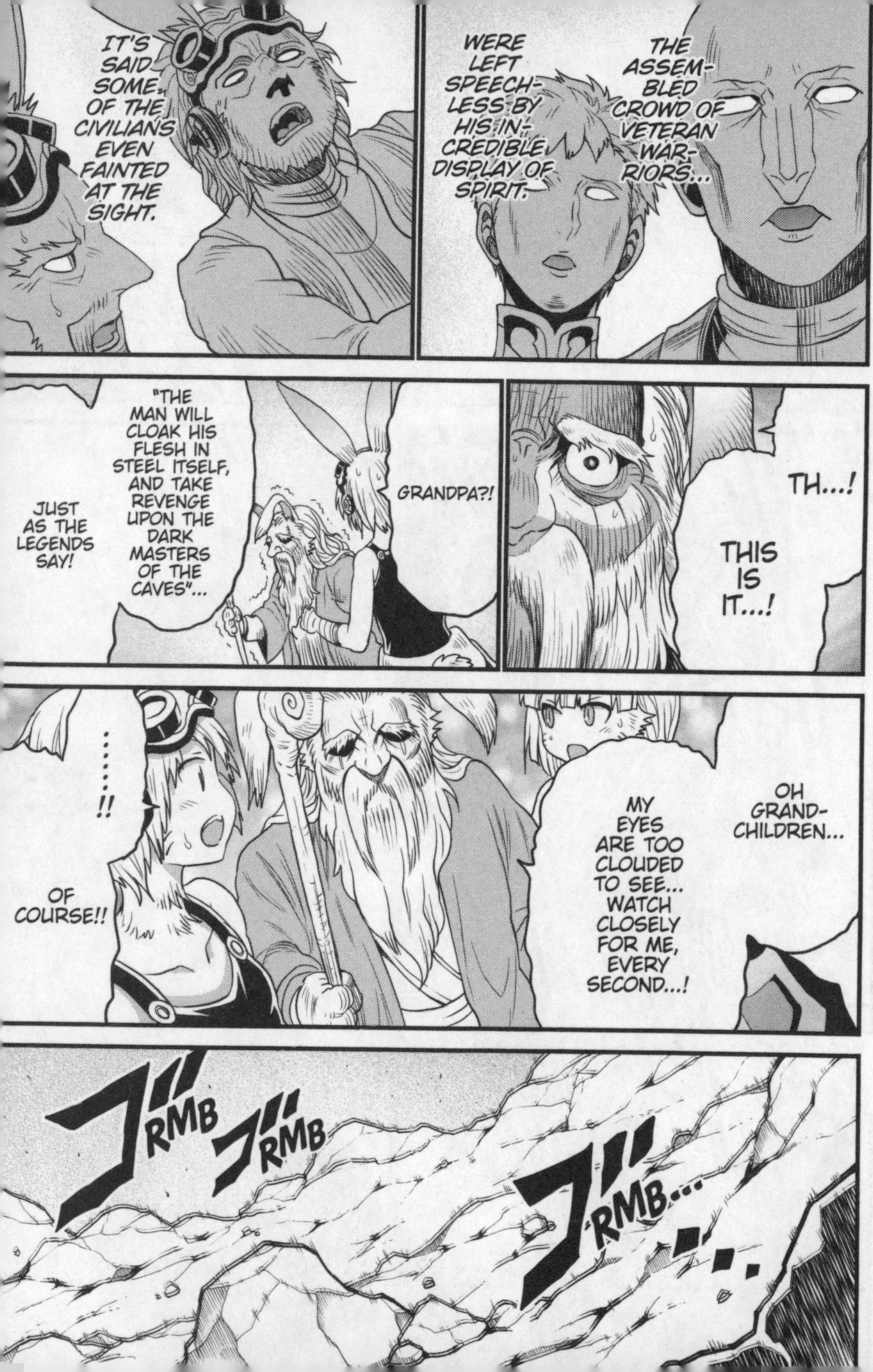
THE ASSEMBLED CROWD OF VETERAN WARRIORS...
WERE LEFT SPEECHLESS BY HIS INCREDIBLE DISPLAY OF SPIRIT.
IT'S SAID SOME OF THE CIVILIANS EVEN FAINTED AT THE SIGHT.
TH...!
THIS IS IT...!
GRANDPA?!
"THE MAN WILL CLOAK HIS FLESH IN STEEL ITSELF, AND TAKE REVENGE UPON THE DARK MASTERS OF THE CAVES"...
JUST AS THE LEGENDS SAY!
OH GRANDCHILDREN...
MY EYES ARE TOO CLOUDED TO SEE... WATCH CLOSELY FOR ME, EVERY SECOND...!
......!!
OF COURSE!!
RMB
RMB
RMB.......

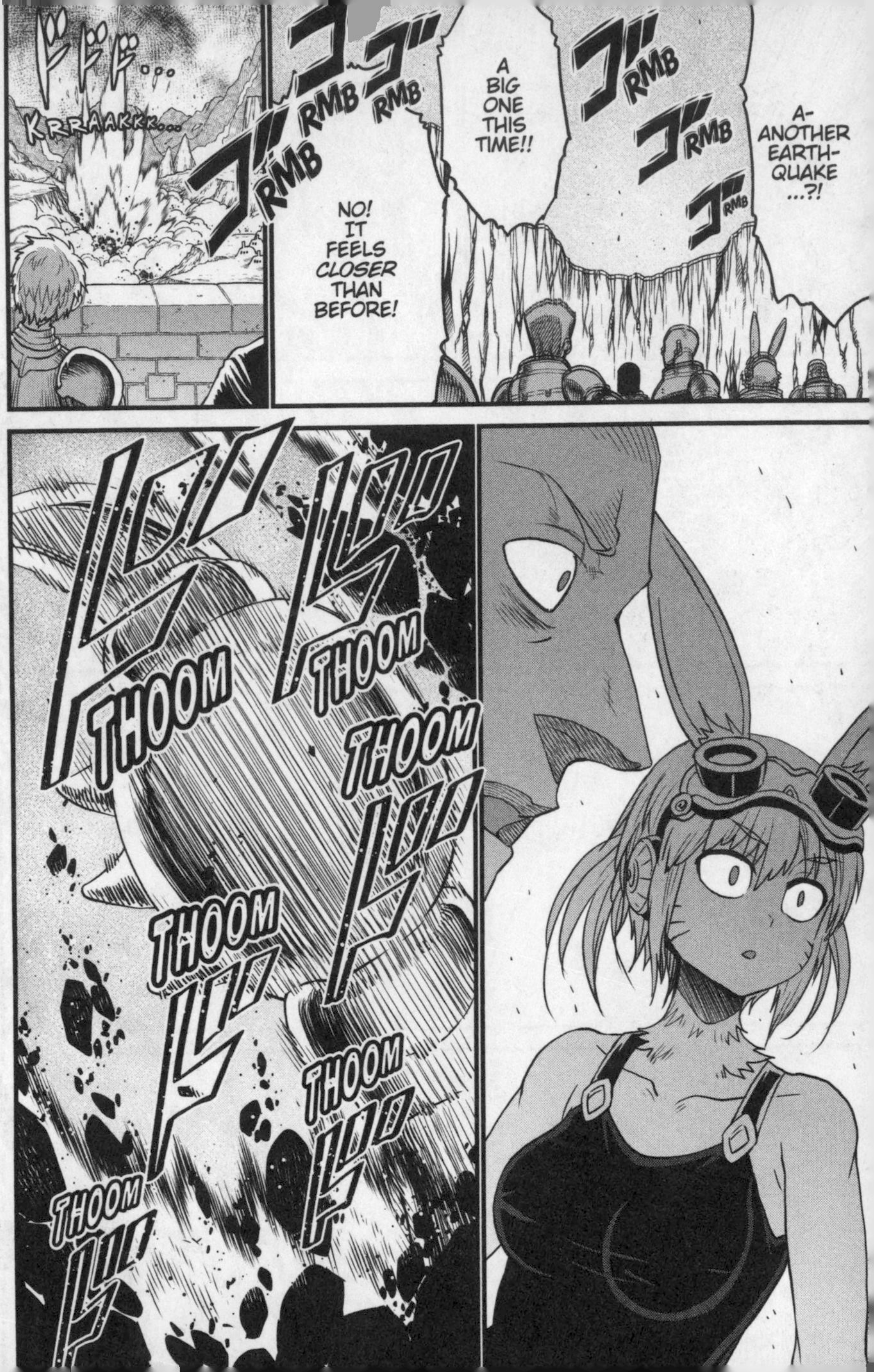
A-
ANOTHER
EARTH-
QUAKE
...?!
RMB
RMB
RMB
A BIG ONE THIS TIME!!
NO! IT FEELS CLOSER THAN BEFORE!
RMB RMB RMB RMB
ドドド...
KRRAAKKK...
THOOM
THOOM
THOOM
THOOM
THOOM
THOOM

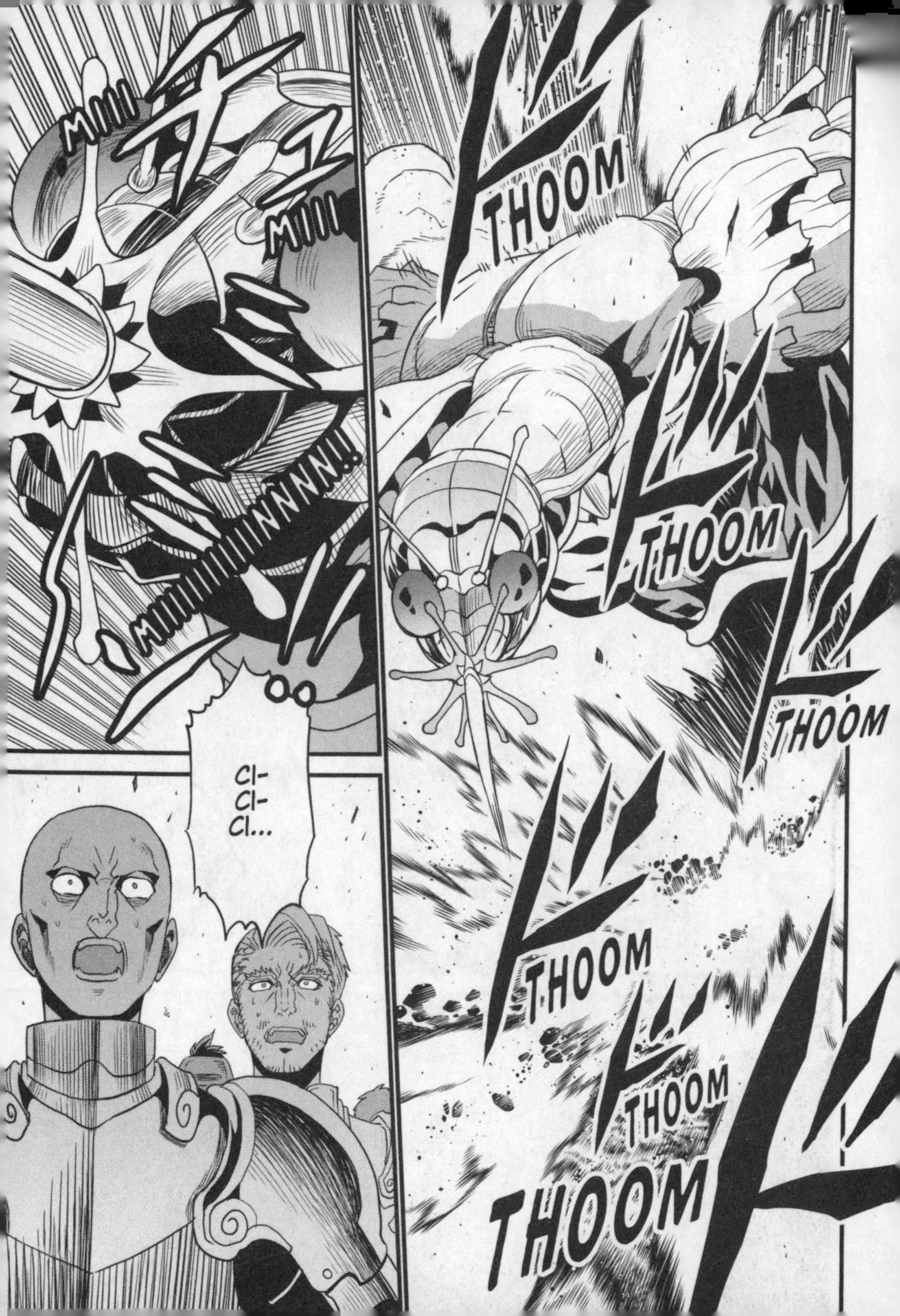
THOOM
THOOM
THOOM
THOOM
THOOM
THOOM
MIII
MIII
MIIIIIIIIIIIIINNNNNN!!
CI-
CI-
CI...

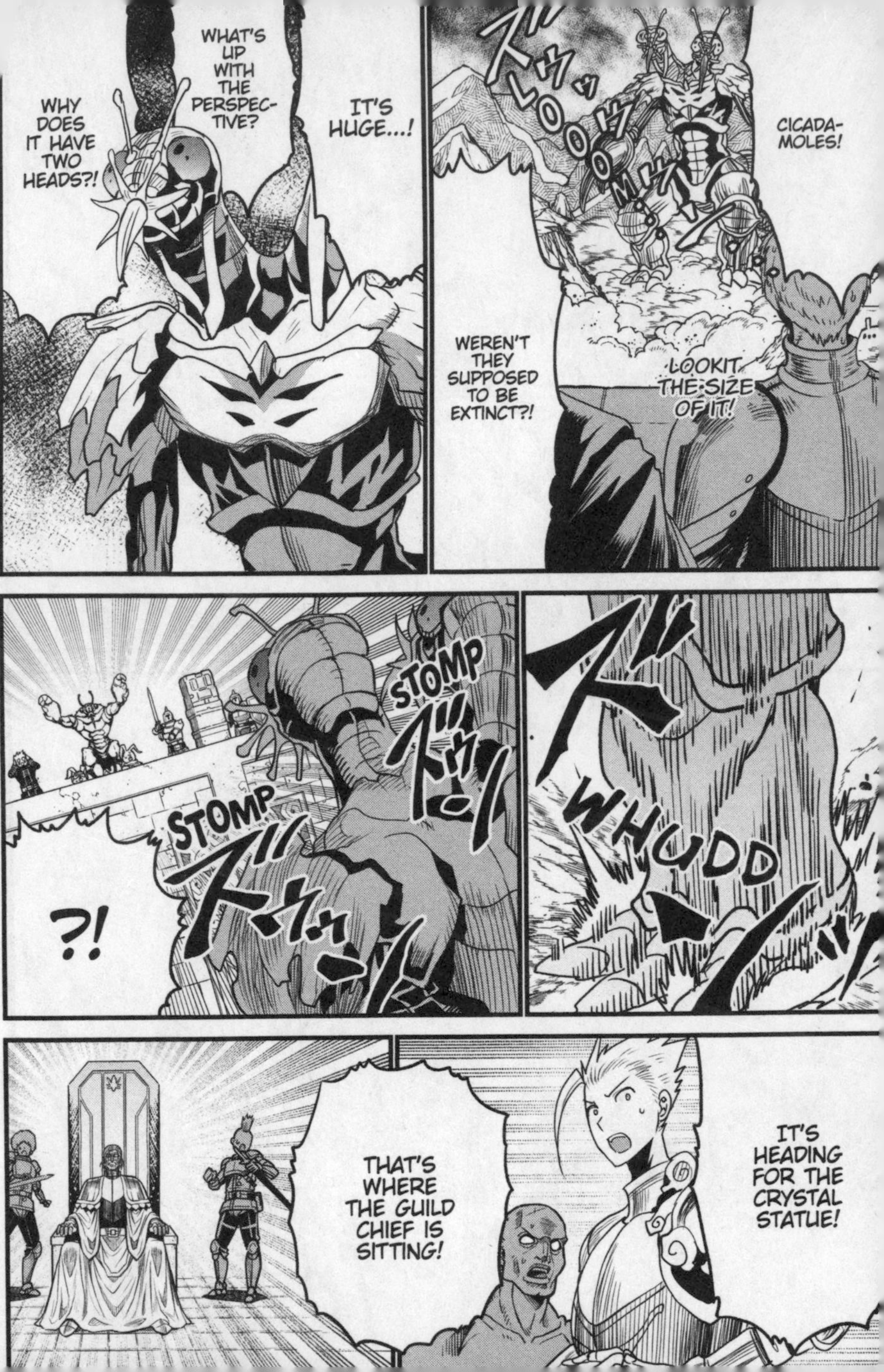
LOOOOM
CICADA-MOLES!
LOOKIT THE SIZE OF IT!
WEREN'T THEY SUPPOSED TO BE EXTINCT?!
IT'S HUGE...!
WHAT'S UP WITH THE PERSPECTIVE?
WHY DOES IT HAVE TWO HEADS?!
WHUDD
STOMP
STOMP
?!
IT'S HEADING FOR THE CRYSTAL STATUE!
THAT'S WHERE THE GUILD CHIEF IS SITTING!

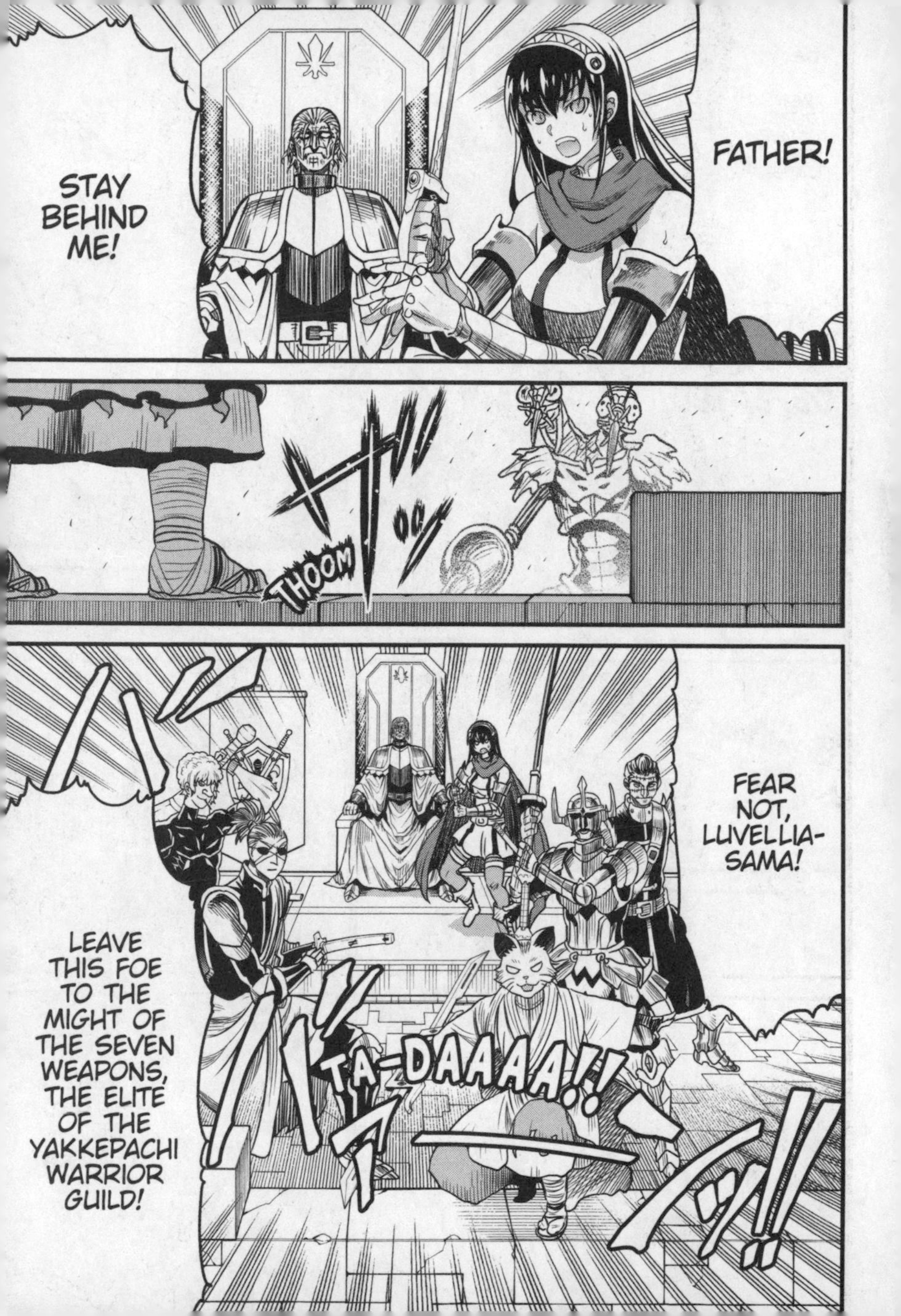
FATHER!
STAY BEHIND ME!
THOOM
FEAR NOT, LUVELLIA-SAMA!
LEAVE THIS FOE TO THE MIGHT OF THE SEVEN WEAPONS, THE ELITE OF THE YAKKEPACHI WARRIOR GUILD!
TA-DAAAAA!!

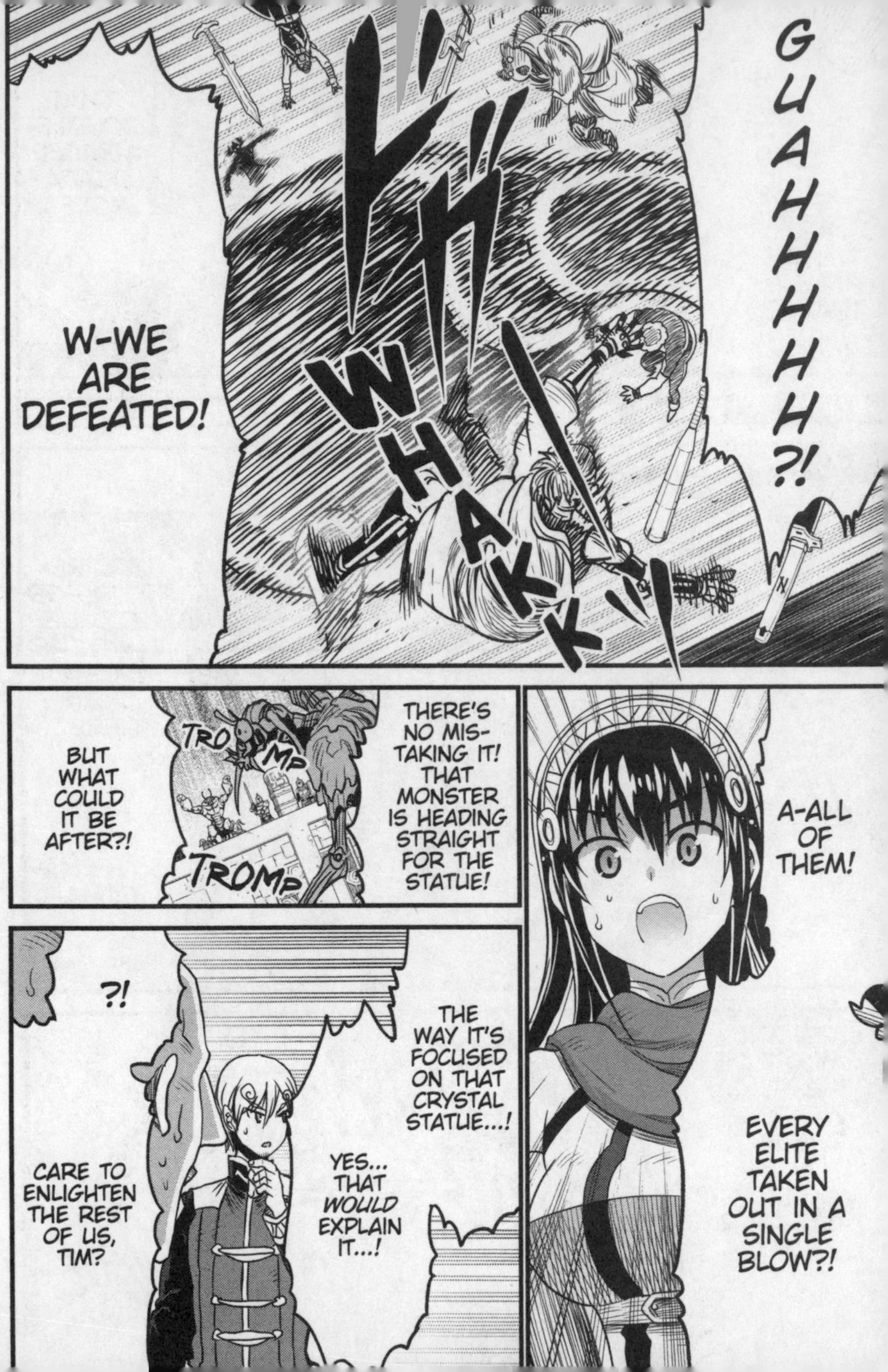
GUAHHHHHHH?!
WHAKK
W-WE ARE DEFEATED!
A-ALL OF THEM!
EVERY ELITE TAKEN OUT IN A SINGLE BLOW?!
THERE'S NO MIS-TAKING IT! THAT MONSTER IS HEADING STRAIGHT FOR THE STATUE!
TROMP
BUT WHAT COULD IT BE AFTER?!
TROMP
THE WAY IT'S FOCUSED ON THAT CRYSTAL STATUE...!
?!
YES... THAT *WOULD* EXPLAIN IT...!
CARE TO ENLIGHTEN THE REST OF US, TIM?

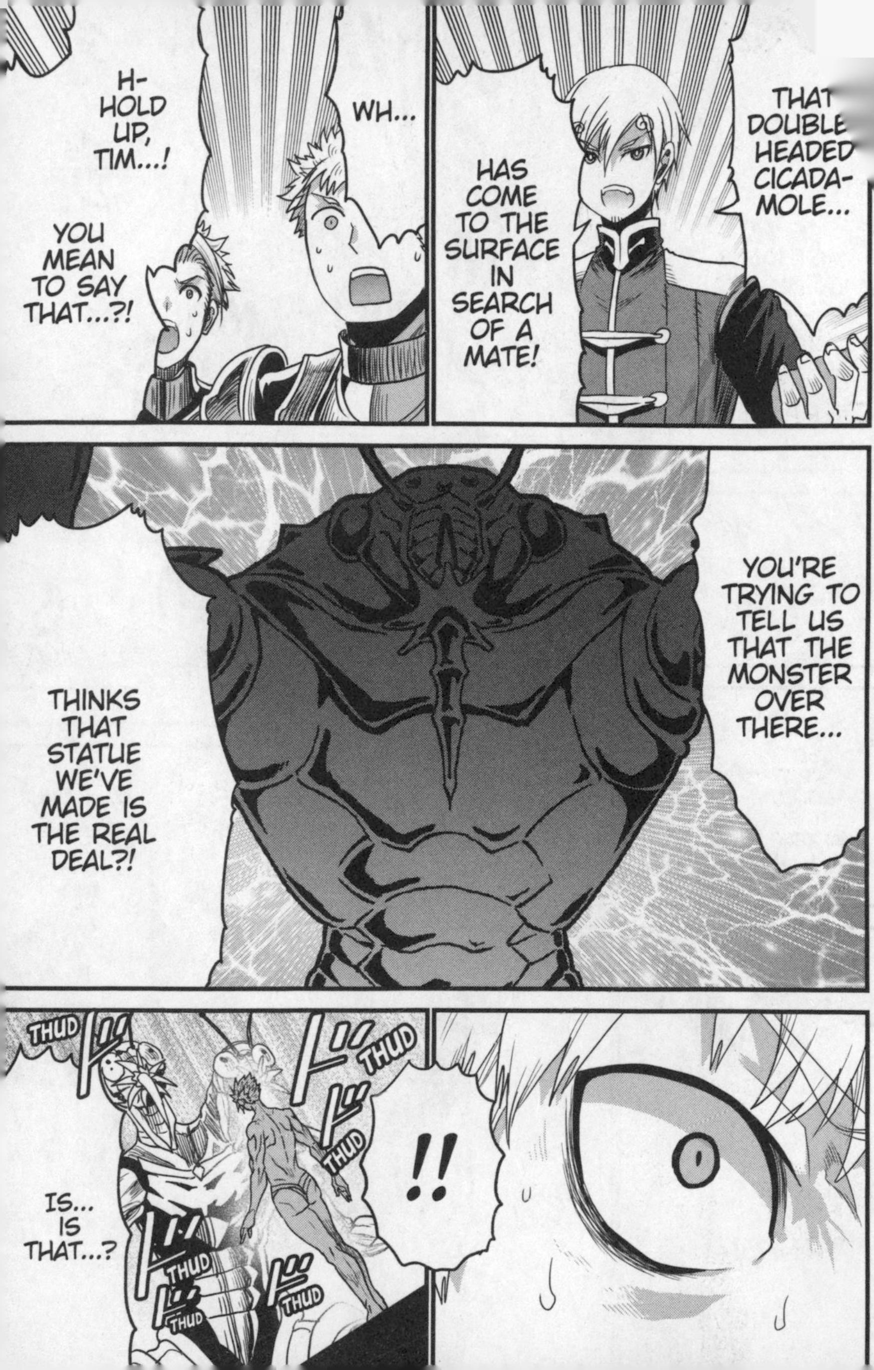
THAT DOUBLE HEADED CICADA-MOLE...
HAS COME TO THE SURFACE IN SEARCH OF A MATE!
WH...
H- HOLD UP, TIM...!
YOU MEAN TO SAY THAT...?!
YOU'RE TRYING TO TELL US THAT THE MONSTER OVER THERE...
THINKS THAT STATUE WE'VE MADE IS THE REAL DEAL?!
!!
THUD
THUD
THUD
IS... IS THAT...?
THUD
THUD
THUD

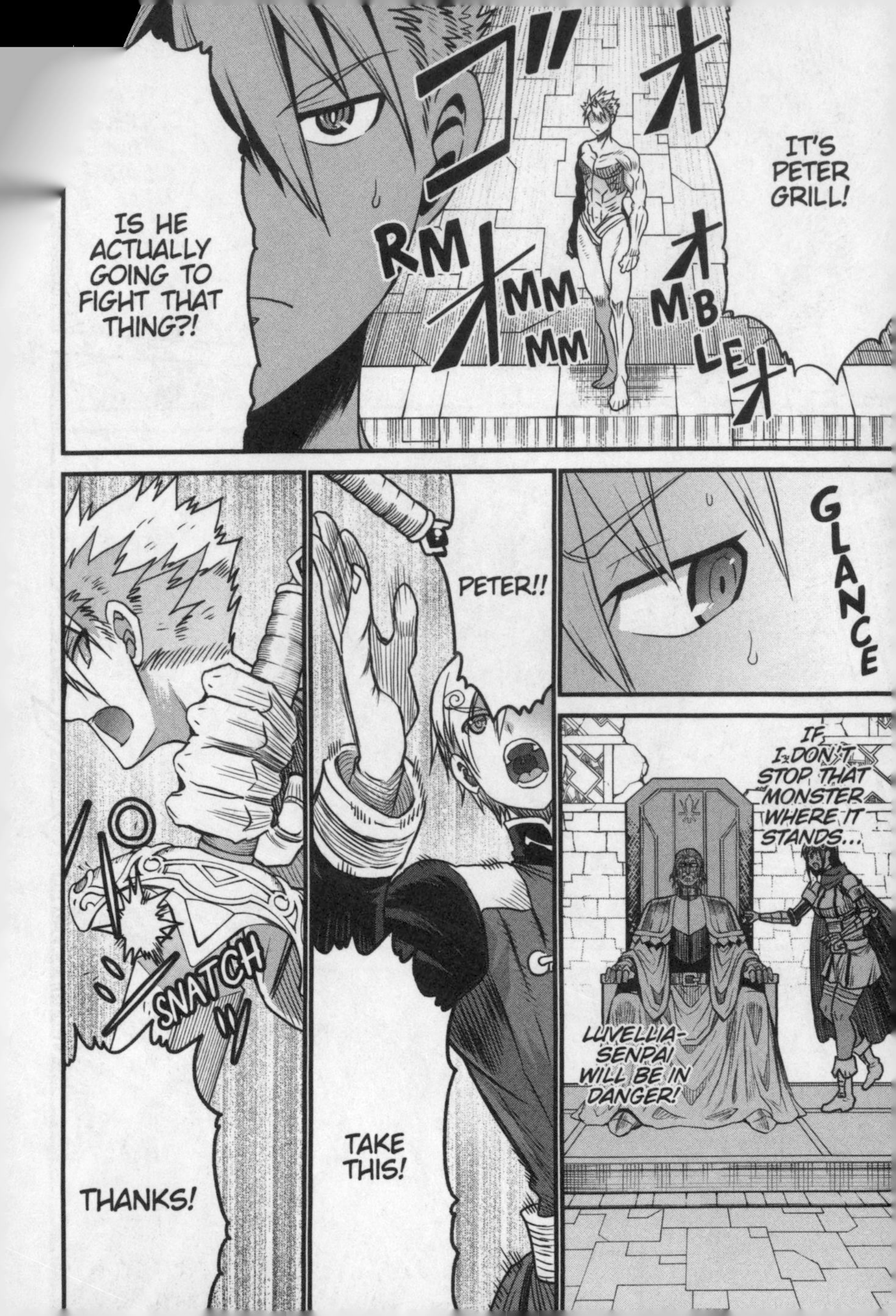
IT'S PETER GRILL!
ゴオオオオ
RMMMMMMBLE
IS HE ACTUALLY GOING TO FIGHT THAT THING?!
GLANCE
IF I DON'T STOP THAT MONSTER WHERE IT STANDS...
LUVELLIA-SENPAI WILL BE IN DANGER!
PETER!!
TAKE THIS!
SNATCH
THANKS!

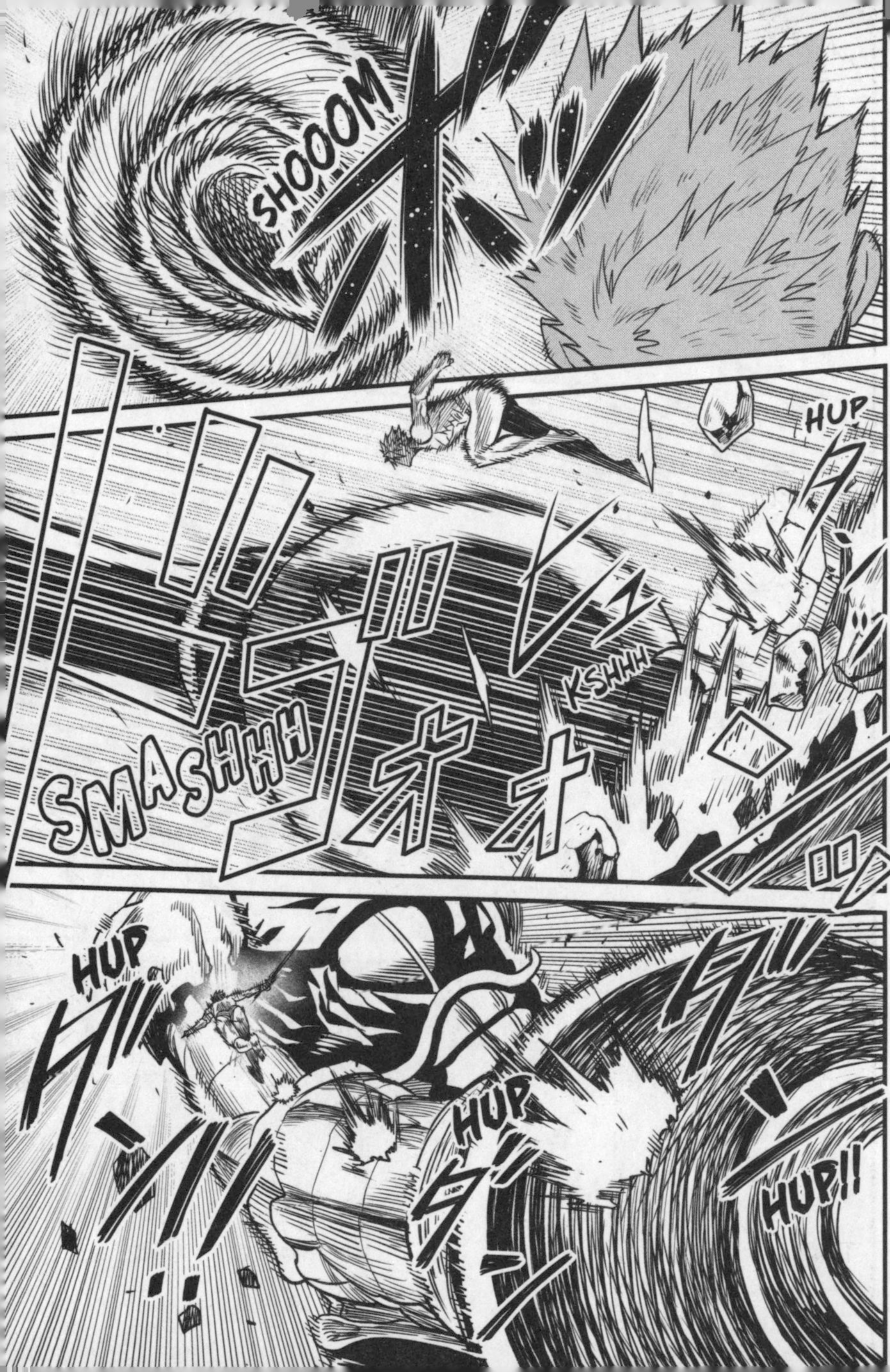
SHOOOM
HUP
KSHHH
SMASHHH
HUP!!
HUP
HUP

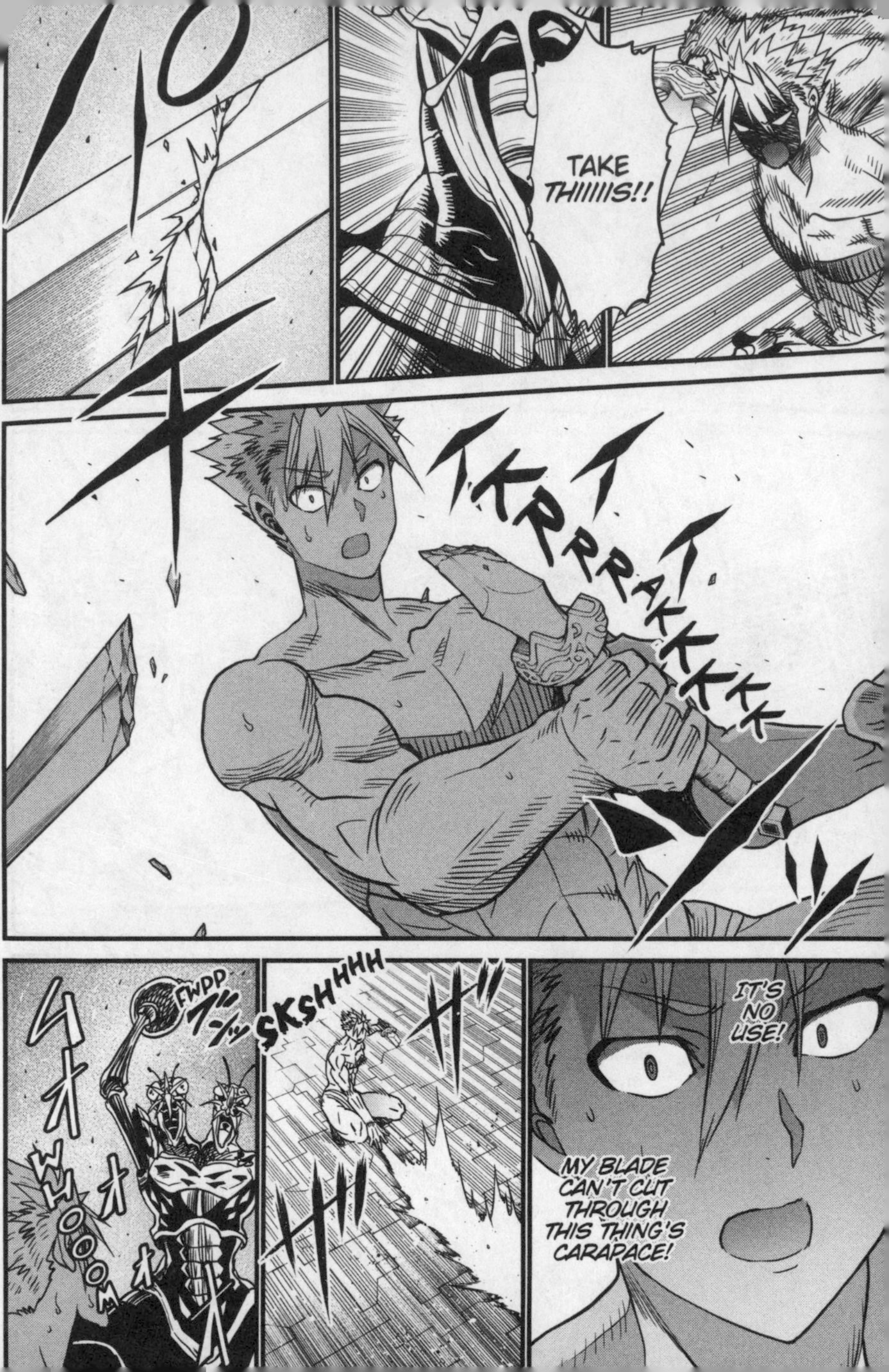
TAKE THIIIIIS!!
TKRRRAKKKKK
IT'S NO USE!
MY BLADE CAN'T CUT THROUGH THIS THING'S CARAPACE!
SKSHHHH
FWPP
WHOOOOM

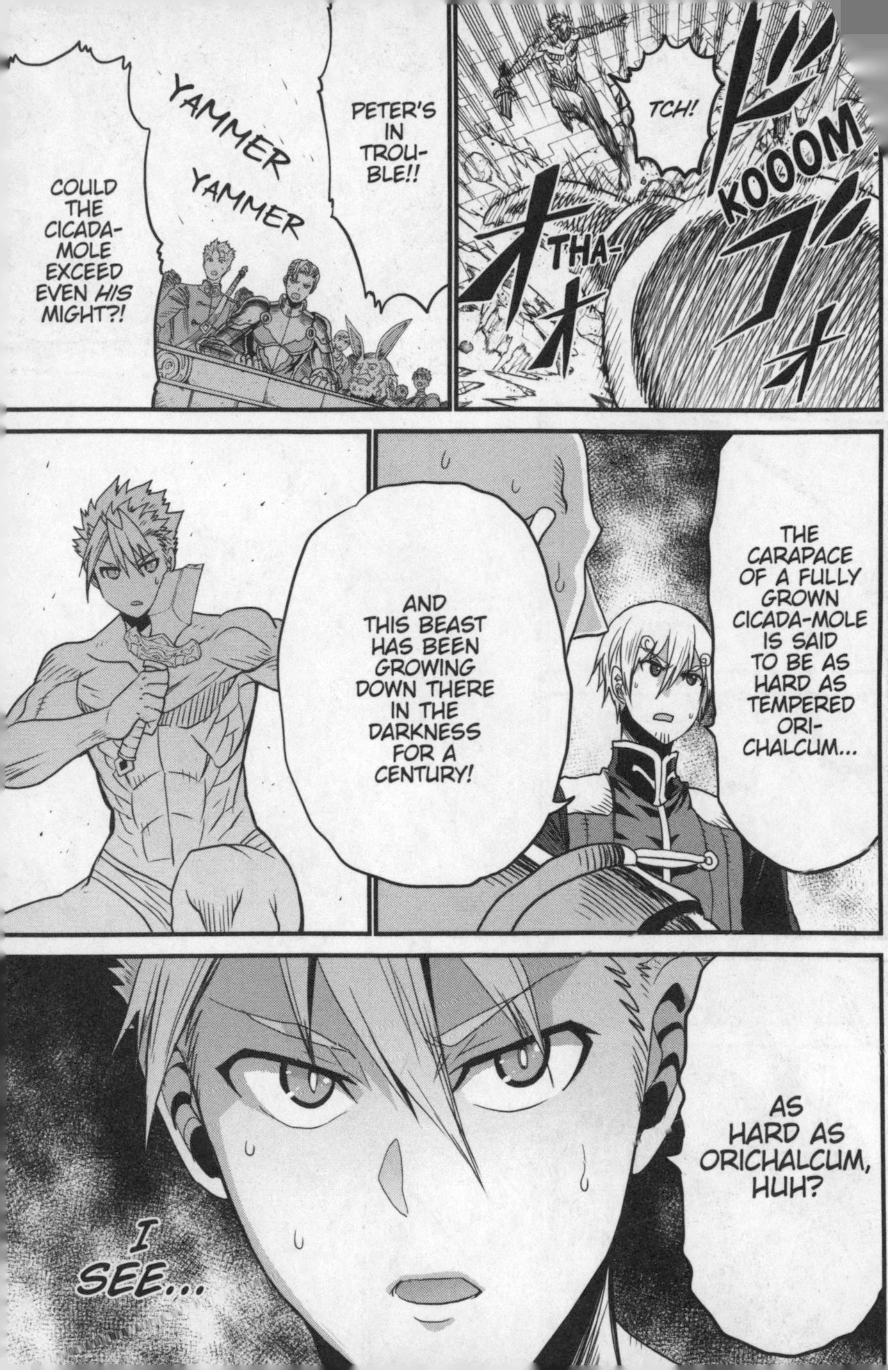
TCH!
KOOOM
THA-
PETER'S IN TROUBLE!!
YAMMER
YAMMER
COULD THE CICADA-MOLE EXCEED EVEN HIS MIGHT?!
THE CARAPACE OF A FULLY GROWN CICADA-MOLE IS SAID TO BE AS HARD AS TEMPERED ORICHALCUM...
AND THIS BEAST HAS BEEN GROWING DOWN THERE IN THE DARKNESS FOR A CENTURY!
AS HARD AS ORICHALCUM, HUH?
I SEE...

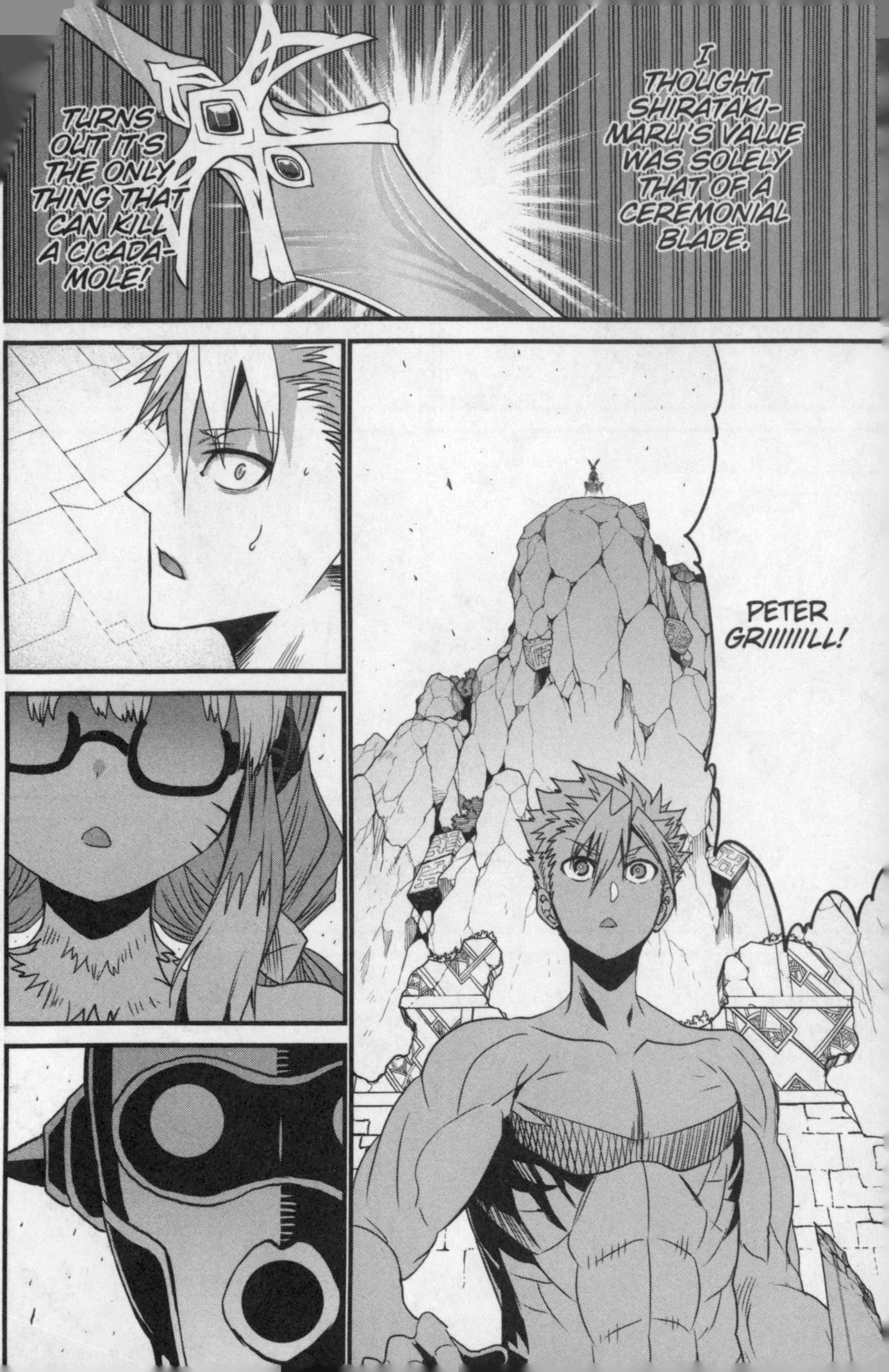
I THOUGHT SHIRATAKI-MARU'S VALUE WAS SOLELY THAT OF A CEREMONIAL BLADE.
TURNS OUT IT'S THE ONLY THING THAT CAN KILL A CICADA-MOLE!
PETER GRIIIIIILL!

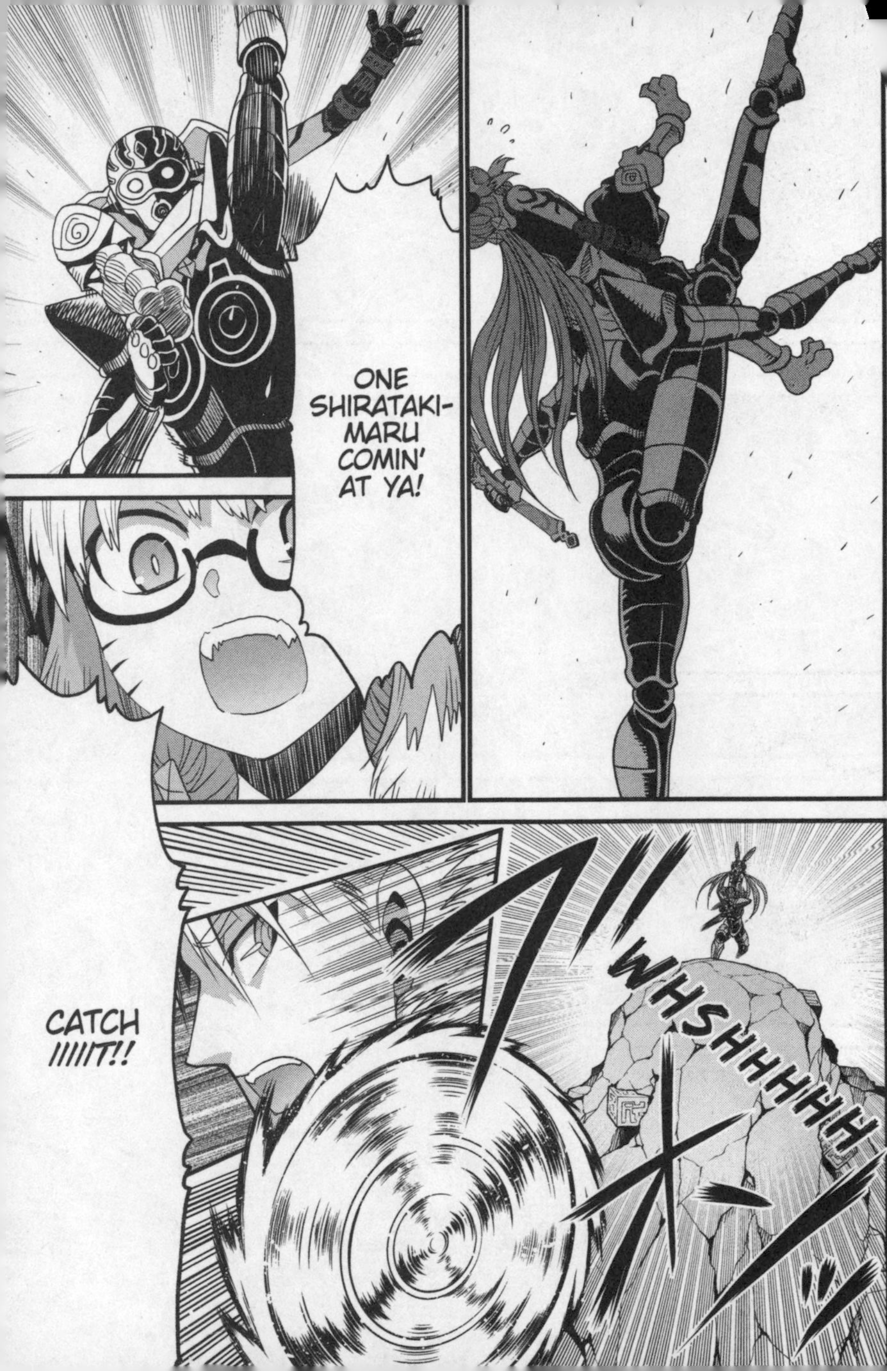
ONE SHIRATAKI-MARU COMIN' AT YA!
WHSHHHHH
CATCH IIIIIT!!

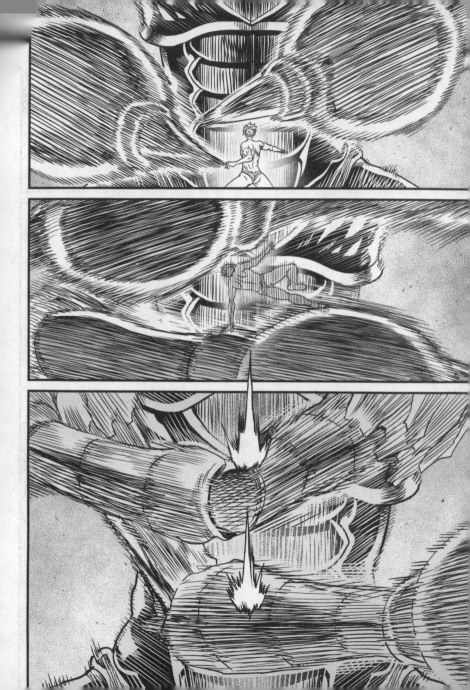

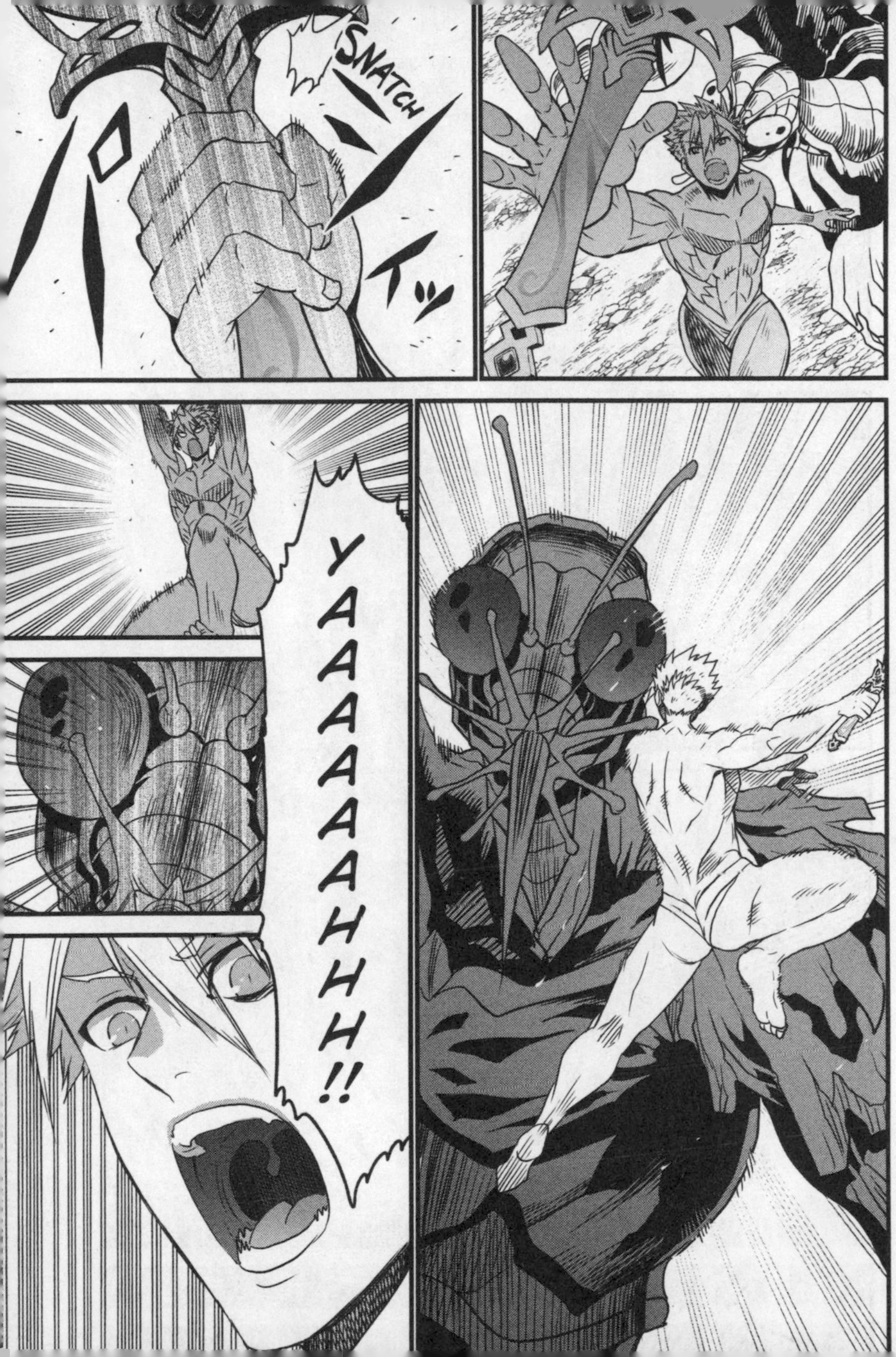
SNATCH
パ
ッ
YAAAAAAAHHH!!

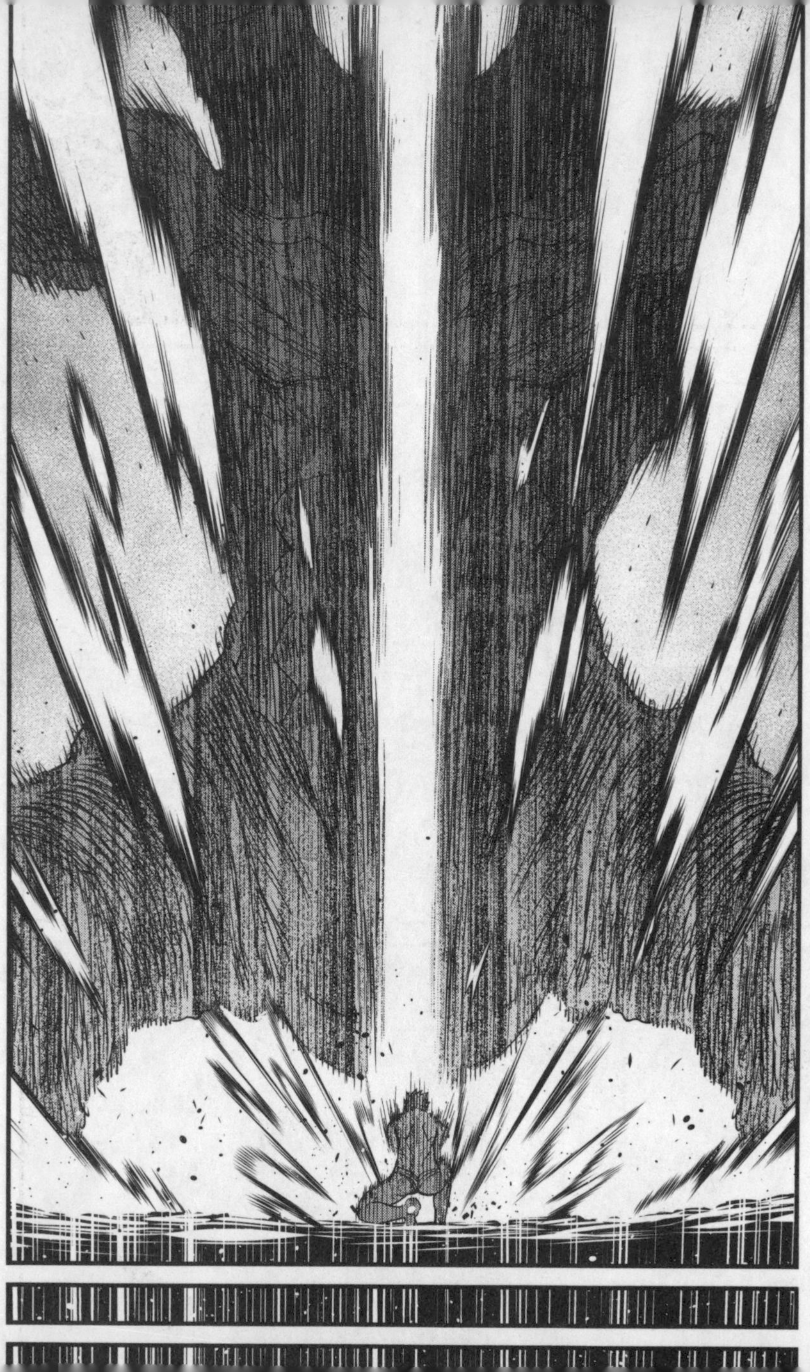

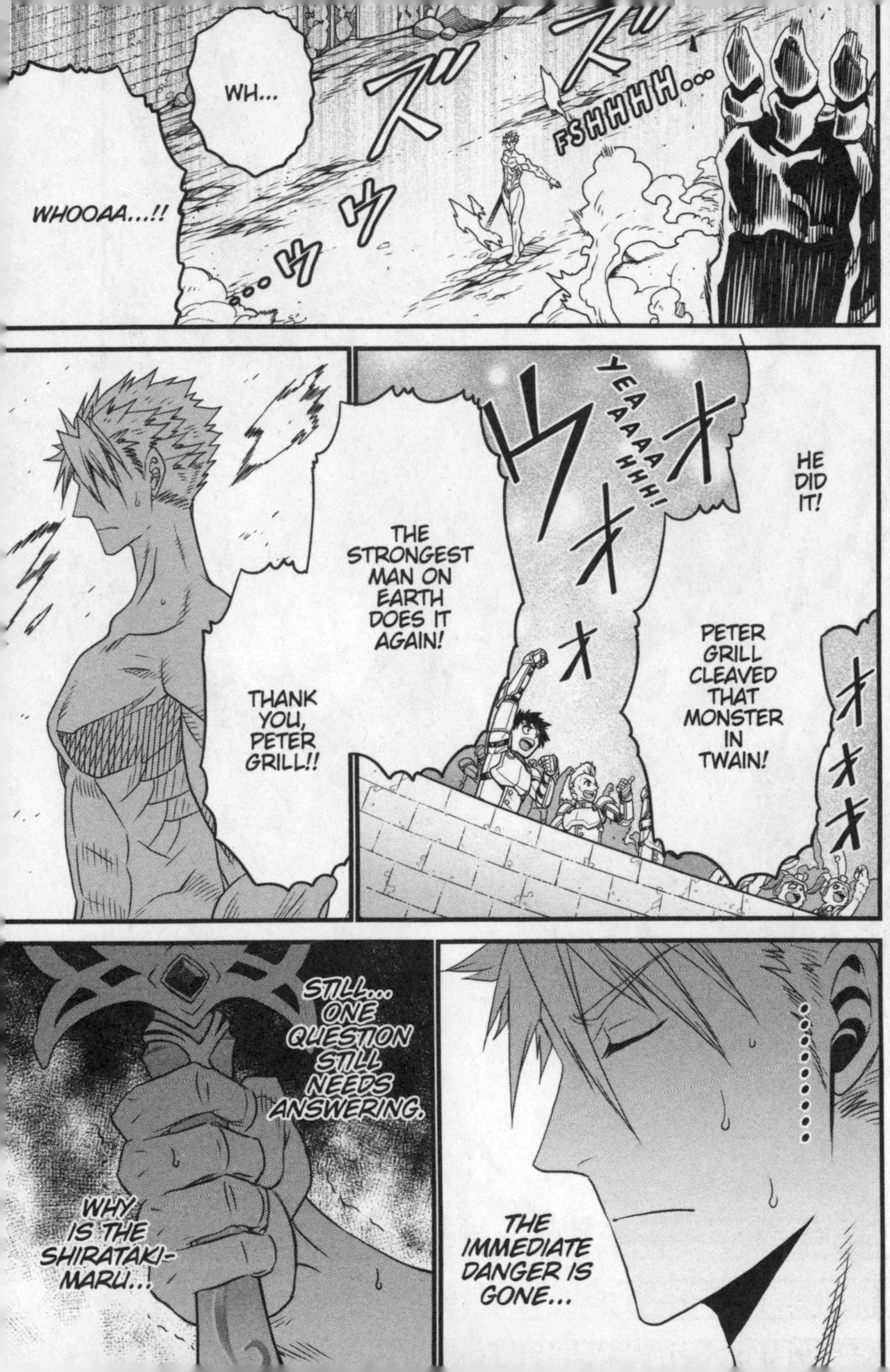
FSHHHHH...
WH...
WHOOAA...!!
HE DID IT!
YEAAAAAHHH!
PETER GRILL CLEAVED THAT MONSTER IN TWAIN!
THE STRONGEST MAN ON EARTH DOES IT AGAIN!
THANK YOU, PETER GRILL!!
....
THE IMMEDIATE DANGER IS GONE...
STILL... ONE QUESTION STILL NEEDS ANSWERING.
WHY IS THE SHIRATAKI-MARU...

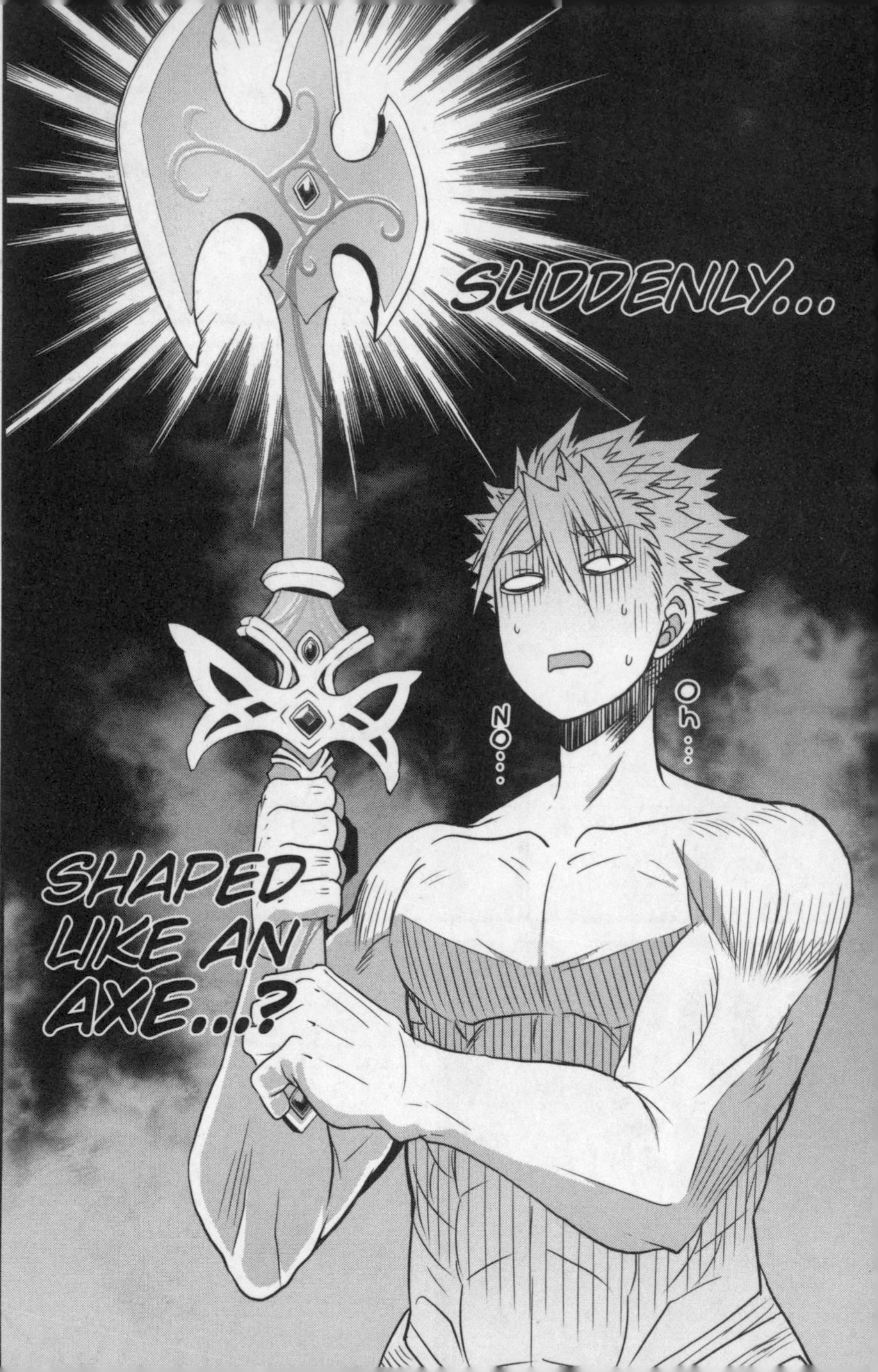
SUDDENLY...
Oh...
NO...
SHAPED LIKE AN AXE...?

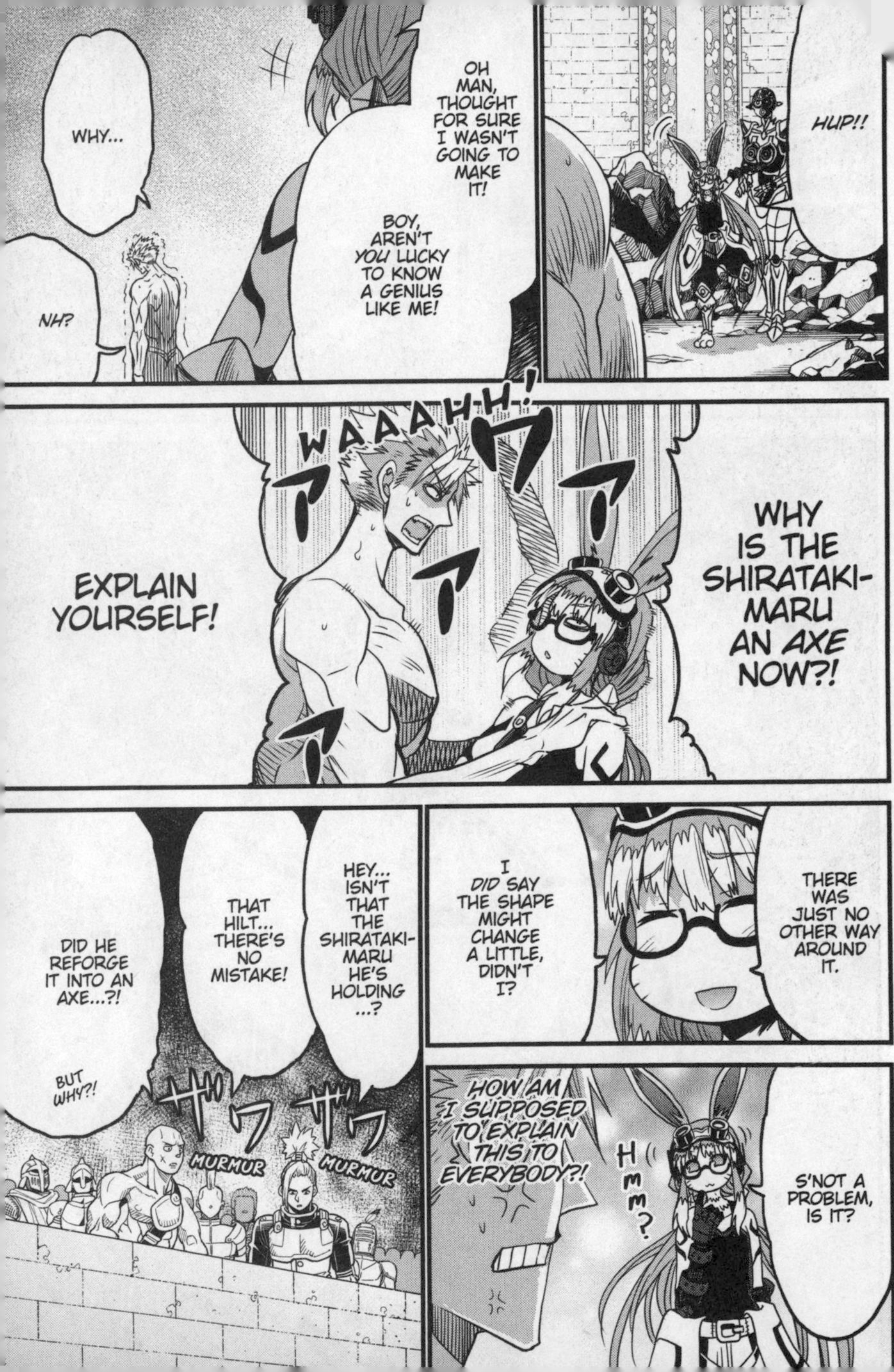
HUP!!
OH MAN, THOUGHT FOR SURE I WASN'T GOING TO MAKE IT!
BOY, AREN'T *YOU* LUCKY TO KNOW A GENIUS LIKE ME!
WHY...
NH?
WAAAAHH!
WHY IS THE SHIRATAKI-MARU AN AXE NOW?!
EXPLAIN YOURSELF!
THERE WAS JUST NO OTHER WAY AROUND IT.
I *DID* SAY THE SHAPE MIGHT CHANGE A LITTLE, DIDN'T I?
S'NOT A PROBLEM, IS IT?
HMM?
HOW AM I SUPPOSED TO EXPLAIN THIS TO EVERYBODY?!
HEY... ISN'T THAT THE SHIRATAKI-MARU HE'S HOLDING ...?
THAT HILT... THERE'S NO MISTAKE!
DID HE REFORGE IT INTO AN AXE...?!
MURMUR
MURMUR
BUT WHY?!

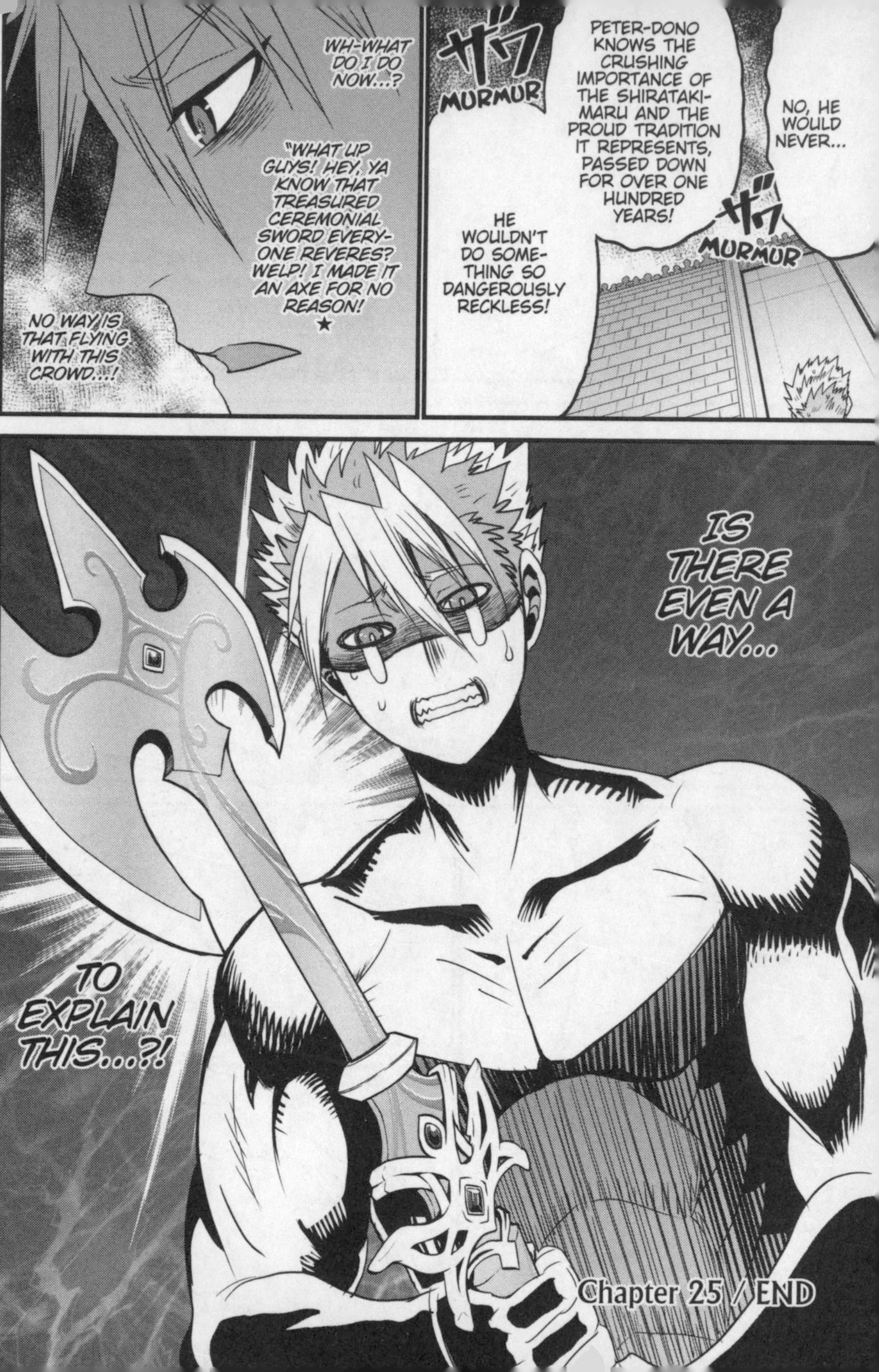
NO, HE WOULD NEVER...
PETER-DONO KNOWS THE CRUSHING IMPORTANCE OF THE SHIRATAKI-MARU AND THE PROUD TRADITION IT REPRESENTS, PASSED DOWN FOR OVER ONE HUNDRED YEARS!
ザワ MURMUR
ザワ MURMUR
HE WOULDN'T DO SOME-THING SO DANGEROUSLY RECKLESS!
WH-WHAT DO I DO NOW...?
"WHAT UP GUYS! HEY, YA KNOW THAT TREASURED CEREMONIAL SWORD EVERY-ONE REVERES? WELP! I MADE IT AN AXE FOR NO REASON! ★
NO WAY IS THAT FLYING WITH THIS CROWD...!
IS THERE EVEN A WAY...
TO EXPLAIN THIS...?!
Chapter 25 / END

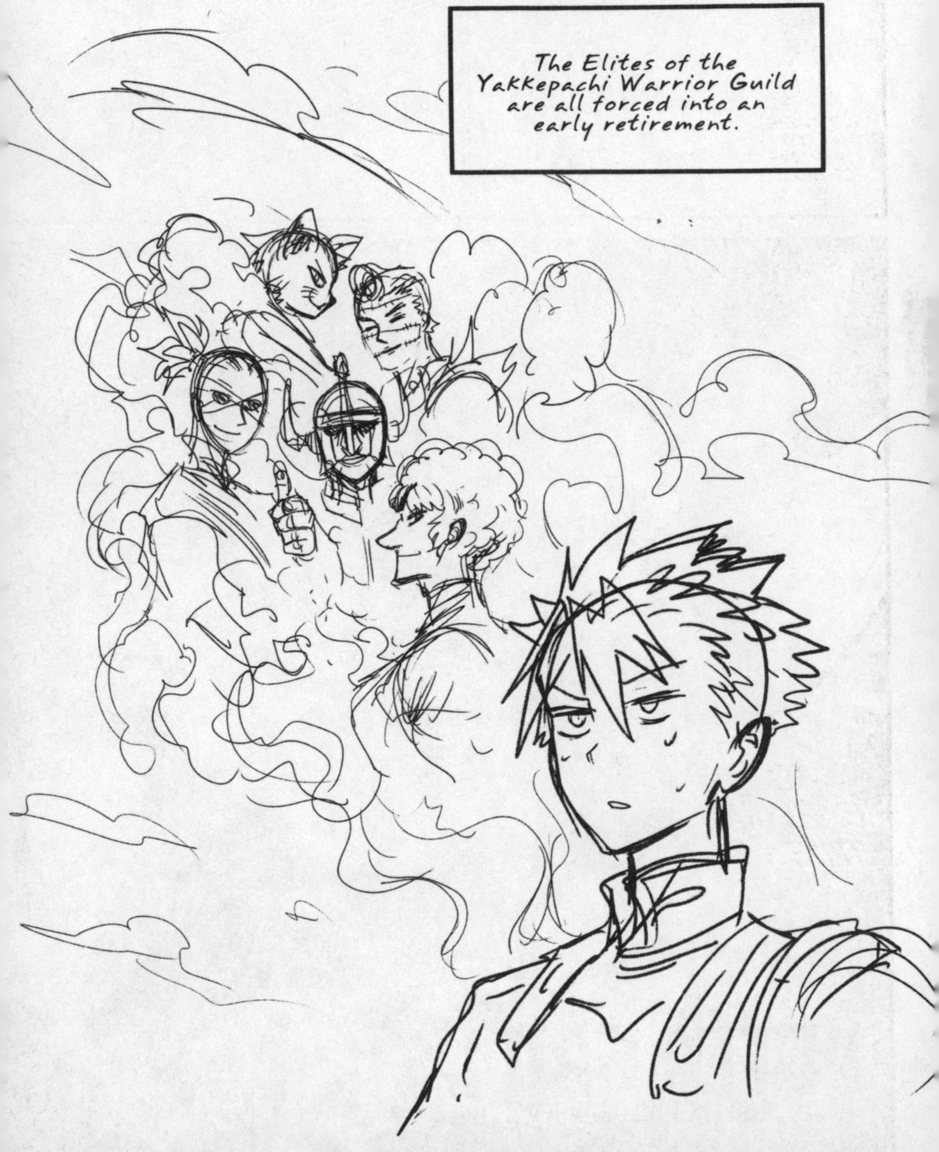
The Elites of the Yakkepachi Warrior Guild are all forced into an early retirement.

PETER GRILL
AND THE PHILOSOPHER'S TIME

Previously, on *Peter Grill*...

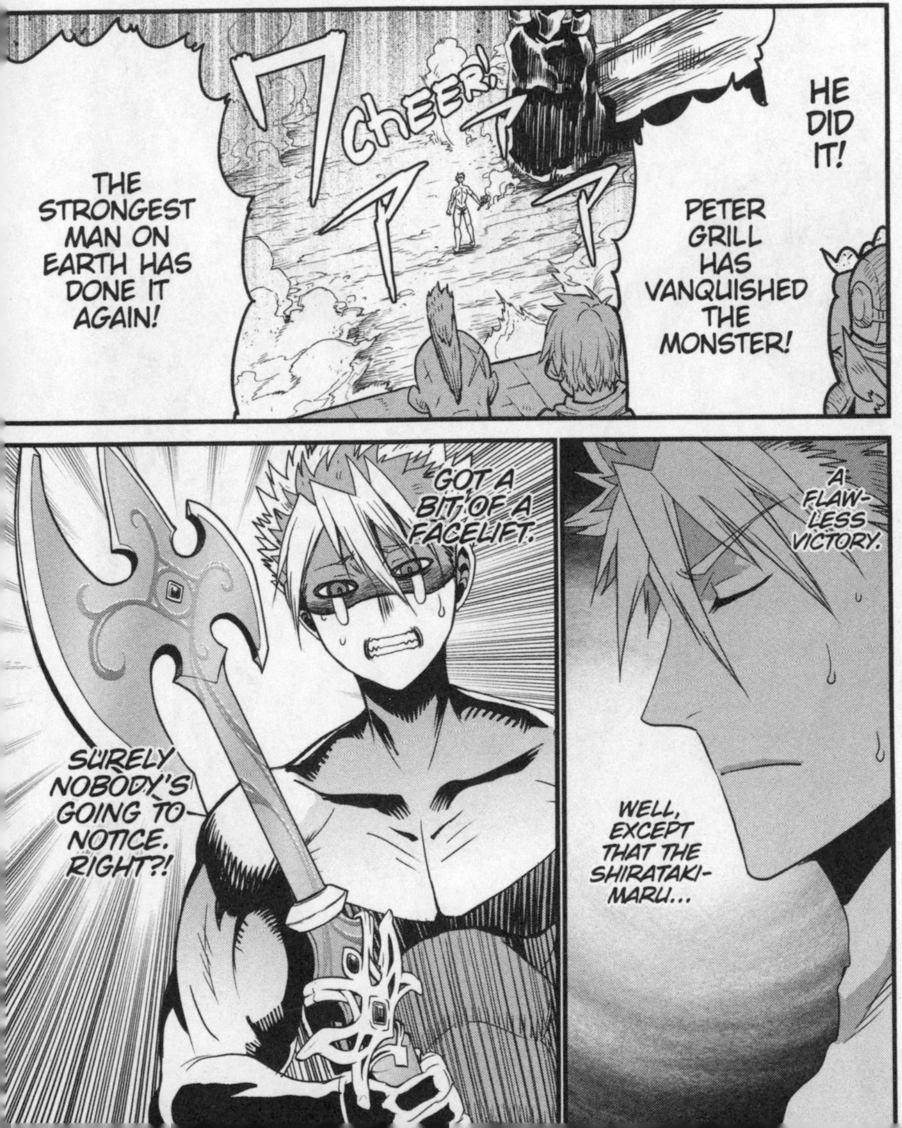
HE DID IT!
PETER GRILL HAS VANQUISHED THE MONSTER!
ワアア
CHEER!
THE STRONGEST MAN ON EARTH HAS DONE IT AGAIN!
A FLAWLESS VICTORY.
WELL, EXCEPT THAT THE SHIRATAKI-MARU...
GOT A BIT OF A FACELIFT.
SURELY NOBODY'S GOING TO NOTICE. RIGHT?!

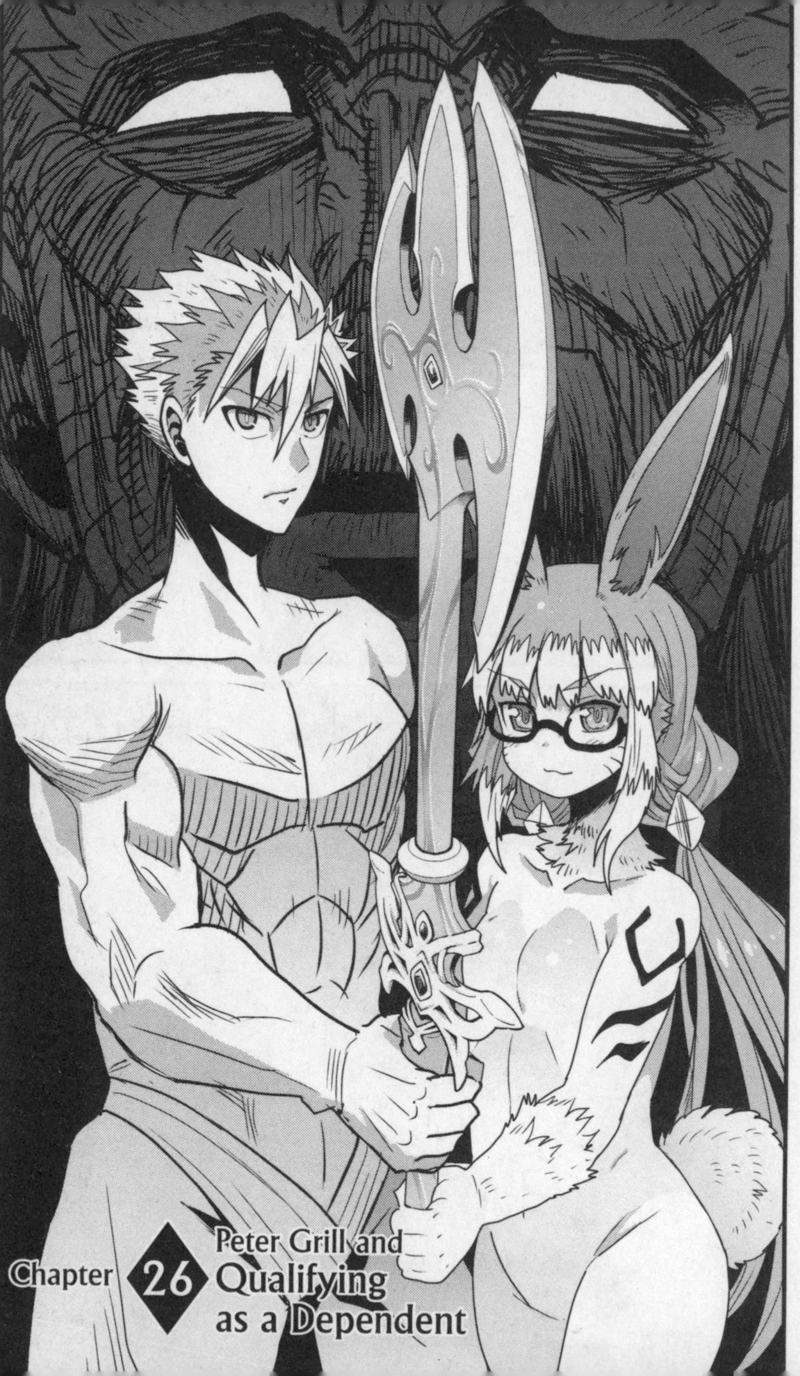
Chapter 26
Peter Grill and Qualifying as a Dependent

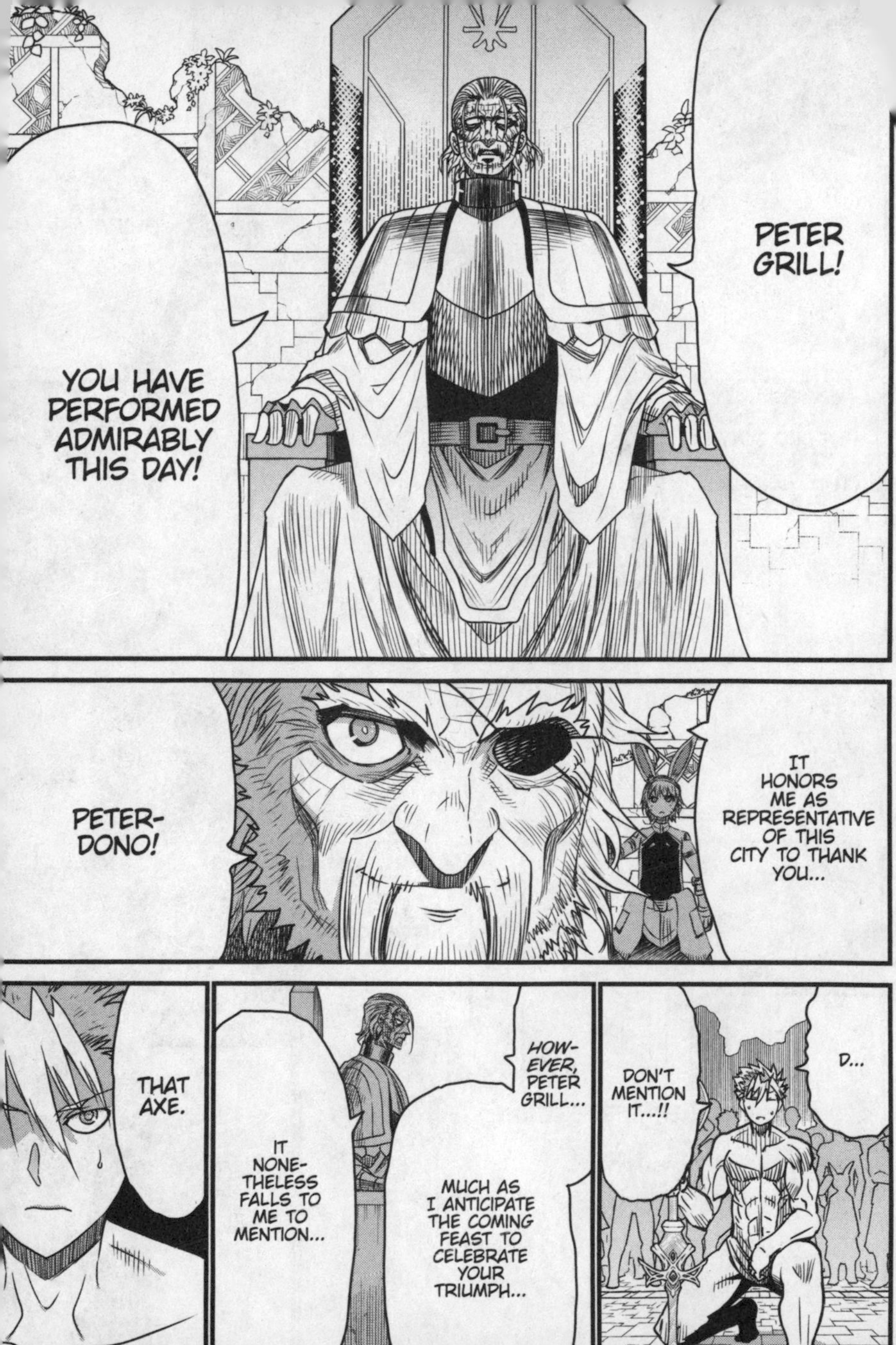
PETER GRILL!
YOU HAVE PERFORMED ADMIRABLY THIS DAY!
IT HONORS ME AS REPRESENTATIVE OF THIS CITY TO THANK YOU...
PETER-DONO!
D...
DON'T MENTION IT...!!
HOW-EVER, PETER GRILL...
MUCH AS I ANTICIPATE THE COMING FEAST TO CELEBRATE YOUR TRIUMPH...
IT NONE-THELESS FALLS TO ME TO MENTION...
THAT AXE.

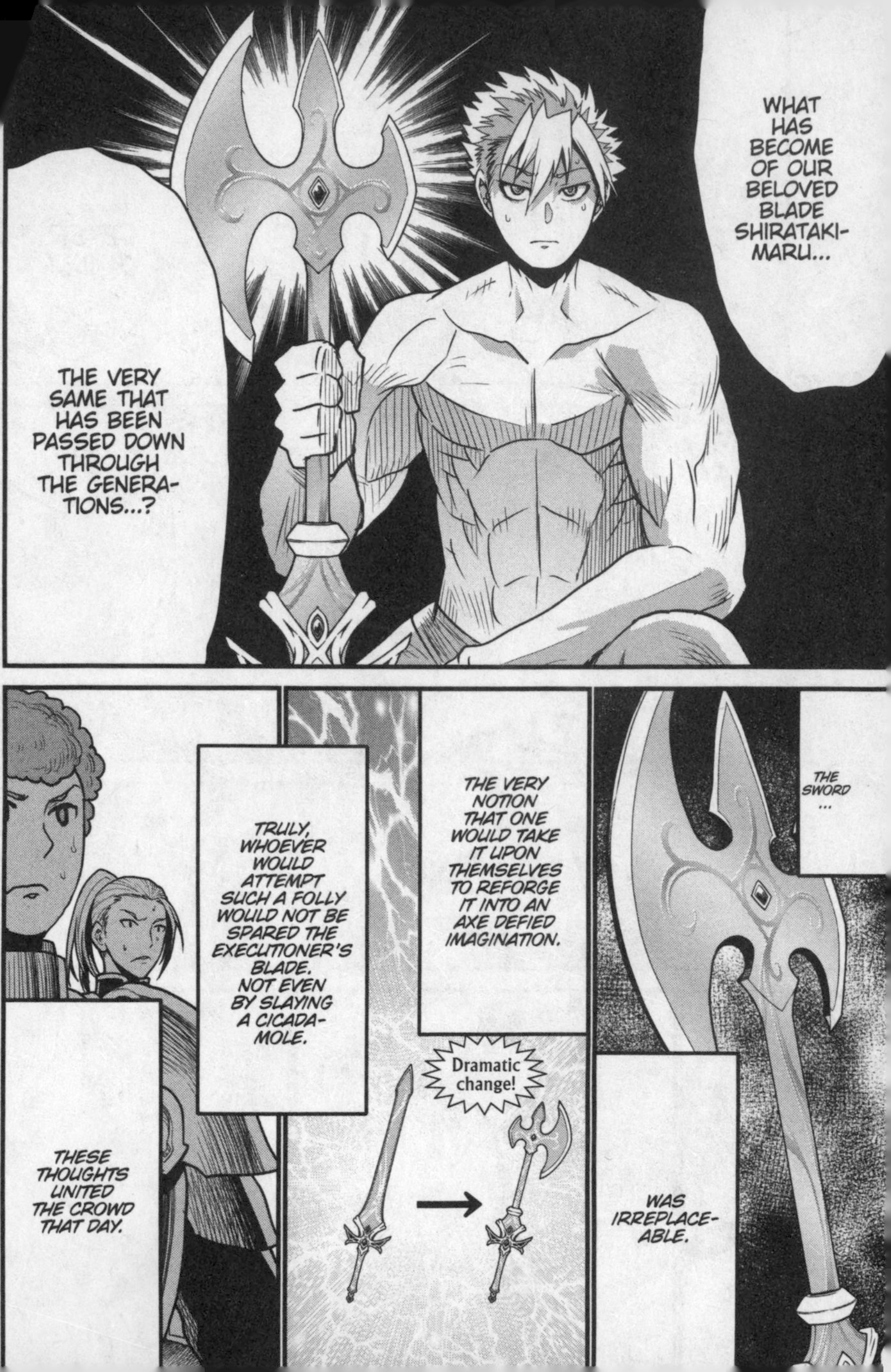

WHAT HAS BECOME OF OUR BELOVED BLADE SHIRATAKI-MARU...
THE VERY SAME THAT HAS BEEN PASSED DOWN THROUGH THE GENERA-TIONS...?
THE SWORD ...
WAS IRREPLACE-ABLE.
THE VERY NOTION THAT ONE WOULD TAKE IT UPON THEMSELVES TO REFORGE IT INTO AN AXE DEFIED IMAGINATION.
Dramatic change!
TRULY, WHOEVER WOULD ATTEMPT SUCH A FOLLY WOULD NOT BE SPARED THE EXECUTIONER'S BLADE. NOT EVEN BY SLAYING A CICADA-MOLE.
THESE THOUGHTS UNITED THE CROWD THAT DAY.

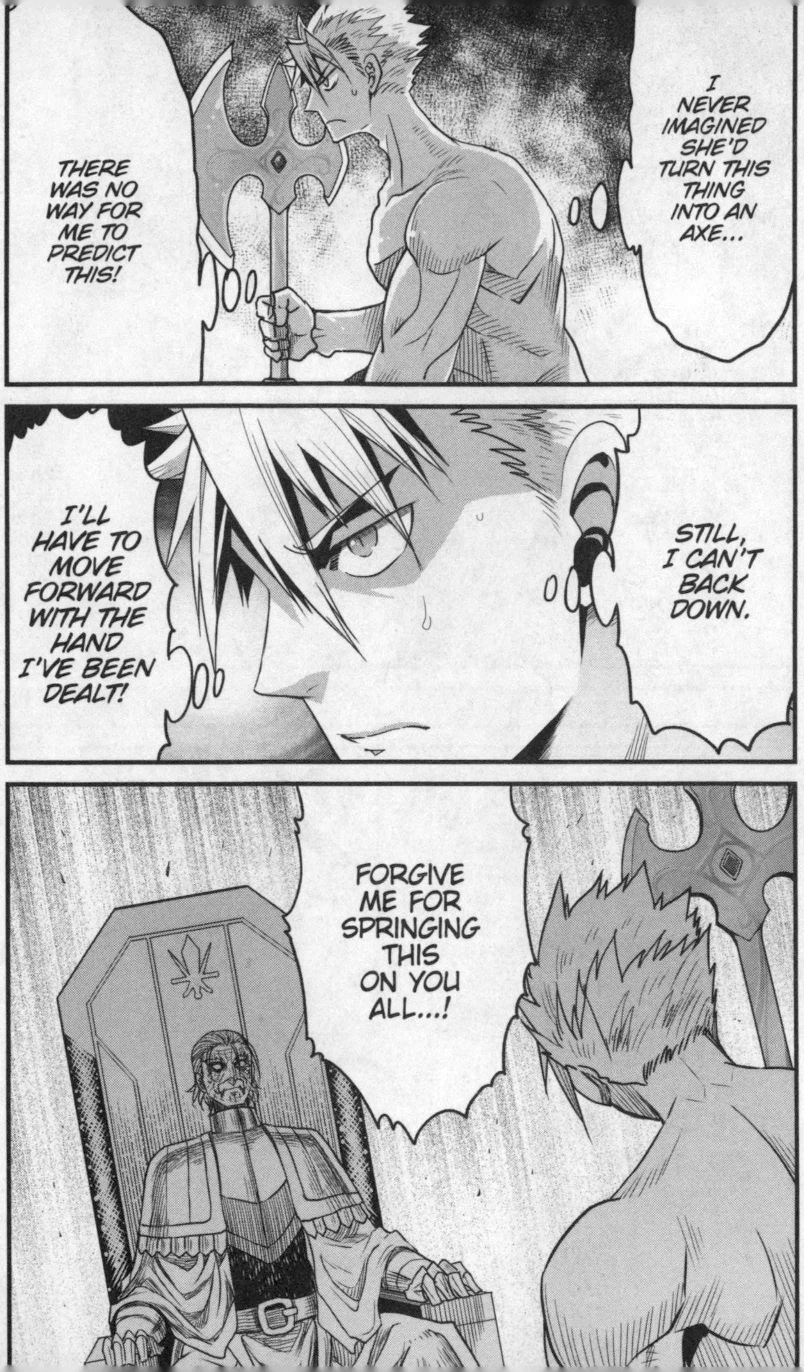
I NEVER IMAGINED SHE'D TURN THIS THING INTO AN AXE...
THERE WAS NO WAY FOR ME TO PREDICT THIS!
STILL, I CAN'T BACK DOWN.
I'LL HAVE TO MOVE FORWARD WITH THE HAND I'VE BEEN DEALT!
FORGIVE ME FOR SPRINGING THIS ON YOU ALL...!

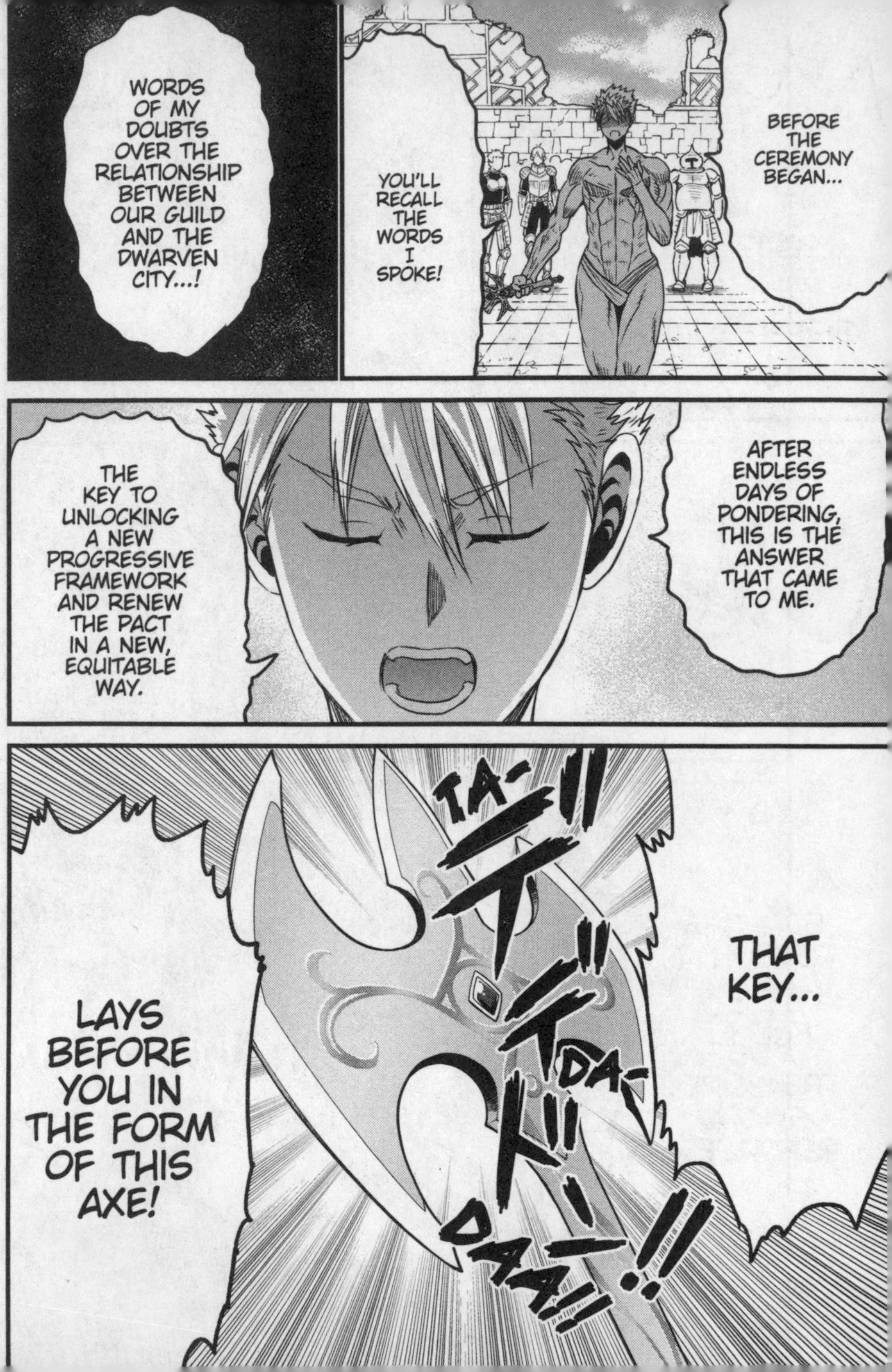

BEFORE THE CEREMONY BEGAN...
YOU'LL RECALL THE WORDS I SPOKE!
WORDS OF MY DOUBTS OVER THE RELATIONSHIP BETWEEN OUR GUILD AND THE DWARVEN CITY...!
AFTER ENDLESS DAYS OF PONDERING, THIS IS THE ANSWER THAT CAME TO ME.
THE KEY TO UNLOCKING A NEW PROGRESSIVE FRAMEWORK AND RENEW THE PACT IN A NEW, EQUITABLE WAY.
THAT KEY...
TA-
DA-
DAA!!
LAYS BEFORE YOU IN THE FORM OF THIS AXE!

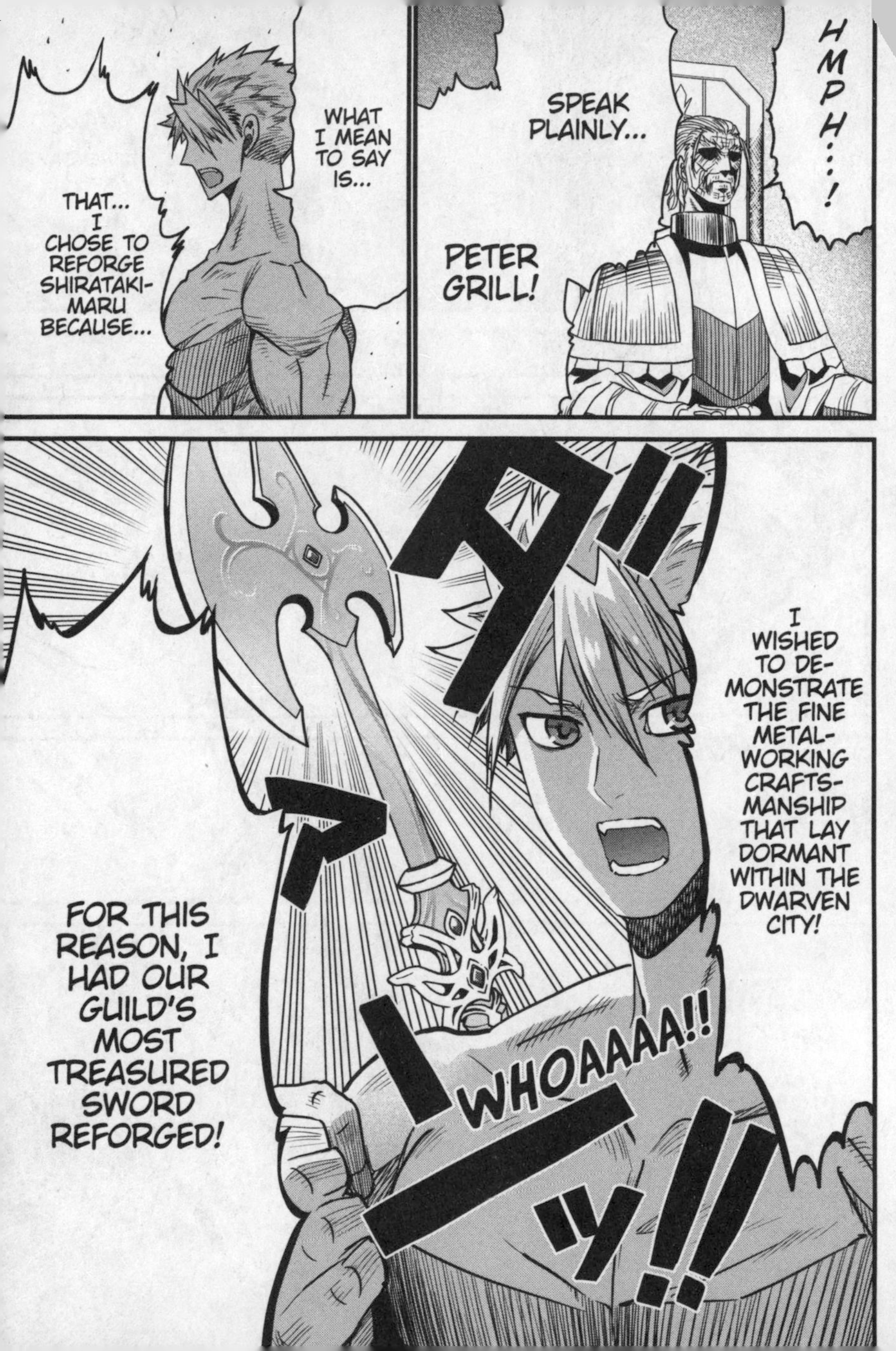
HMPH...!
SPEAK PLAINLY...
PETER GRILL!
WHAT I MEAN TO SAY IS...
THAT... I CHOSE TO REFORGE SHIRATAKI-MARU BECAUSE...
I WISHED TO DE-MONSTRATE THE FINE METAL-WORKING CRAFTS-MANSHIP THAT LAY DORMANT WITHIN THE DWARVEN CITY!
FOR THIS REASON, I HAD OUR GUILD'S MOST TREASURED SWORD REFORGED!
WHOAAAA!!
ダアーーッ!!

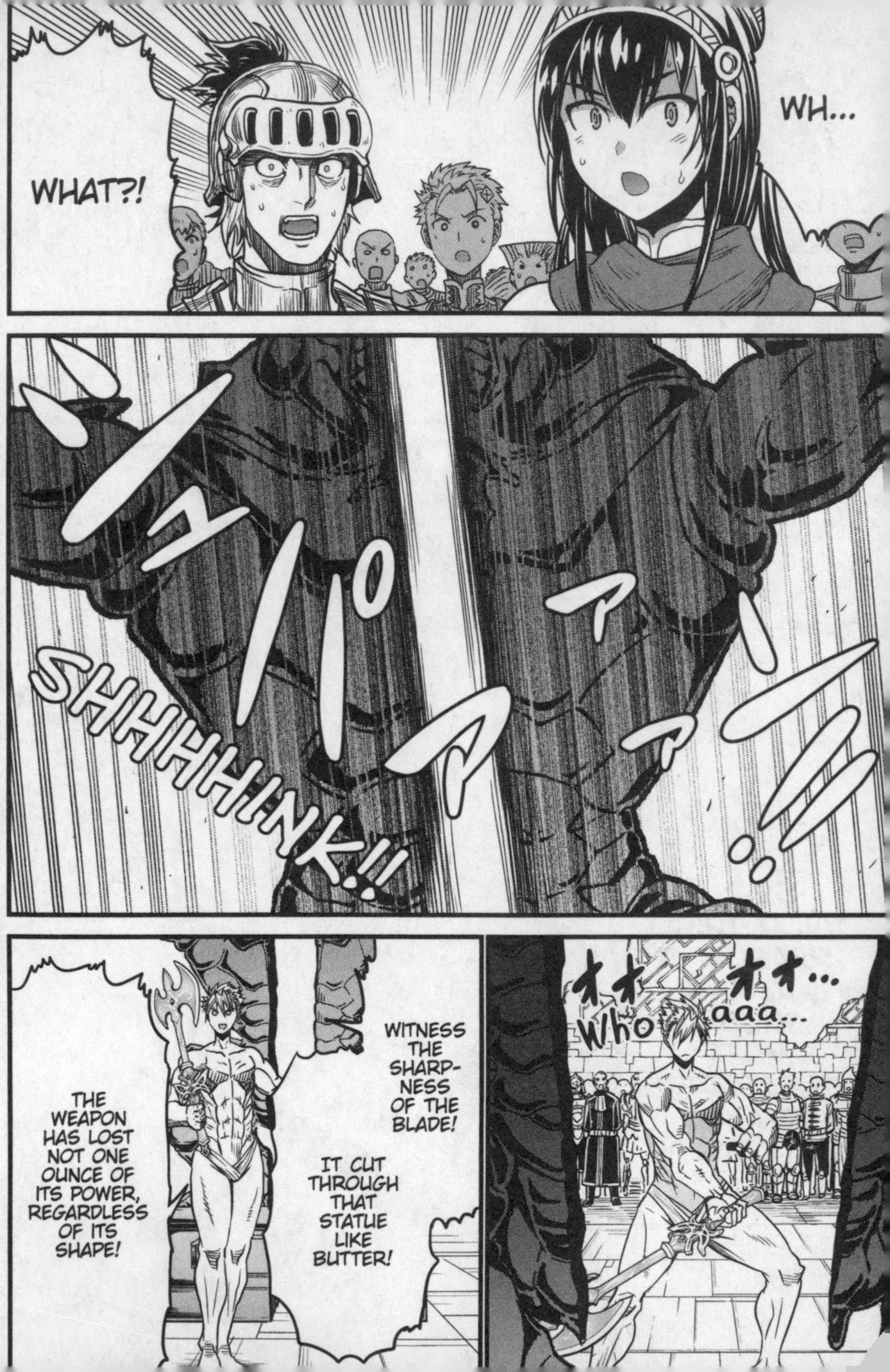
WH...
WHAT?!
シャパァァァ
SHHHHHINK!!!
オオ オオ…
Whoaaa...
WITNESS THE SHARPNESS OF THE BLADE!
IT CUT THROUGH THAT STATUE LIKE BUTTER!
THE WEAPON HAS LOST NOT ONE OUNCE OF ITS POWER, REGARDLESS OF ITS SHAPE!

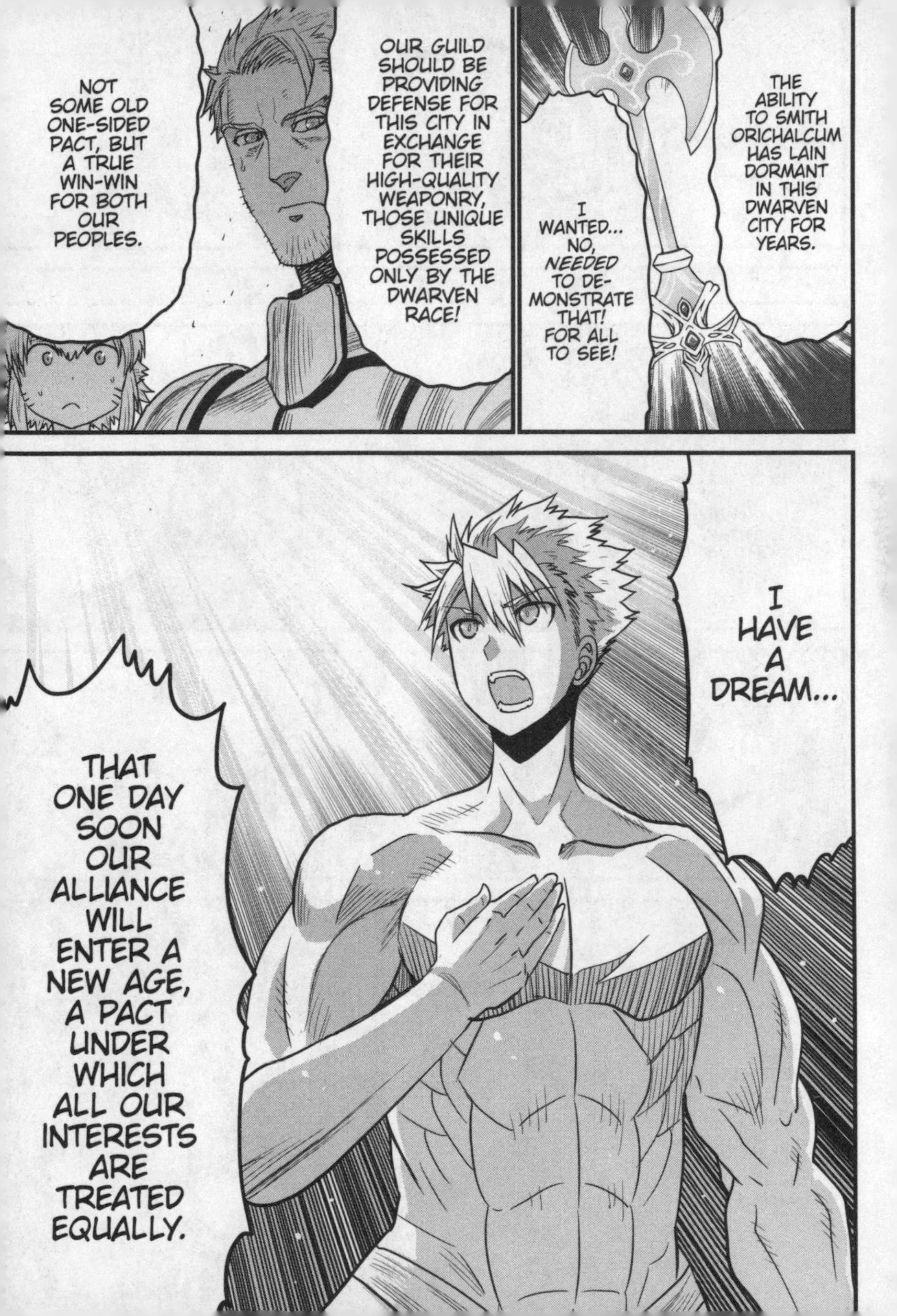
THE ABILITY TO SMITH ORICHALCUM HAS LAIN DORMANT IN THIS DWARVEN CITY FOR YEARS.
I WANTED... NO, *NEEDED* TO DE-MONSTRATE THAT! FOR ALL TO SEE!
OUR GUILD SHOULD BE PROVIDING DEFENSE FOR THIS CITY IN EXCHANGE FOR THEIR HIGH-QUALITY WEAPONRY, THOSE UNIQUE SKILLS POSSESSED ONLY BY THE DWARVEN RACE!
NOT SOME OLD ONE-SIDED PACT, BUT A TRUE WIN-WIN FOR BOTH OUR PEOPLES.
I HAVE A DREAM...
THAT ONE DAY SOON OUR ALLIANCE WILL ENTER A NEW AGE, A PACT UNDER WHICH ALL OUR INTERESTS ARE TREATED EQUALLY.

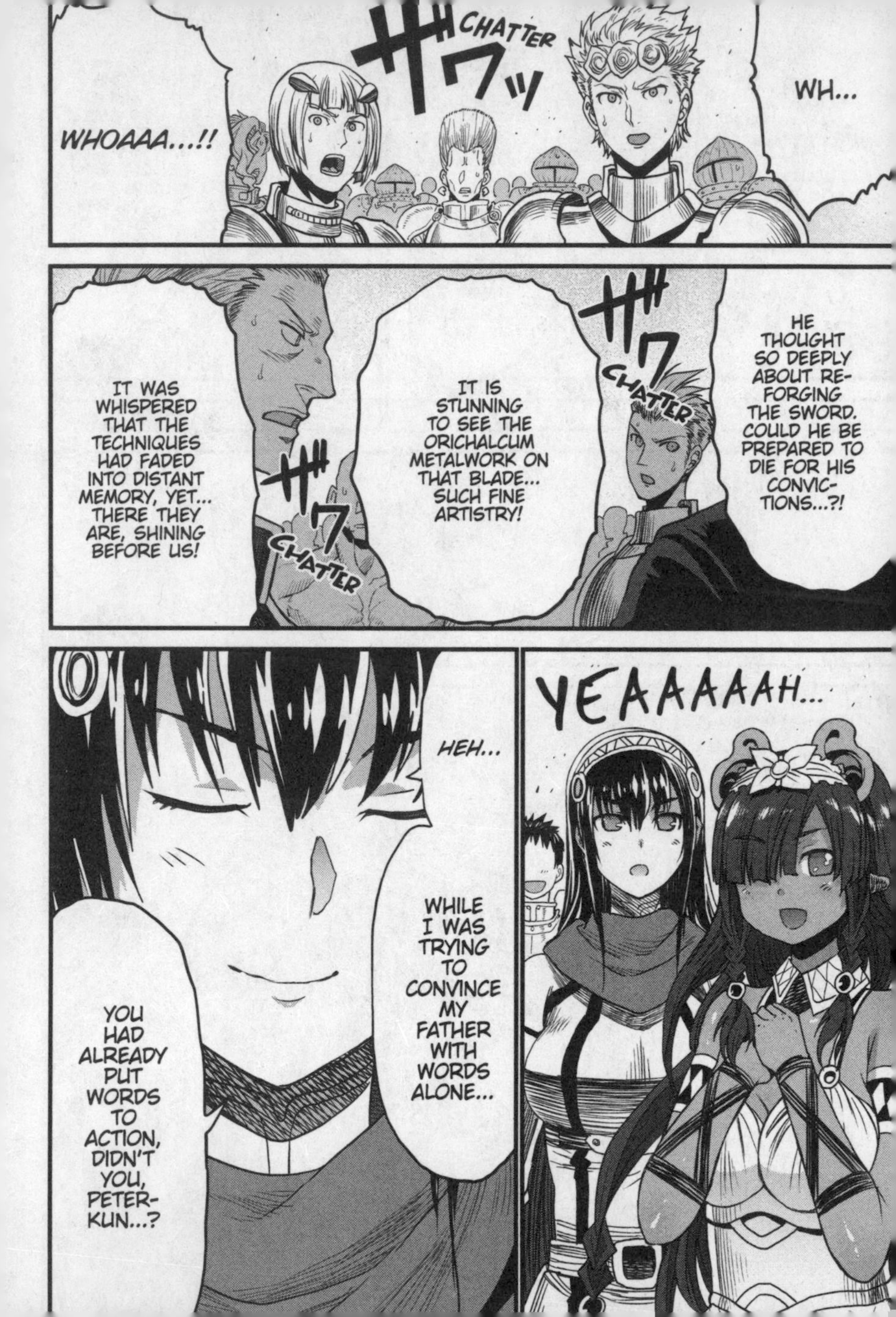
CHATTER
WH...
WHOAAA...!!
HE THOUGHT SO DEEPLY ABOUT RE-FORGING THE SWORD. COULD HE BE PREPARED TO DIE FOR HIS CONVIC-TIONS...?!
CHATTER
IT IS STUNNING TO SEE THE ORICHALCUM METALWORK ON THAT BLADE... SUCH FINE ARTISTRY!
IT WAS WHISPERED THAT THE TECHNIQUES HAD FADED INTO DISTANT MEMORY, YET... THERE THEY ARE, SHINING BEFORE US!
CHATTER
YEAAAAAH...
HEH...
WHILE I WAS TRYING TO CONVINCE MY FATHER WITH WORDS ALONE...
YOU HAD ALREADY PUT WORDS TO ACTION, DIDN'T YOU, PETER-KUN...?

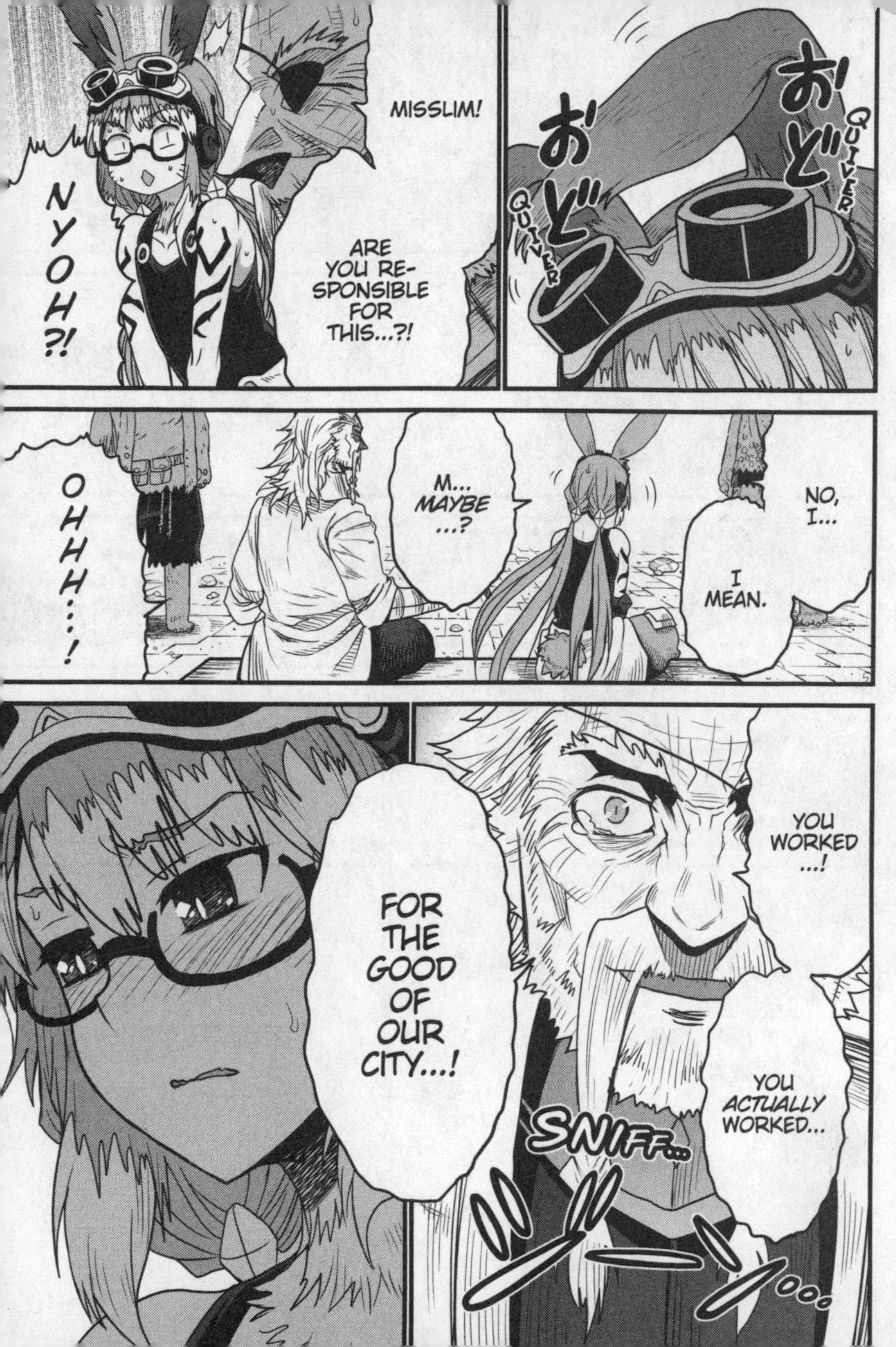
おど
おど
QUIVER
QUIVER
MISSLIM!
ARE YOU RE-SPONSIBLE FOR THIS...?!
NYOHH?!
NO, I...
I MEAN.
M... MAYBE ...?
OHHHH...!
YOU WORKED ...!
YOU ACTUALLY WORKED...
SNIFF...
FOR THE GOOD OF OUR CITY...!

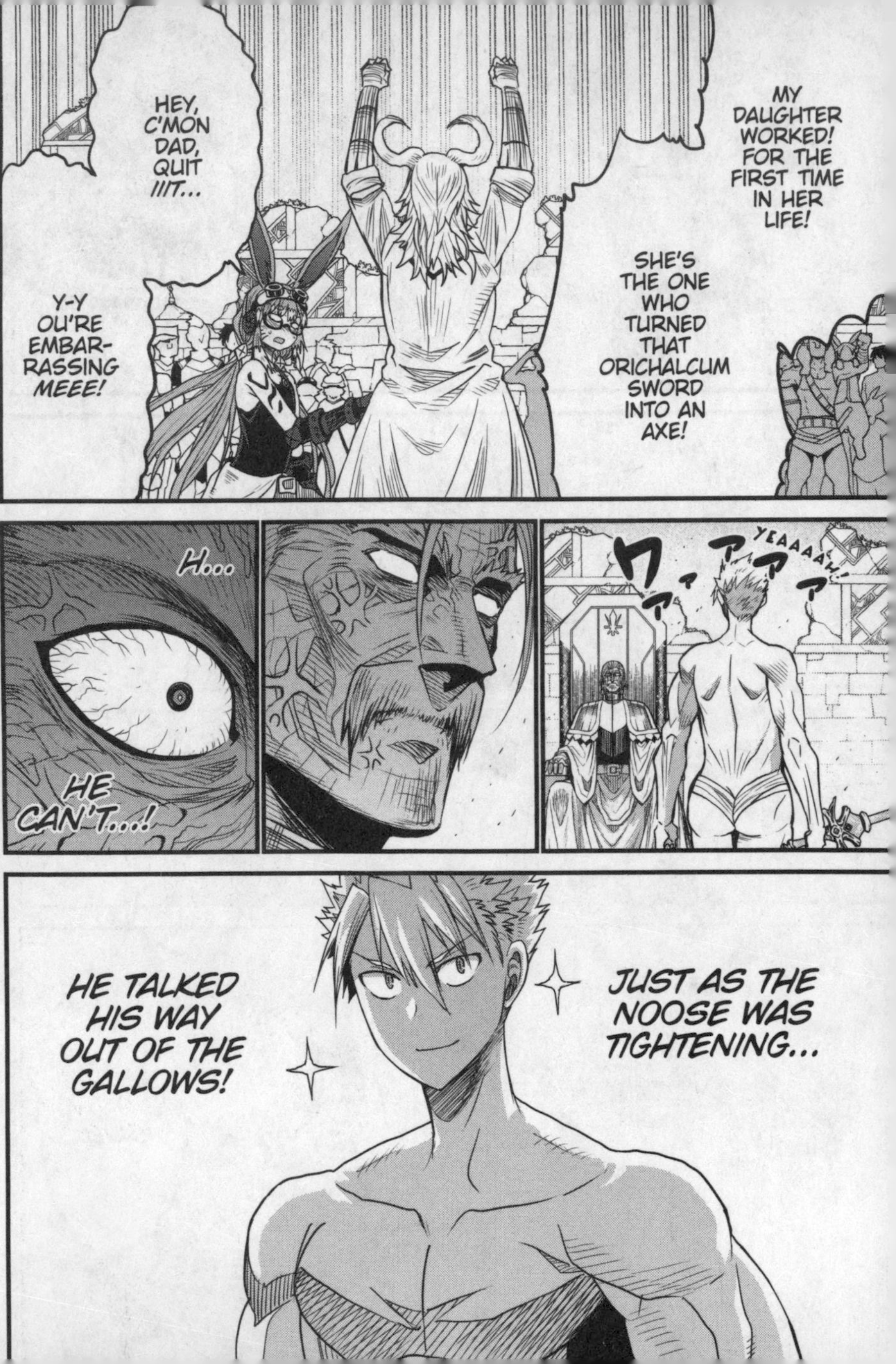
MY DAUGHTER WORKED! FOR THE FIRST TIME IN HER LIFE!
SHE'S THE ONE WHO TURNED THAT ORICHALCUM SWORD INTO AN AXE!
HEY, C'MON DAD, QUIT IIIT...
Y-Y OU'RE EMBARRASSING MEEE!
YEAAAAAH!
H...
HE CAN'T...!
JUST AS THE NOOSE WAS TIGHTENING...
HE TALKED HIS WAY OUT OF THE GALLOWS!

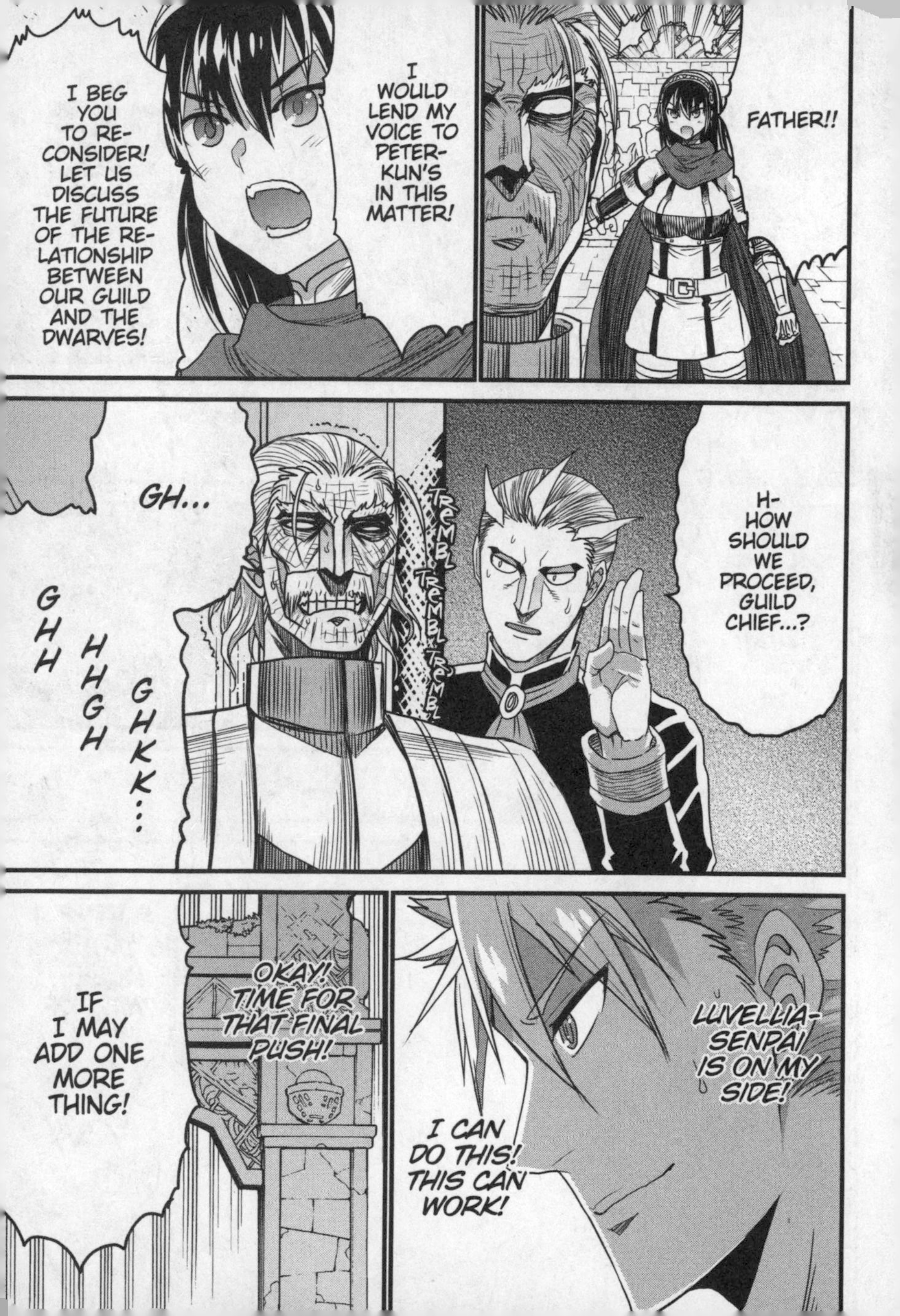
FATHER!!
I WOULD LEND MY VOICE TO PETER-KUN'S IN THIS MATTER!
I BEG YOU TO RECONSIDER! LET US DISCUSS THE FUTURE OF THE RELATIONSHIP BETWEEN OUR GUILD AND THE DWARVES!
H-HOW SHOULD WE PROCEED, GUILD CHIEF...?
TREMBL TREMBL TREMBL
GH...
GHHHHGHGHKK...
LUVELLIA-SENPAI IS ON MY SIDE!
I CAN DO THIS! THIS CAN WORK!
OKAY! TIME FOR THAT FINAL PUSH!
IF I MAY ADD ONE MORE THING!

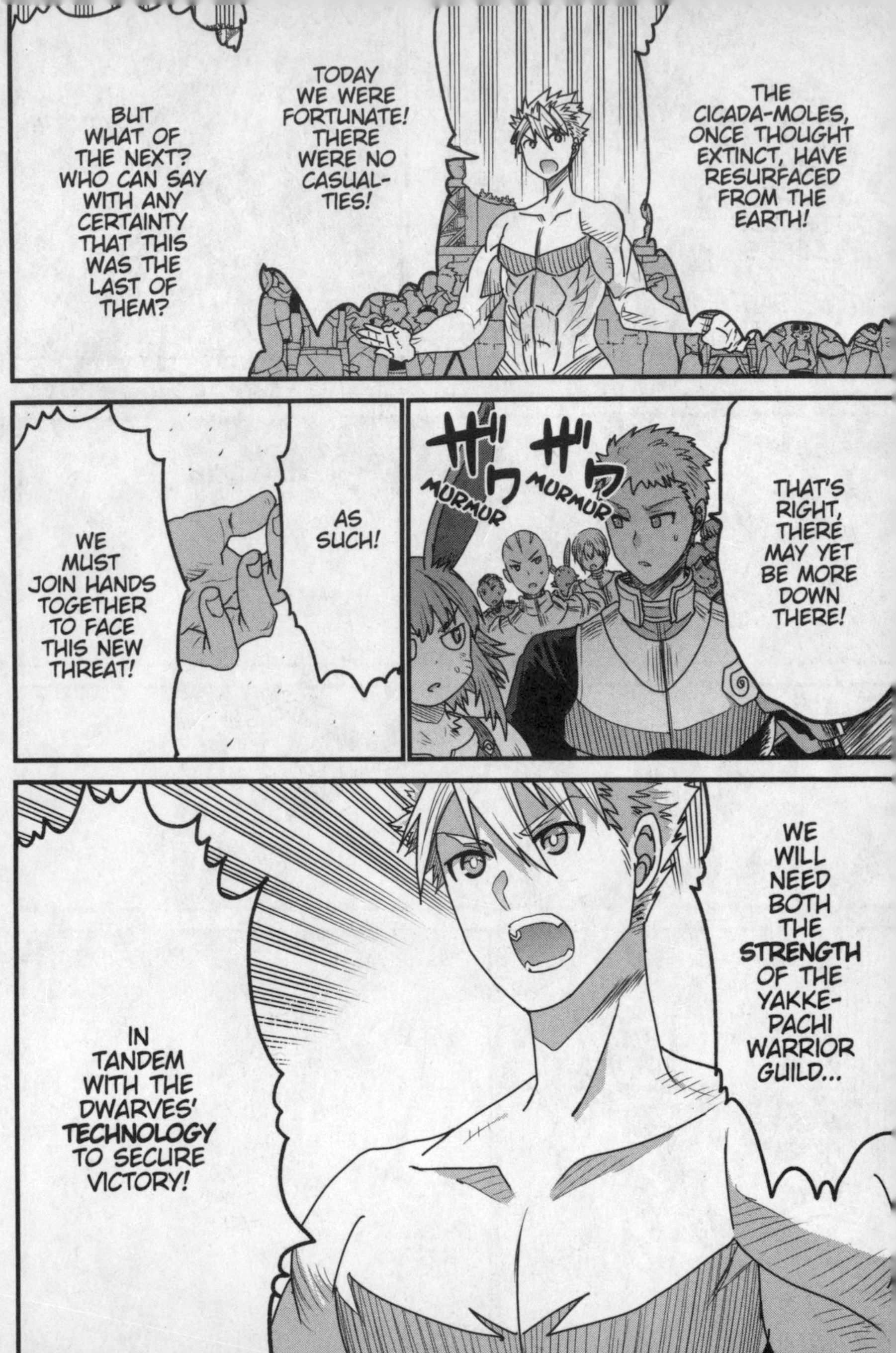
THE CICADA-MOLES, ONCE THOUGHT EXTINCT, HAVE RESURFACED FROM THE EARTH!
TODAY WE WERE FORTUNATE! THERE WERE NO CASUAL-TIES!
BUT WHAT OF THE NEXT? WHO CAN SAY WITH ANY CERTAINTY THAT THIS WAS THE LAST OF THEM?
ザワ
ザワ
MURMUR
MURMUR
THAT'S RIGHT, THERE MAY YET BE MORE DOWN THERE!
AS SUCH!
WE MUST JOIN HANDS TOGETHER TO FACE THIS NEW THREAT!
WE WILL NEED BOTH THE STRENGTH OF THE YAKKE-PACHI WARRIOR GUILD...
IN TANDEM WITH THE DWARVES' TECHNOLOGY TO SECURE VICTORY!

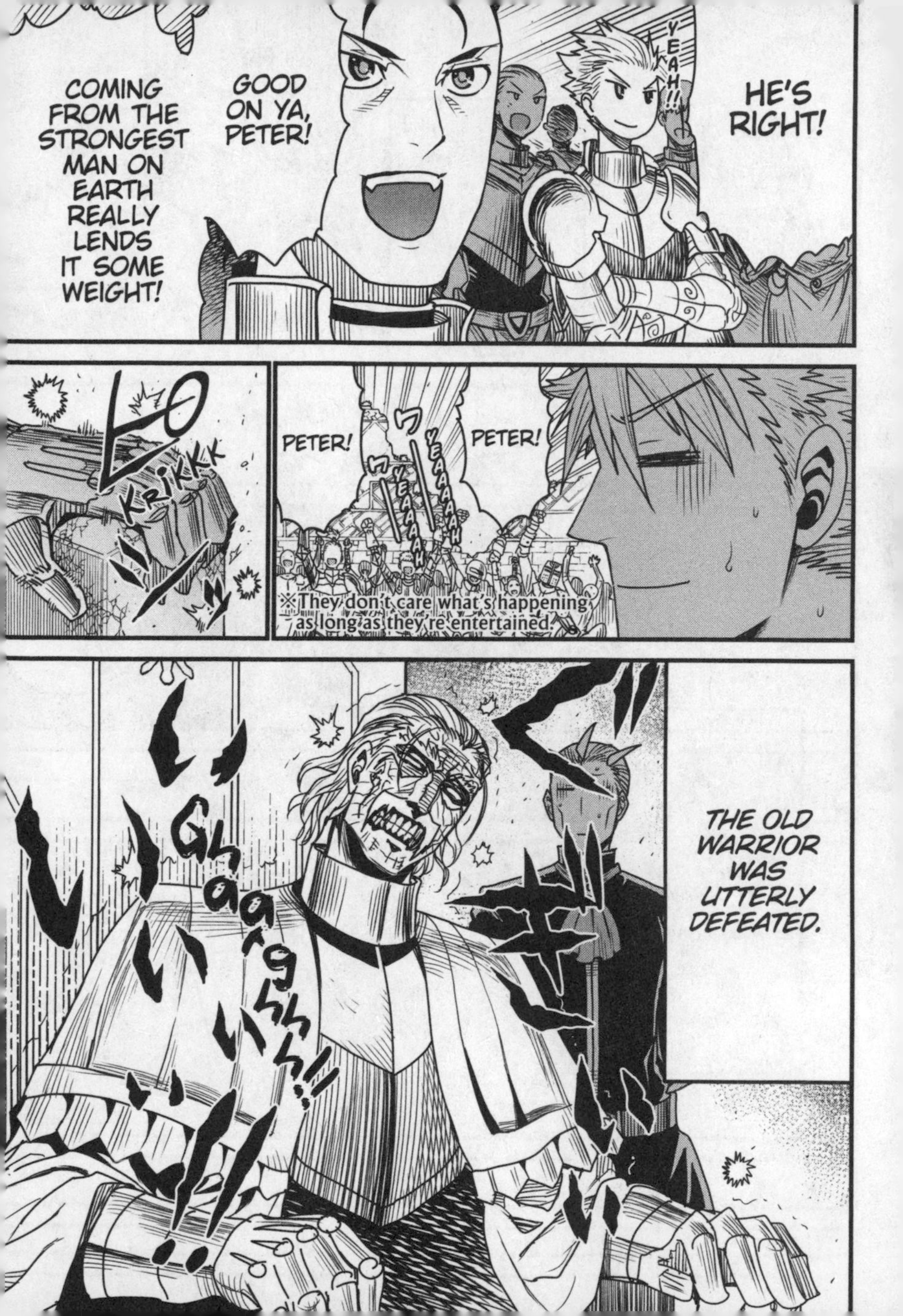
HE'S RIGHT!
YEAH!!
GOOD ON YA, PETER!
COMING FROM THE STRONGEST MAN ON EARTH REALLY LENDS IT SOME WEIGHT!
PETER!
YEAAAAAAH
YEAAAAH
PETER!
※They don't care what's happening as long as they're entertained.
KRIKKK
THE OLD WARRIOR WAS UTTERLY DEFEATED.
Ghaarghhh!!

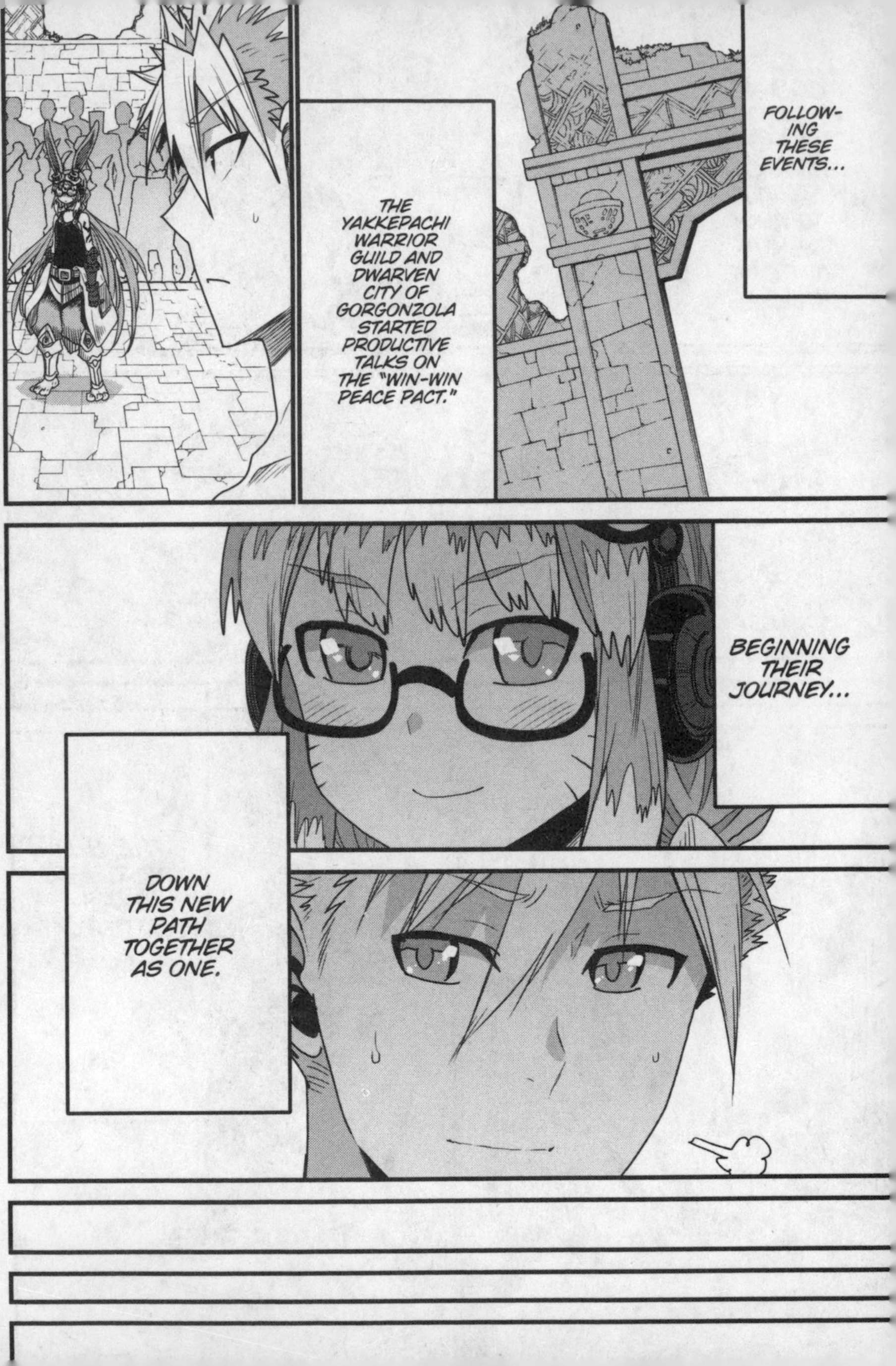
FOLLOW-ING THESE EVENTS...
THE YAKKEPACHI WARRIOR GUILD AND DWARVEN CITY OF GORGONZOLA STARTED PRODUCTIVE TALKS ON THE "WIN-WIN PEACE PACT."
BEGINNING THEIR JOURNEY...
DOWN THIS NEW PATH TOGETHER AS ONE.

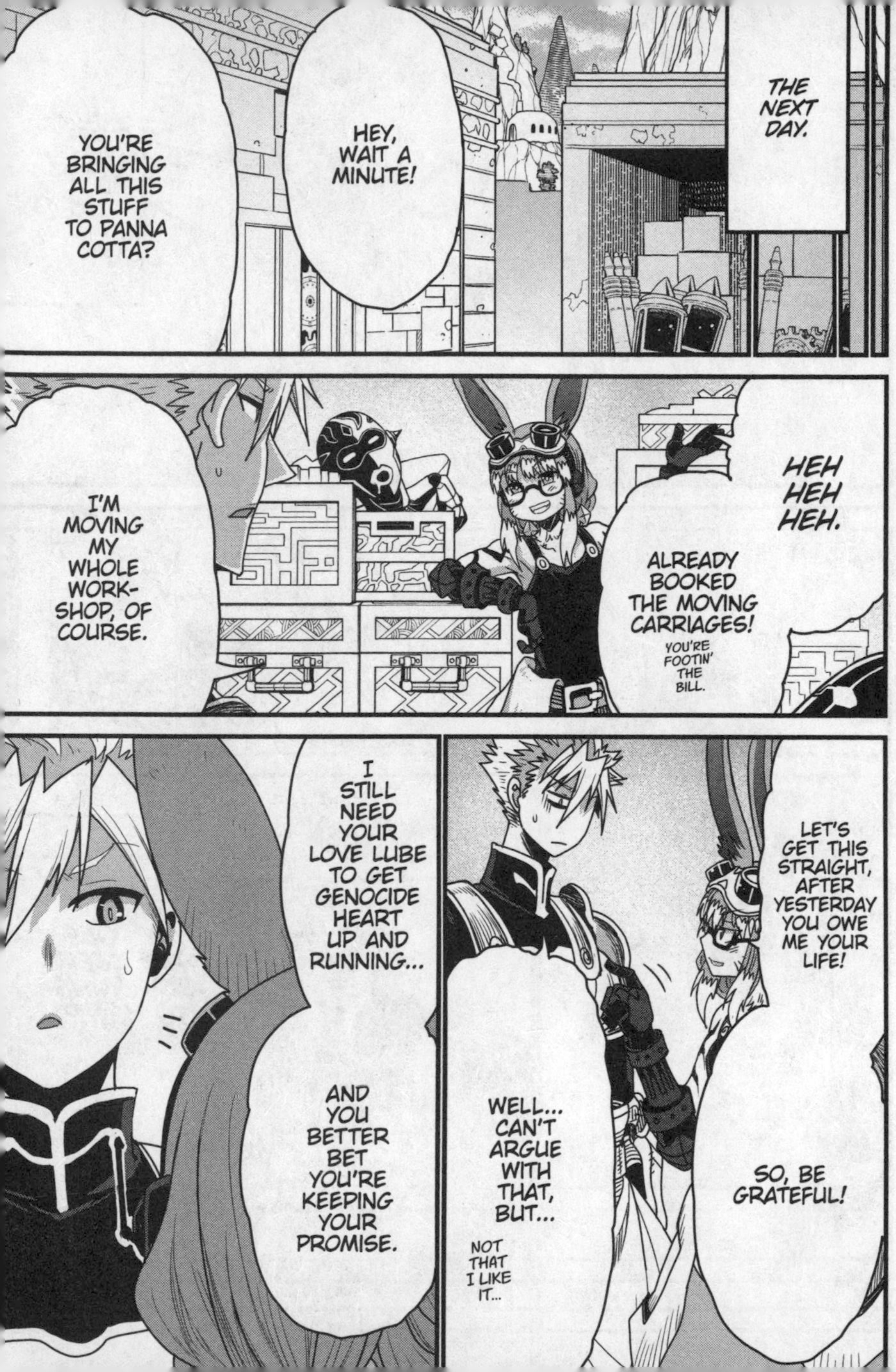
THE NEXT DAY.
HEY, WAIT A MINUTE!
YOU'RE BRINGING ALL THIS STUFF TO PANNA COTTA?
I'M MOVING MY WHOLE WORKSHOP, OF COURSE.
HEH HEH HEH.
ALREADY BOOKED THE MOVING CARRIAGES!
YOU'RE FOOTIN' THE BILL.
LET'S GET THIS STRAIGHT, AFTER YESTERDAY YOU OWE ME YOUR LIFE!
SO, BE GRATEFUL!
WELL... CAN'T ARGUE WITH THAT, BUT...
NOT THAT I LIKE IT...
I STILL NEED YOUR LOVE LUBE TO GET GENOCIDE HEART UP AND RUNNING...
AND YOU BETTER BET YOU'RE KEEPING YOUR PROMISE.

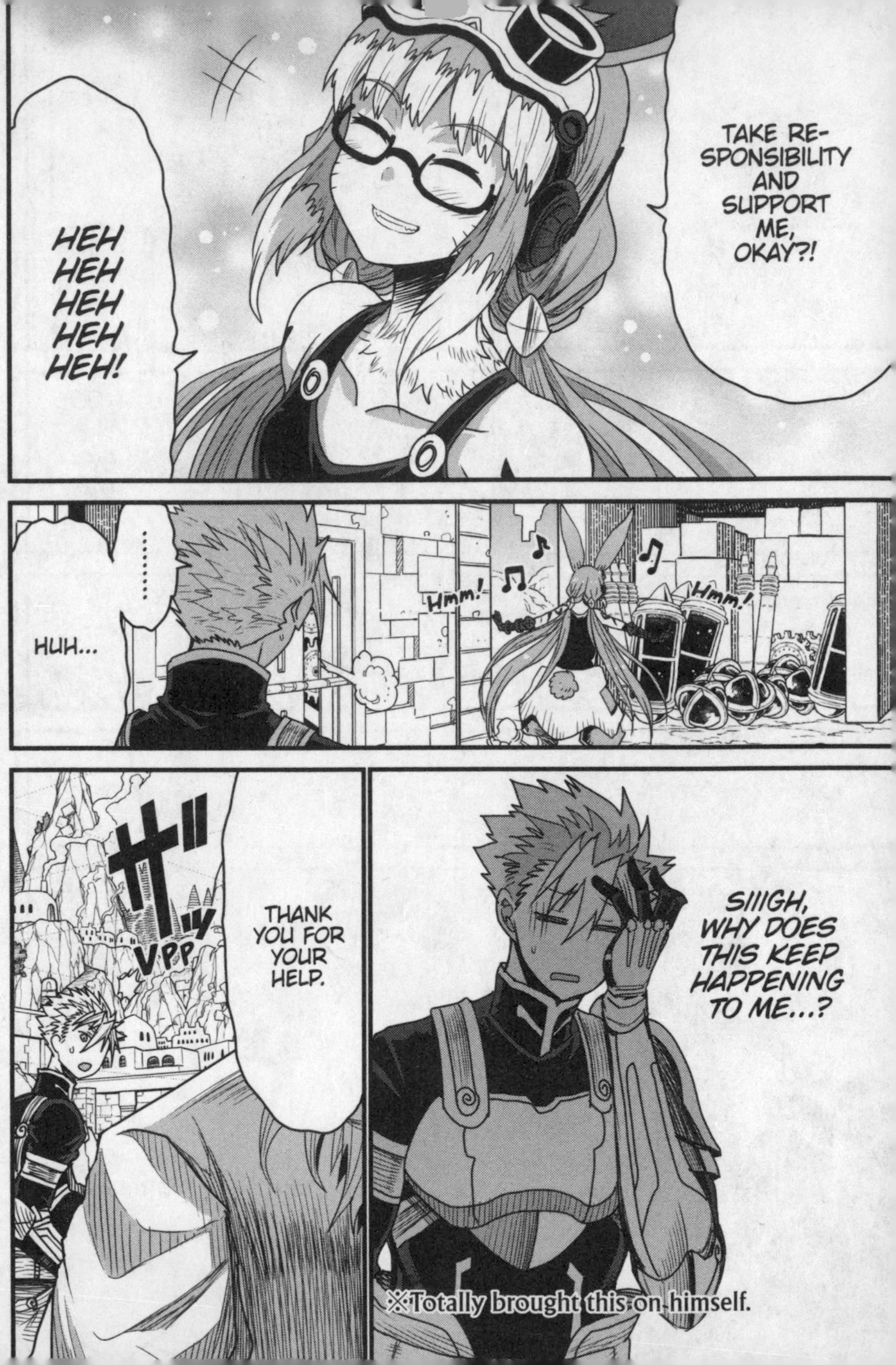
TAKE RE-SPONSIBILITY AND SUPPORT ME, OKAY?!
HEH HEH HEH HEH HEH!
Hmm!
Hmm!
......
HUH...
SIIIGH, WHY DOES THIS KEEP HAPPENING TO ME...?
※Totally brought this on himself.
THANK YOU FOR YOUR HELP.
VPP

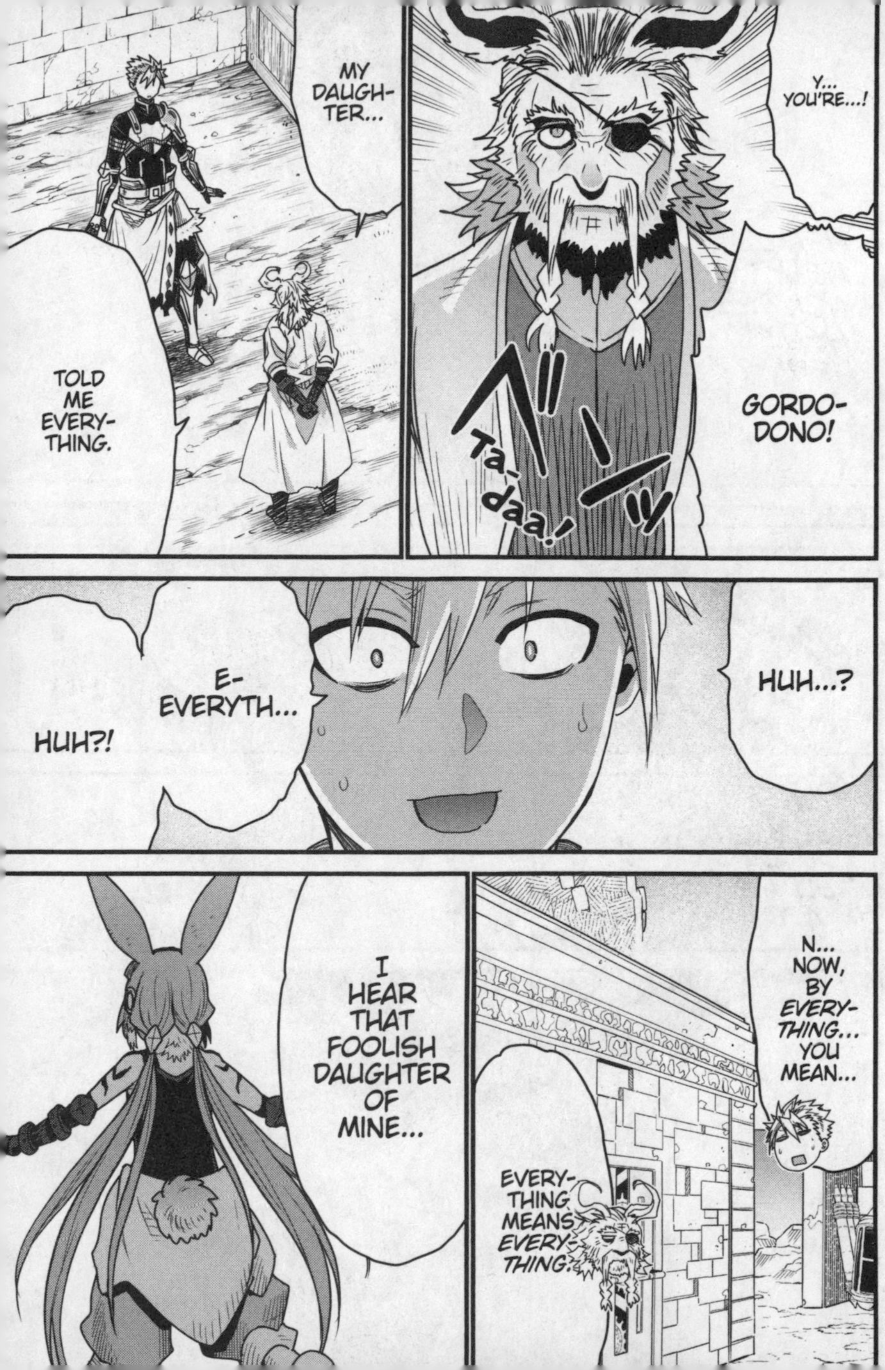
Y... YOU'RE...!
GORDO-DONO!
Ta-daa!
MY DAUGHTER...
TOLD ME EVERYTHING.
HUH...?
E- EVERYTH...
HUH?!
N... NOW, BY EVERYTHING... YOU MEAN...
EVERYTHING MEANS EVERYTHING.
I HEAR THAT FOOLISH DAUGHTER OF MINE...

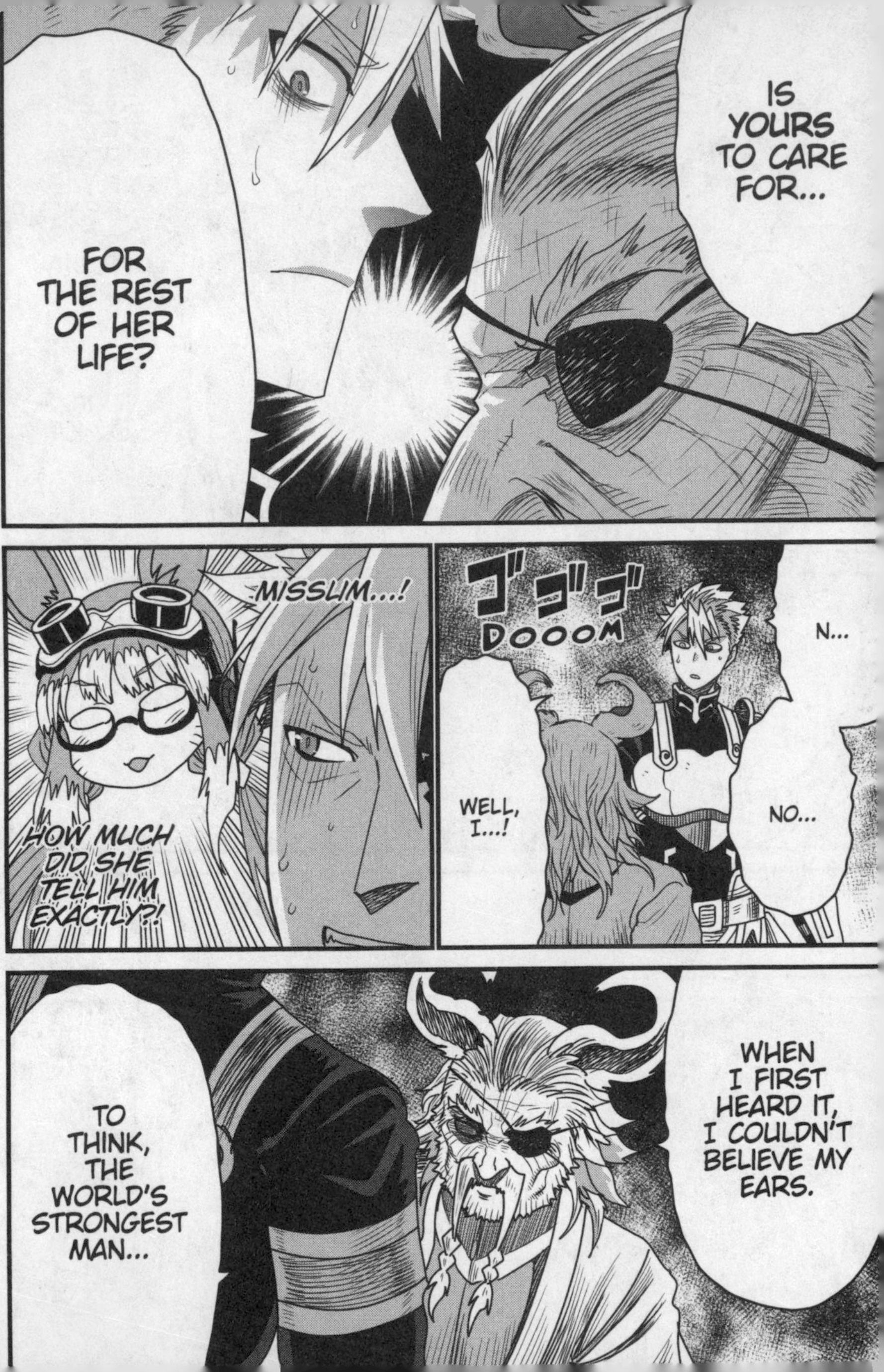
IS YOURS TO CARE FOR...
FOR THE REST OF HER LIFE?
ゴゴゴ
DOOOM
N...
NO...
WELL, I...!
MISSLIM...!
HOW MUCH DID SHE TELL HIM EXACTLY?!
WHEN I FIRST HEARD IT, I COULDN'T BELIEVE MY EARS.
TO THINK, THE WORLD'S STRONGEST MAN...

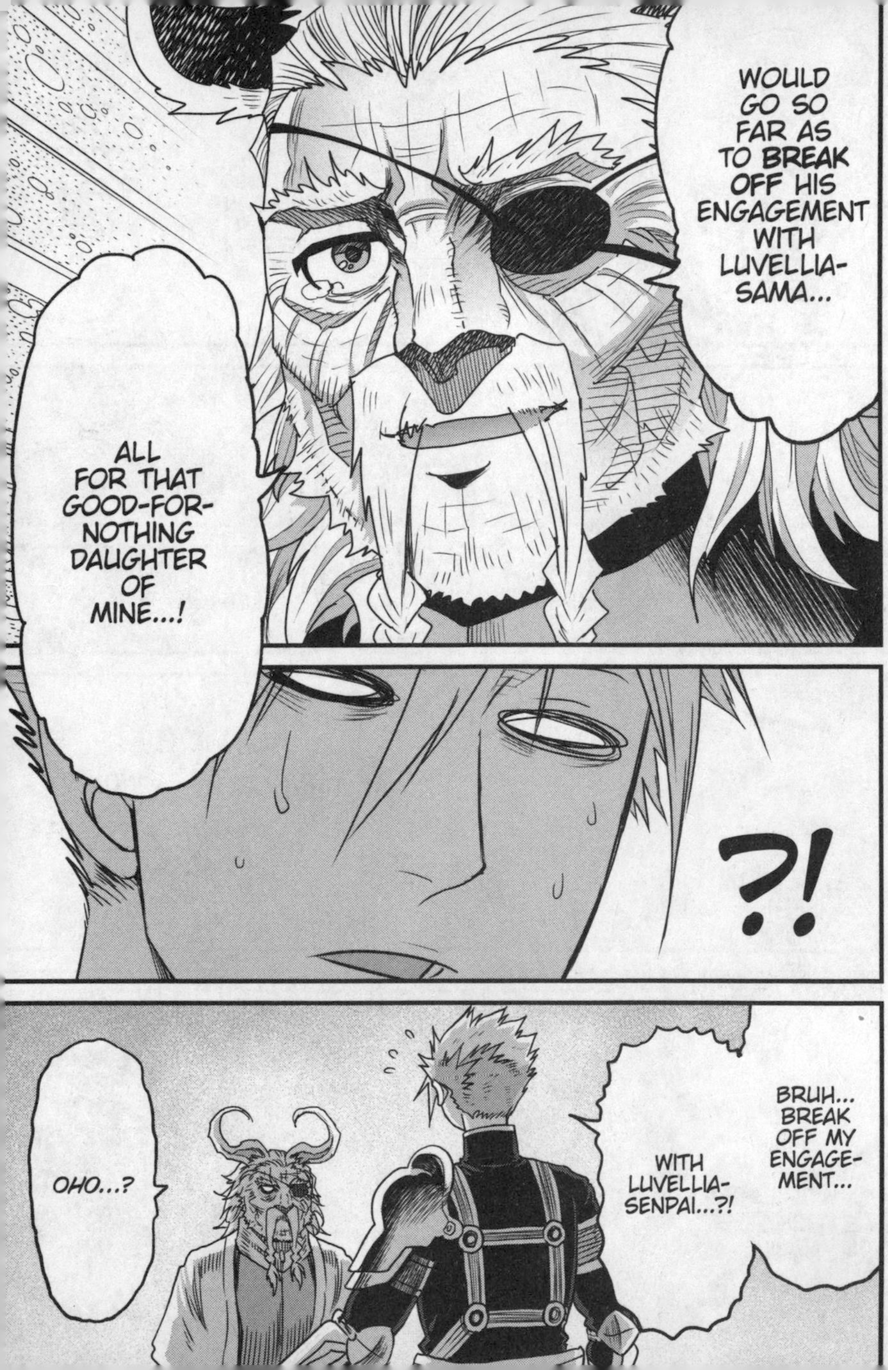
WOULD GO SO FAR AS TO BREAK OFF HIS ENGAGEMENT WITH LUVELLIA-SAMA...
ALL FOR THAT GOOD-FOR-NOTHING DAUGHTER OF MINE...!
?!
BRUH... BREAK OFF MY ENGAGEMENT...
WITH LUVELLIA-SENPAI...?!
OHO...?

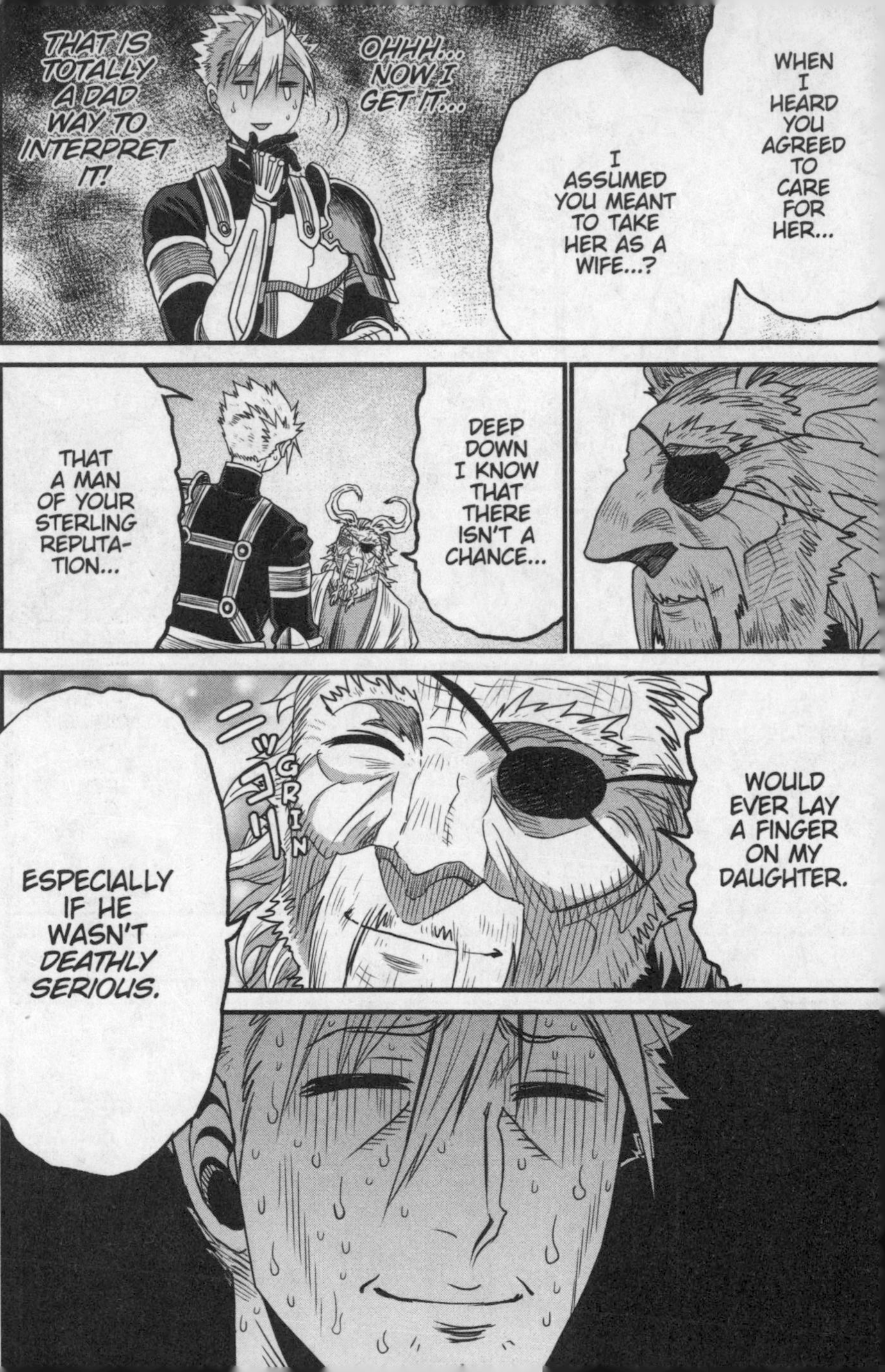
WHEN I HEARD YOU AGREED TO CARE FOR HER...
I ASSUMED YOU MEANT TO TAKE HER AS A WIFE...?
OHHH... NOW I GET IT...
THAT IS TOTALLY A DAD WAY TO INTERPRET IT!
DEEP DOWN I KNOW THAT THERE ISN'T A CHANCE...
THAT A MAN OF YOUR STERLING REPUTATION...
WOULD EVER LAY A FINGER ON MY DAUGHTER.
GRIN
ESPECIALLY IF HE WASN'T DEATHLY SERIOUS.

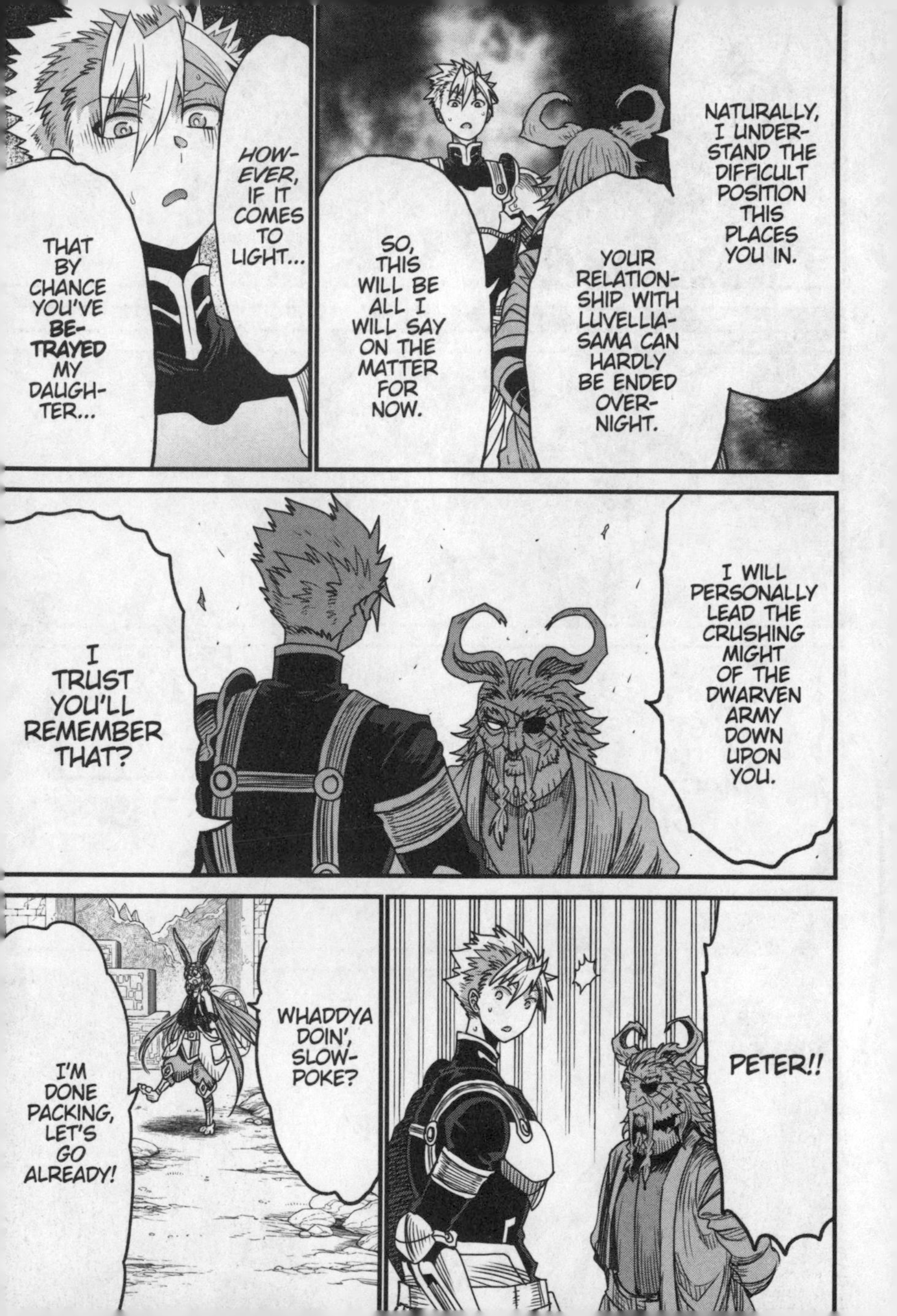
NATURALLY, I UNDERSTAND THE DIFFICULT POSITION THIS PLACES YOU IN.
YOUR RELATIONSHIP WITH LUVELLIA-SAMA CAN HARDLY BE ENDED OVERNIGHT.
SO, THIS WILL BE ALL I WILL SAY ON THE MATTER FOR NOW.
HOWEVER, IF IT COMES TO LIGHT...
THAT BY CHANCE YOU'VE BETRAYED MY DAUGHTER...
I WILL PERSONALLY LEAD THE CRUSHING MIGHT OF THE DWARVEN ARMY DOWN UPON YOU.
I TRUST YOU'LL REMEMBER THAT?
PETER!!
WHADDYA DOIN', SLOWPOKE?
I'M DONE PACKING, LET'S GO ALREADY!

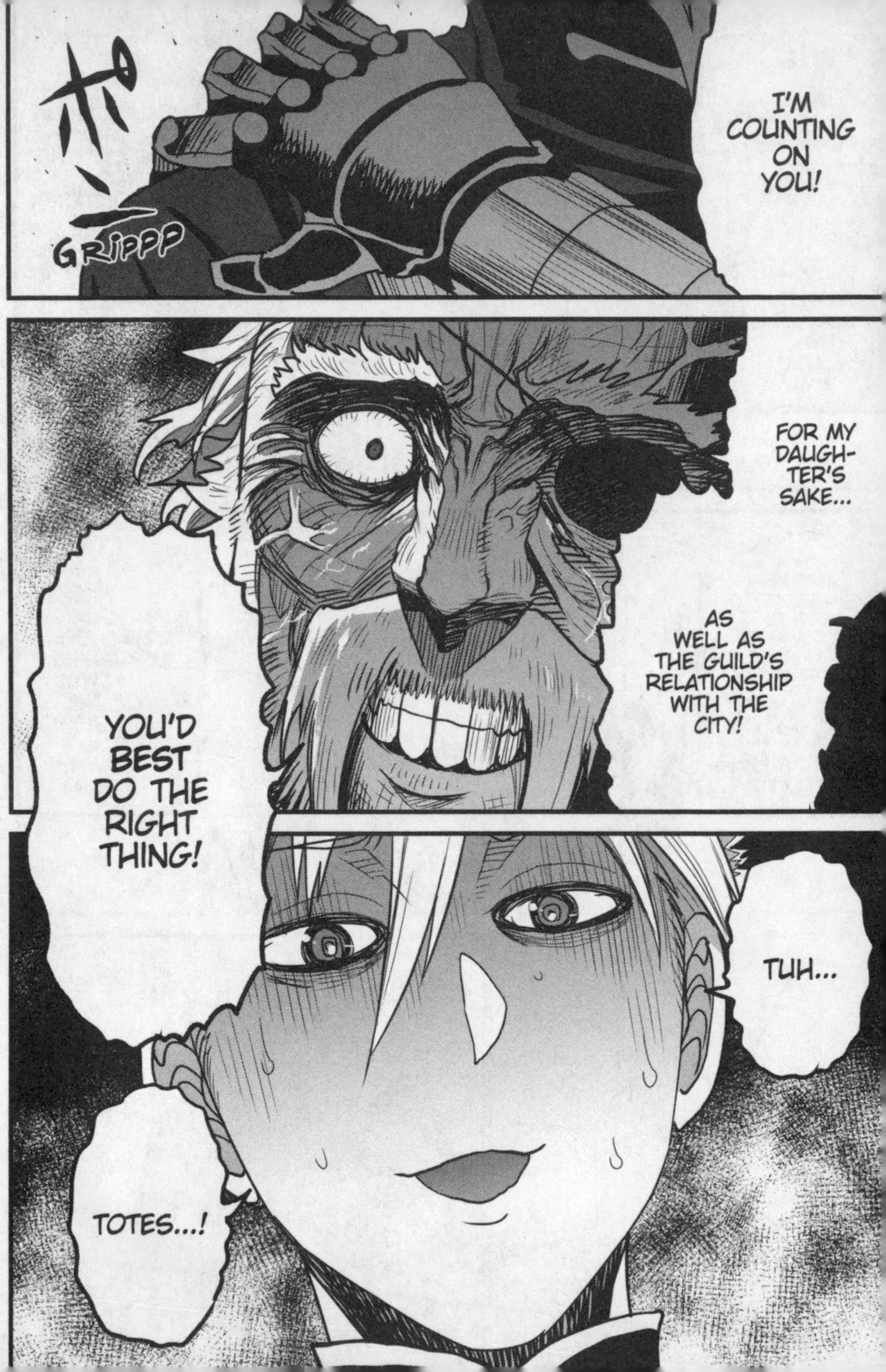
I'M COUNTING ON YOU!
GRIPPP
FOR MY DAUGHTER'S SAKE...
AS WELL AS THE GUILD'S RELATIONSHIP WITH THE CITY!
YOU'D BEST DO THE RIGHT THING!
TUH...
TOTES...!

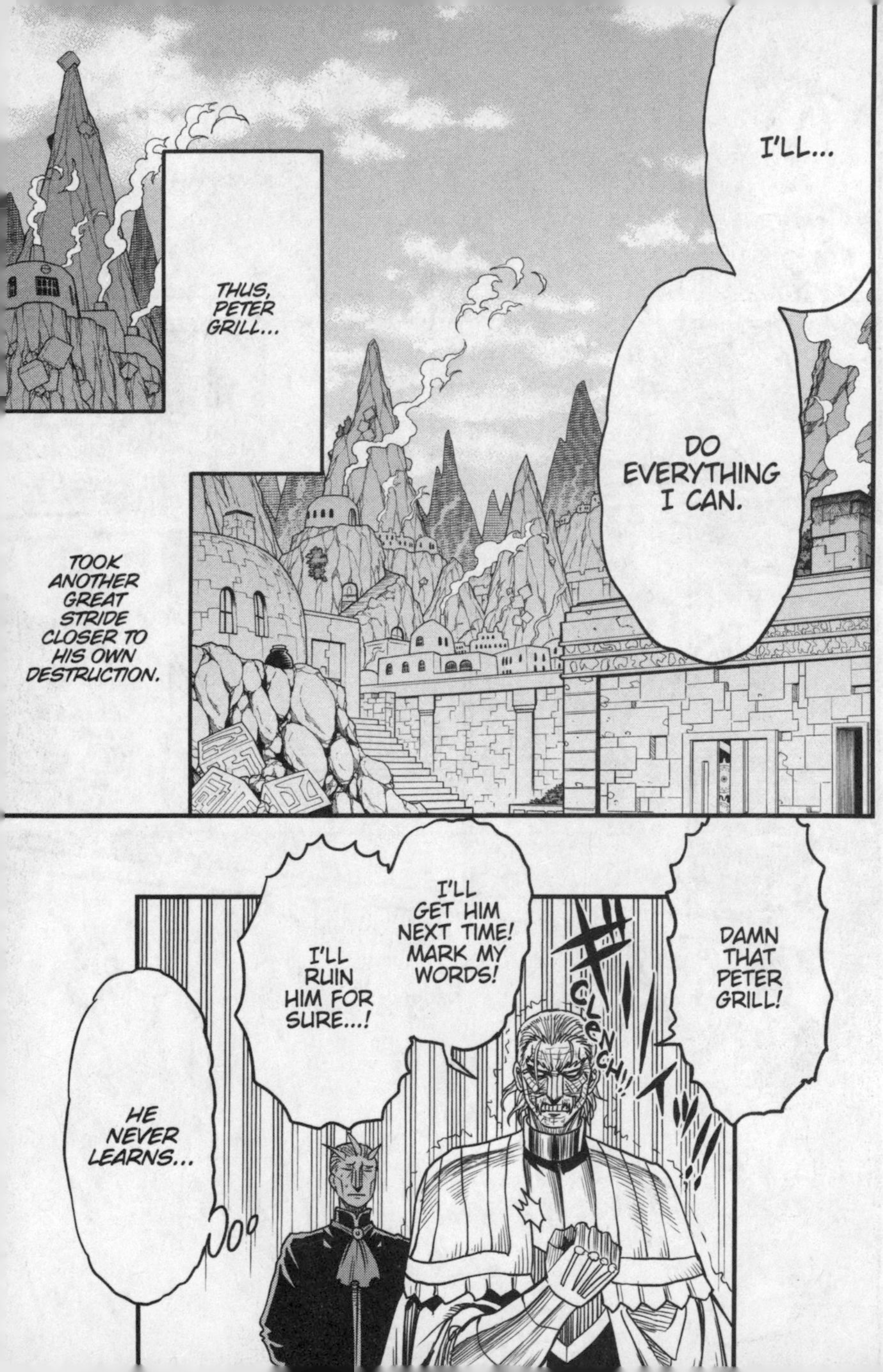
I'LL...
DO EVERYTHING I CAN.
THUS, PETER GRILL...
TOOK ANOTHER GREAT STRIDE CLOSER TO HIS OWN DESTRUCTION.
DAMN THAT PETER GRILL!
CLENCH!!
I'LL GET HIM NEXT TIME! MARK MY WORDS!
I'LL RUIN HIM FOR SURE...!
HE NEVER LEARNS...

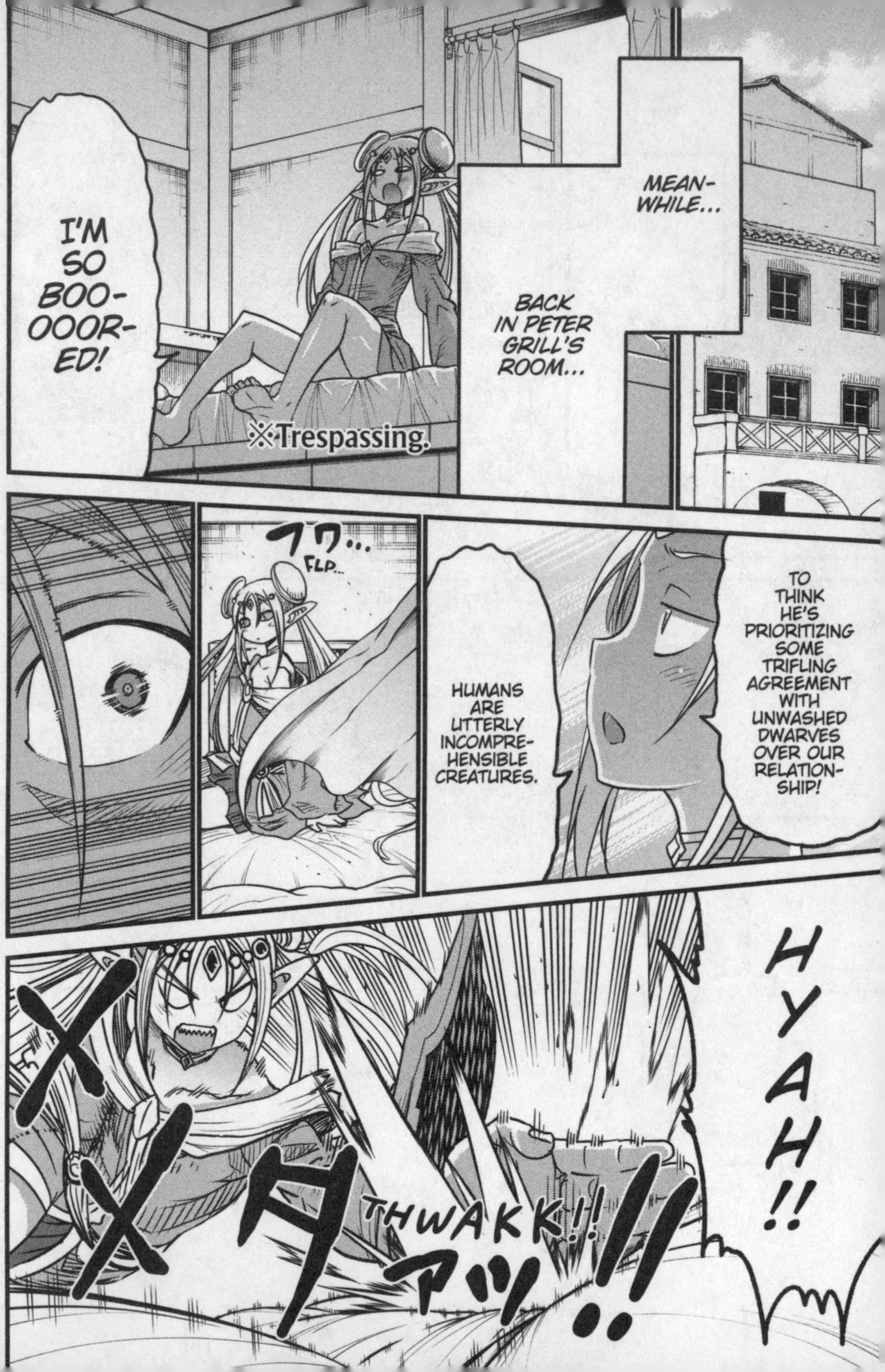
MEAN-WHILE...
BACK IN PETER GRILL'S ROOM...
I'M SO BOOOOORED!
※Trespassing.
TO THINK HE'S PRIORITIZING SOME TRIFLING AGREEMENT WITH UNWASHED DWARVES OVER OUR RELATIONSHIP!
HUMANS ARE UTTERLY INCOMPREHENSIBLE CREATURES.
フワ...
FLP...
HYAH!!
THWAKK!!

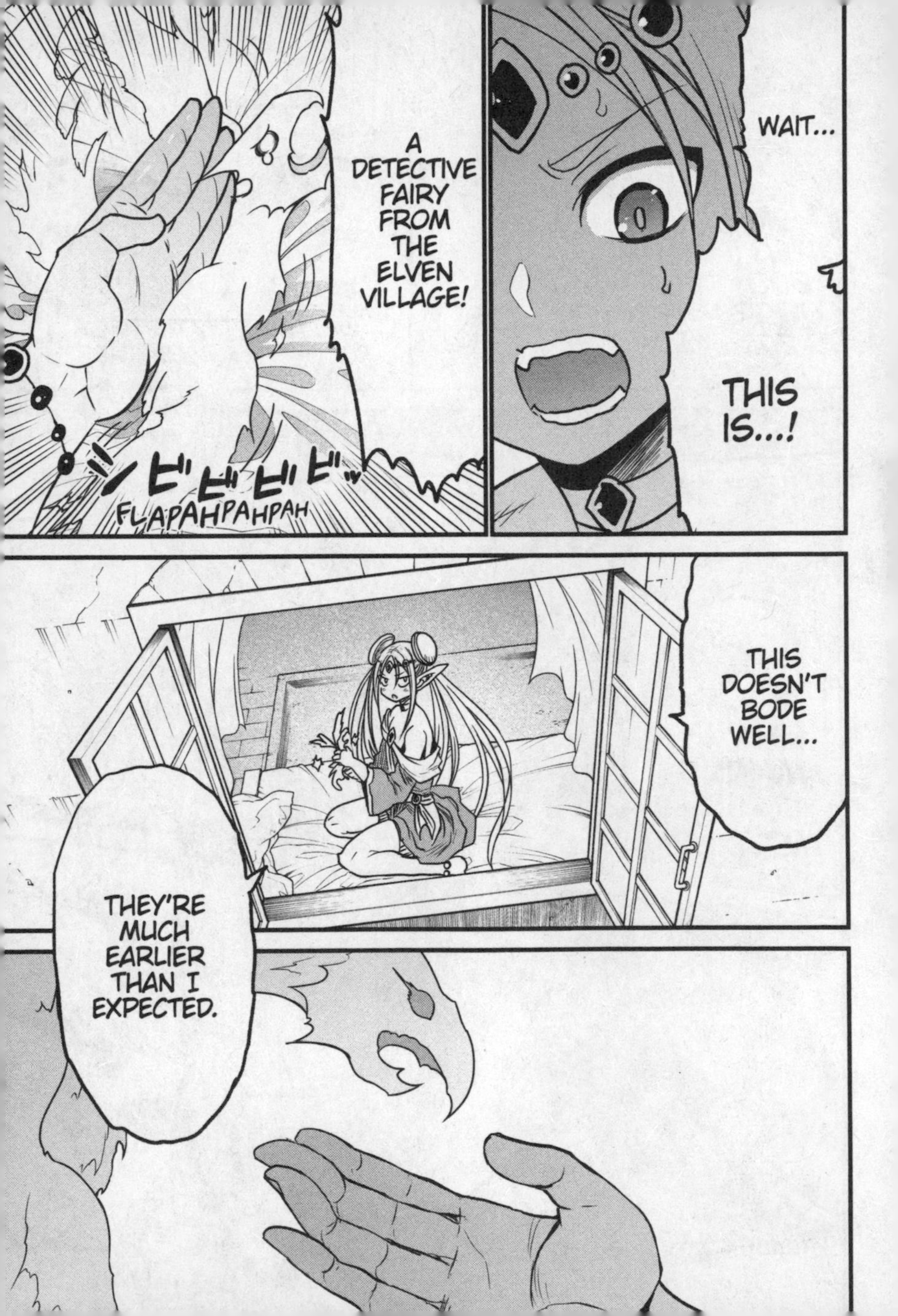
WAIT...
THIS IS...!
A DETECTIVE FAIRY FROM THE ELVEN VILLAGE!
FLAPAHPAHPAH
THIS DOESN'T BODE WELL...
THEY'RE MUCH EARLIER THAN I EXPECTED.

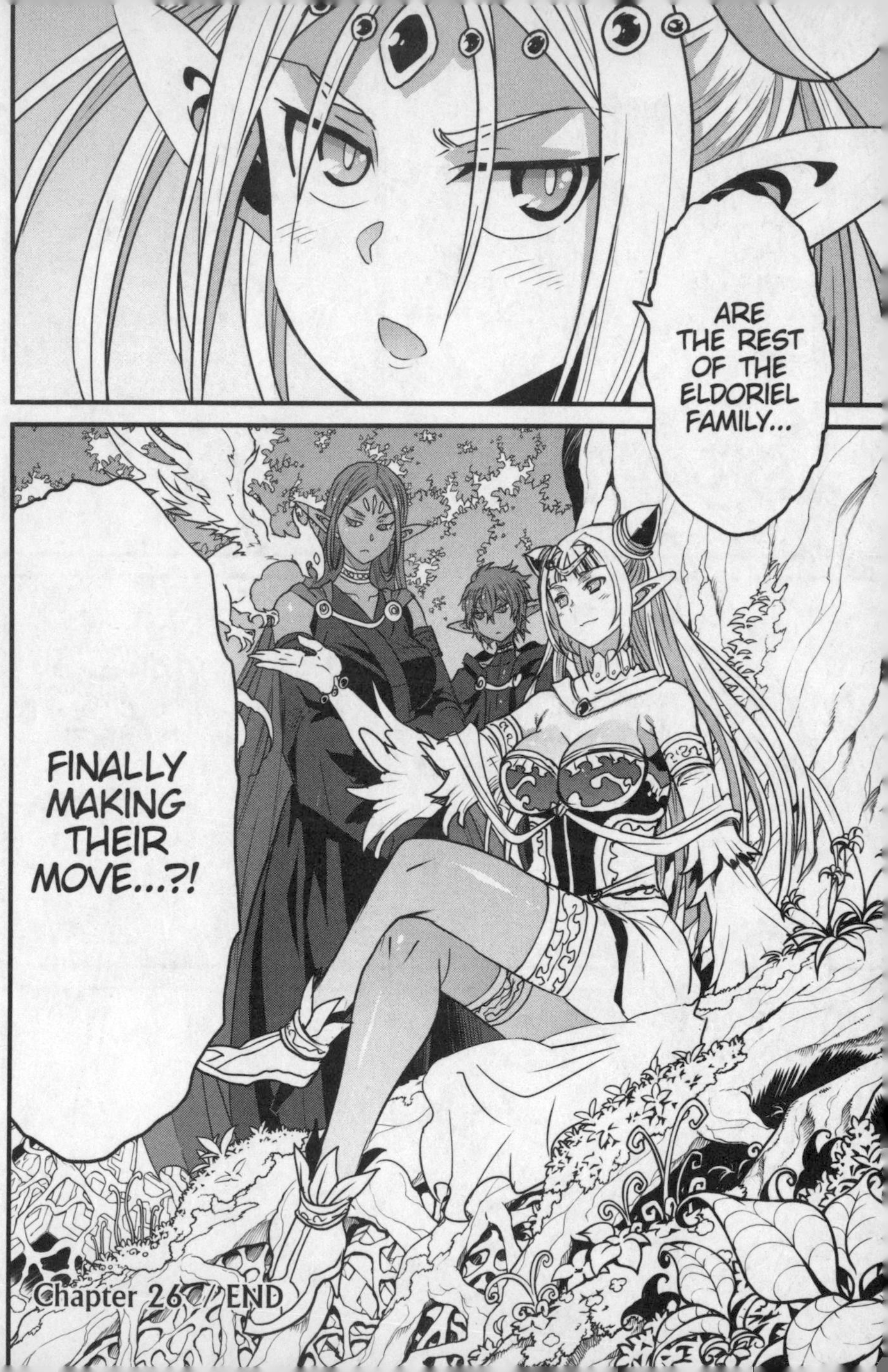
ARE THE REST OF THE ELDORIEL FAMILY...
FINALLY MAKING THEIR MOVE...?!
Chapter 26 / END

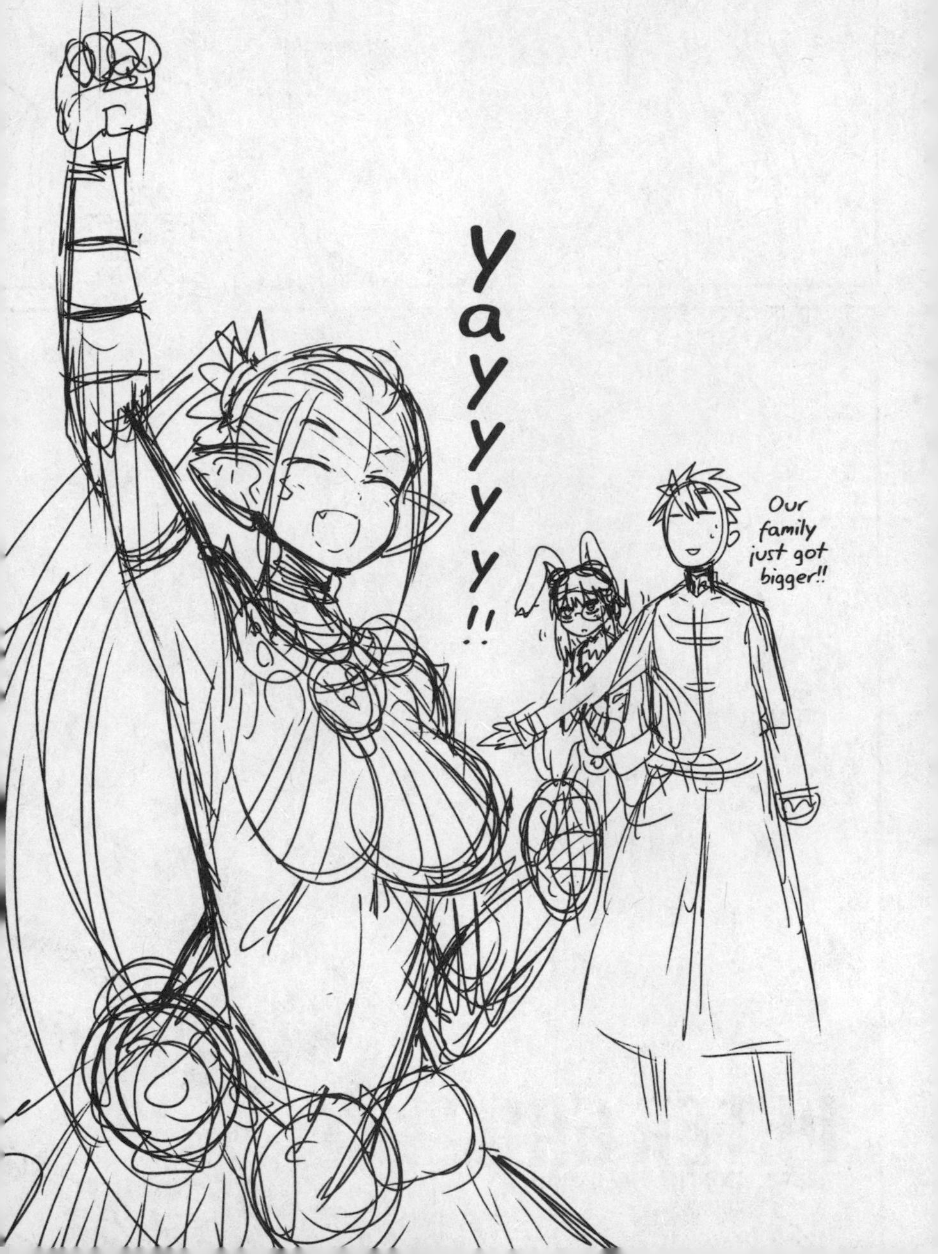
Yayyyy!!
Our family just got bigger!!

PETER GRILL
AND THE PHILOSOPHER'S TIME

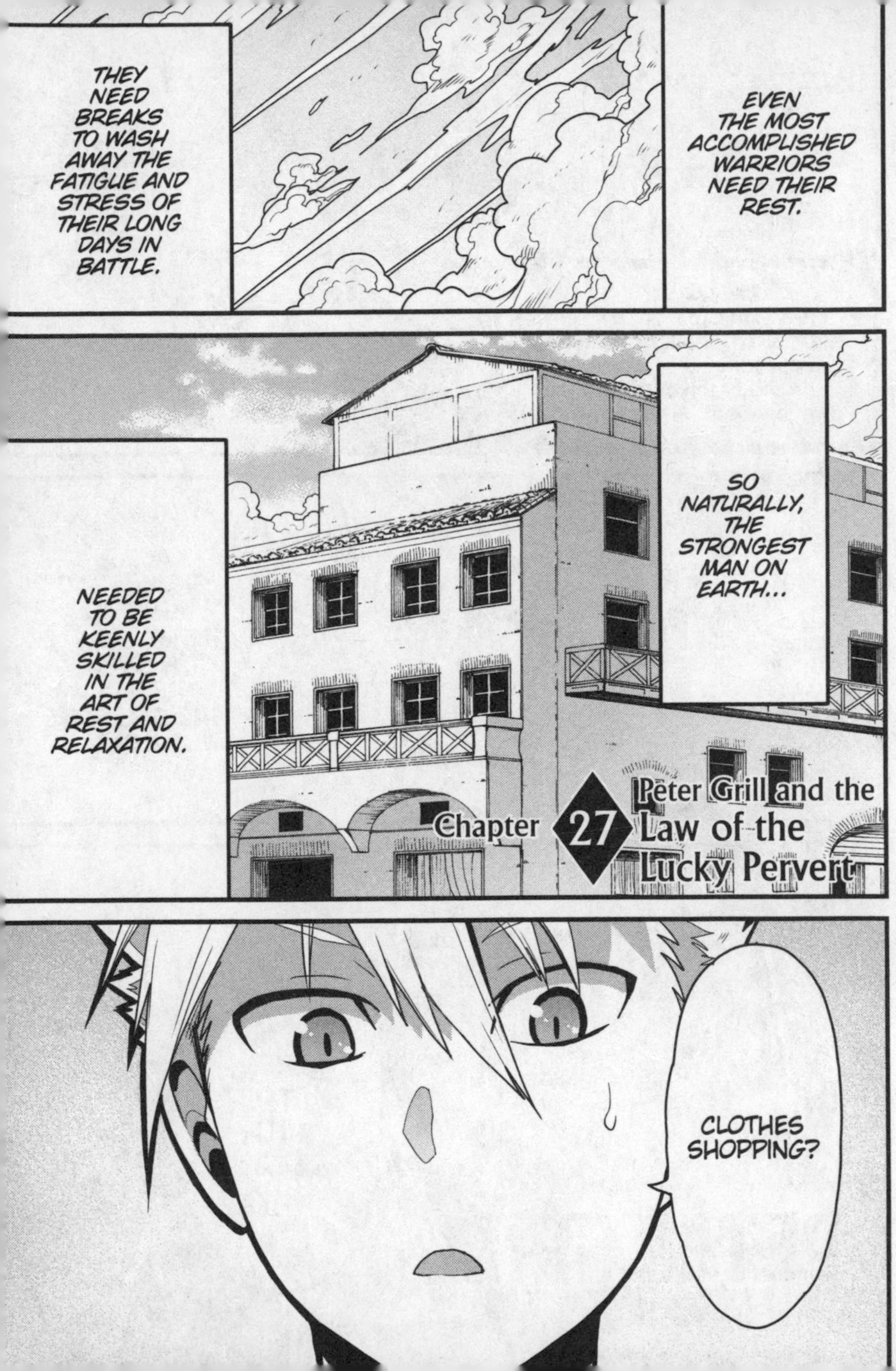
EVEN THE MOST ACCOMPLISHED WARRIORS NEED THEIR REST.
THEY NEED BREAKS TO WASH AWAY THE FATIGUE AND STRESS OF THEIR LONG DAYS IN BATTLE.
SO NATURALLY, THE STRONGEST MAN ON EARTH...
NEEDED TO BE KEENLY SKILLED IN THE ART OF REST AND RELAXATION.
Chapter 27 Peter Grill and the Law of the Lucky Pervert
CLOTHES SHOPPING?

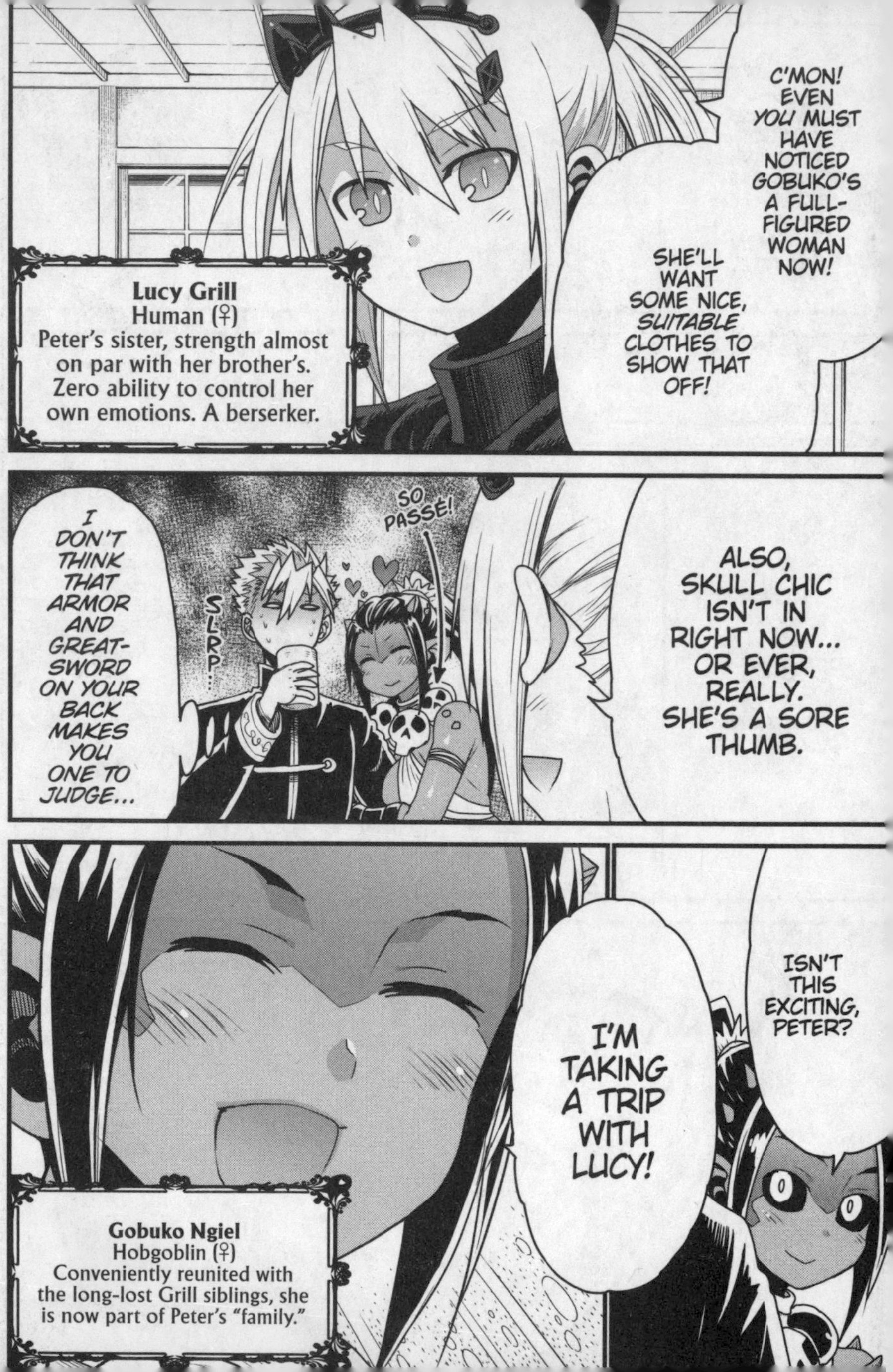
C'MON! EVEN YOU MUST HAVE NOTICED GOBUKO'S A FULL-FIGURED WOMAN NOW!
SHE'LL WANT SOME NICE, SUITABLE CLOTHES TO SHOW THAT OFF!
Lucy Grill
Human (♀)
Peter's sister, strength almost on par with her brother's. Zero ability to control her own emotions. A berserker.
ALSO, SKULL CHIC ISN'T IN RIGHT NOW... OR EVER, REALLY. SHE'S A SORE THUMB.
SO PASSÉ!
SLRP...
I DON'T THINK THAT ARMOR AND GREAT-SWORD ON YOUR BACK MAKES YOU ONE TO JUDGE...
ISN'T THIS EXCITING, PETER?
I'M TAKING A TRIP WITH LUCY!
Gobuko Ngiel
Hobgoblin (♀)
Conveniently reunited with the long-lost Grill siblings, she is now part of Peter's "family."

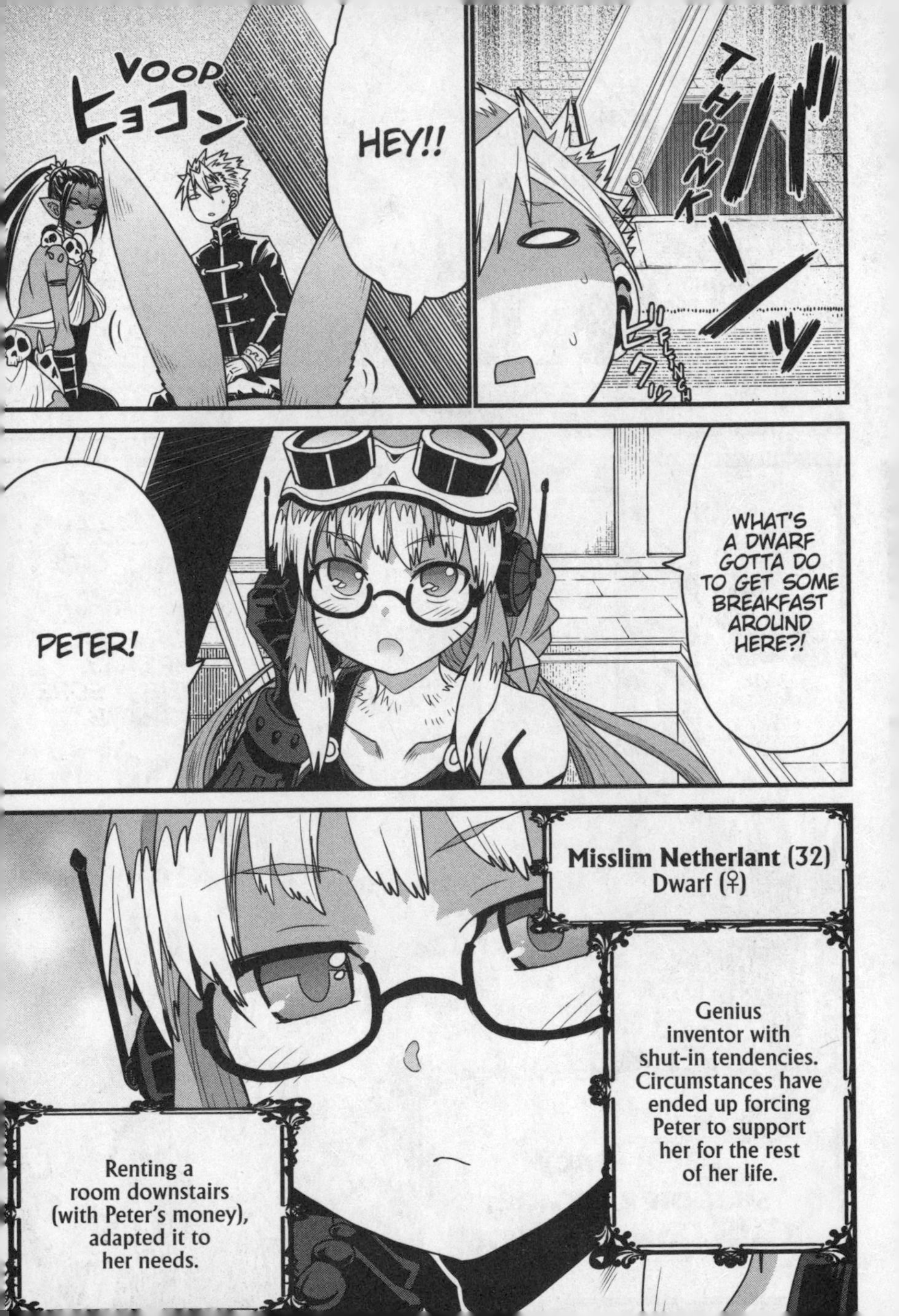
THUNK
FLINCH
ビクッ
HEY!!
VOOP
ヒョコン
WHAT'S A DWARF GOTTA DO TO GET SOME BREAKFAST AROUND HERE?!
PETER!
Misslim Netherlant (32)
Dwarf (♀)
Genius inventor with shut-in tendencies. Circumstances have ended up forcing Peter to support her for the rest of her life.
Renting a room downstairs (with Peter's money), adapted it to her needs.

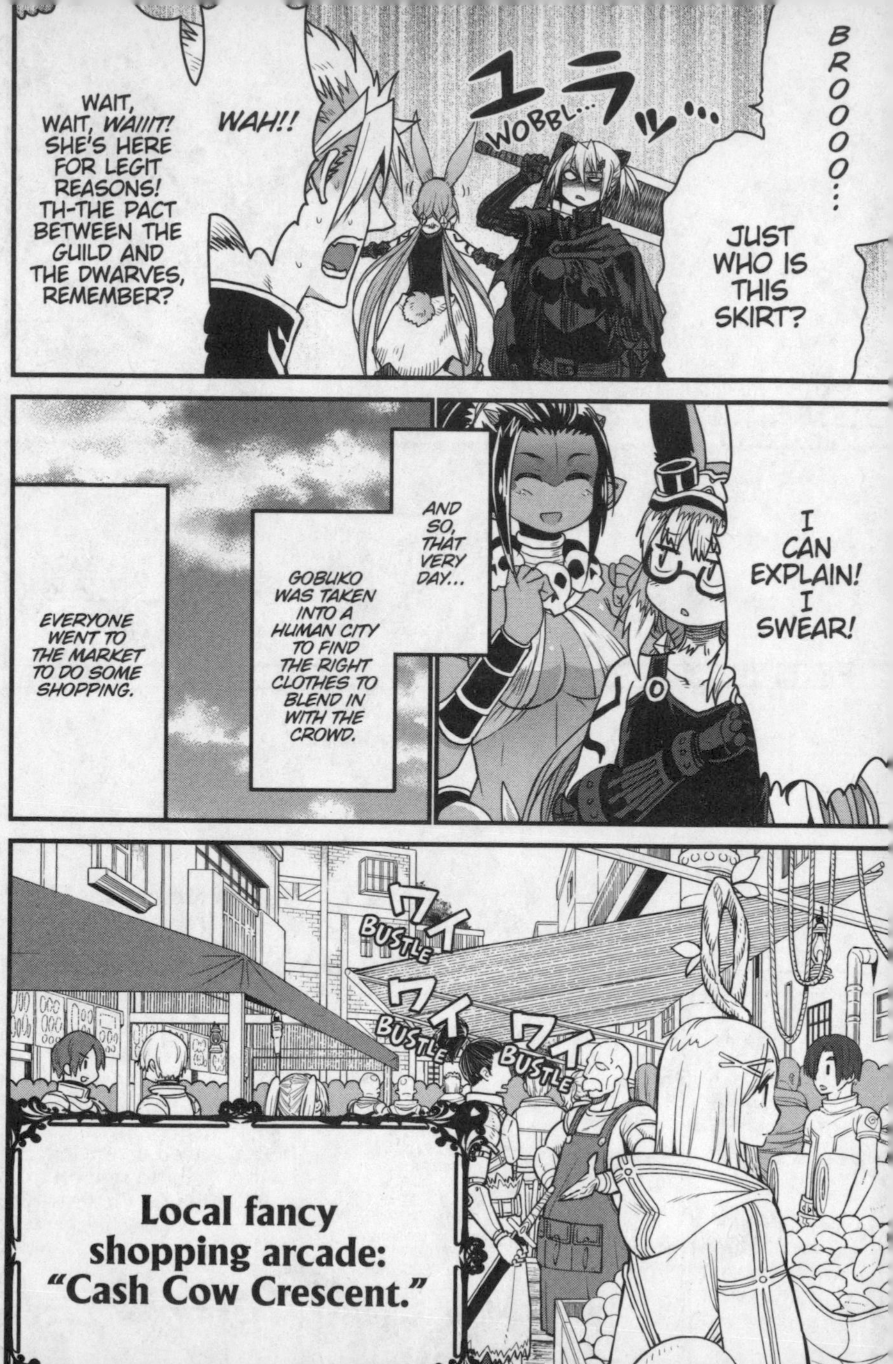
BROOOOO...
JUST WHO IS THIS SKIRT?
ユラ WOBBL... ッ...
WAH!!
WAIT, WAIT, WAIIIT! SHE'S HERE FOR LEGIT REASONS! TH-THE PACT BETWEEN THE GUILD AND THE DWARVES, REMEMBER?
I CAN EXPLAIN! I SWEAR!
AND SO, THAT VERY DAY...
GOBUKO WAS TAKEN INTO A HUMAN CITY TO FIND THE RIGHT CLOTHES TO BLEND IN WITH THE CROWD.
EVERYONE WENT TO THE MARKET TO DO SOME SHOPPING.
ワイ BUSTLE
ワイ BUSTLE
ワイ BUSTLE
Local fancy shopping arcade: “Cash Cow Crescent.”

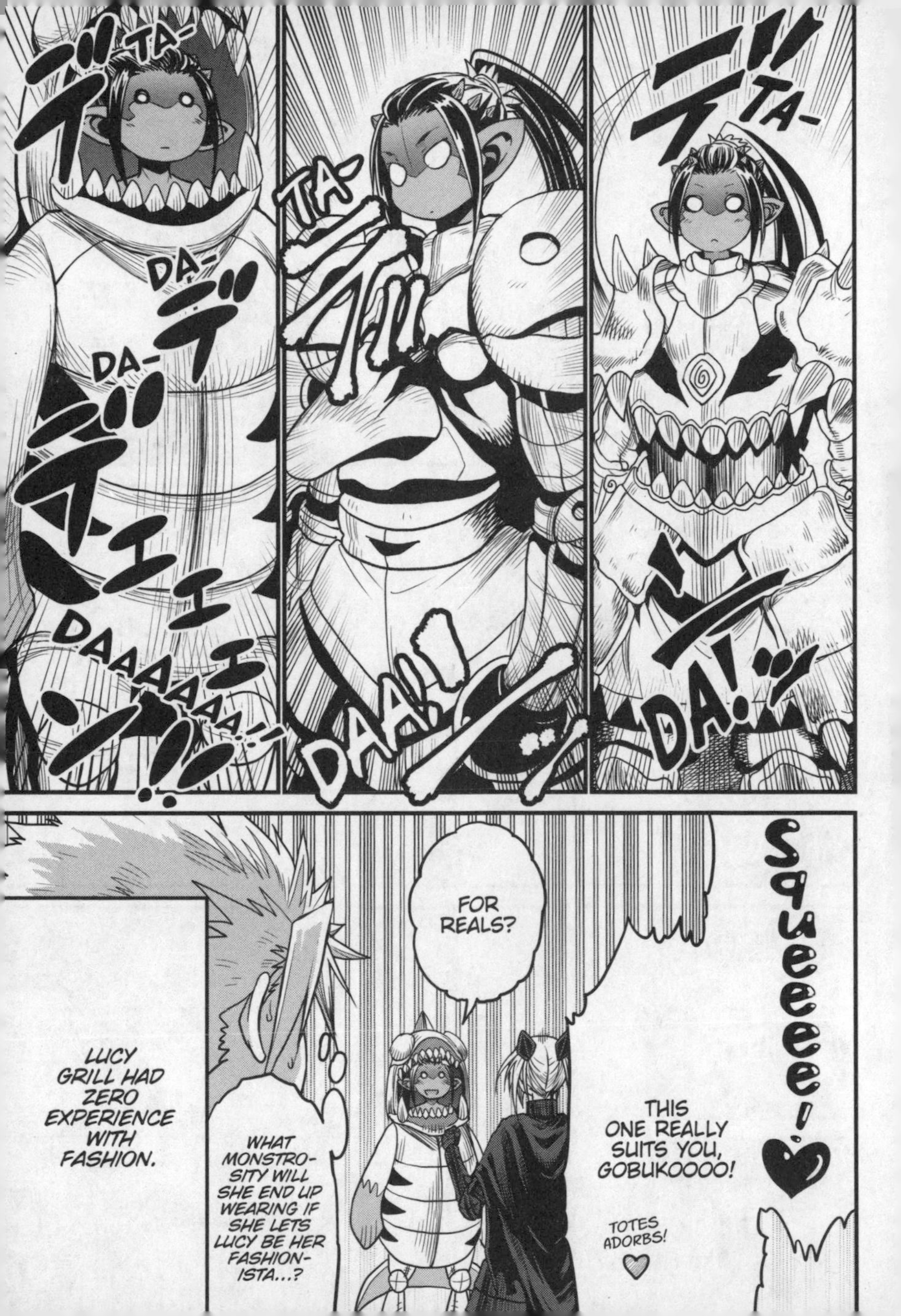
TA-
DA!!
TA-
DA!!
TA-
DA-
DA-
DAAAAAAA!!
Squeeeeee!
THIS ONE REALLY SUITS YOU, GOBUKOOOO!
TOTES ADORBS!
FOR REALS?
WHAT MONSTROSITY WILL SHE END UP WEARING IF SHE LETS LUCY BE HER FASHIONISTA...?
LUCY GRILL HAD ZERO EXPERIENCE WITH FASHION.

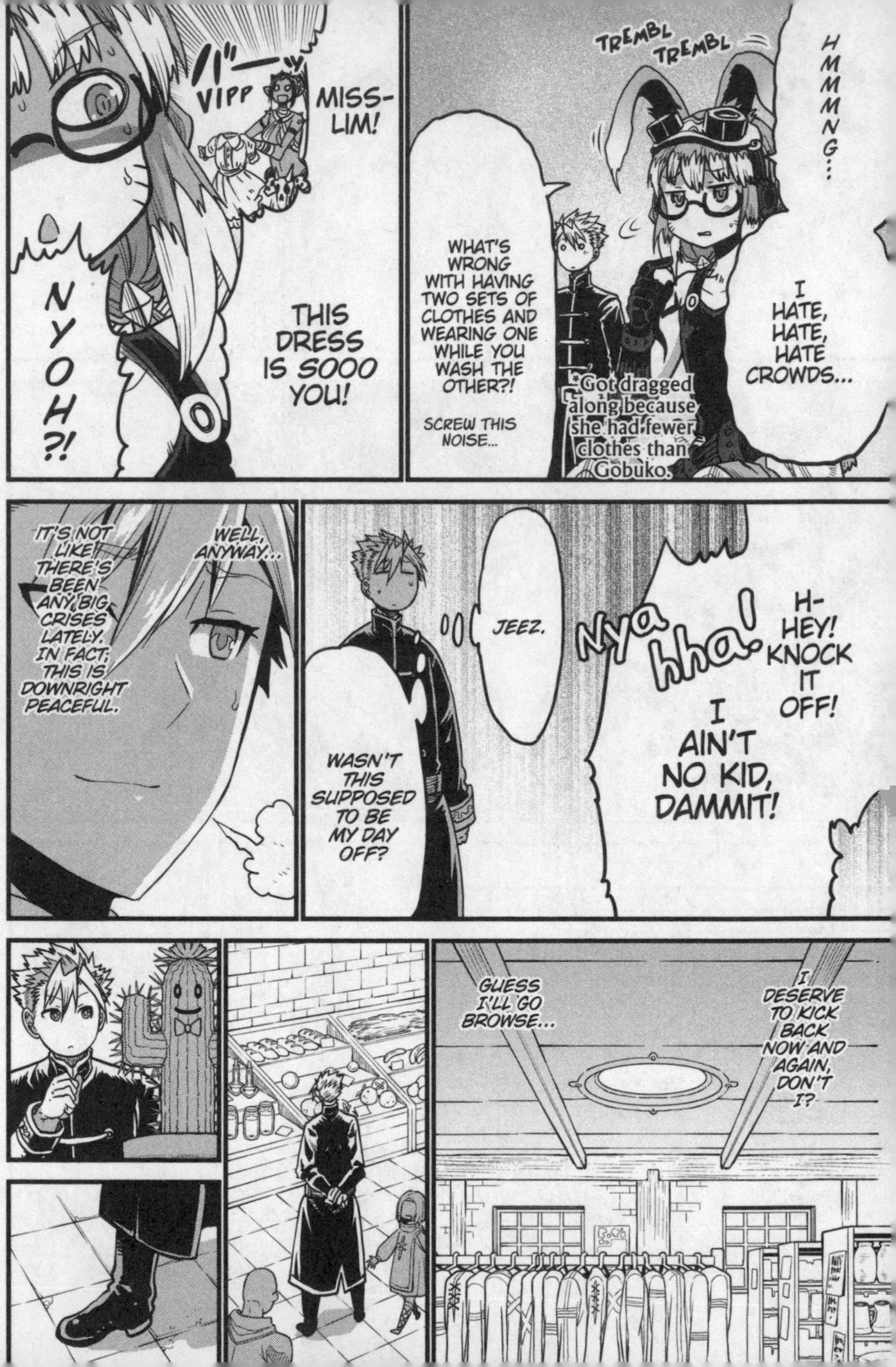
TREMBL TREMBL
HMMMNG...
I HATE, HATE, HATE CROWDS...
WHAT'S WRONG WITH HAVING TWO SETS OF CLOTHES AND WEARING ONE WHILE YOU WASH THE OTHER?!
SCREW THIS NOISE...
*Got dragged along because she had fewer clothes than Gobuko.
VIPP
MISS-LIM!
THIS DRESS IS SOOO YOU!
NYOH?!
H-HEY! KNOCK IT OFF!
I AIN'T NO KID, DAMMIT!
Nyahha!
JEEZ.
WASN'T THIS SUPPOSED TO BE MY DAY OFF?
WELL, ANYWAY...
IT'S NOT LIKE THERE'S BEEN ANY BIG CRISES LATELY. IN FACT, THIS IS DOWNRIGHT PEACEFUL.
I DESERVE TO KICK BACK NOW AND AGAIN, DON'T I?
GUESS I'LL GO BROWSE...

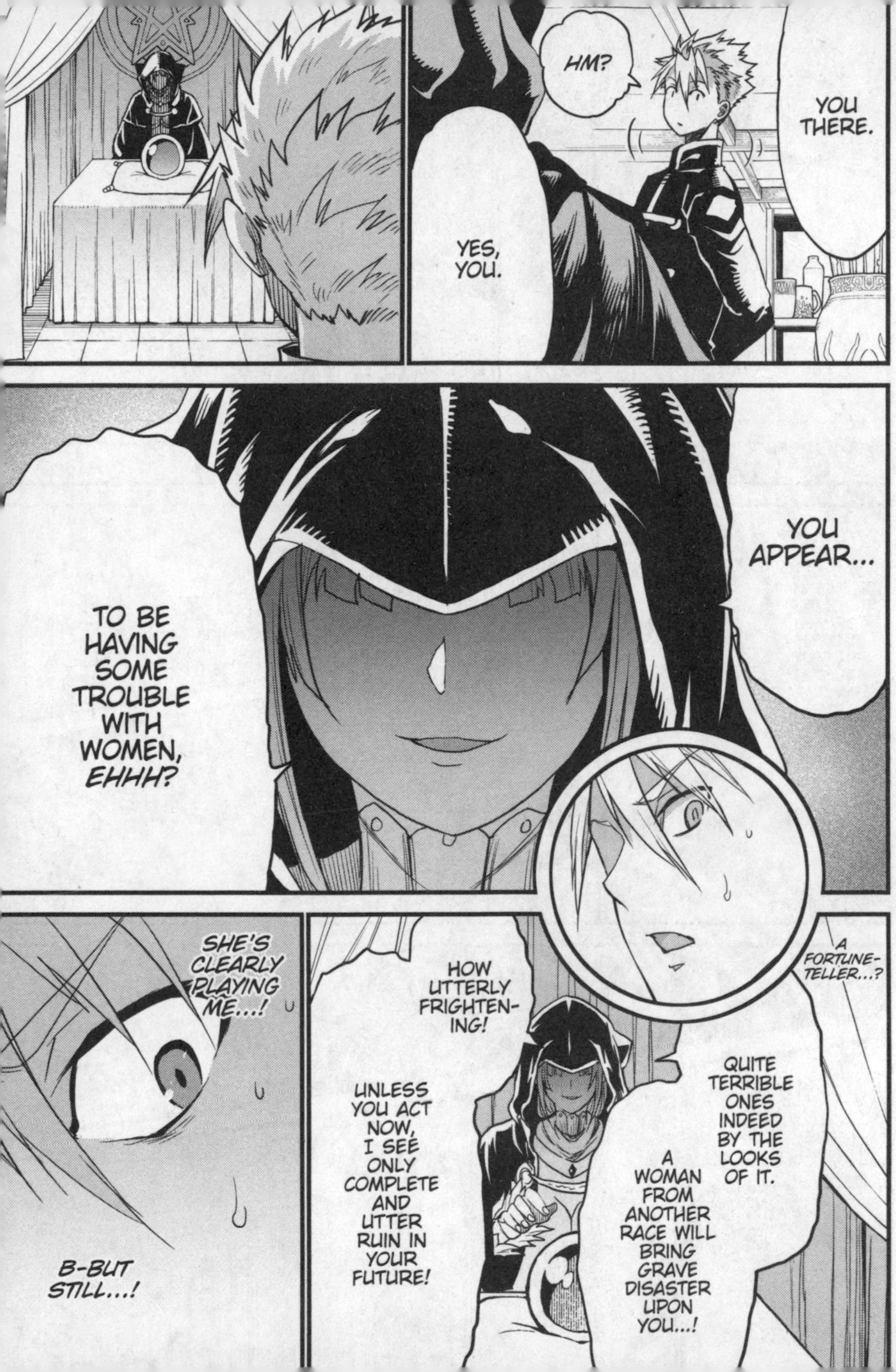
YOU THERE.
HM?
YES, YOU.
YOU APPEAR...
TO BE HAVING SOME TROUBLE WITH WOMEN, EHHH?
A FORTUNE-TELLER...?
QUITE TERRIBLE ONES INDEED BY THE LOOKS OF IT.
A WOMAN FROM ANOTHER RACE WILL BRING GRAVE DISASTER UPON YOU...!
HOW UTTERLY FRIGHTENING!
UNLESS YOU ACT NOW, I SEE ONLY COMPLETE AND UTTER RUIN IN YOUR FUTURE!
SHE'S CLEARLY PLAYING ME...!
B-BUT STILL...!

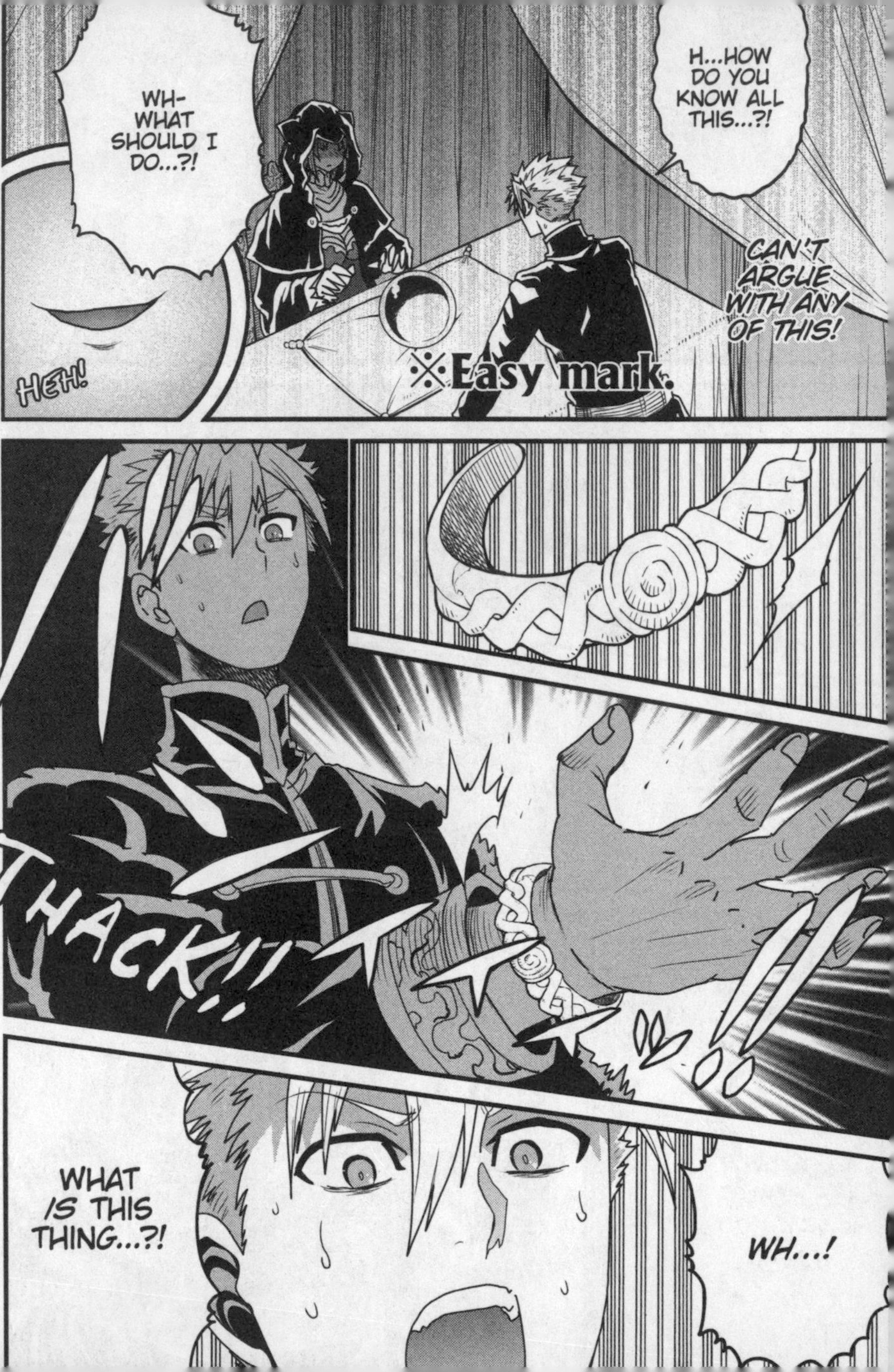
H...HOW DO YOU KNOW ALL THIS...?!
CAN'T ARGUE WITH ANY OF THIS!
WH- WHAT SHOULD I DO...?!
※Easy mark.
HEH!
THACK!!
WH...!
WHAT IS THIS THING...?!

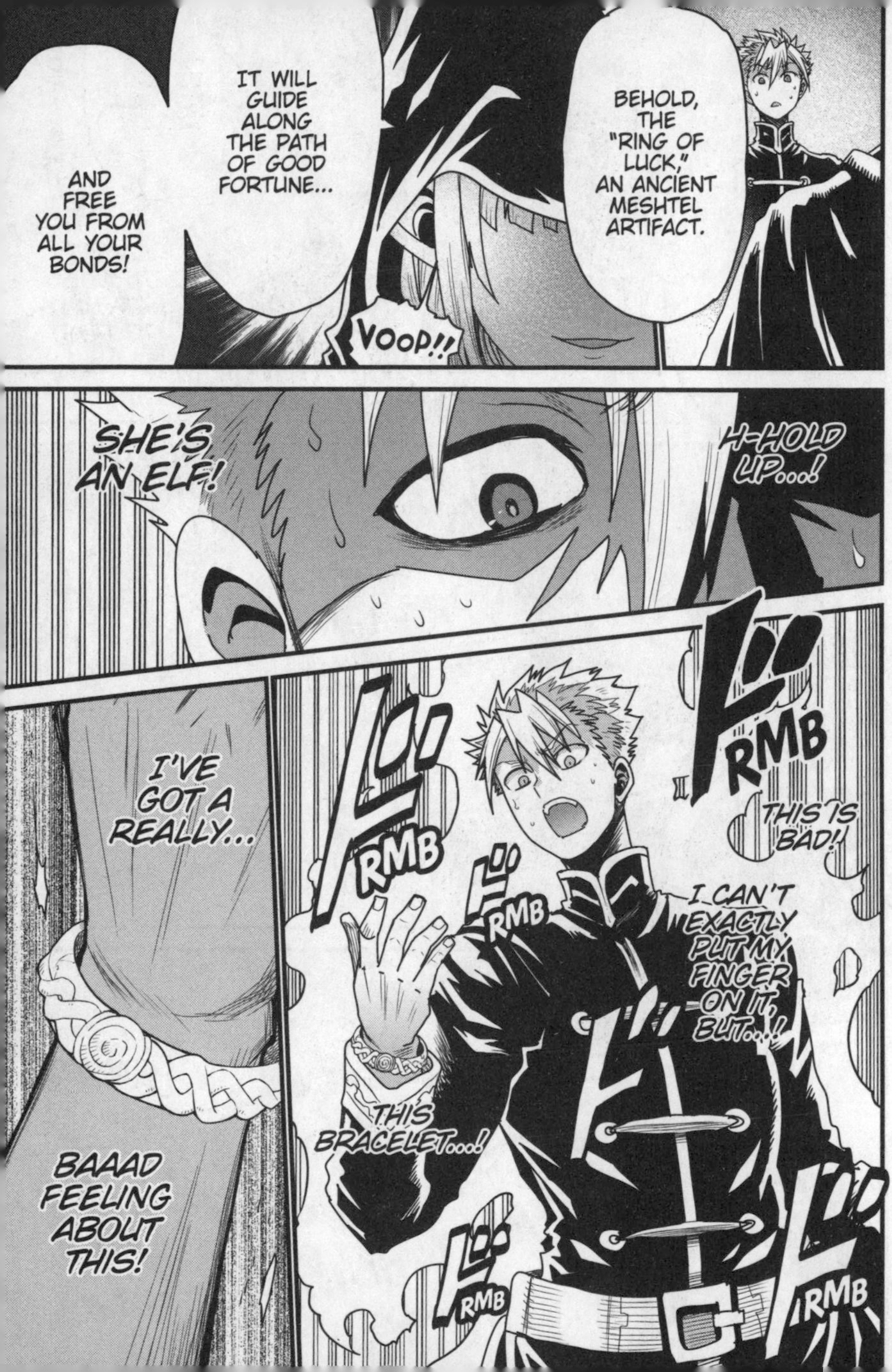
BEHOLD, THE "RING OF LUCK," AN ANCIENT MESHTEL ARTIFACT.
IT WILL GUIDE ALONG THE PATH OF GOOD FORTUNE...
AND FREE YOU FROM ALL YOUR BONDS!
VOOP!!
H-HOLD UP...!
SHE'S AN ELF!
RMB
THIS IS BAD!
I CAN'T EXACTLY PUT MY FINGER ON IT, BUT...!
RMB
RMB
THIS BRACELET...!
RMB
RMB
I'VE GOT A REALLY...
BAAAD FEELING ABOUT THIS!

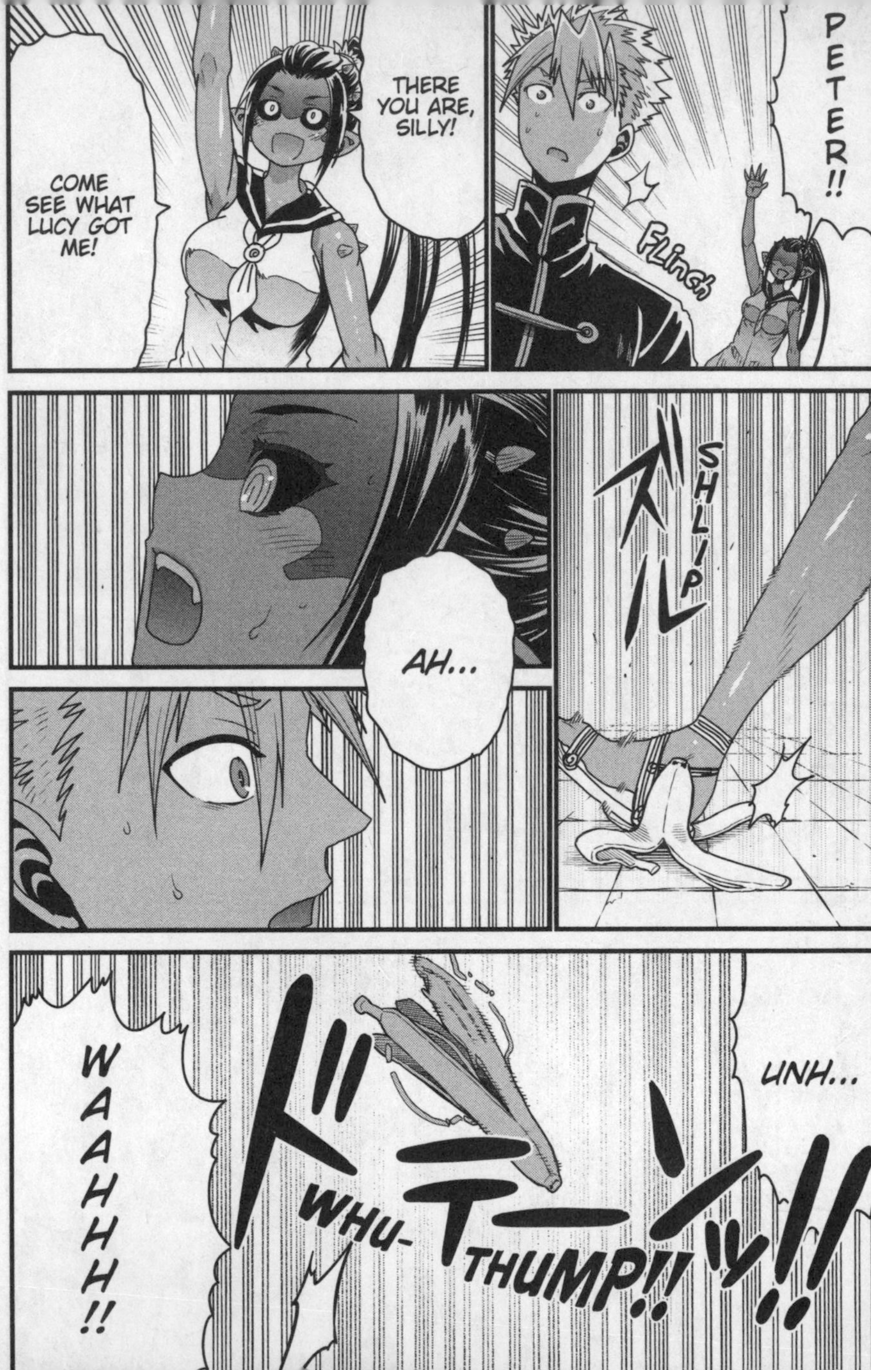
PETER!!
FLinch
THERE YOU ARE, SILLY!
COME SEE WHAT LUCY GOT ME!
SHLIP
AH...
UNH...
WHU-THUMP!!
WAAHHHH!!

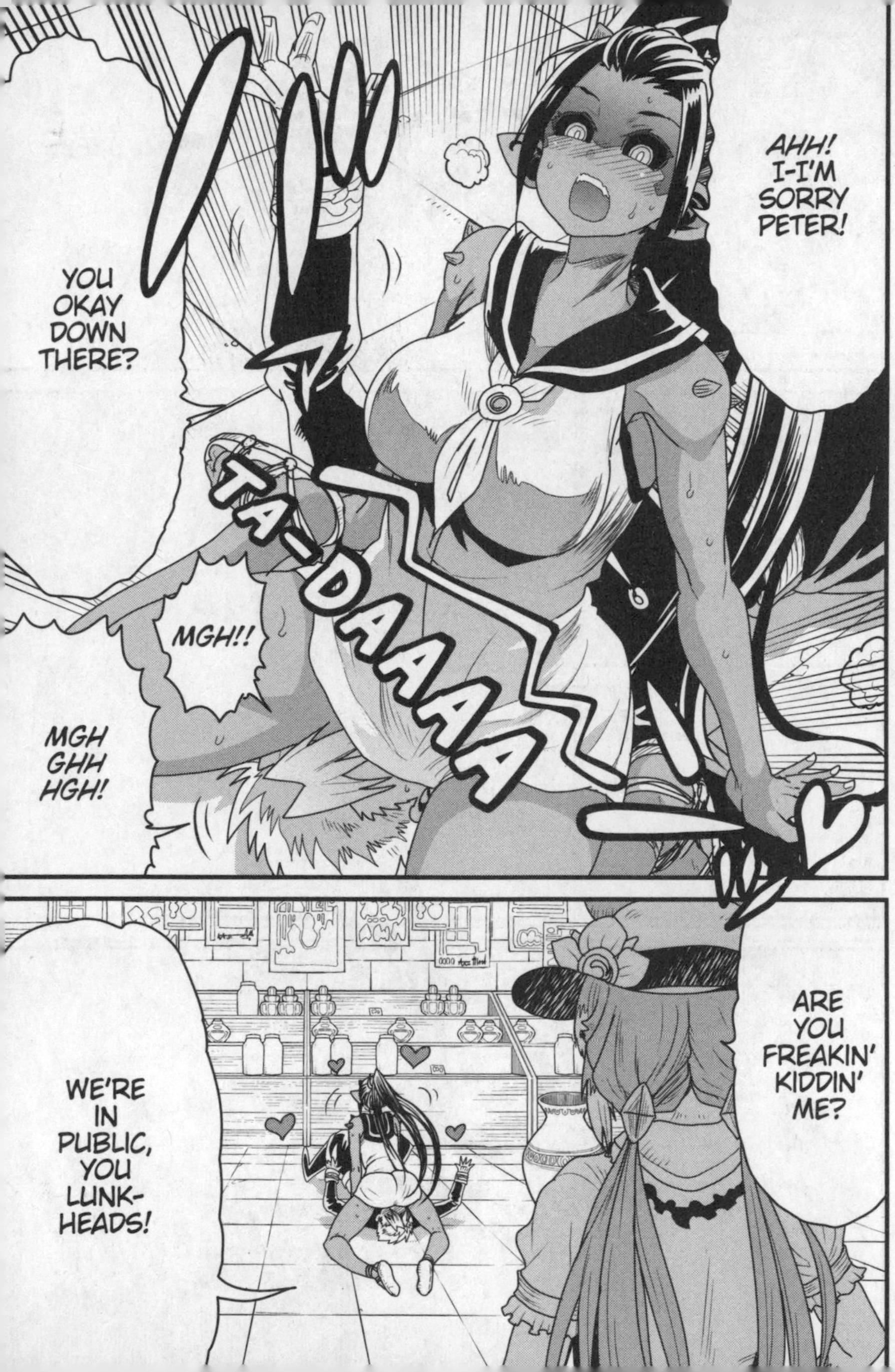
AHH! I-I'M SORRY PETER!
YOU OKAY DOWN THERE?
TA-DAAAAA
MGH!!
MGH GHH HGH!
ARE YOU FREAKIN' KIDDIN' ME?
WE'RE IN PUBLIC, YOU LUNK-HEADS!

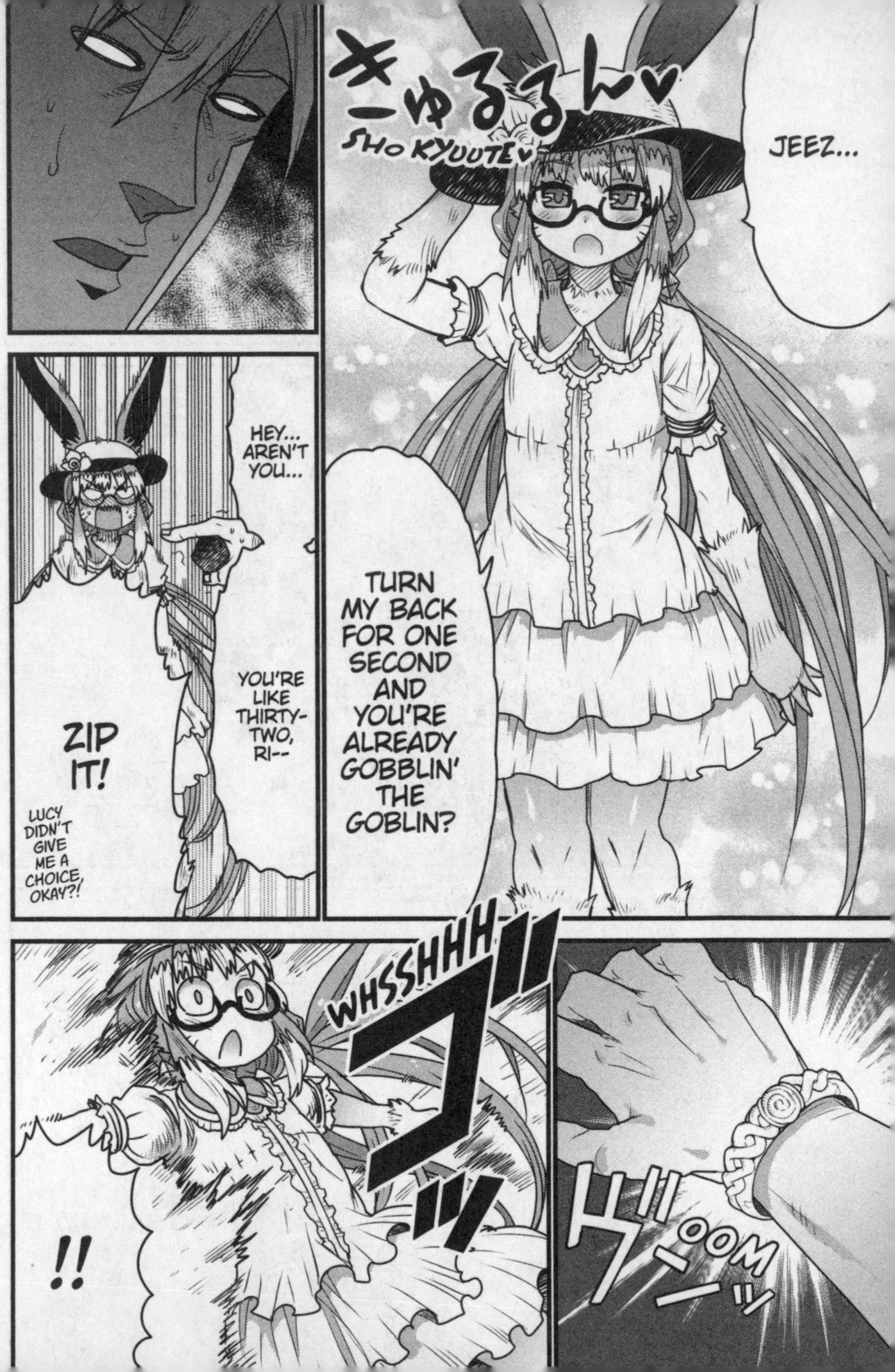
きゅるるん♥
SHOKYUUTE♥
JEEZ...
TURN MY BACK FOR ONE SECOND AND YOU'RE ALREADY GOBBLIN' THE GOBLIN?
HEY... AREN'T YOU...
YOU'RE LIKE THIRTY-TWO, RI--
ZIP IT!
LUCY DIDN'T GIVE ME A CHOICE, OKAY?!
OOM
WHSSHHH
ゴッ
!!

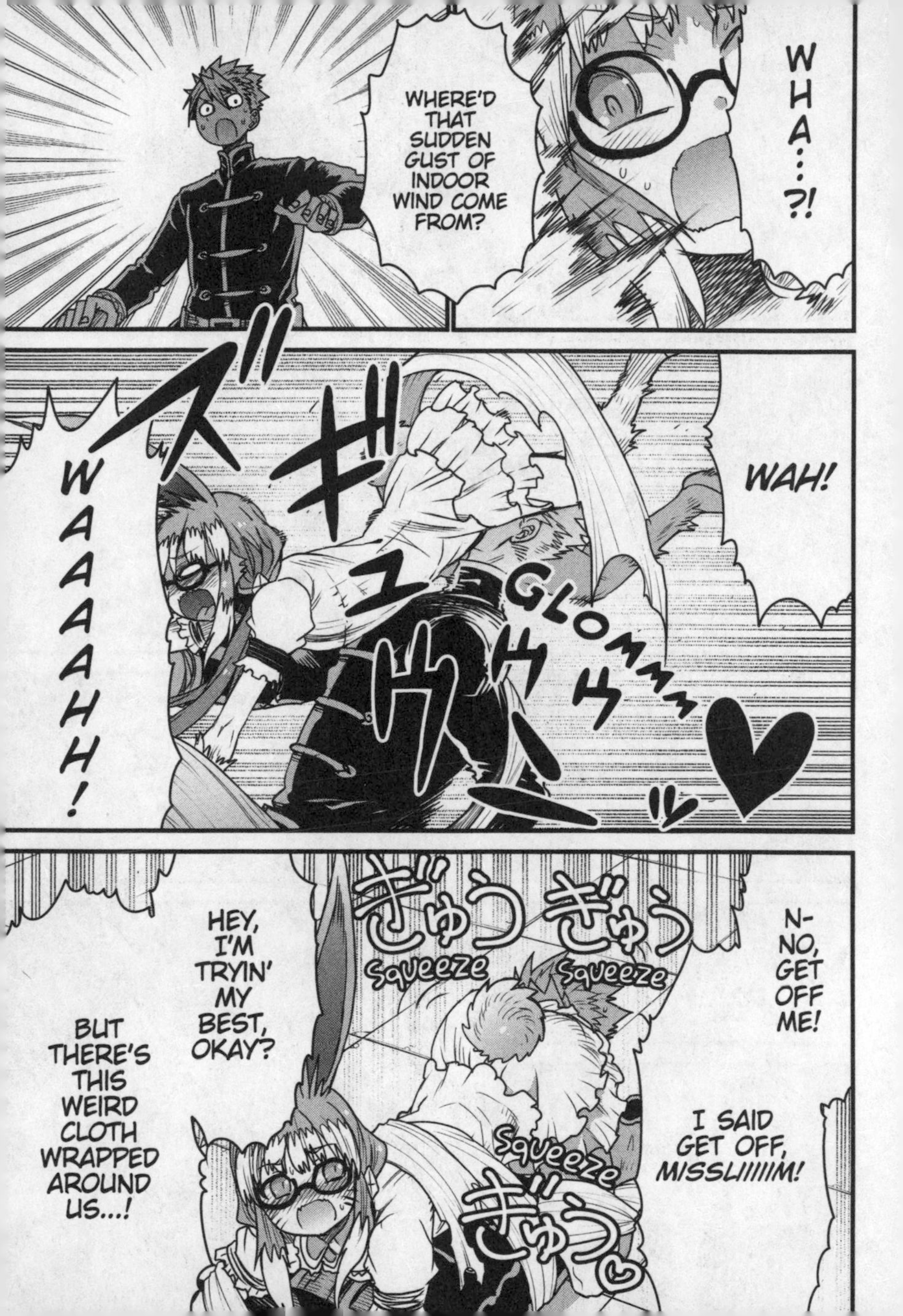
WHA...?!
WHERE'D THAT SUDDEN GUST OF INDOOR WIND COME FROM?
WAH!
ズギュウウッ
GLOMMMM
WAAAAHH!
N-NO, GET OFF ME!
I SAID GET OFF, MISSLIIIIIIM!
ぎゅう ぎゅう
squeeze squeeze
HEY, I'M TRYIN' MY BEST, OKAY?
BUT THERE'S THIS WEIRD CLOTH WRAPPED AROUND US...!
ぎゅう
squeeze

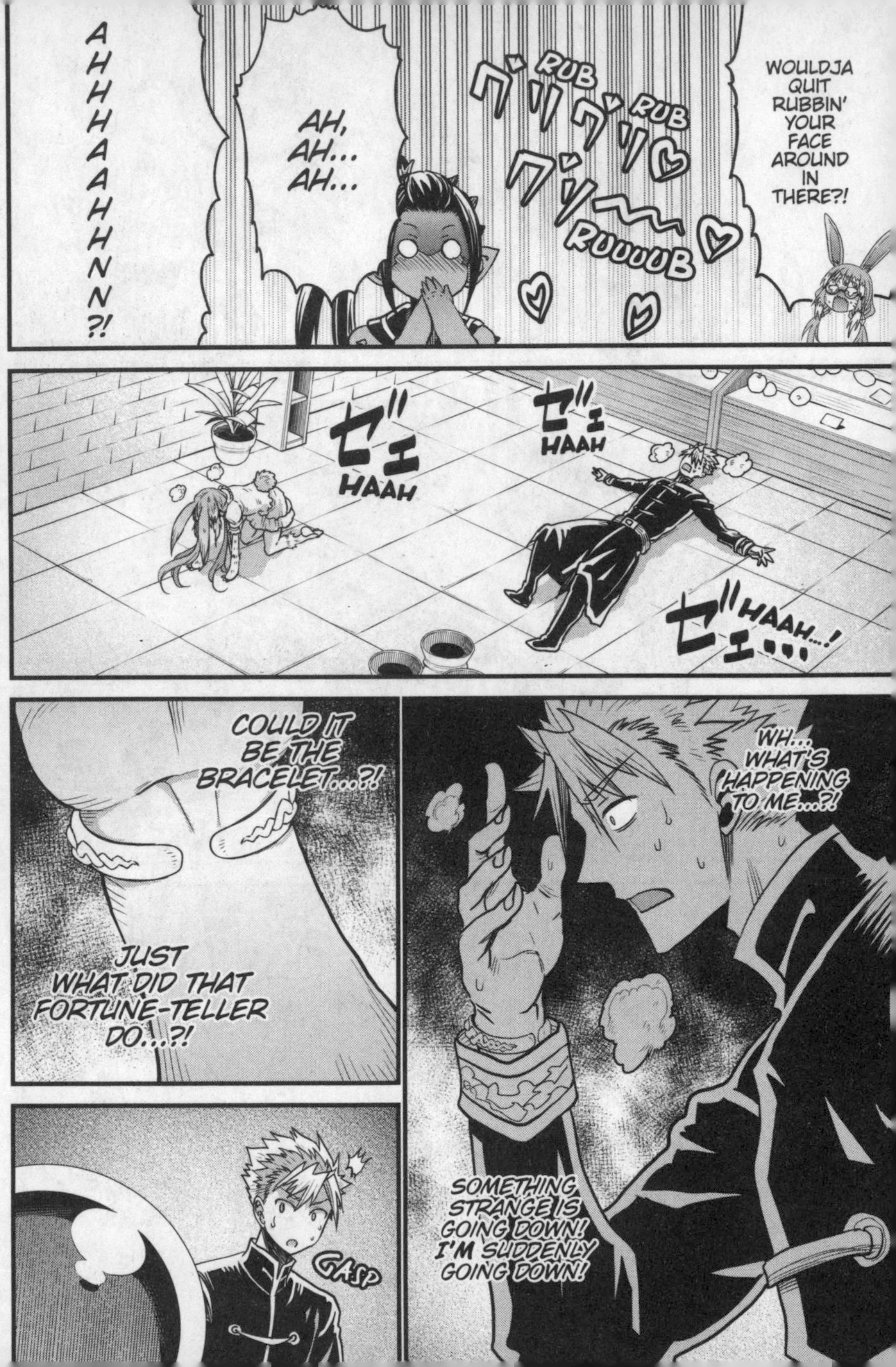
WOULDJA QUIT RUBBIN' YOUR FACE AROUND IN THERE?!
RUB RUB
RUUUUB
AH, AH... AH...
AHHHAAHHNN?!
HAAH
HAAH
HAAH...!
WH... WHAT'S HAPPENING TO ME...?!
SOMETHING STRANGE IS GOING DOWN! I'M SUDDENLY GOING DOWN!
COULD IT BE THE BRACELET...?!
JUST WHAT DID THAT FORTUNE-TELLER DO...?!
GASP

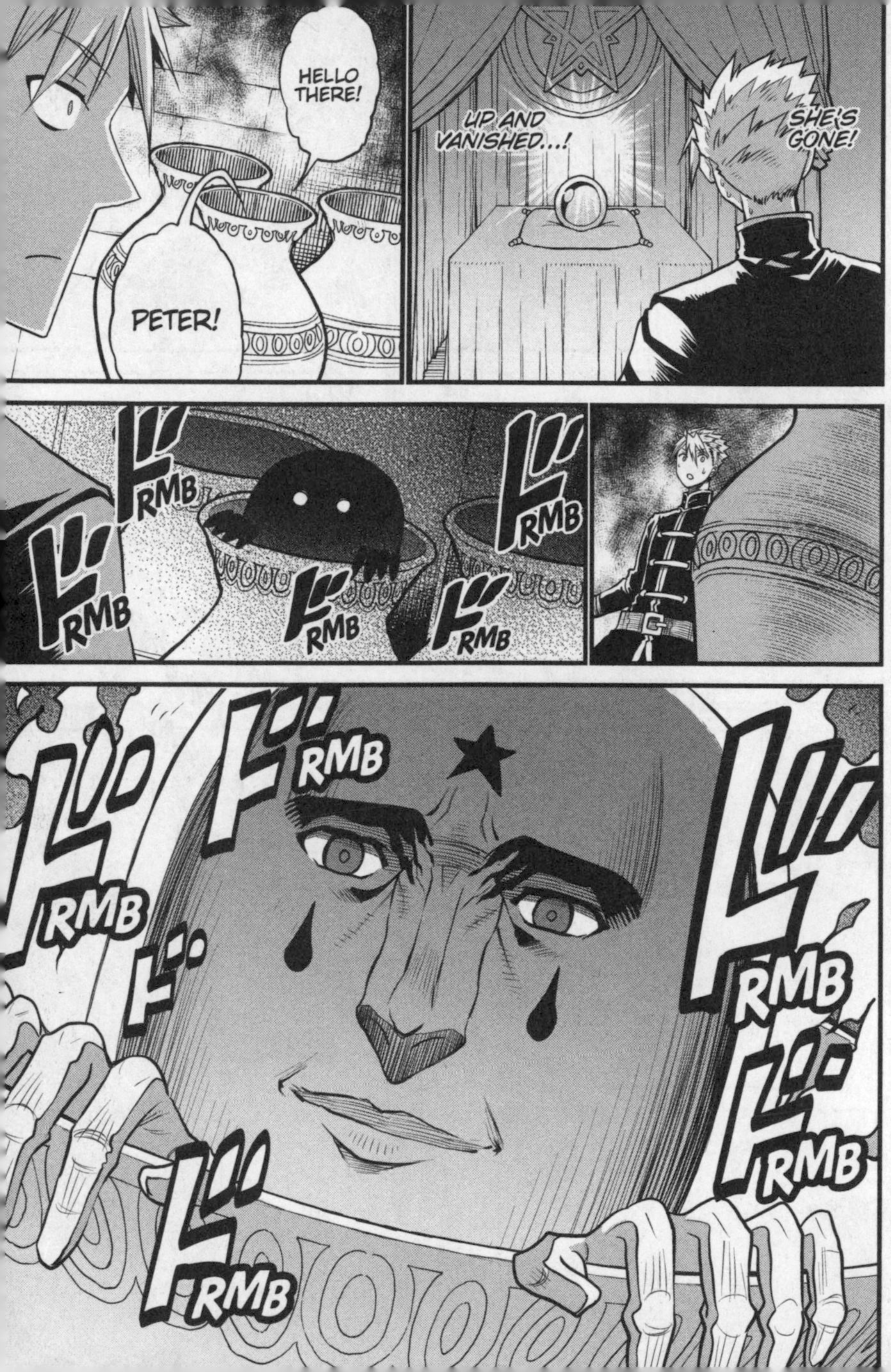
SHE'S GONE!
UP AND VANISHED...!
HELLO THERE!
PETER!
RMB
RMB
RMB
RMB
RMB
RMB
RMB
RMB
RMB
RMB
RMB

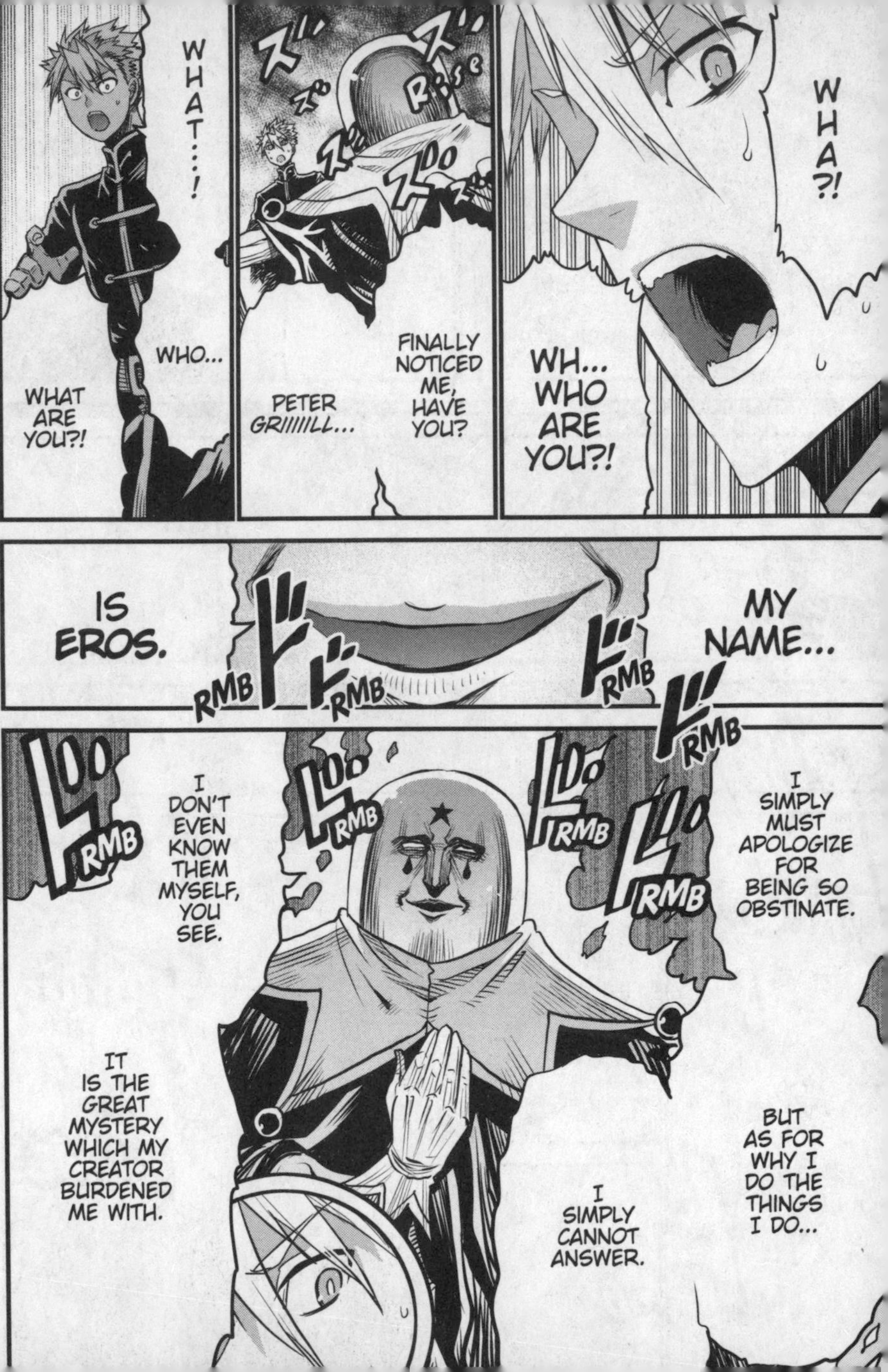
WHA?!
WH... WHO ARE YOU?!
FINALLY NOTICED ME, HAVE YOU?
PETER GRIIIIILL...
WHAT...!
WHO...
WHAT ARE YOU?!
MY NAME...
RMB
RMB
RMB
IS EROS.
I SIMPLY MUST APOLOGIZE FOR BEING SO OBSTINATE.
RMB
RMB
RMB
RMB
RMB
I DON'T EVEN KNOW THEM MYSELF, YOU SEE.
BUT AS FOR WHY I DO THE THINGS I DO...
I SIMPLY CANNOT ANSWER.
IT IS THE GREAT MYSTERY WHICH MY CREATOR BURDENED ME WITH.

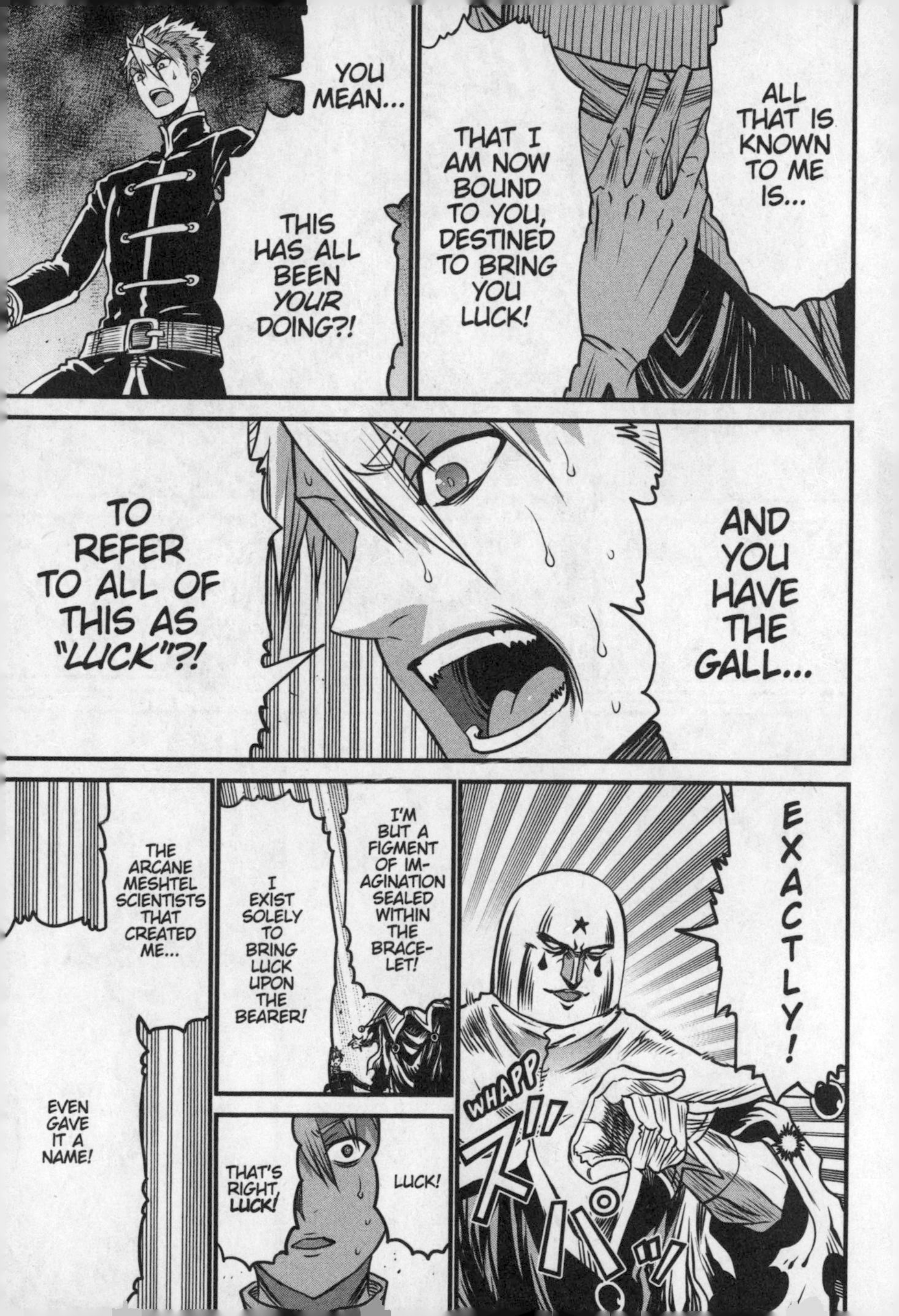
ALL THAT IS KNOWN TO ME IS...
THAT I AM NOW BOUND TO YOU, DESTINED TO BRING YOU LUCK!
YOU MEAN...
THIS HAS ALL BEEN *YOUR* DOING?!
AND YOU HAVE THE GALL...
TO REFER TO ALL OF THIS AS "*LUCK*"?!
EXACTLY!
WHAPP
I'M BUT A FIGMENT OF IMAGINATION SEALED WITHIN THE BRACELET!
I EXIST SOLELY TO BRING LUCK UPON THE BEARER!
THE ARCANE MESHTEL SCIENTISTS THAT CREATED ME...
EVEN GAVE IT A NAME!
LUCK!
THAT'S RIGHT, LUCK!

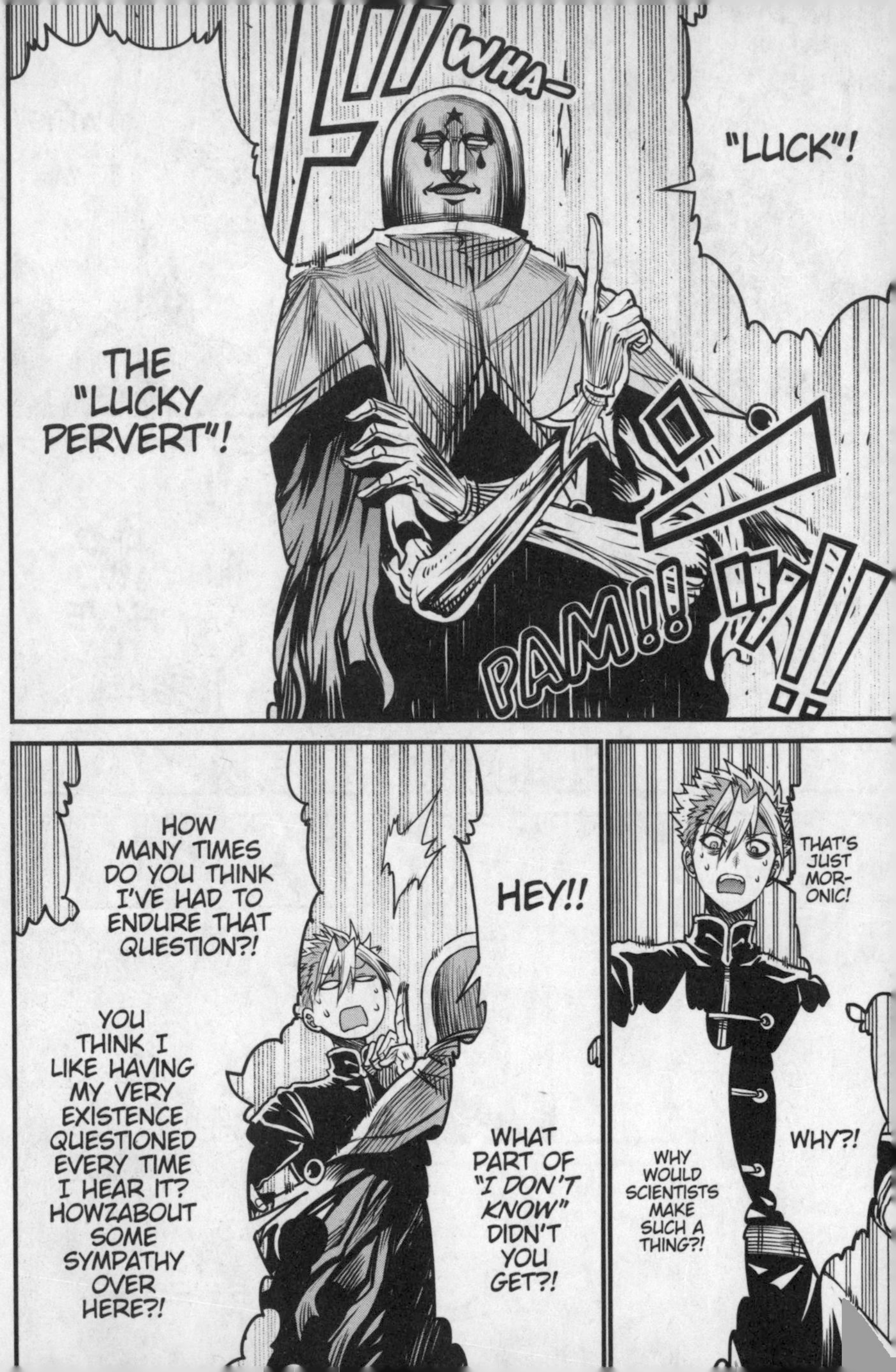
"LUCK"!
THE "LUCKY PERVERT"!
WHA-
PAM!!
THAT'S JUST MOR-ONIC!
WHY?!
WHY WOULD SCIENTISTS MAKE SUCH A THING?!
HEY!!
HOW MANY TIMES DO YOU THINK I'VE HAD TO ENDURE THAT QUESTION?!
WHAT PART OF "I DON'T KNOW" DIDN'T YOU GET?!
YOU THINK I LIKE HAVING MY VERY EXISTENCE QUESTIONED EVERY TIME I HEAR IT? HOWZABOUT SOME SYMPATHY OVER HERE?!

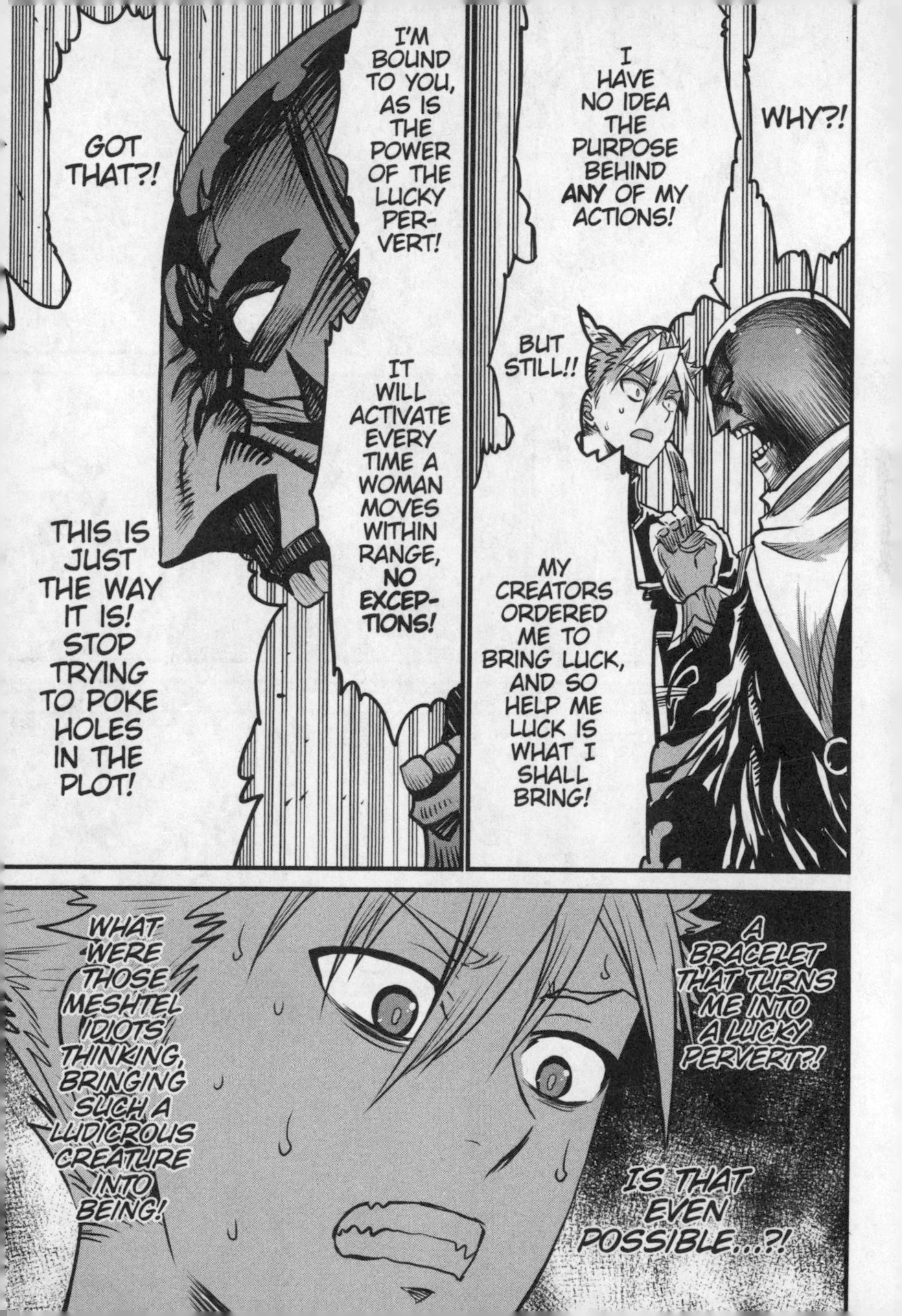
WHY?!
I HAVE NO IDEA THE PURPOSE BEHIND ANY OF MY ACTIONS!
BUT STILL!!
MY CREATORS ORDERED ME TO BRING LUCK, AND SO HELP ME LUCK IS WHAT I SHALL BRING!
I'M BOUND TO YOU, AS IS THE POWER OF THE LUCKY PER-VERT!
GOT THAT?!
IT WILL ACTIVATE EVERY TIME A WOMAN MOVES WITHIN RANGE, NO EXCEP-TIONS!
THIS IS JUST THE WAY IT IS! STOP TRYING TO POKE HOLES IN THE PLOT!
A BRACELET THAT TURNS ME INTO A LUCKY PERVERT?!
WHAT WERE THOSE MESHTEL IDIOTS THINKING, BRINGING SUCH A LUDICROUS CREATURE INTO BEING!
IS THAT EVEN POSSIBLE...?!

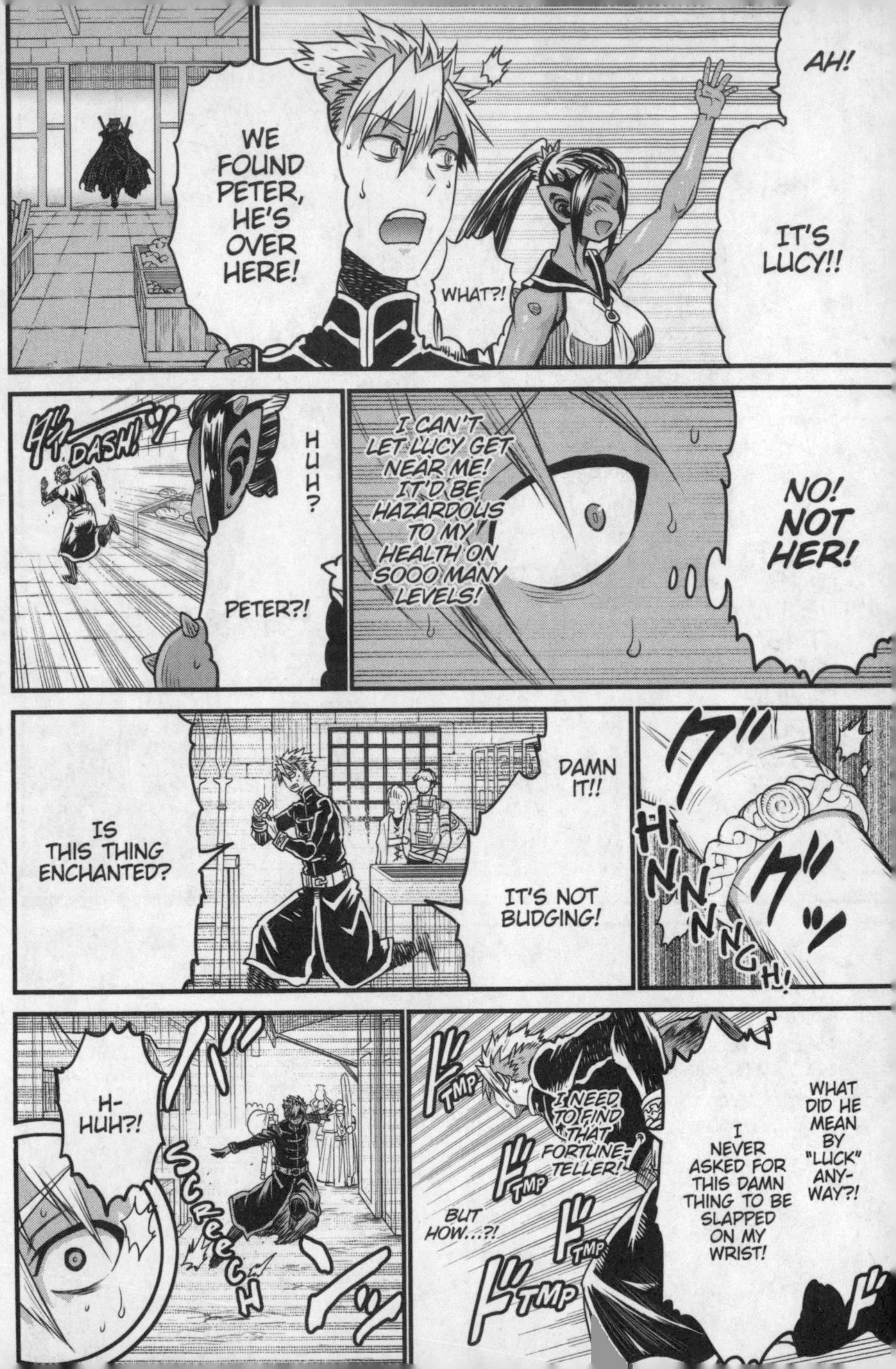
AH!
IT'S LUCY!!
WE FOUND PETER, HE'S OVER HERE!
WHAT?!
NO! NOT HER!
I CAN'T LET LUCY GET NEAR ME! IT'D BE HAZARDOUS TO MY HEALTH ON SOOO MANY LEVELS!
HUH?
DASH!
PETER?!
HNNNNNGH!
DAMN IT!!
IT'S NOT BUDGING!
IS THIS THING ENCHANTED?
WHAT DID HE MEAN BY "LUCK" ANYWAY?!
I NEVER ASKED FOR THIS DAMN THING TO BE SLAPPED ON MY WRIST!
I NEED TO FIND THAT FORTUNE-TELLER!
BUT HOW...?!
TMP
TMP
TMP
TMP
H-HUH?!
SCREECH

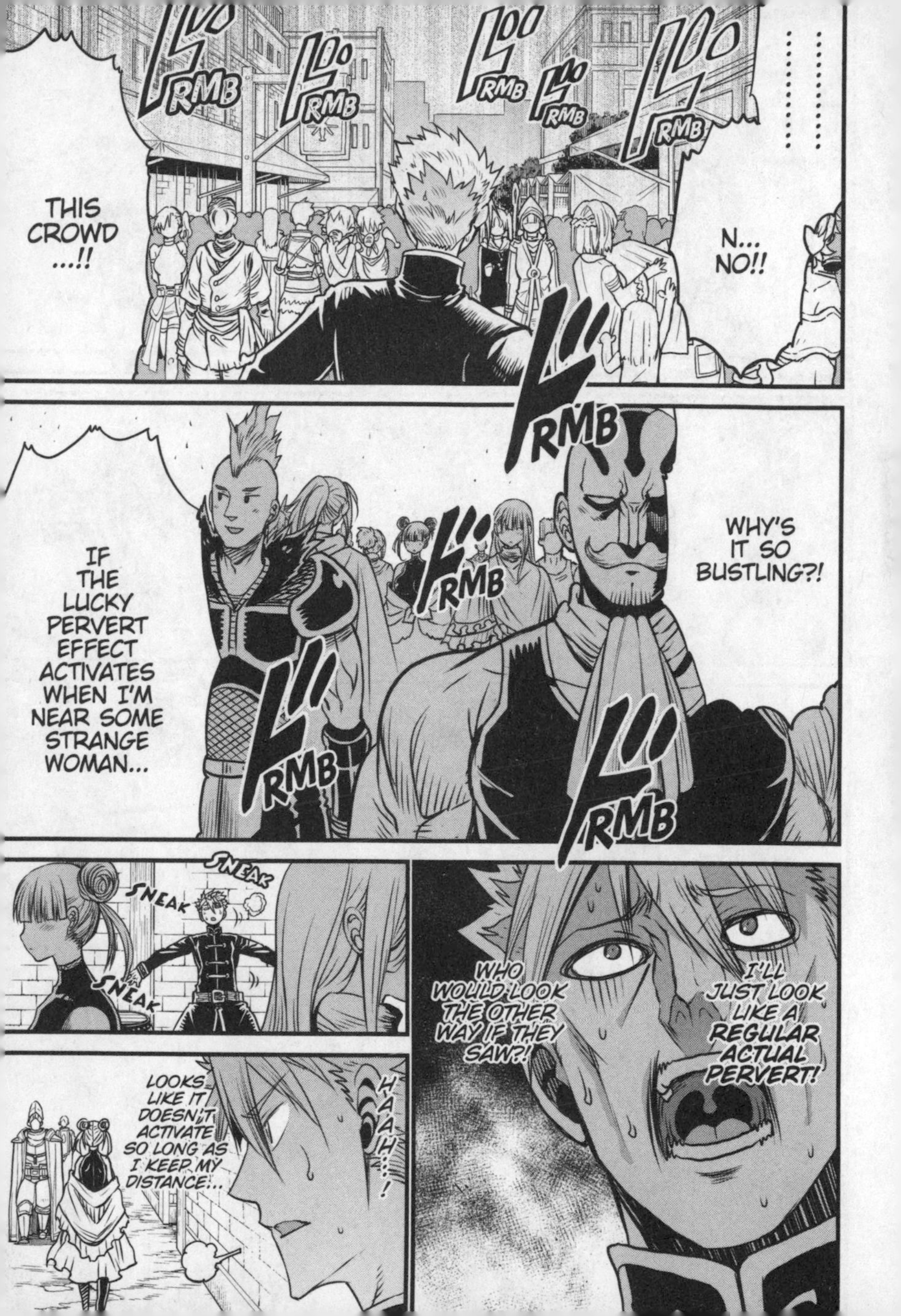
RMB
RMB
RMB
RMB
RMB
......
N... NO!!
THIS CROWD ...!!
RMB
WHY'S IT SO BUSTLING?!
IF THE LUCKY PERVERT EFFECT ACTIVATES WHEN I'M NEAR SOME STRANGE WOMAN...
RMB
RMB
RMB
I'LL JUST LOOK LIKE A REGULAR ACTUAL PERVERT!
WHO WOULD LOOK THE OTHER WAY IF THEY SAW?!
SNEAK
SNEAK
SNEAK
HAAAH...!
LOOKS LIKE IT DOESN'T ACTIVATE SO LONG AS I KEEP MY DISTANCE...

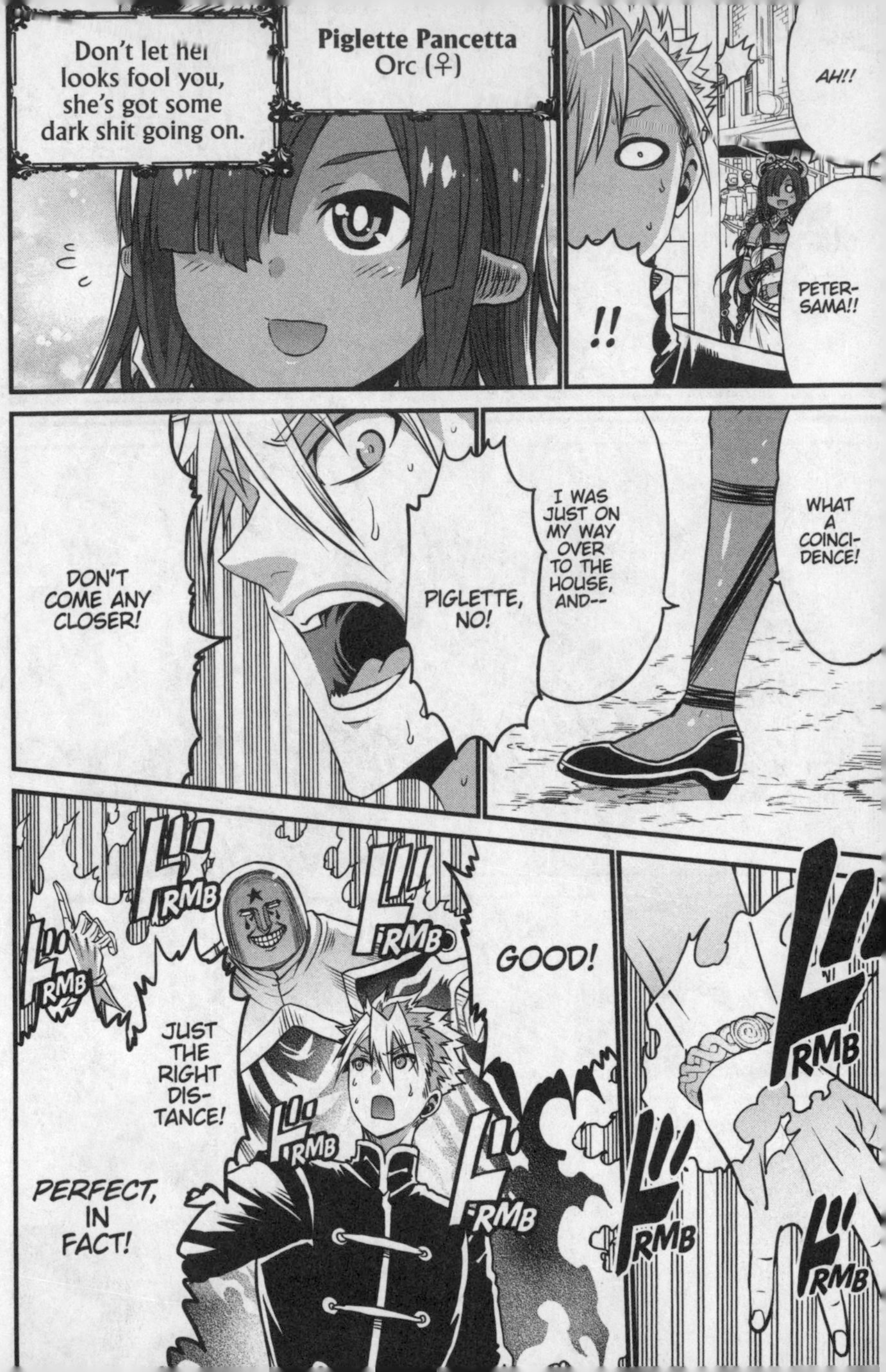
AH!!
PETER-SAMA!!
!!
Piglette Pancetta
Orc (♀)
Don't let her looks fool you, she's got some dark shit going on.
WHAT A COINCIDENCE!
I WAS JUST ON MY WAY OVER TO THE HOUSE, AND--
PIGLETTE, NO!
DON'T COME ANY CLOSER!
RMB
RMB
GOOD!
RMB
RMB
JUST THE RIGHT DISTANCE!
RMB
RMB
PERFECT, IN FACT!
RMB
RMB

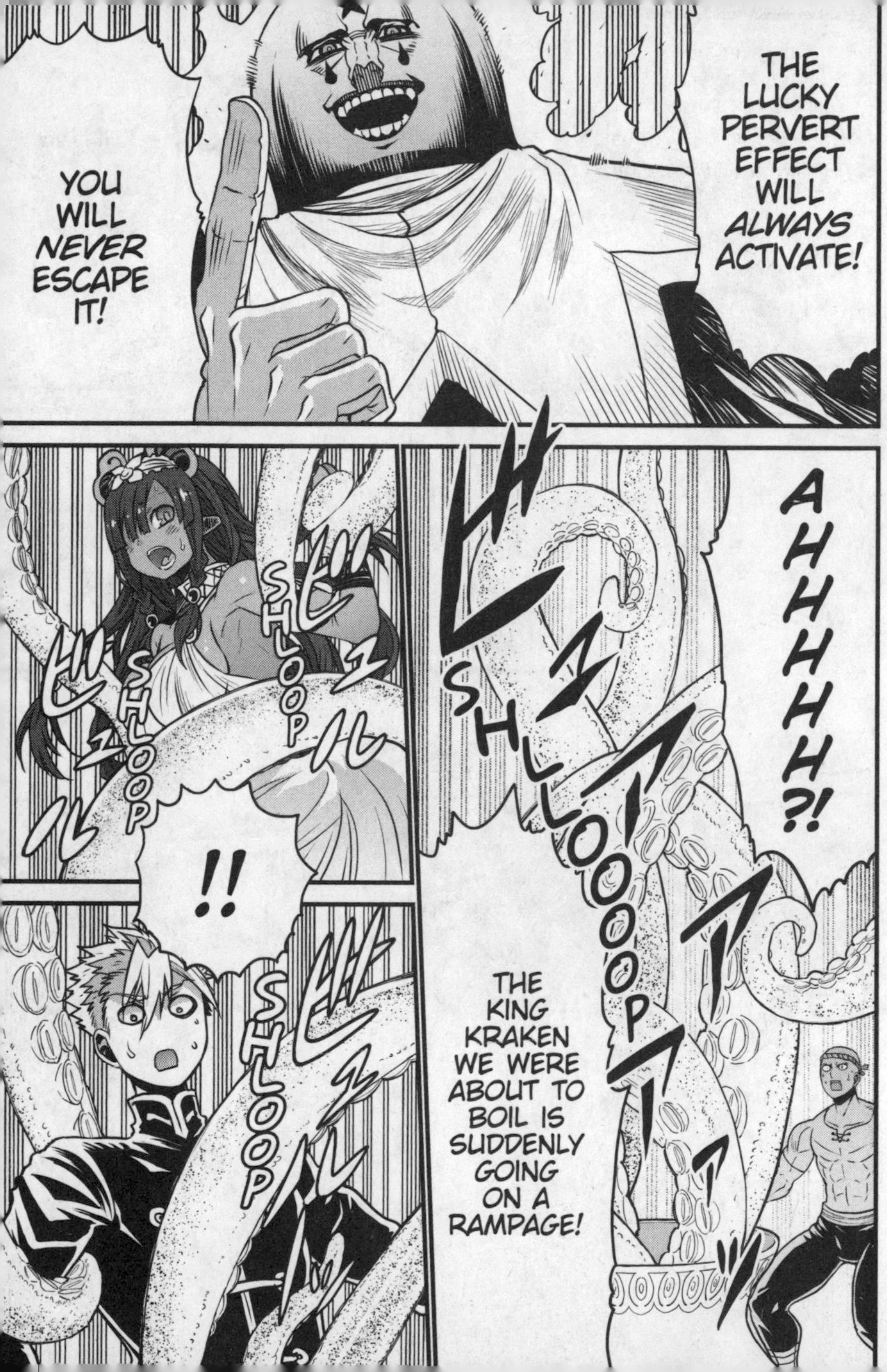
THE LUCKY PERVERT EFFECT WILL ALWAYS ACTIVATE!
YOU WILL NEVER ESCAPE IT!
AHHHHHH?!
SHLLOOOOOOP
THE KING KRAKEN WE WERE ABOUT TO BOIL IS SUDDENLY GOING ON A RAMPAGE!
SHLOOP
SHLOOP
!!
SHLOOP

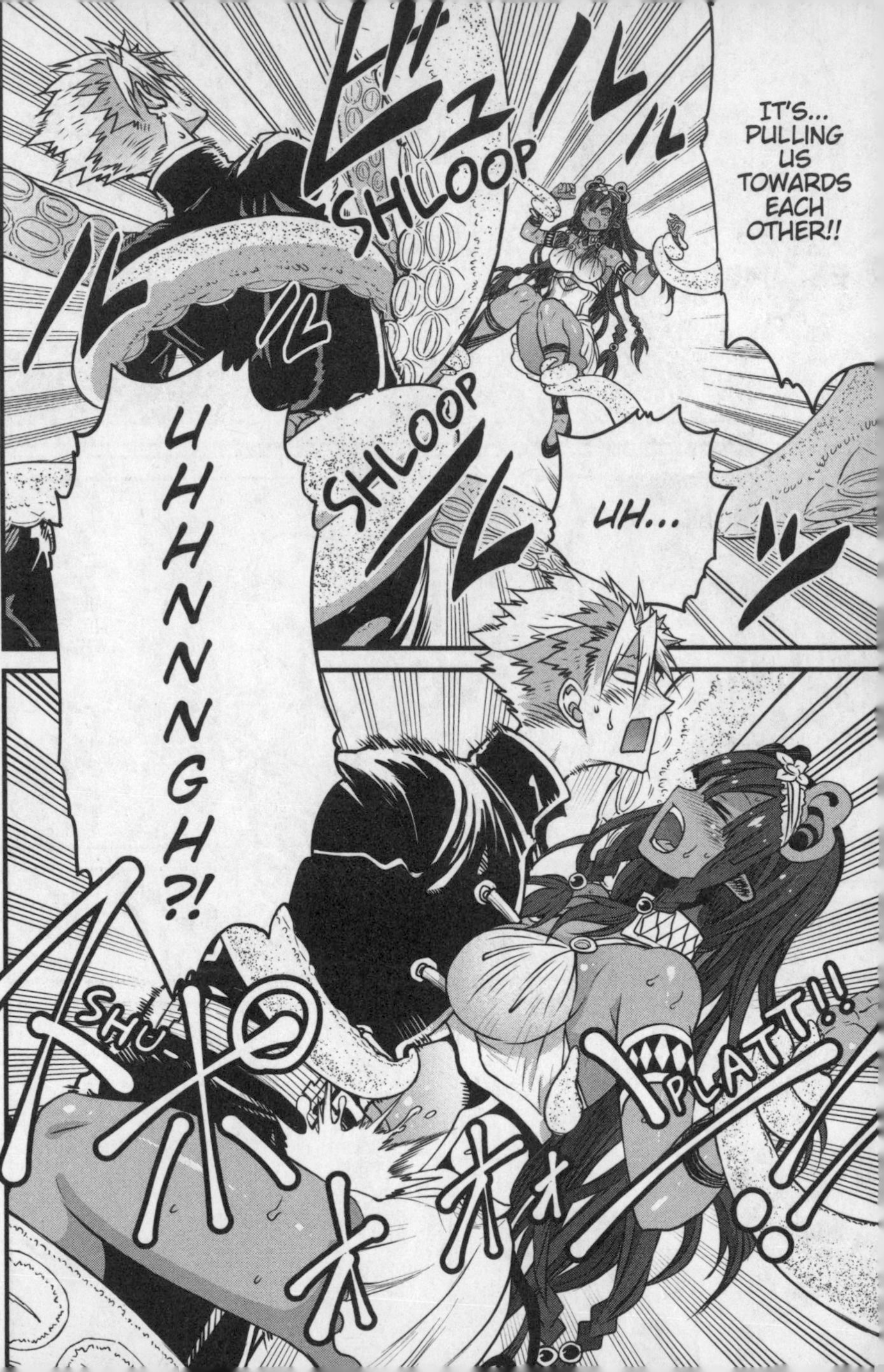
IT'S... PULLING US TOWARDS EACH OTHER!!
SHLOOP
SHLOOP
UH...
UHHHNNNGH?!
SHU-
PLATT!!

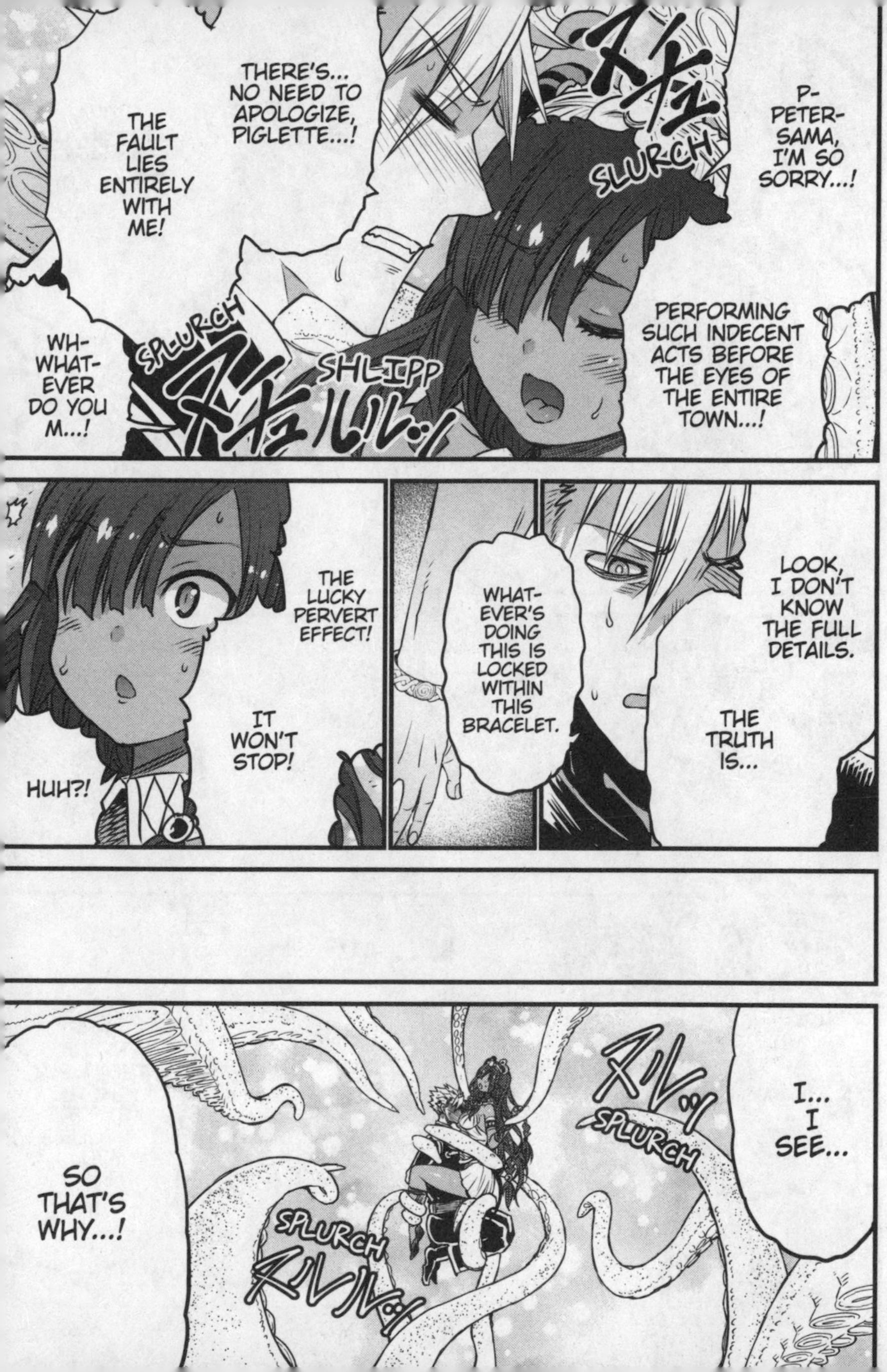
P-PETER-SAMA, I'M SO SORRY...!
SLURCH
PERFORMING SUCH INDECENT ACTS BEFORE THE EYES OF THE ENTIRE TOWN...!
THERE'S... NO NEED TO APOLOGIZE, PIGLETTE...!
THE FAULT LIES ENTIRELY WITH ME!
SHLIPP
SPLURCH
WH-WHATEVER DO YOU M...!
LOOK, I DON'T KNOW THE FULL DETAILS.
THE TRUTH IS...
WHATEVER'S DOING THIS IS LOCKED WITHIN THIS BRACELET.
THE LUCKY PERVERT EFFECT!
IT WON'T STOP!
HUH?!
I... I SEE...
SPLURCH
SPLURCH
SO THAT'S WHY...!

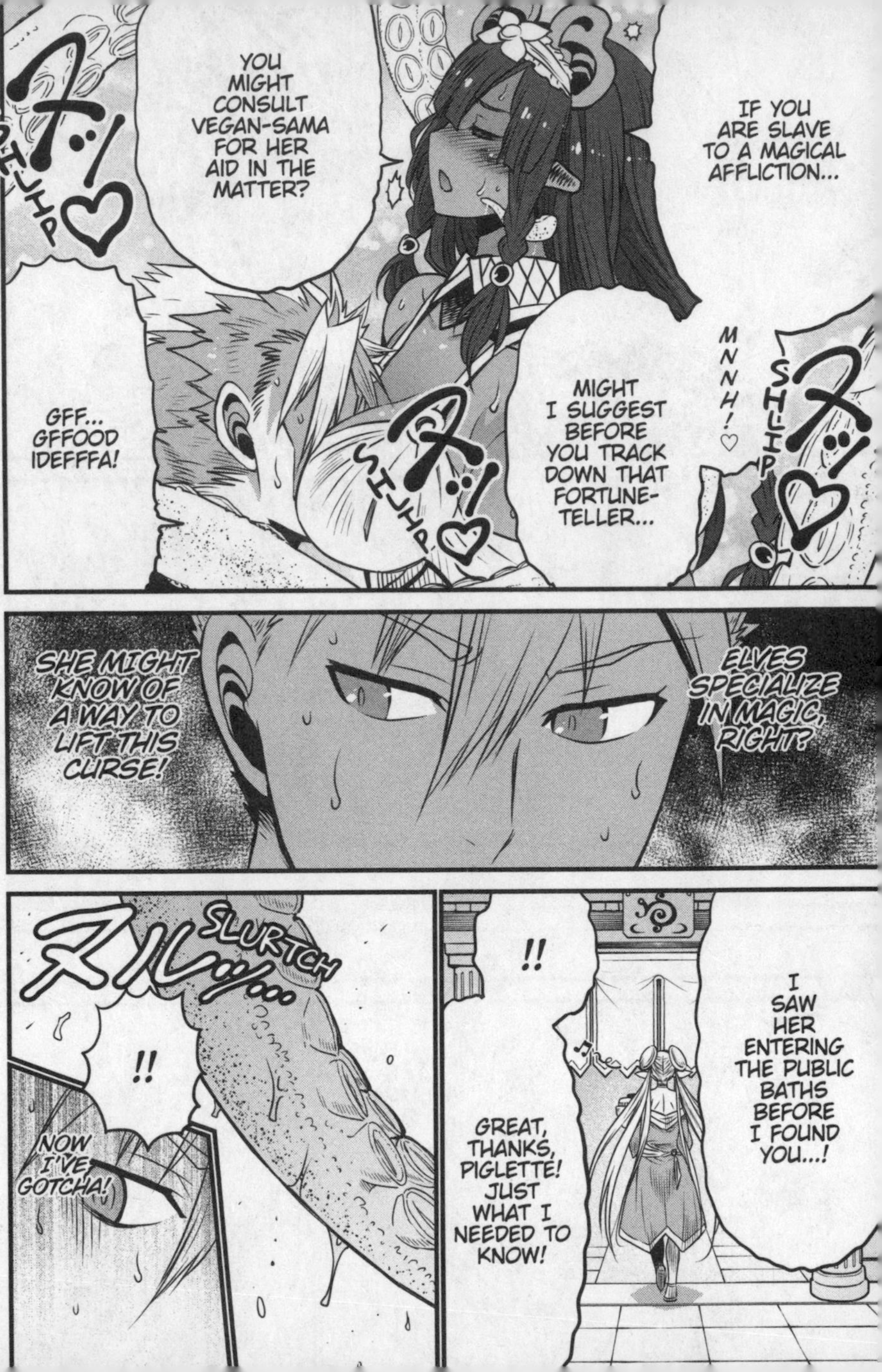
IF YOU ARE SLAVE TO A MAGICAL AFFLICTION...
YOU MIGHT CONSULT VEGAN-SAMA FOR HER AID IN THE MATTER?
SHLIP
SHLIP
MNNH!♡
MIGHT I SUGGEST BEFORE YOU TRACK DOWN THAT FORTUNE-TELLER...
SHLIP
GFF... GFFOOD IDEFFFA!
ELVES SPECIALIZE IN MAGIC, RIGHT?
SHE MIGHT KNOW OF A WAY TO LIFT THIS CURSE!
I SAW HER ENTERING THE PUBLIC BATHS BEFORE I FOUND YOU...!
!!
GREAT, THANKS, PIGLETTE! JUST WHAT I NEEDED TO KNOW!
SLURTCH
!!
NOW I'VE GOTCHA!

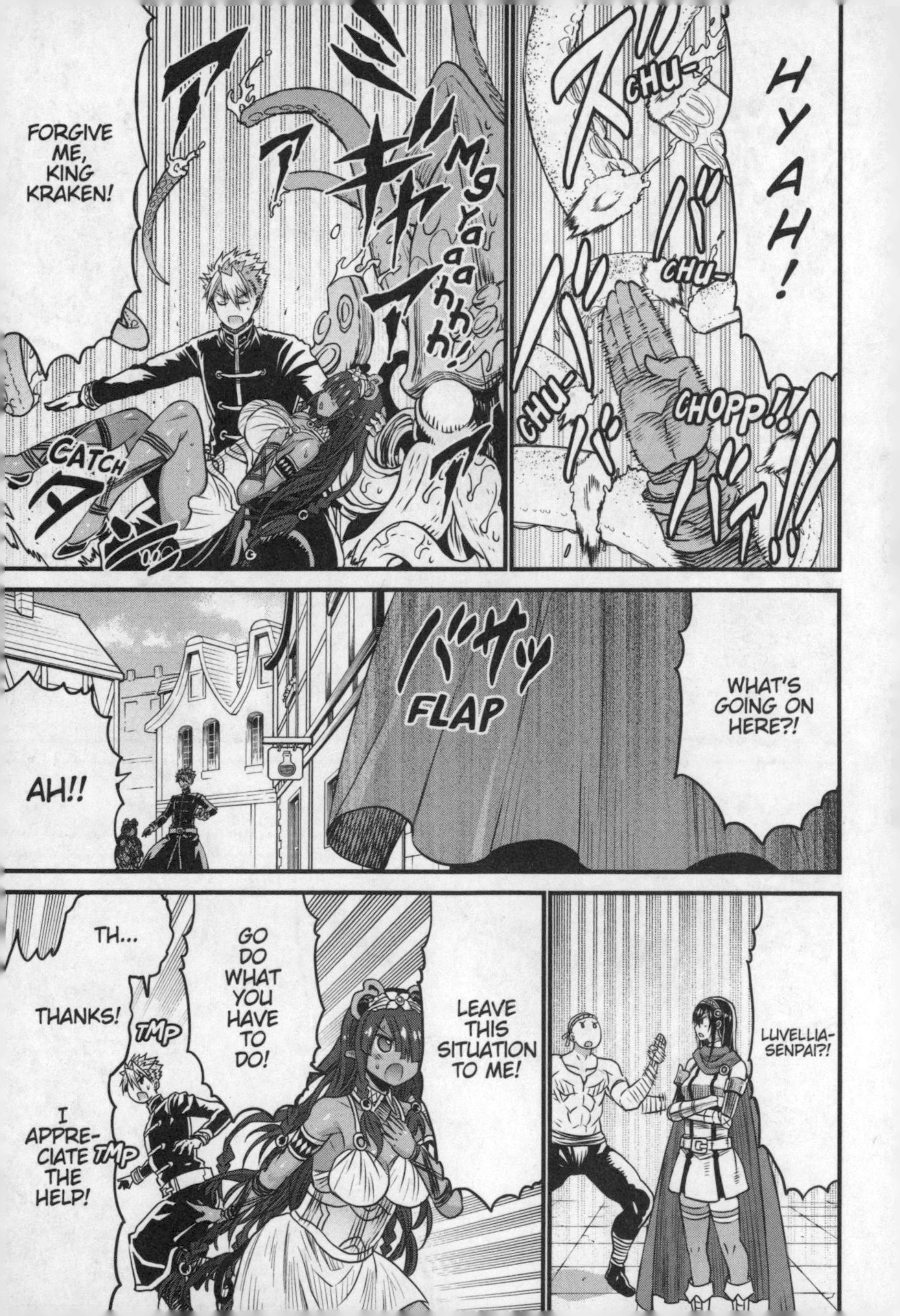
HYAH!
CHU-
CHU-
CHOPP!!
CHU-
FORGIVE ME, KING KRAKEN!
Mgyaaahhhh!!
CATCH
WHAT'S GOING ON HERE?!
FLAP
AH!!
LUVELLIA-SENPAI?!
LEAVE THIS SITUATION TO ME!
GO DO WHAT YOU HAVE TO DO!
TH...
THANKS!
TMP
I APPRE-CIATE THE HELP!
TMP

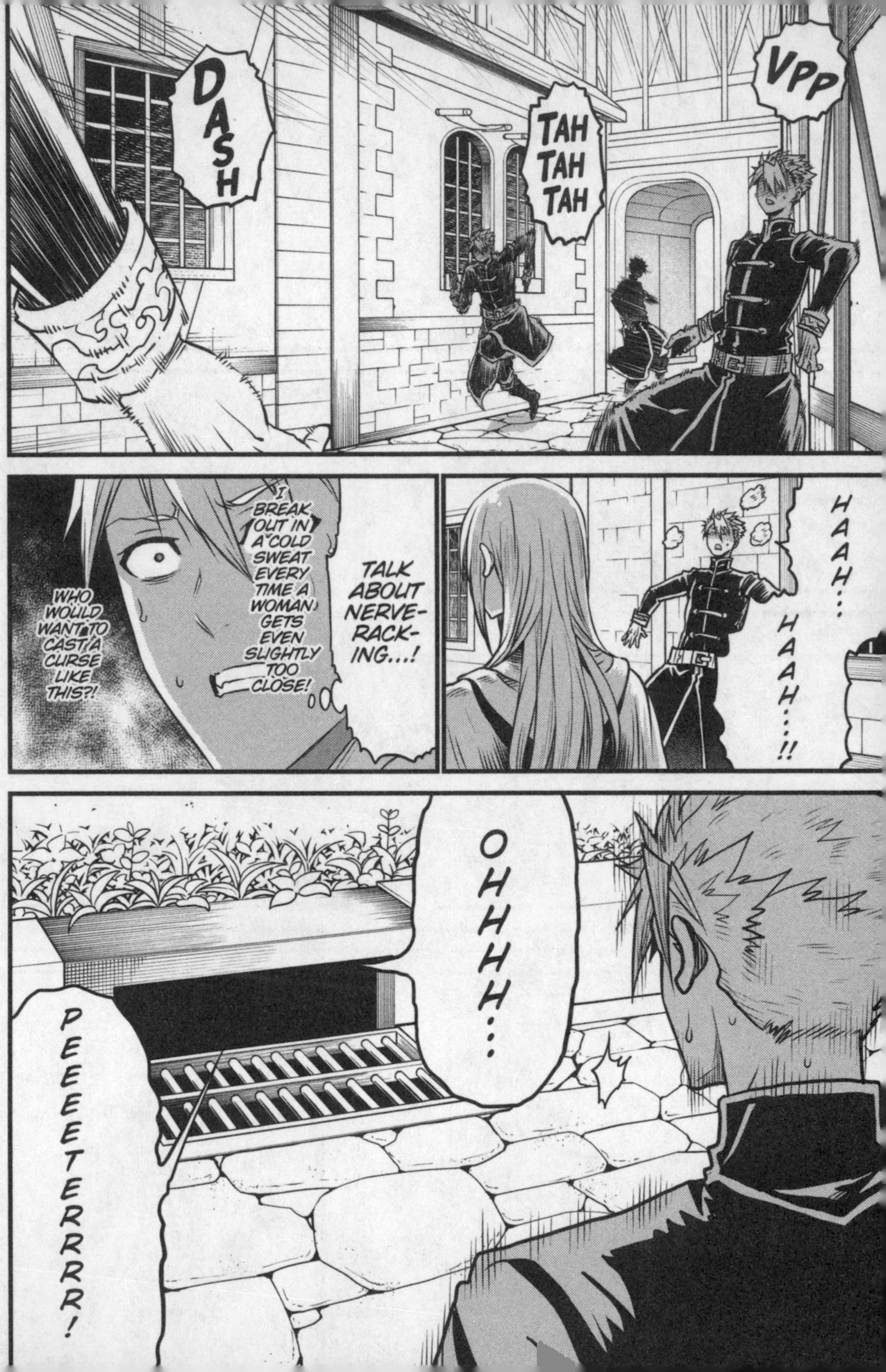
VPP
TAH TAH TAH
DASH
HAAH...
HAAAH...!!
TALK ABOUT NERVE-RACKING...!
I BREAK OUT IN A COLD SWEAT EVERY TIME A WOMAN GETS EVEN SLIGHTLY TOO CLOSE!
WHO WOULD WANT TO CAST A CURSE LIKE THIS?!
OHHHH...
PEEEEETERRRR!

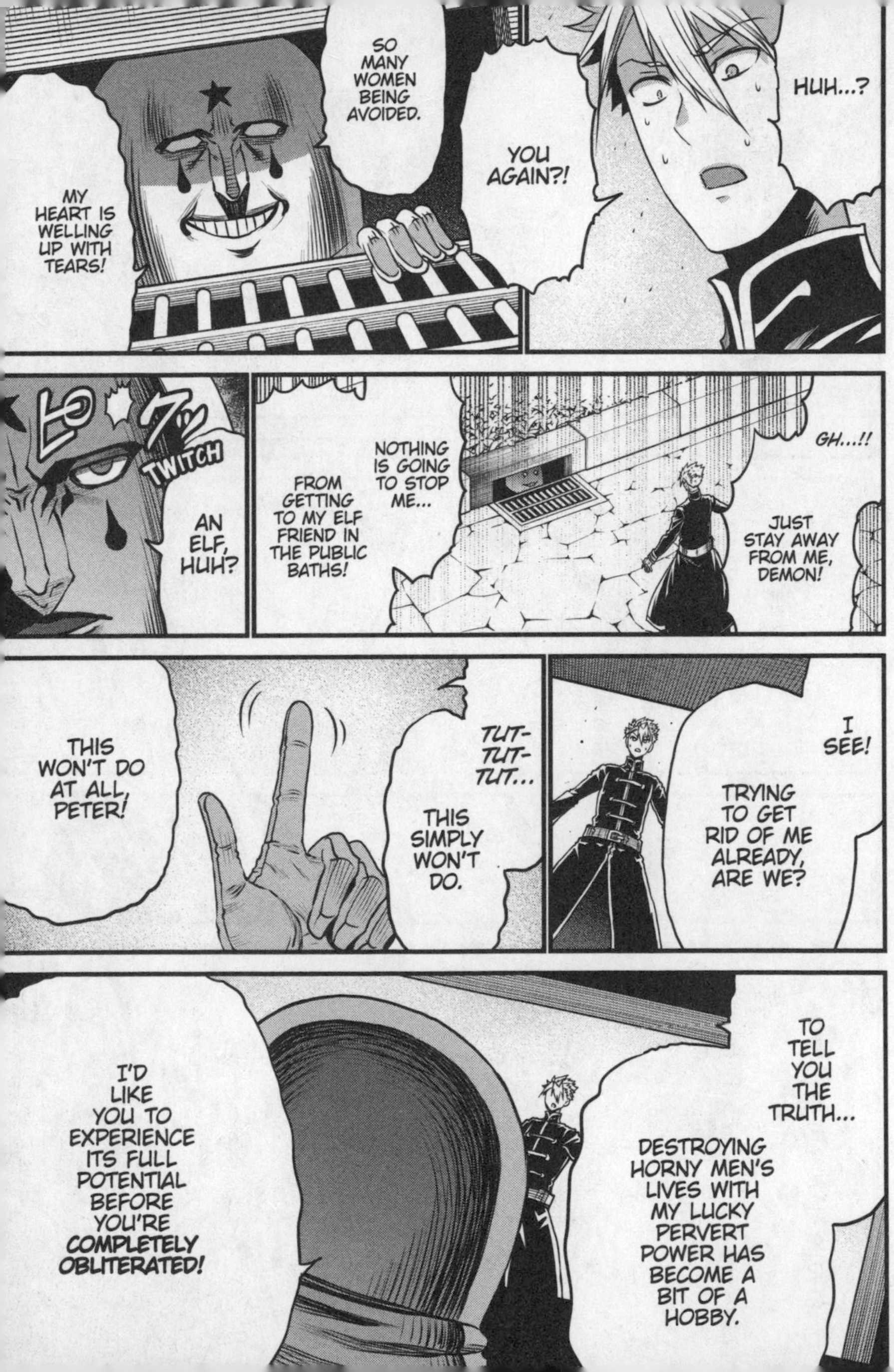
HUH...?
YOU AGAIN?!
SO MANY WOMEN BEING AVOIDED.
MY HEART IS WELLING UP WITH TEARS!
GH...!!
JUST STAY AWAY FROM ME, DEMON!
NOTHING IS GOING TO STOP ME...
FROM GETTING TO MY ELF FRIEND IN THE PUBLIC BATHS!
TWITCH
AN ELF, HUH?
I SEE!
TRYING TO GET RID OF ME ALREADY, ARE WE?
TUT-TUT-TUT...
THIS SIMPLY WON'T DO.
THIS WON'T DO AT ALL, PETER!
TO TELL YOU THE TRUTH...
DESTROYING HORNY MEN'S LIVES WITH MY LUCKY PERVERT POWER HAS BECOME A BIT OF A HOBBY.
I'D LIKE YOU TO EXPERIENCE ITS FULL POTENTIAL BEFORE YOU'RE COMPLETELY OBLITERATED!

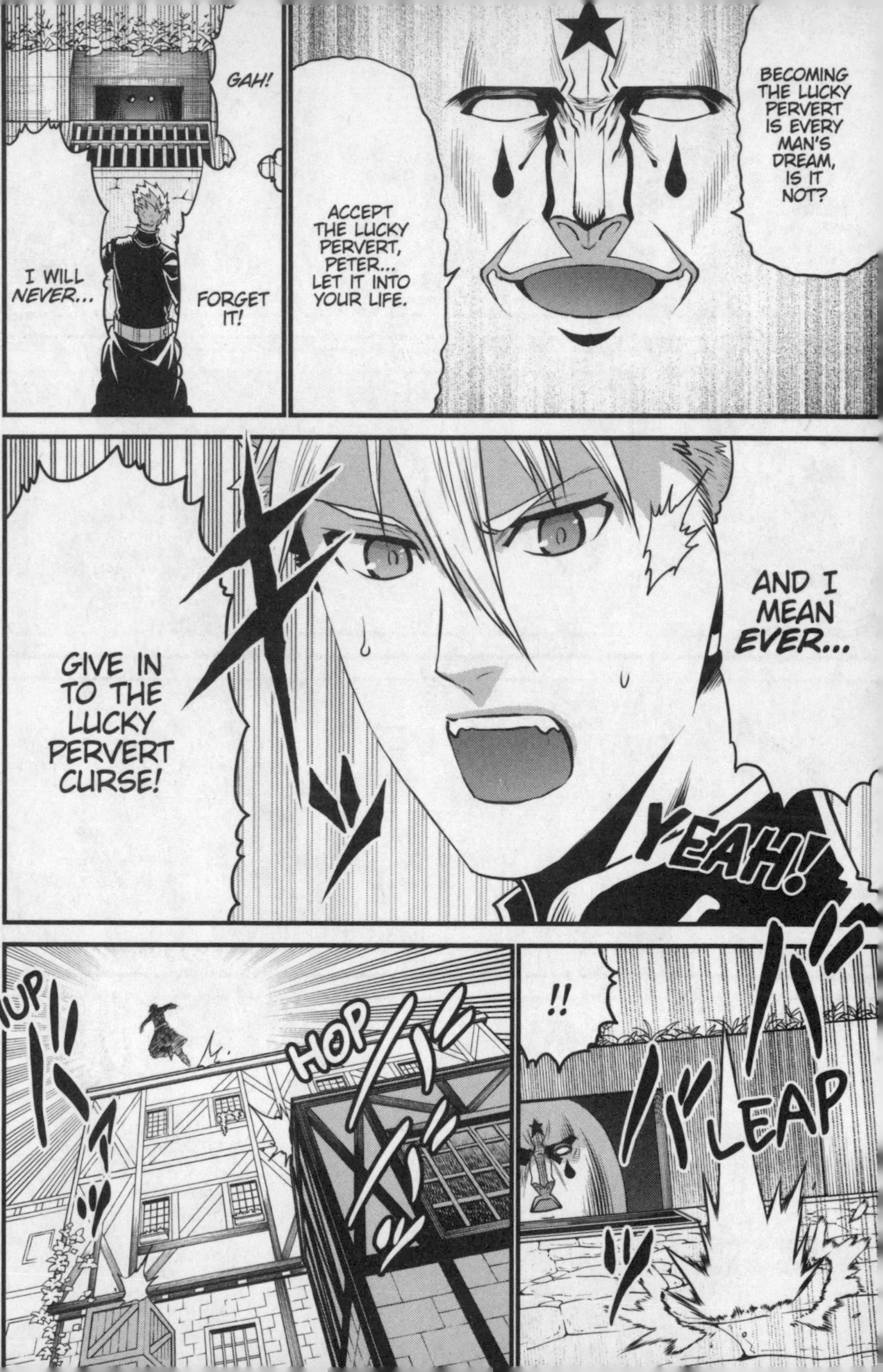
BECOMING THE LUCKY PERVERT IS EVERY MAN'S DREAM, IS IT NOT?
ACCEPT THE LUCKY PERVERT, PETER... LET IT INTO YOUR LIFE.
GAH!
I WILL NEVER...
FORGET IT!
AND I MEAN EVER...
GIVE IN TO THE LUCKY PERVERT CURSE!
YEAH!
LEAP
!!
HOP
HUP

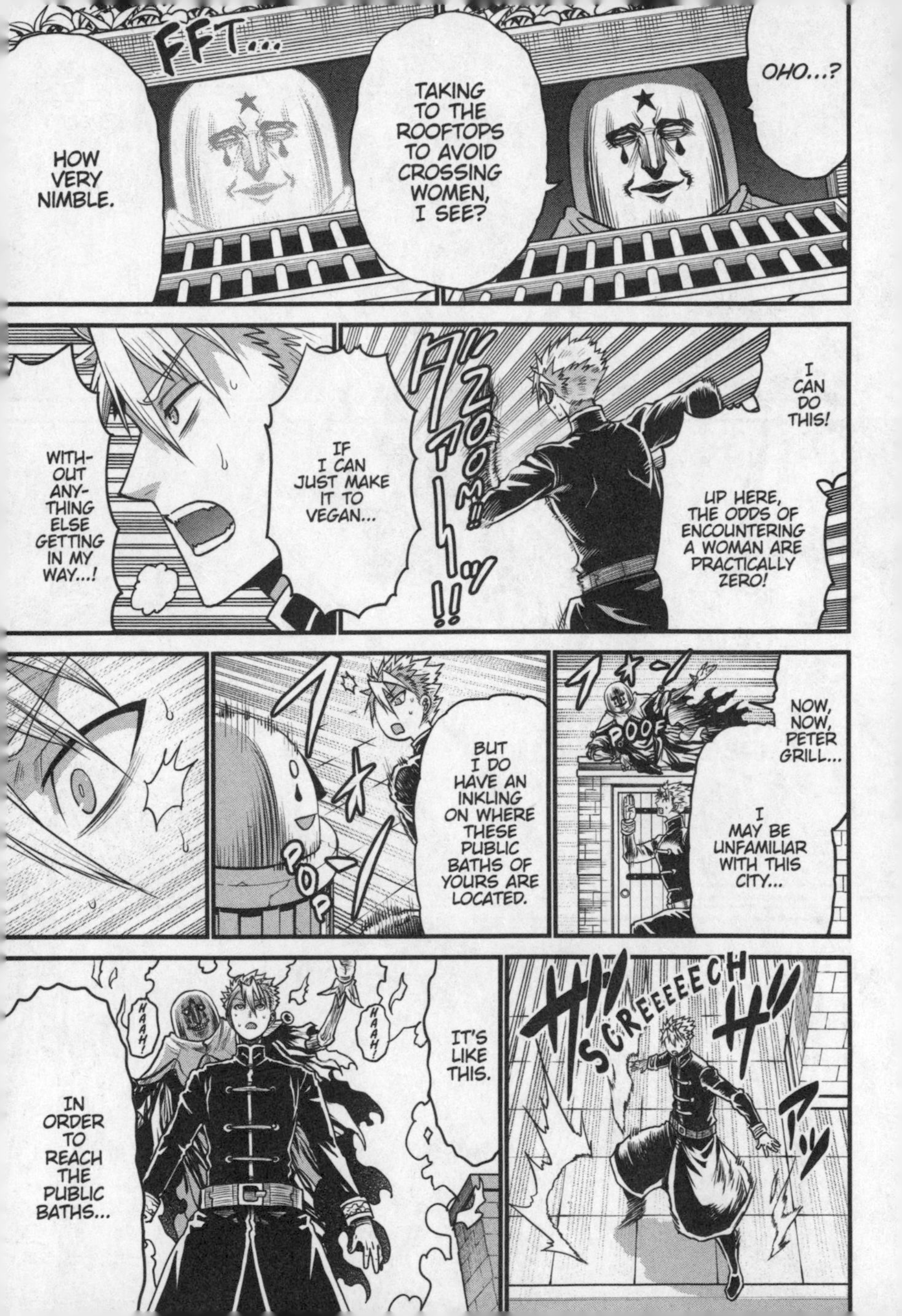
OHO...?
TAKING TO THE ROOFTOPS TO AVOID CROSSING WOMEN, I SEE?
FFT...
HOW VERY NIMBLE.
I CAN DO THIS!
UP HERE, THE ODDS OF ENCOUNTERING A WOMAN ARE PRACTICALLY ZERO!
ZOOM!!
IF I CAN JUST MAKE IT TO VEGAN...
WITH-OUT ANY-THING ELSE GETTING IN MY WAY...!
POOF
NOW, NOW, PETER GRILL...
I MAY BE UNFAMILIAR WITH THIS CITY...
BUT I DO HAVE AN INKLING ON WHERE THESE PUBLIC BATHS OF YOURS ARE LOCATED.
POP
SCREEEEECH
IT'S LIKE THIS.
IN ORDER TO REACH THE PUBLIC BATHS...
HAAH!
HAAH!

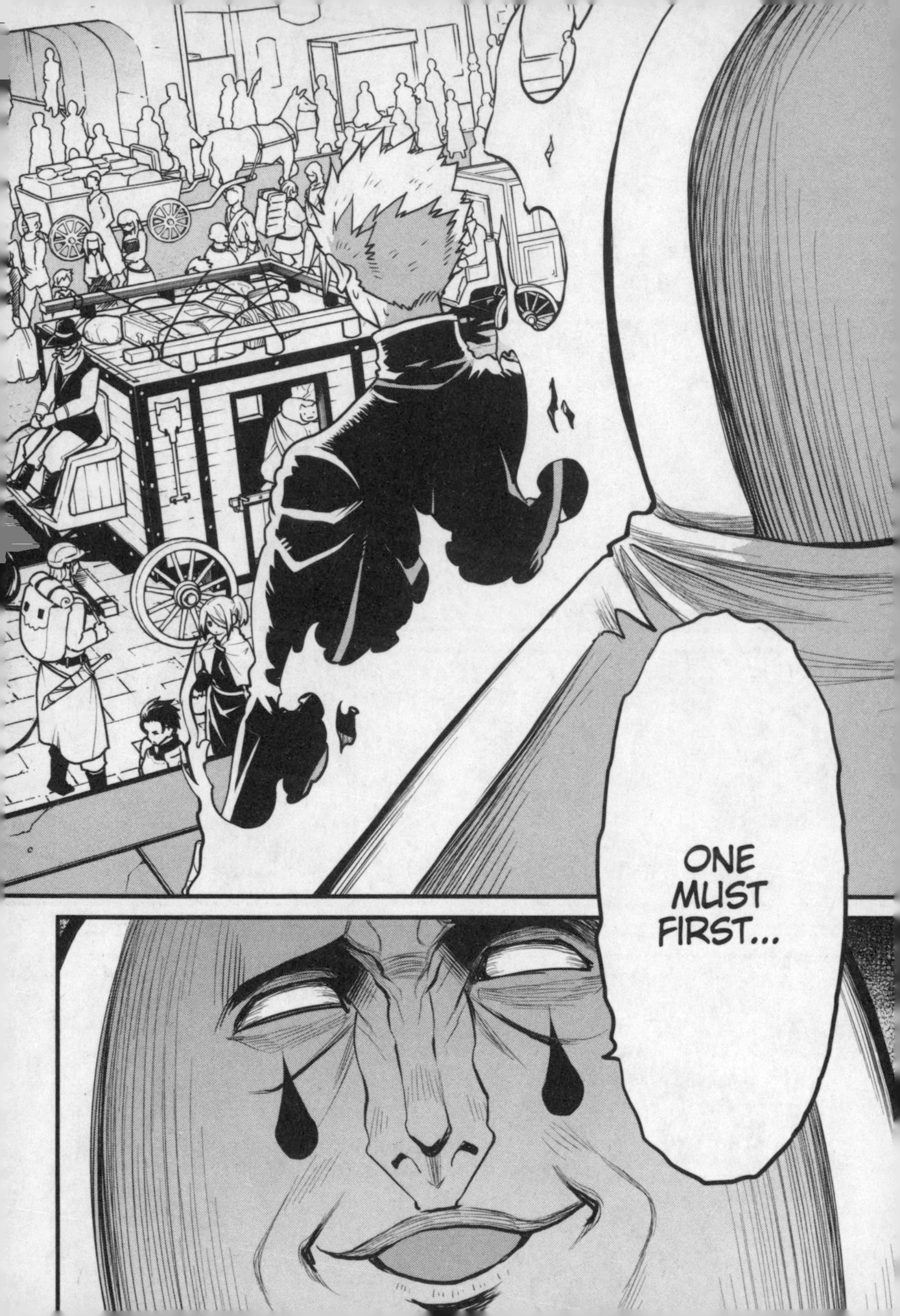
ONE MUST FIRST...

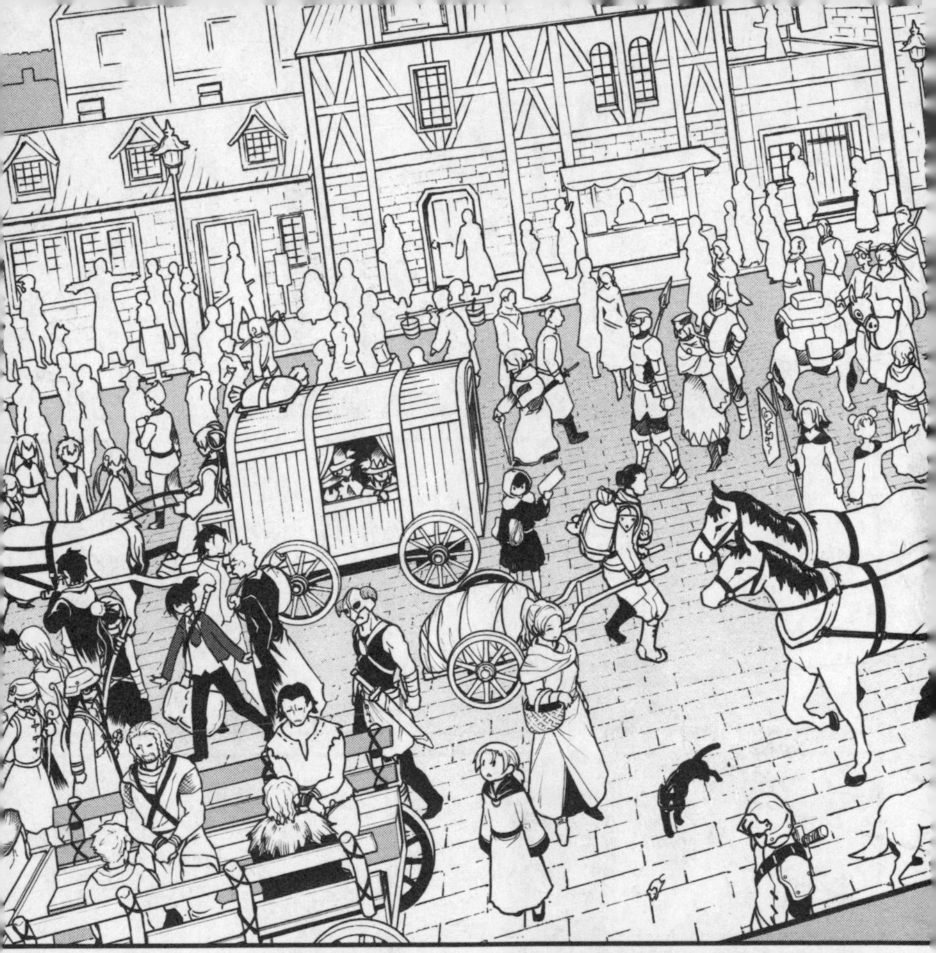

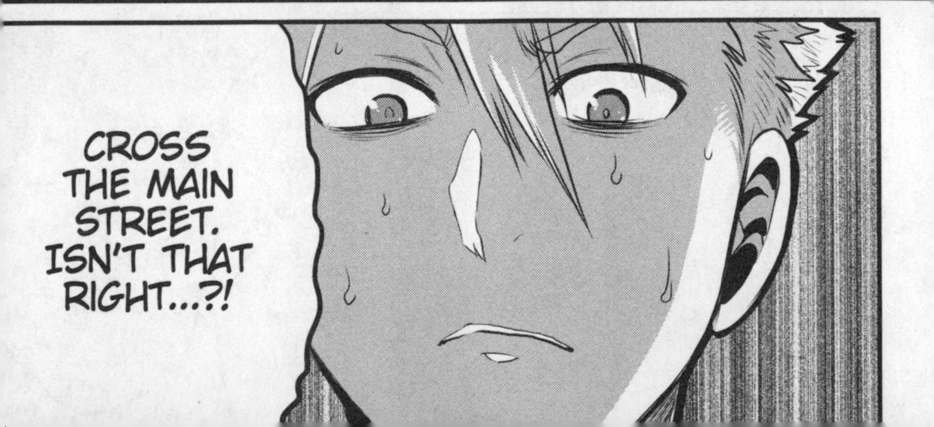
CROSS THE MAIN STREET. ISN'T THAT RIGHT...?!

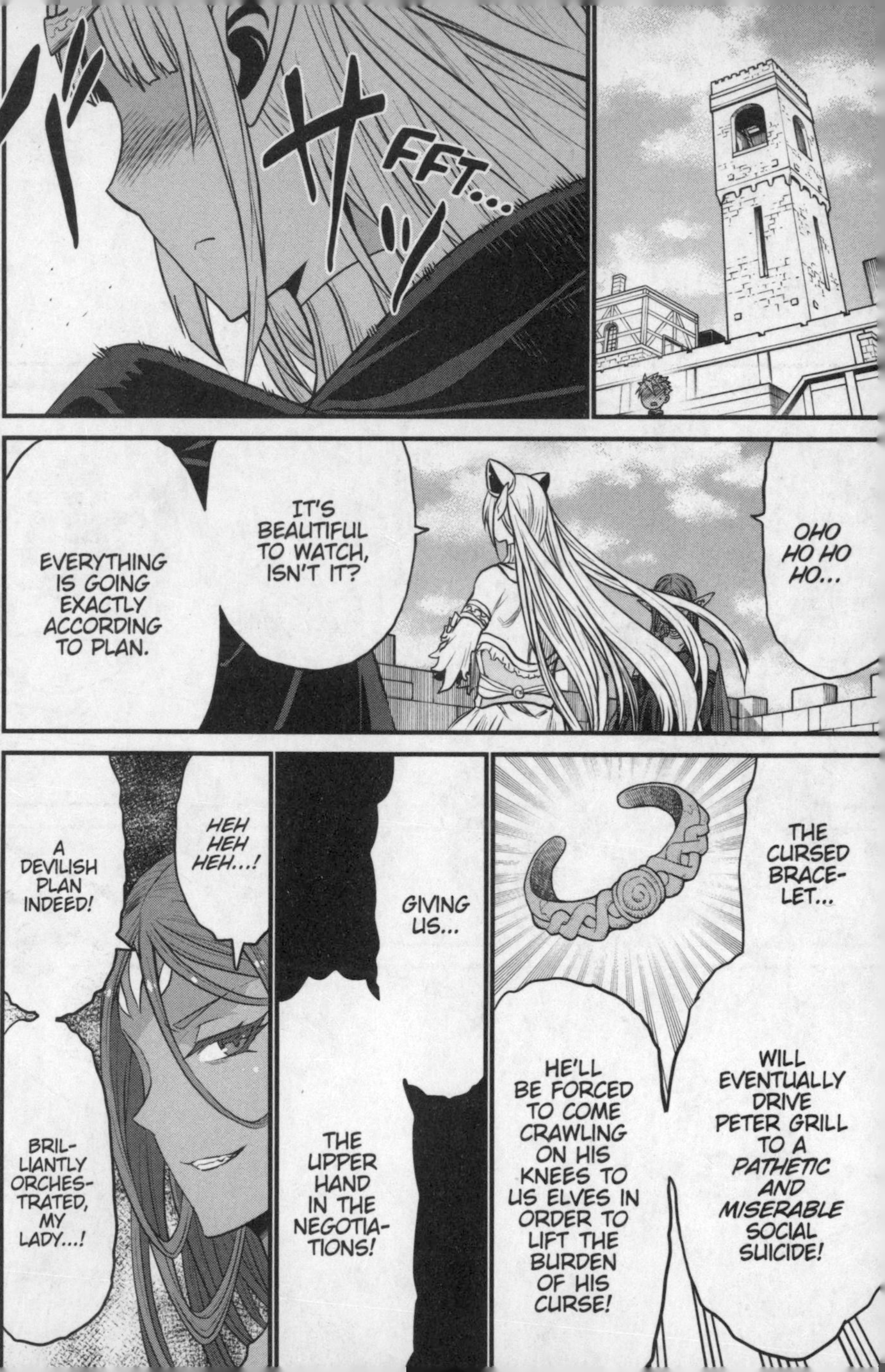
FFT...
OHO HO HO HO...
IT'S BEAUTIFUL TO WATCH, ISN'T IT?
EVERYTHING IS GOING EXACTLY ACCORDING TO PLAN.
THE CURSED BRACE-LET...
WILL EVENTUALLY DRIVE PETER GRILL TO A *PATHETIC AND MISERABLE* SOCIAL SUICIDE!
HE'LL BE FORCED TO COME CRAWLING ON HIS KNEES TO US ELVES IN ORDER TO LIFT THE BURDEN OF HIS CURSE!
GIVING US...
THE UPPER HAND IN THE NEGOTIA-TIONS!
HEH HEH HEH...!
A DEVILISH PLAN INDEED!
BRIL-LIANTLY ORCHES-TRATED, MY LADY...!

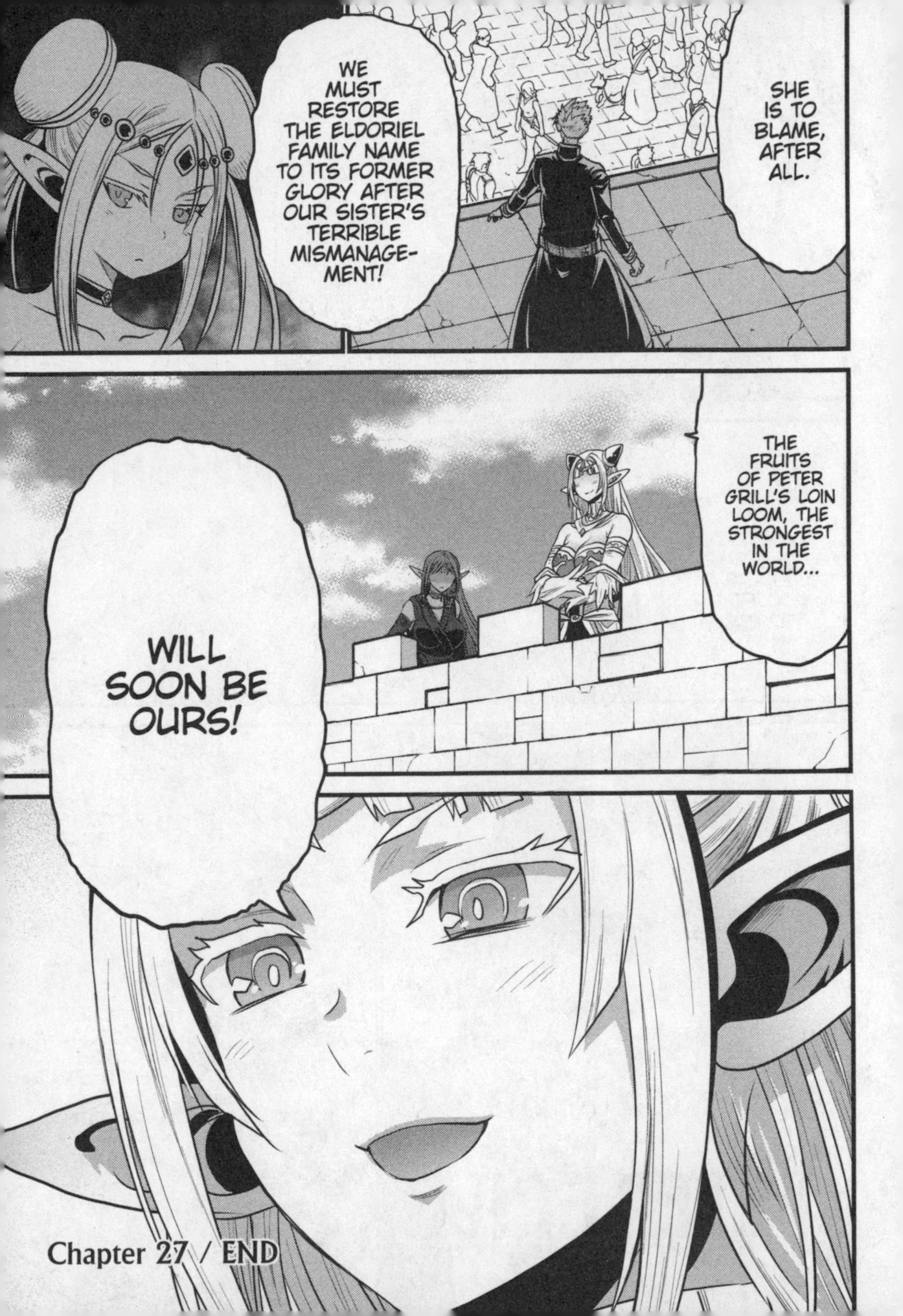
SHE IS TO BLAME, AFTER ALL.
WE MUST RESTORE THE ELDORIEL FAMILY NAME TO ITS FORMER GLORY AFTER OUR SISTER'S TERRIBLE MISMANAGEMENT!
THE FRUITS OF PETER GRILL'S LOIN LOOM, THE STRONGEST IN THE WORLD...
WILL SOON BE OURS!

Chapter 27 / END

PETER GRILL
AND THE PHILOSOPHER'S TIME

Previously, on *Peter Grill...*

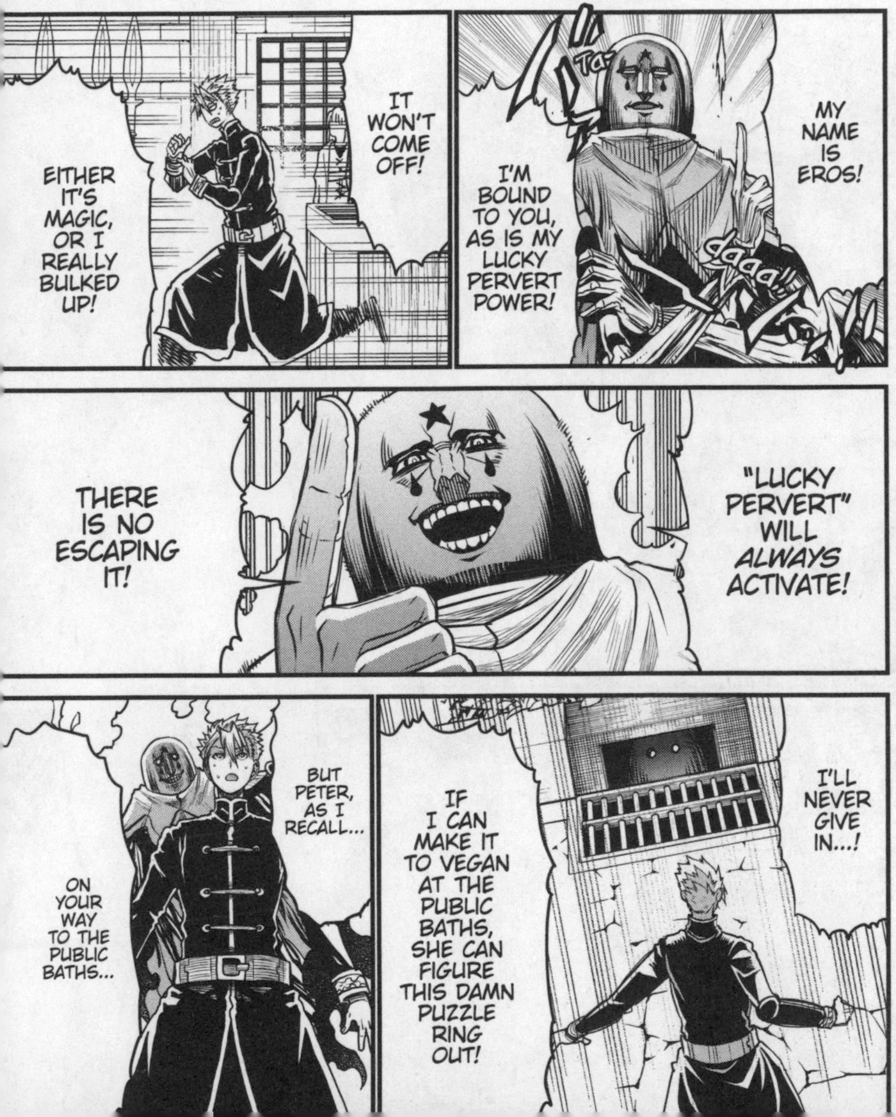
MY NAME IS EROS!
I'M BOUND TO YOU, AS IS MY LUCKY PERVERT POWER!
IT WON'T COME OFF!
EITHER IT'S MAGIC, OR I REALLY BULKED UP!
"LUCKY PERVERT" WILL ALWAYS ACTIVATE!
THERE IS NO ESCAPING IT!
I'LL NEVER GIVE IN...!
IF I CAN MAKE IT TO VEGAN AT THE PUBLIC BATHS, SHE CAN FIGURE THIS DAMN PUZZLE RING OUT!
BUT PETER, AS I RECALL...
ON YOUR WAY TO THE PUBLIC BATHS...

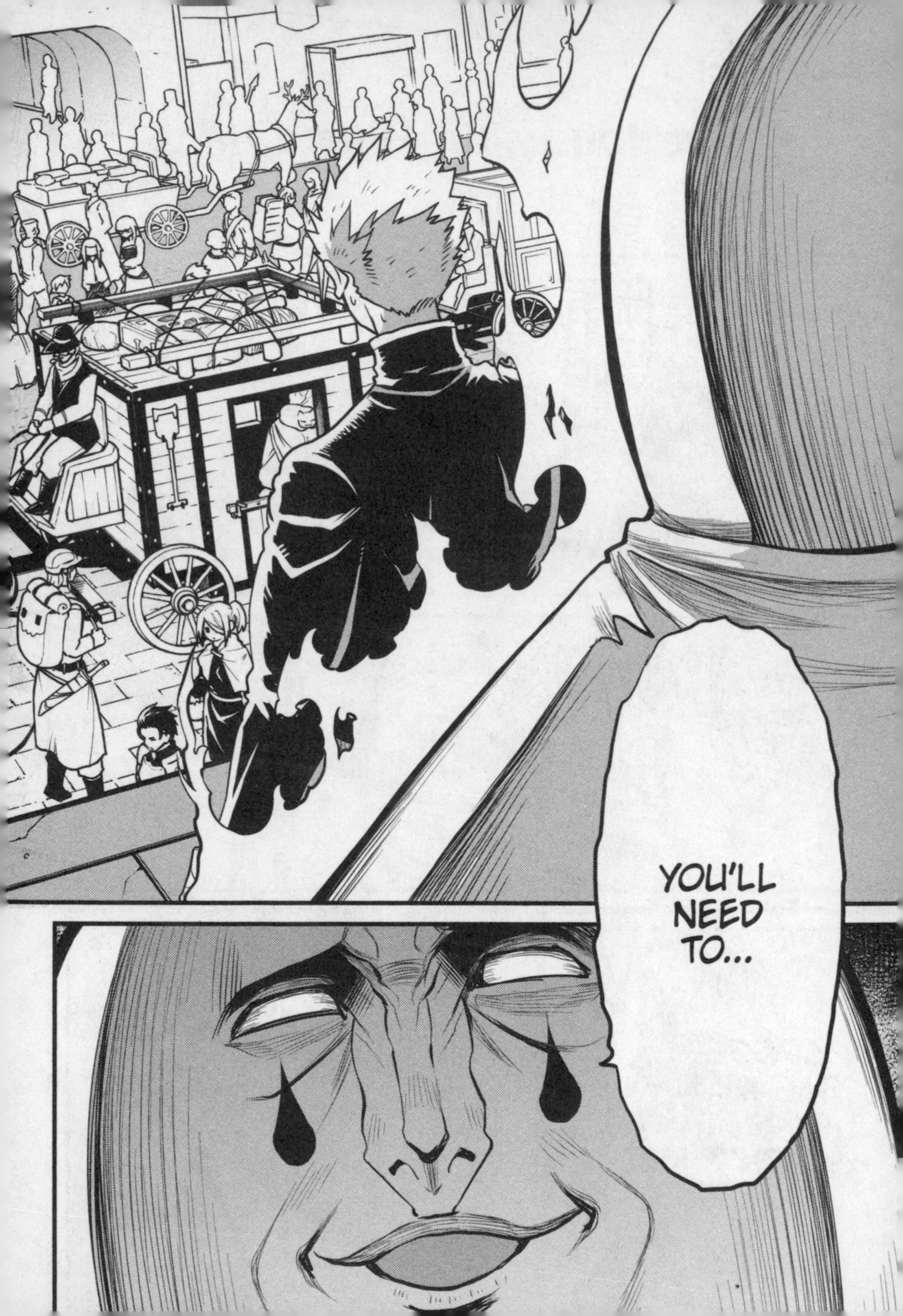
YOU'LL NEED TO...

Chapter 28 Peter Grill and the Revealed Truth

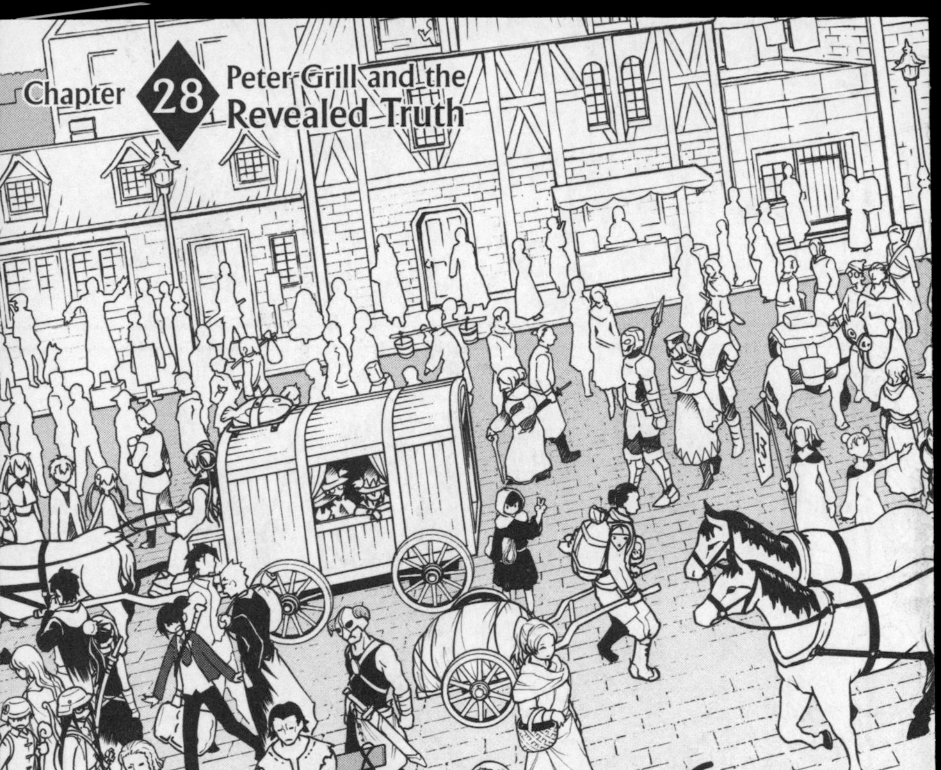

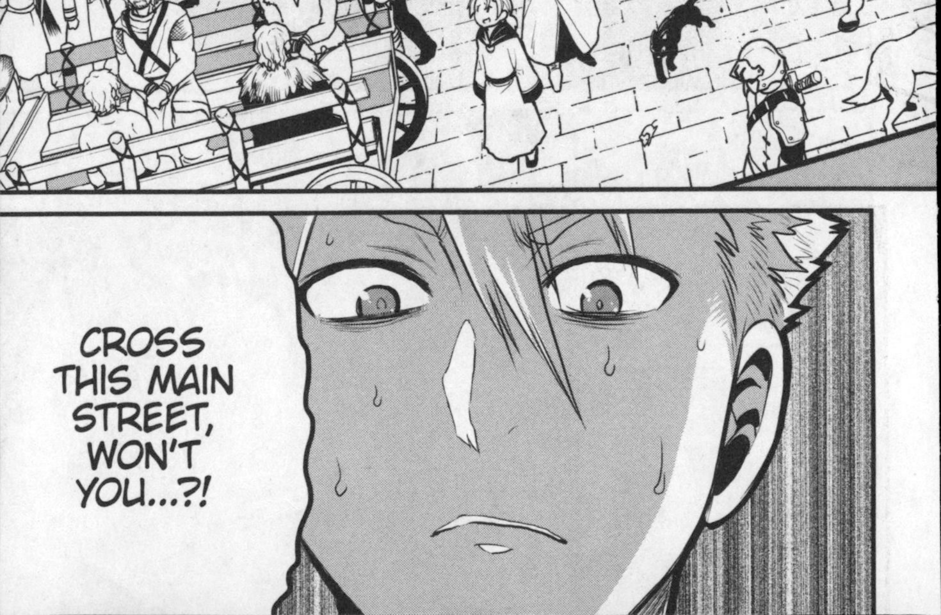
CROSS THIS MAIN STREET, WON'T YOU...?!

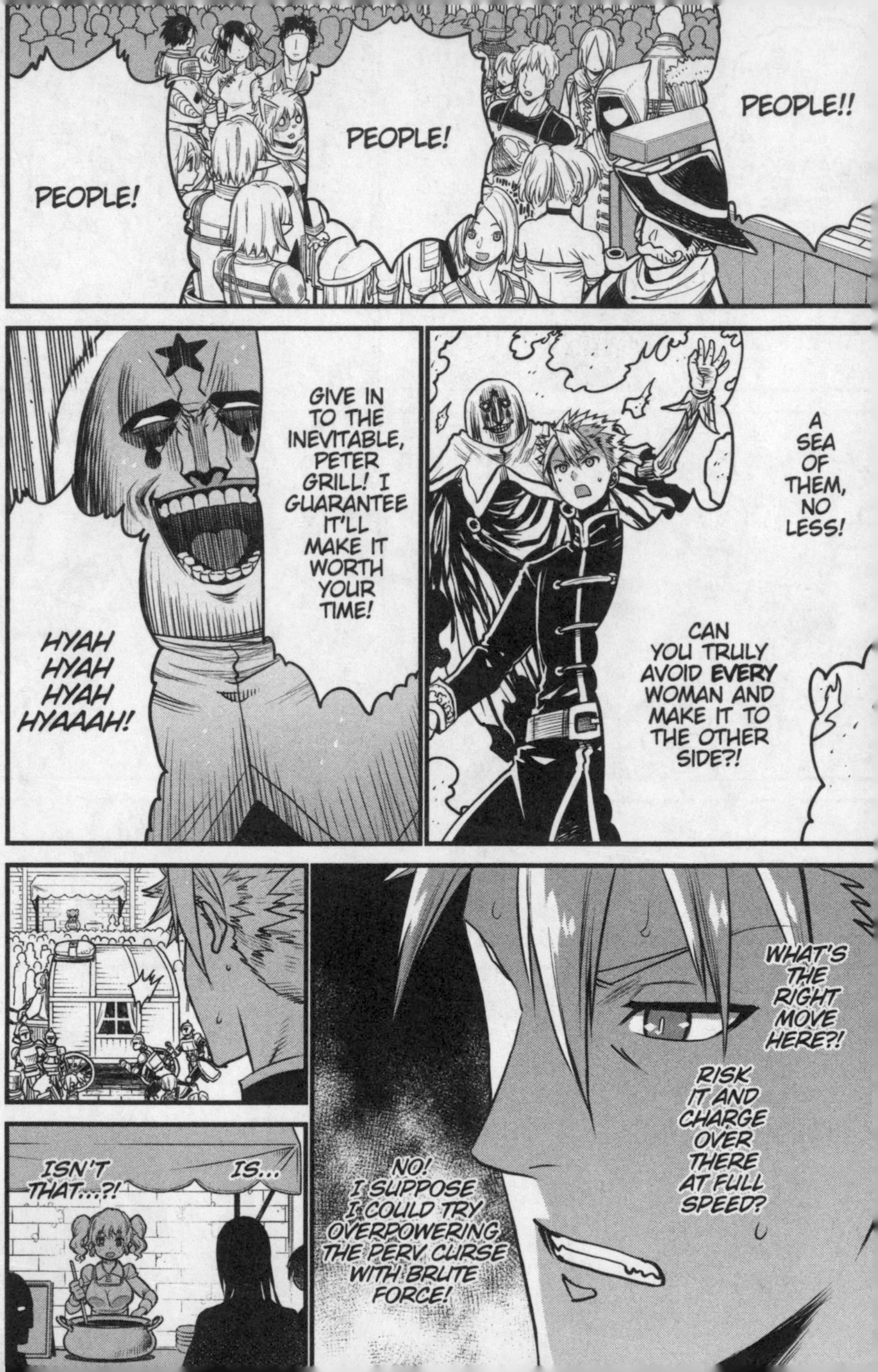
PEOPLE!!
PEOPLE!
PEOPLE!
A SEA OF THEM, NO LESS!
CAN YOU TRULY AVOID EVERY WOMAN AND MAKE IT TO THE OTHER SIDE?!
GIVE IN TO THE INEVITABLE, PETER GRILL! I GUARANTEE IT'LL MAKE IT WORTH YOUR TIME!
HYAH HYAH HYAH HYAAAH!
WHAT'S THE RIGHT MOVE HERE?!
RISK IT AND CHARGE OVER THERE AT FULL SPEED?
NO! I SUPPOSE I COULD TRY OVERPOWERING THE PERV CURSE WITH BRUTE FORCE!
IS...
ISN'T THAT...?!

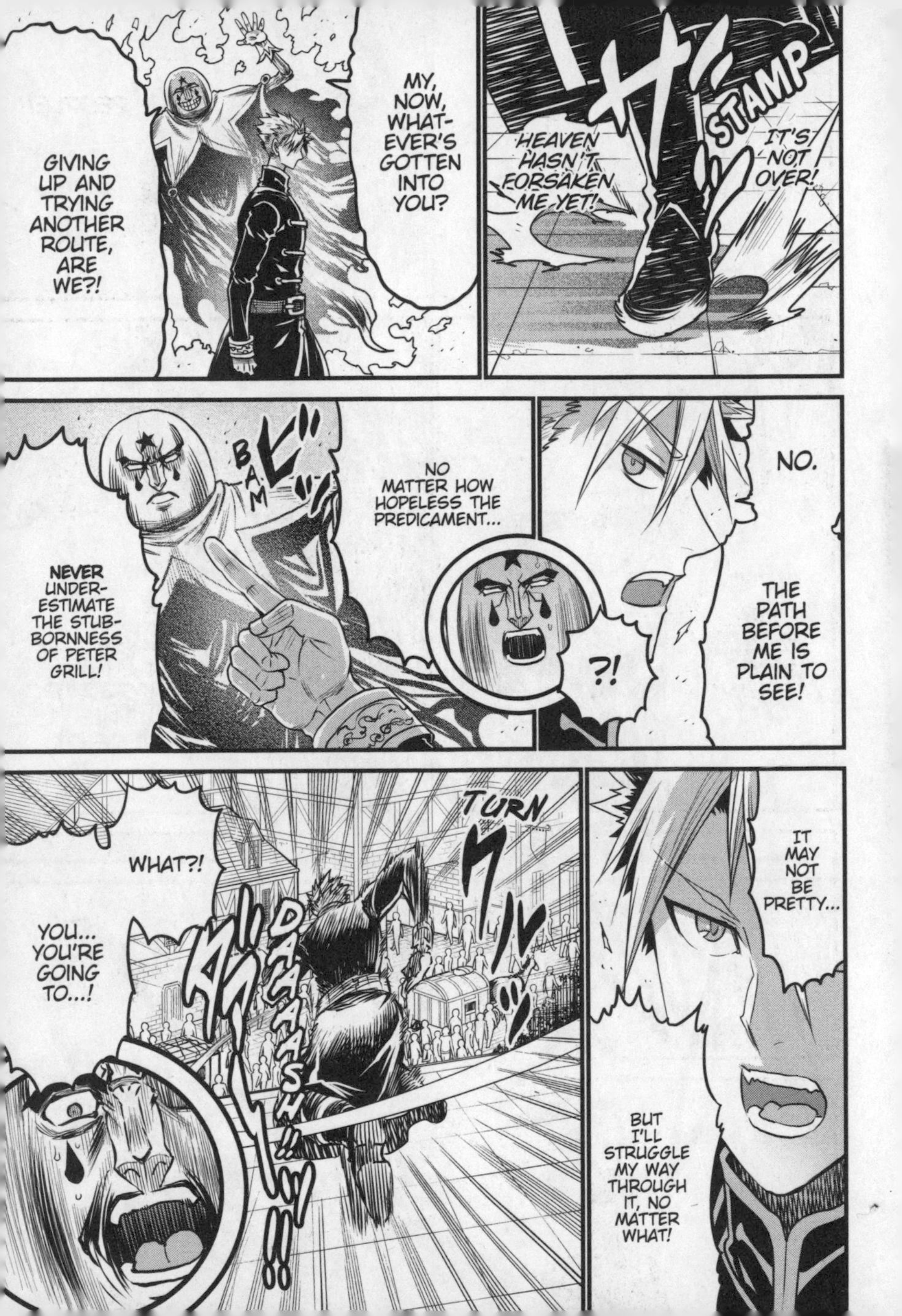
STAMP
IT'S NOT OVER!
HEAVEN HASN'T FORSAKEN ME YET!
MY, NOW, WHAT-EVER'S GOTTEN INTO YOU?
GIVING UP AND TRYING ANOTHER ROUTE, ARE WE?!
NO.
THE PATH BEFORE ME IS PLAIN TO SEE!
?!
NO MATTER HOW HOPELESS THE PREDICAMENT...
BAM
NEVER UNDER-ESTIMATE THE STUB-BORNNESS OF PETER GRILL!
IT MAY NOT BE PRETTY...
BUT I'LL STRUGGLE MY WAY THROUGH IT, NO MATTER WHAT!
TURN
WHAT?!
DAAAASH!!
YOU... YOU'RE GOING TO...!

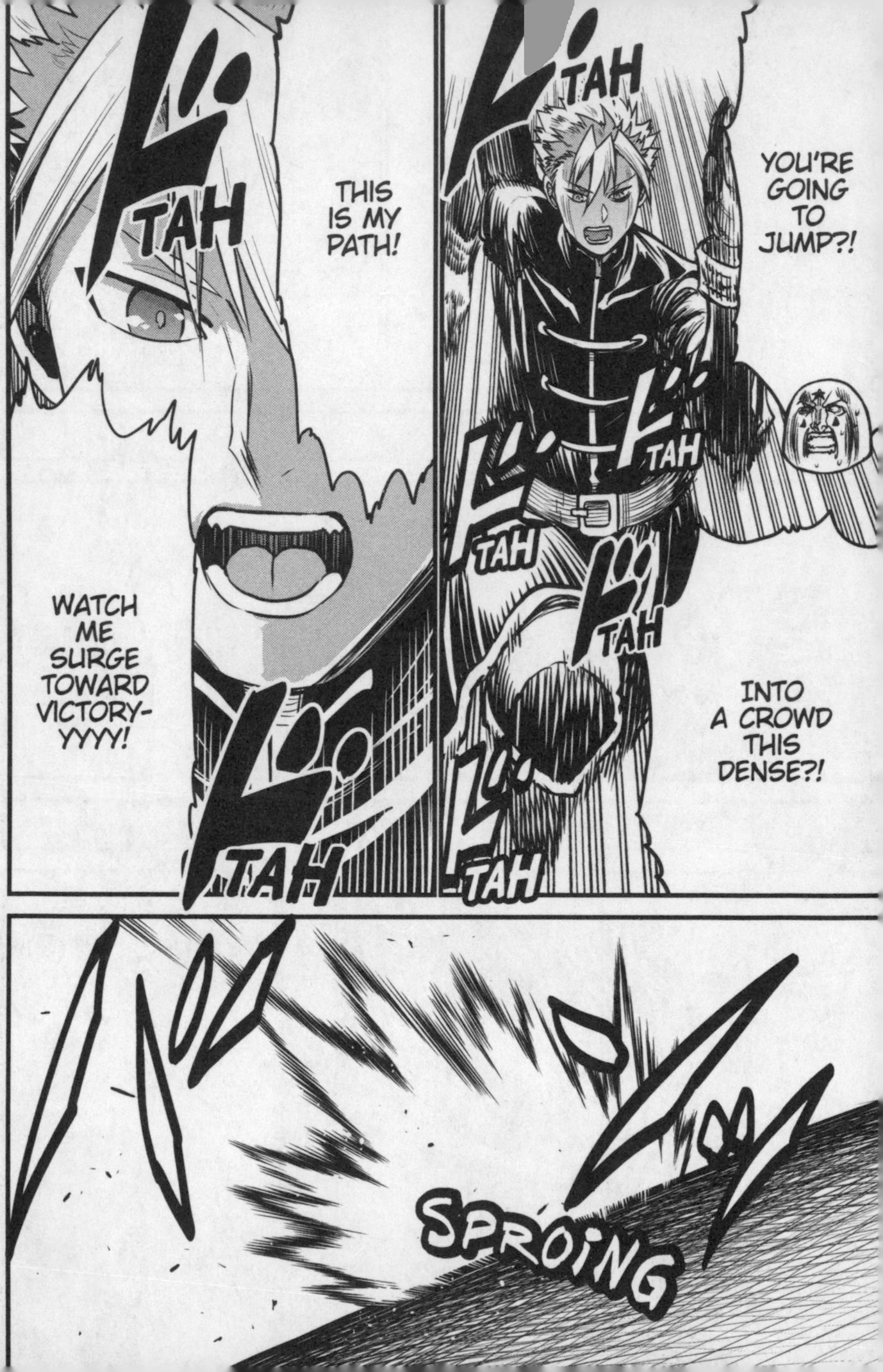
TAH
YOU'RE GOING TO JUMP?!
TAH
TAH
TAH
INTO A CROWD THIS DENSE?!
TAH
TAH
THIS IS MY PATH!
WATCH ME SURGE TOWARD VICTORY-YYYY!
TAH
SPROING

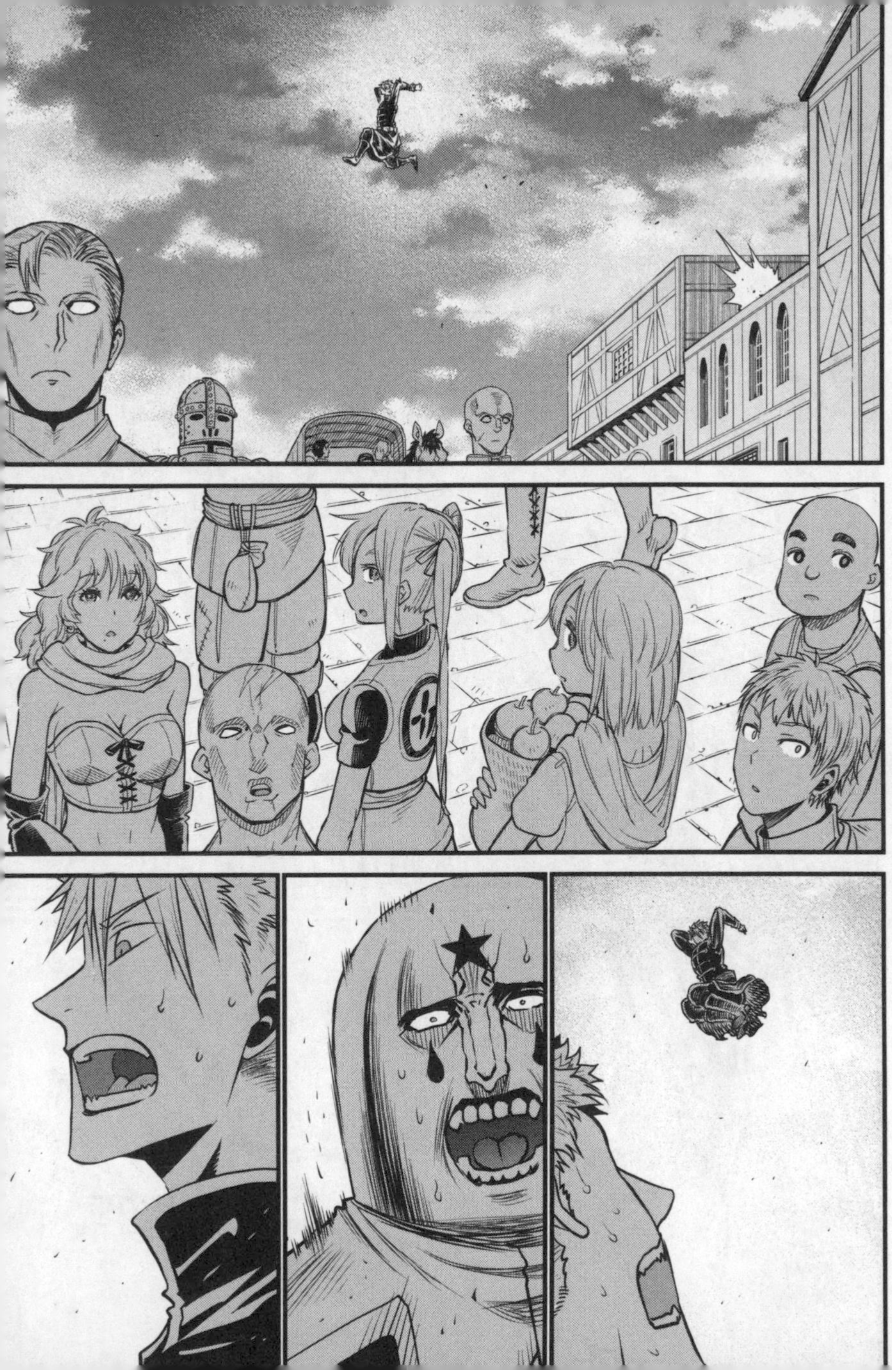

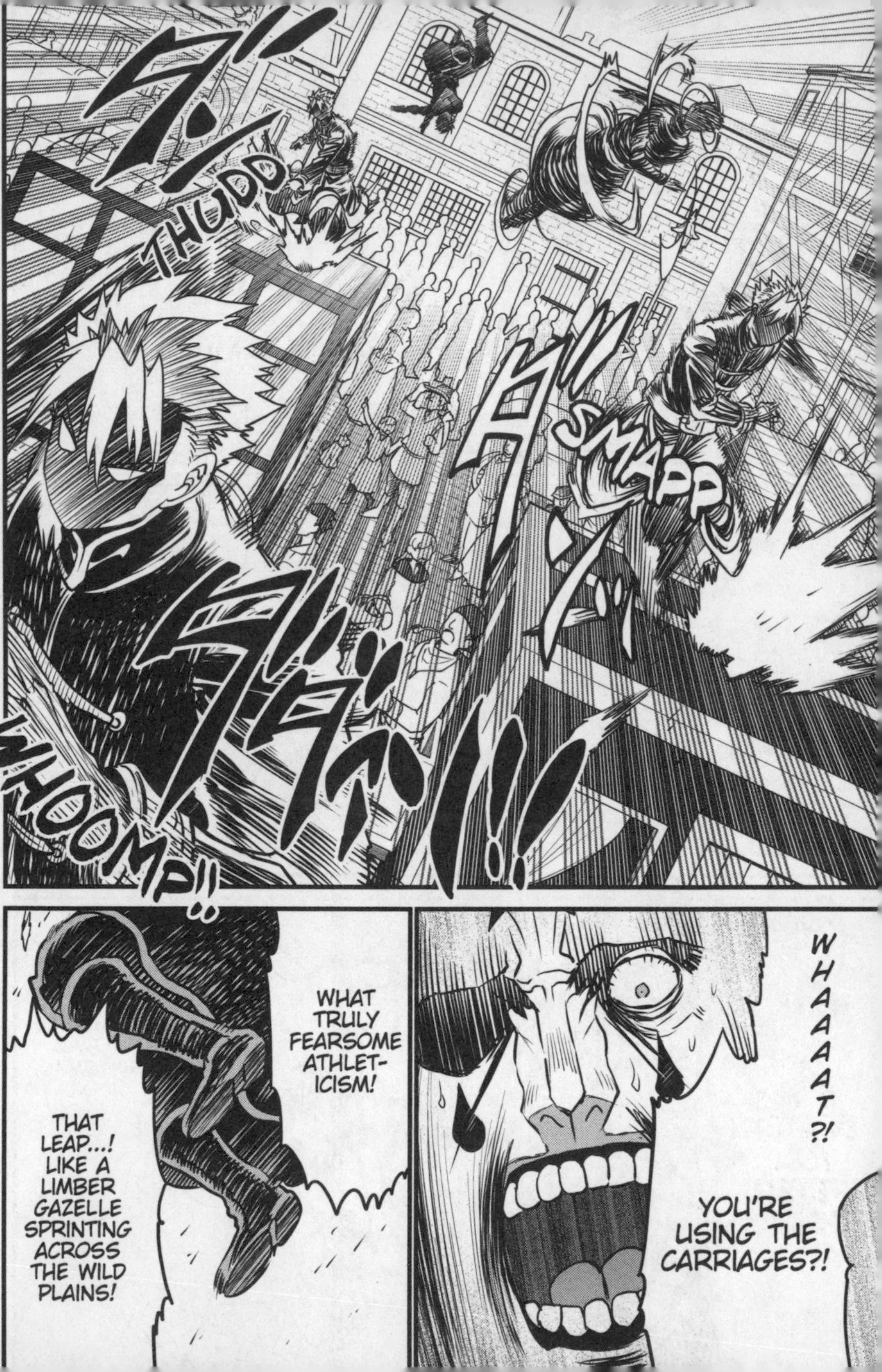
THUDD
SMAPP
WHOOMP!!
WHAAAAAT?!
YOU'RE USING THE CARRIAGES?!
WHAT TRULY FEARSOME ATHLETICISM!
THAT LEAP...! LIKE A LIMBER GAZELLE SPRINTING ACROSS THE WILD PLAINS!

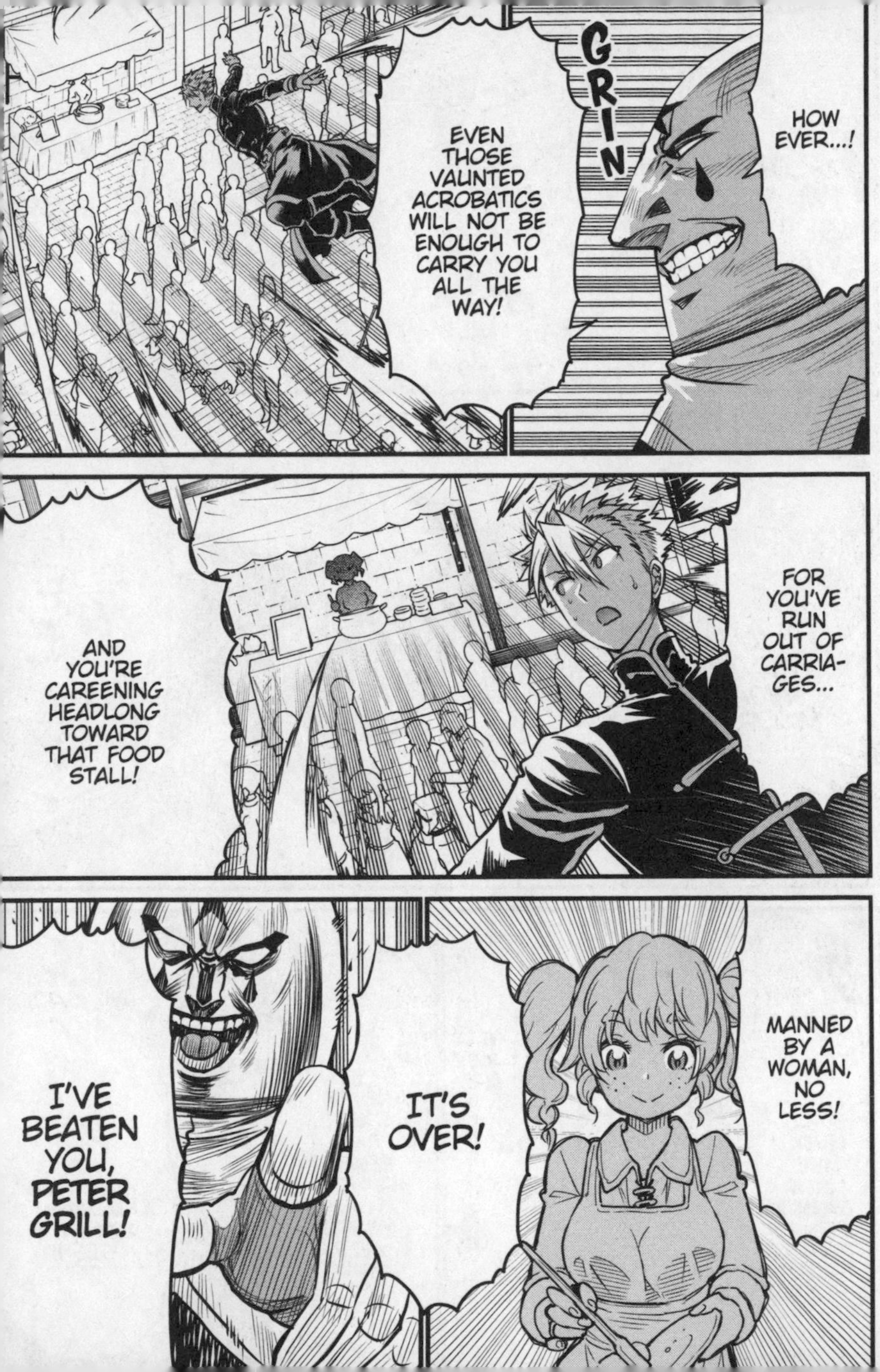
GRIN
HOW EVER...!
EVEN THOSE VAUNTED ACROBATICS WILL NOT BE ENOUGH TO CARRY YOU ALL THE WAY!
FOR YOU'VE RUN OUT OF CARRIA-GES...
AND YOU'RE CAREENING HEADLONG TOWARD THAT FOOD STALL!
MANNED BY A WOMAN, NO LESS!
IT'S OVER!
I'VE BEATEN YOU, PETER GRILL!

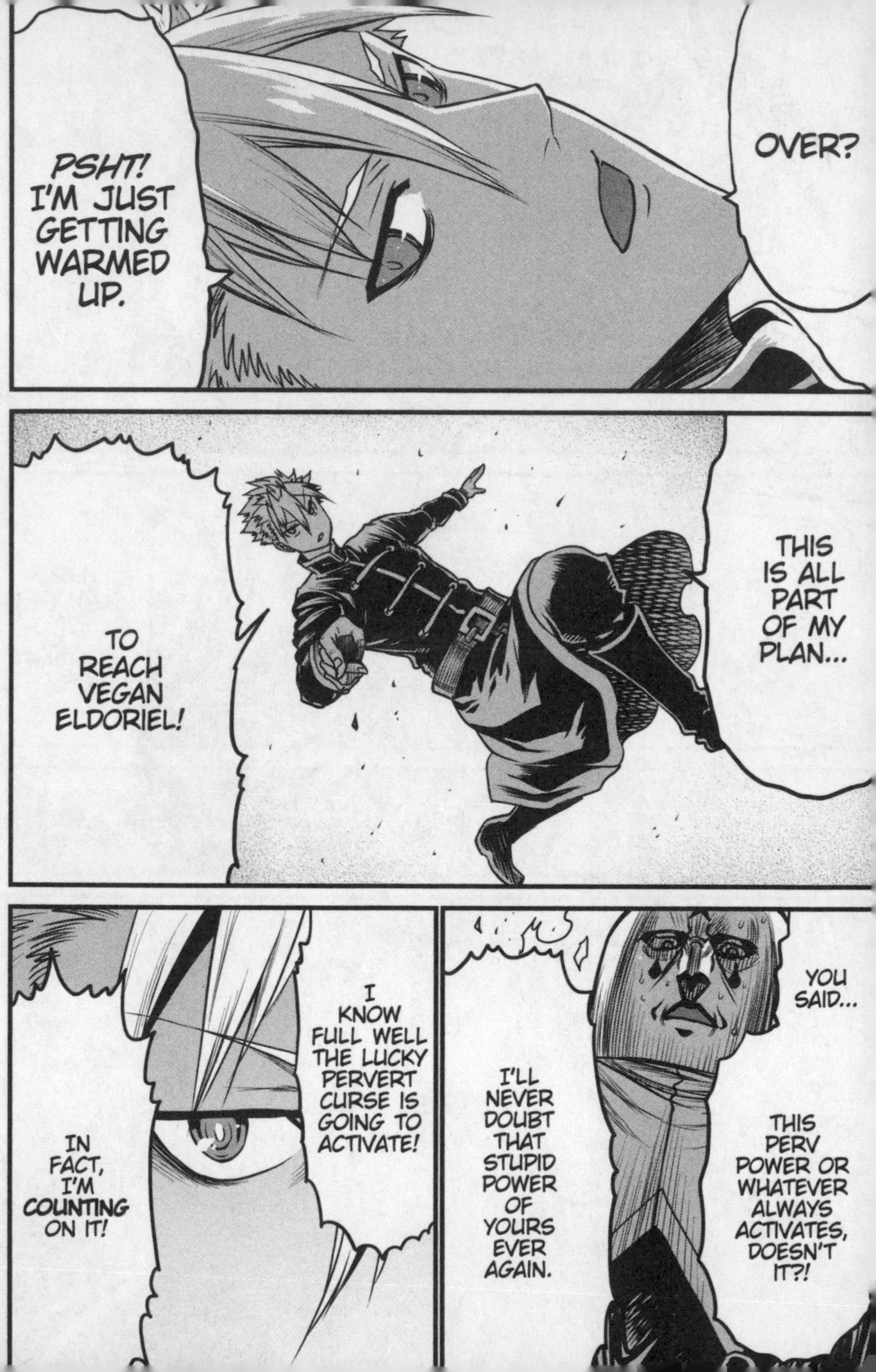
OVER?
PSHT! I'M JUST GETTING WARMED UP.
THIS IS ALL PART OF MY PLAN...
TO REACH VEGAN ELDORIEL!
YOU SAID...
THIS PERV POWER OR WHATEVER ALWAYS ACTIVATES, DOESN'T IT?!
I'LL NEVER DOUBT THAT STUPID POWER OF YOURS EVER AGAIN.
I KNOW FULL WELL THE LUCKY PERVERT CURSE IS GOING TO ACTIVATE!
IN FACT, I'M COUNTING ON IT!

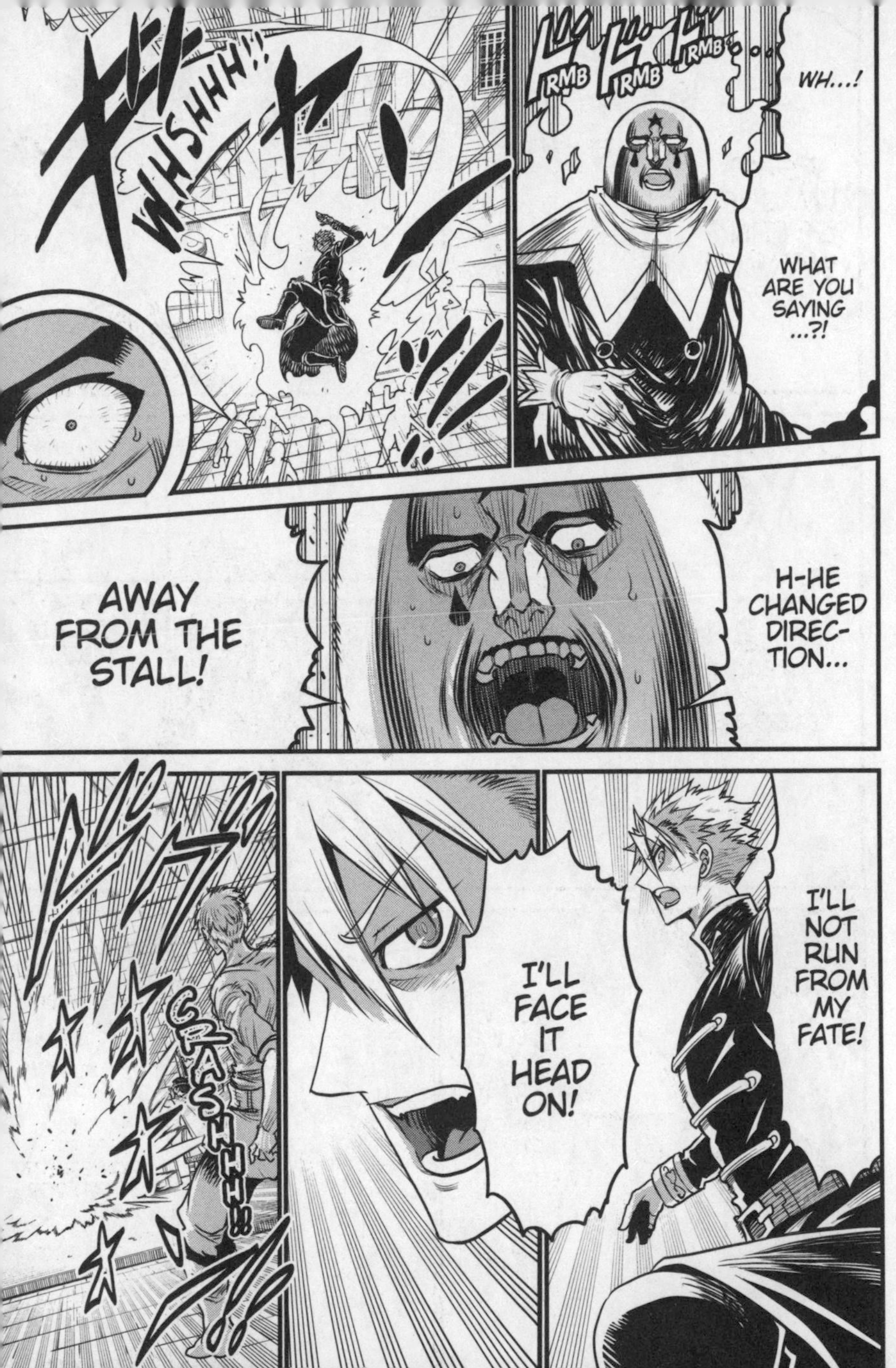

RMB RMB RMB
WH...!
WHAT ARE YOU SAYING ...?!
WHSHHH!!
H-HE CHANGED DIREC-TION...
AWAY FROM THE STALL!
I'LL NOT RUN FROM MY FATE!
I'LL FACE IT HEAD ON!
CRASHHH!!

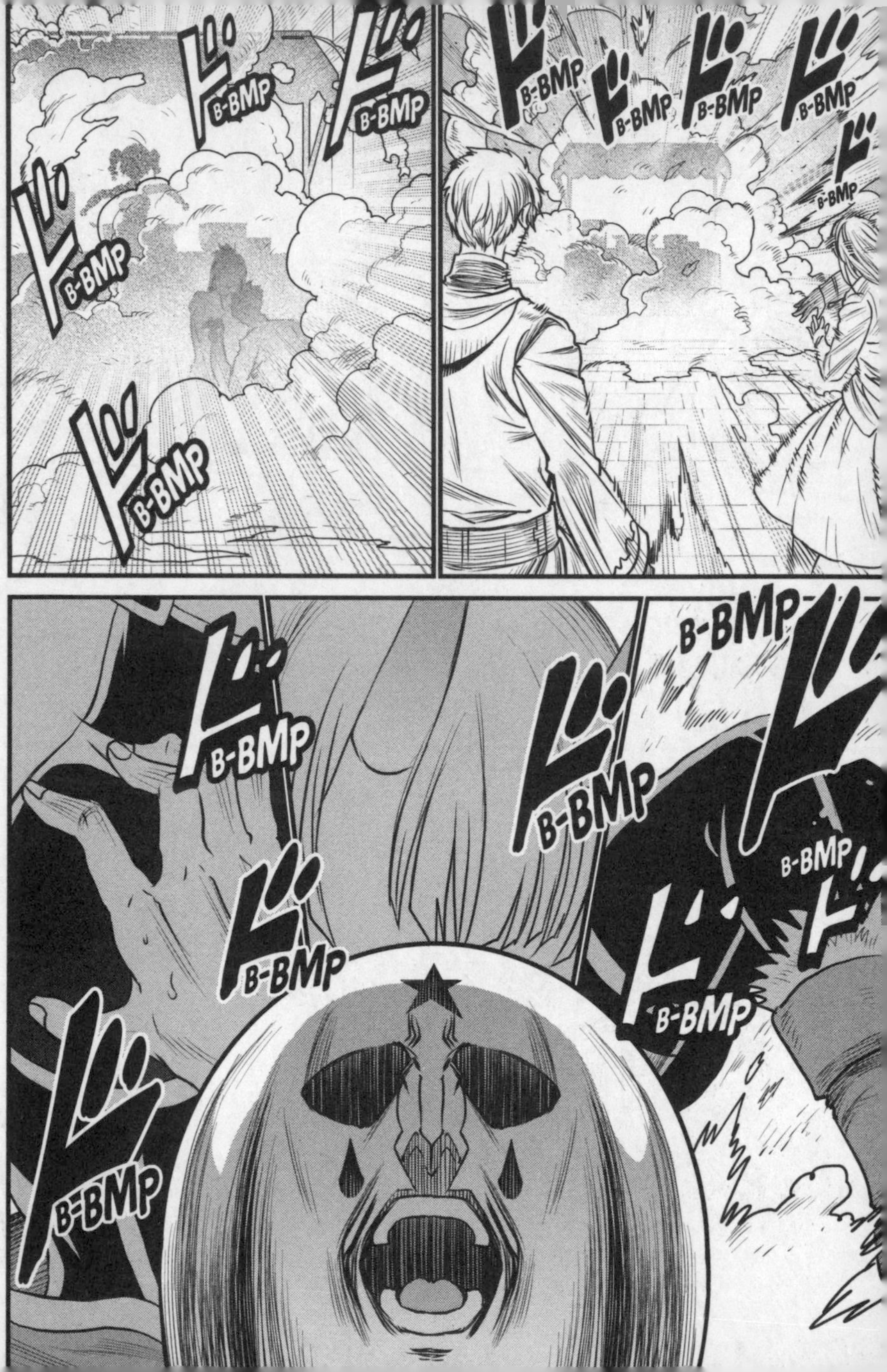
B-BMP
B-BMP
B-BMP
B-BMP
B-BMP
B-BMP
B-BMP
B-BMP
B-BMP
B-BMP
B-BMP
B-BMP
B-BMP
B-BMP
B-BMP
B-BMP

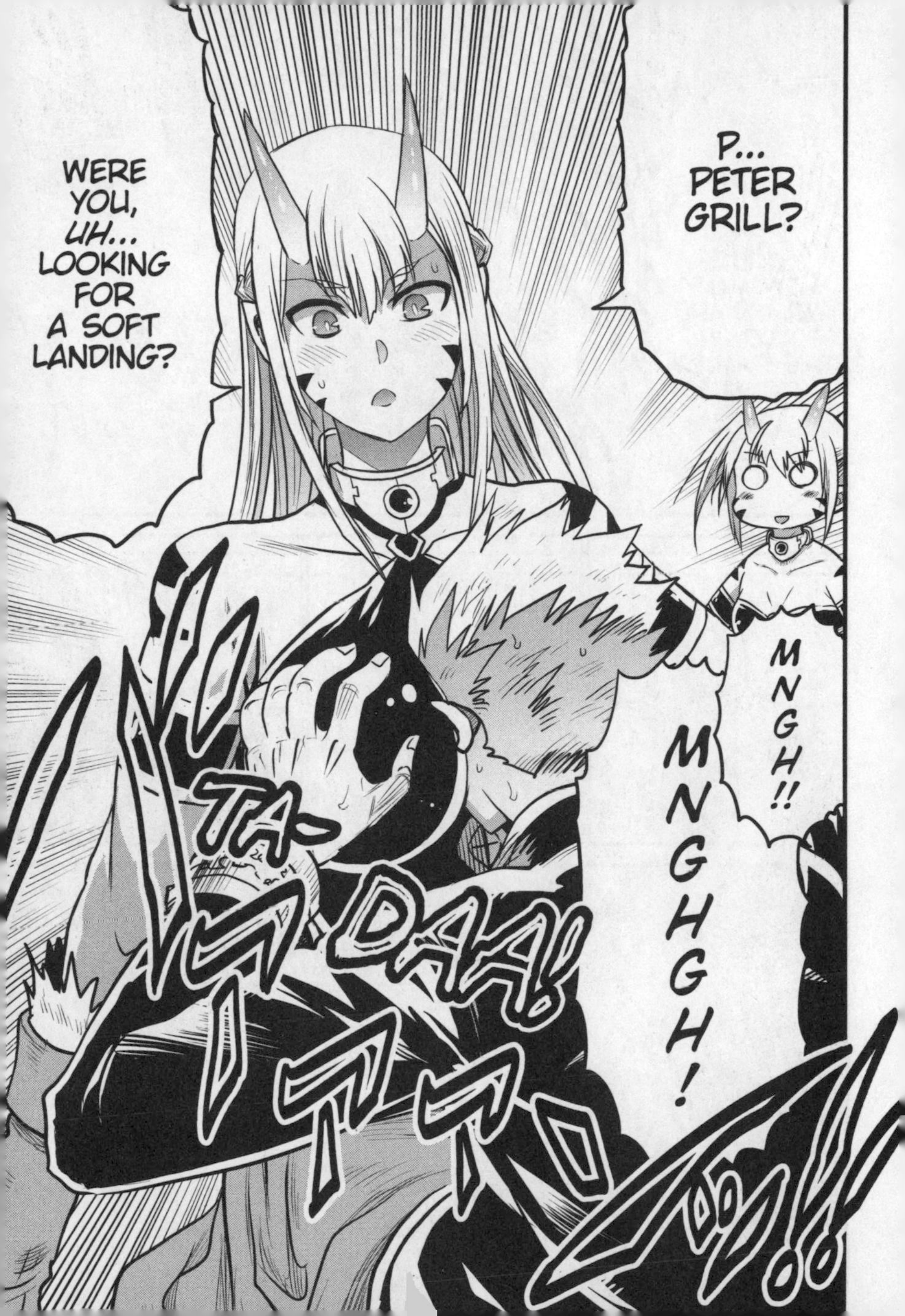
P... PETER GRILL?
WERE YOU, UH... LOOKING FOR A SOFT LANDING?
MNGH MNGH!!
MNGHGH!
TA-DAA!

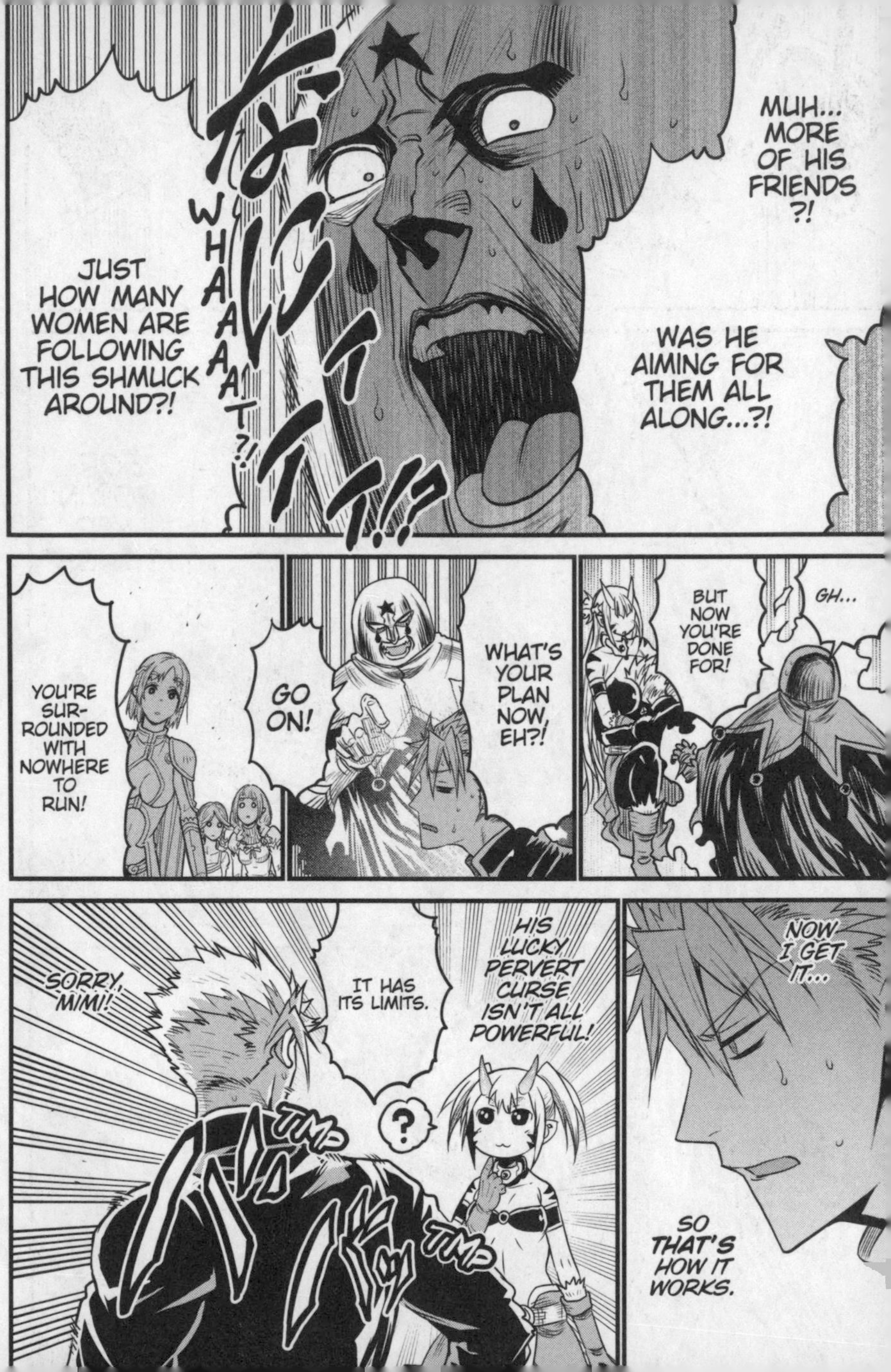
MUH... MORE OF HIS FRIENDS?!
WAS HE AIMING FOR THEM ALL ALONG...?!
WHAAAAAT?!
JUST HOW MANY WOMEN ARE FOLLOWING THIS SHMUCK AROUND?!
GH...
BUT NOW YOU'RE DONE FOR!
WHAT'S YOUR PLAN NOW, EH?!
GO ON!
YOU'RE SURROUNDED WITH NOWHERE TO RUN!
NOW I GET IT...
SO THAT'S HOW IT WORKS.
HIS LUCKY PERVERT CURSE ISN'T ALL POWERFUL!
IT HAS ITS LIMITS.
?
SORRY, MIMI!
TMP
TMP

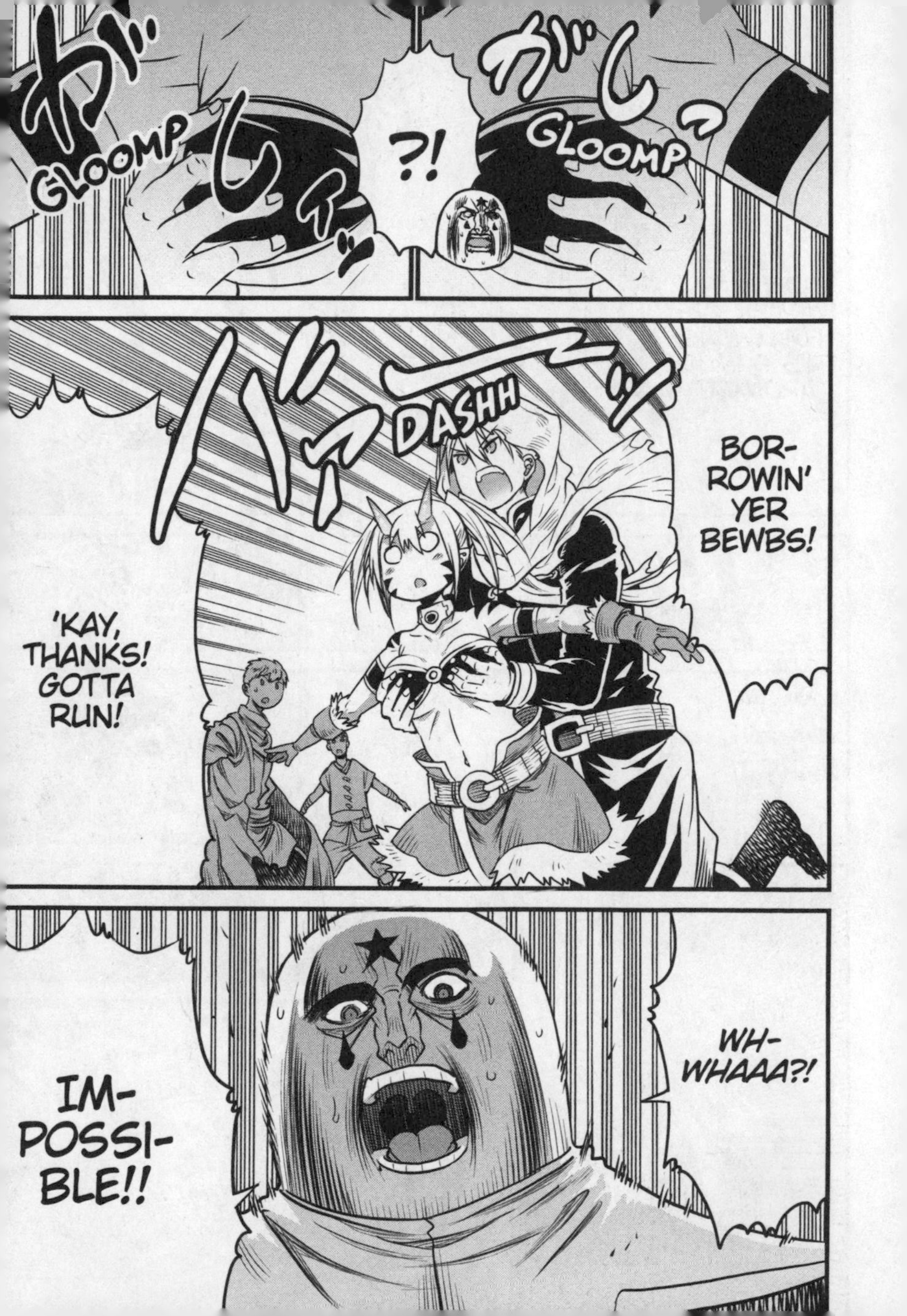
がしっ
GLOOMP
GLOOMP
?!
DASHH
BOR-ROWIN' YER BEWBS!
'KAY, THANKS! GOTTA RUN!
WH-WHAAA?!
IM-POSSI-BLE!!

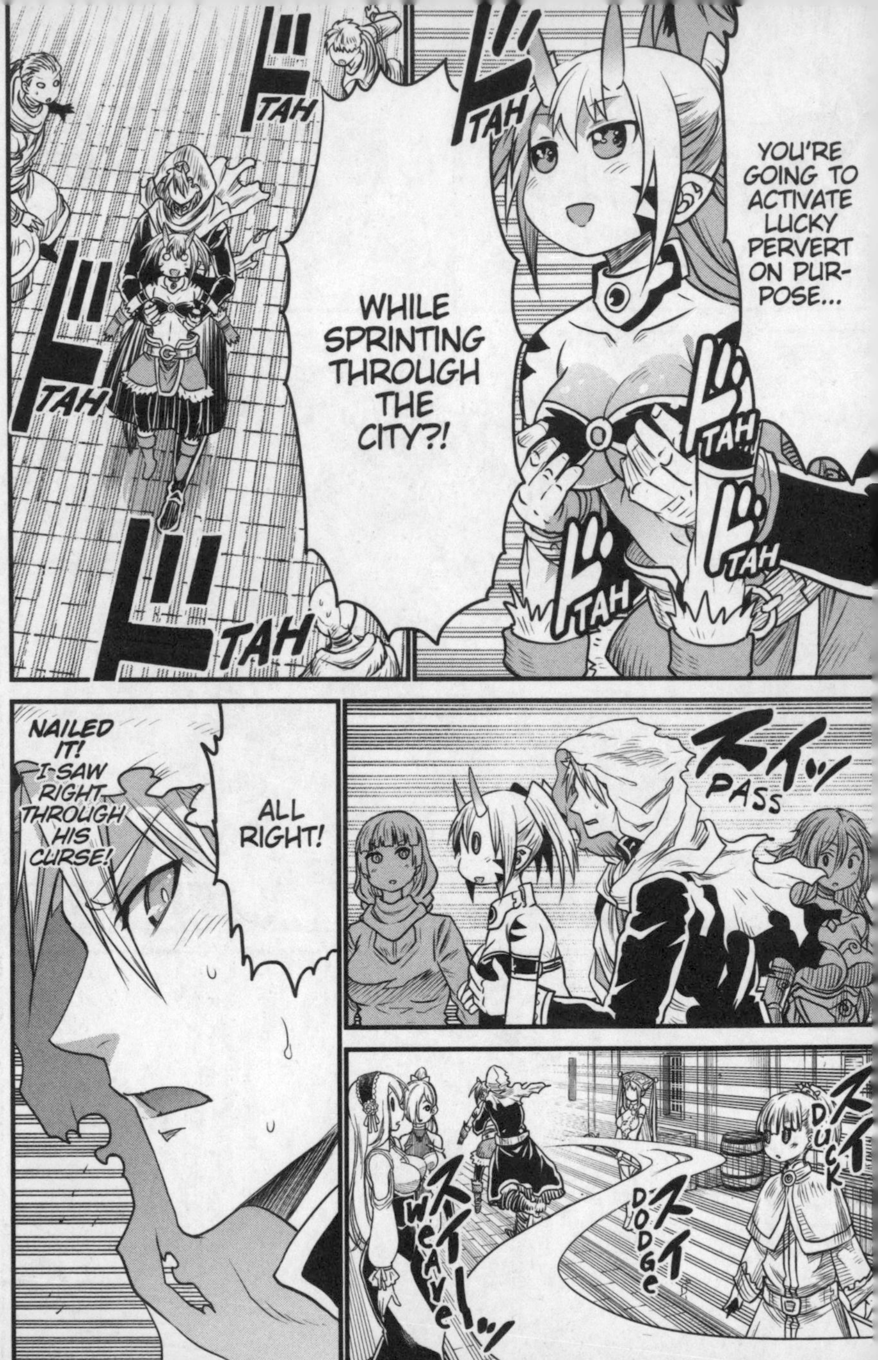
YOU'RE GOING TO ACTIVATE LUCKY PERVERT ON PUR-POSE...
WHILE SPRINTING THROUGH THE CITY?!
TAH
TAH
TAH
TAH
TAH
TAH
TAH
TAH
PASS
DUCK
DODGE
WEAVE
ALL RIGHT!
NAILED IT! I SAW RIGHT THROUGH HIS CURSE!

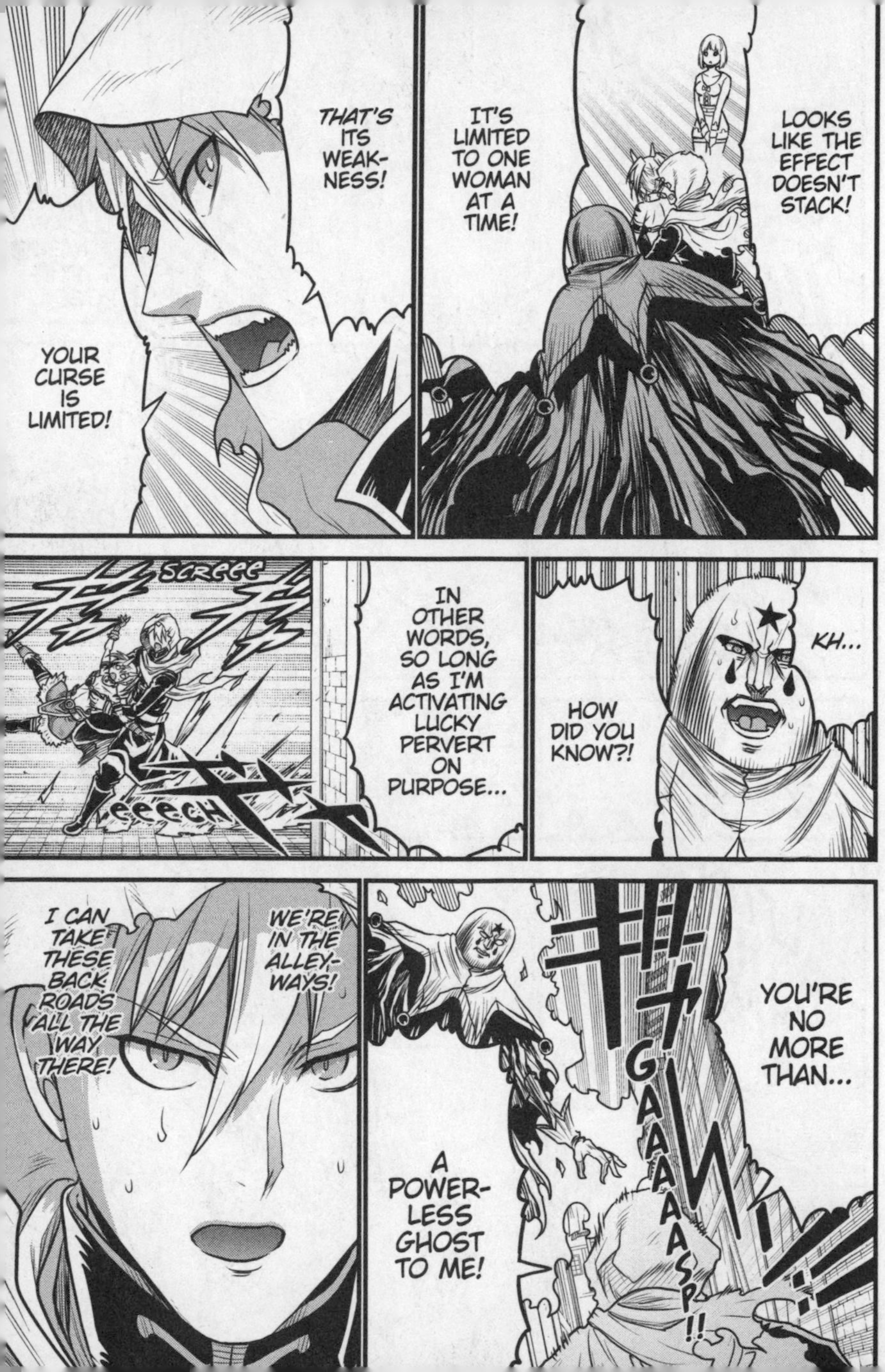
LOOKS LIKE THE EFFECT DOESN'T STACK!
IT'S LIMITED TO ONE WOMAN AT A TIME!
THAT'S ITS WEAKNESS!
YOUR CURSE IS LIMITED!
KH...
HOW DID YOU KNOW?!
IN OTHER WORDS, SO LONG AS I'M ACTIVATING LUCKY PERVERT ON PURPOSE...
screeee
eeeCH
YOU'RE NO MORE THAN...
A POWERLESS GHOST TO ME!
GAAAAASP!!
WE'RE IN THE ALLEYWAYS!
I CAN TAKE THESE BACK ROADS ALL THE WAY THERE!

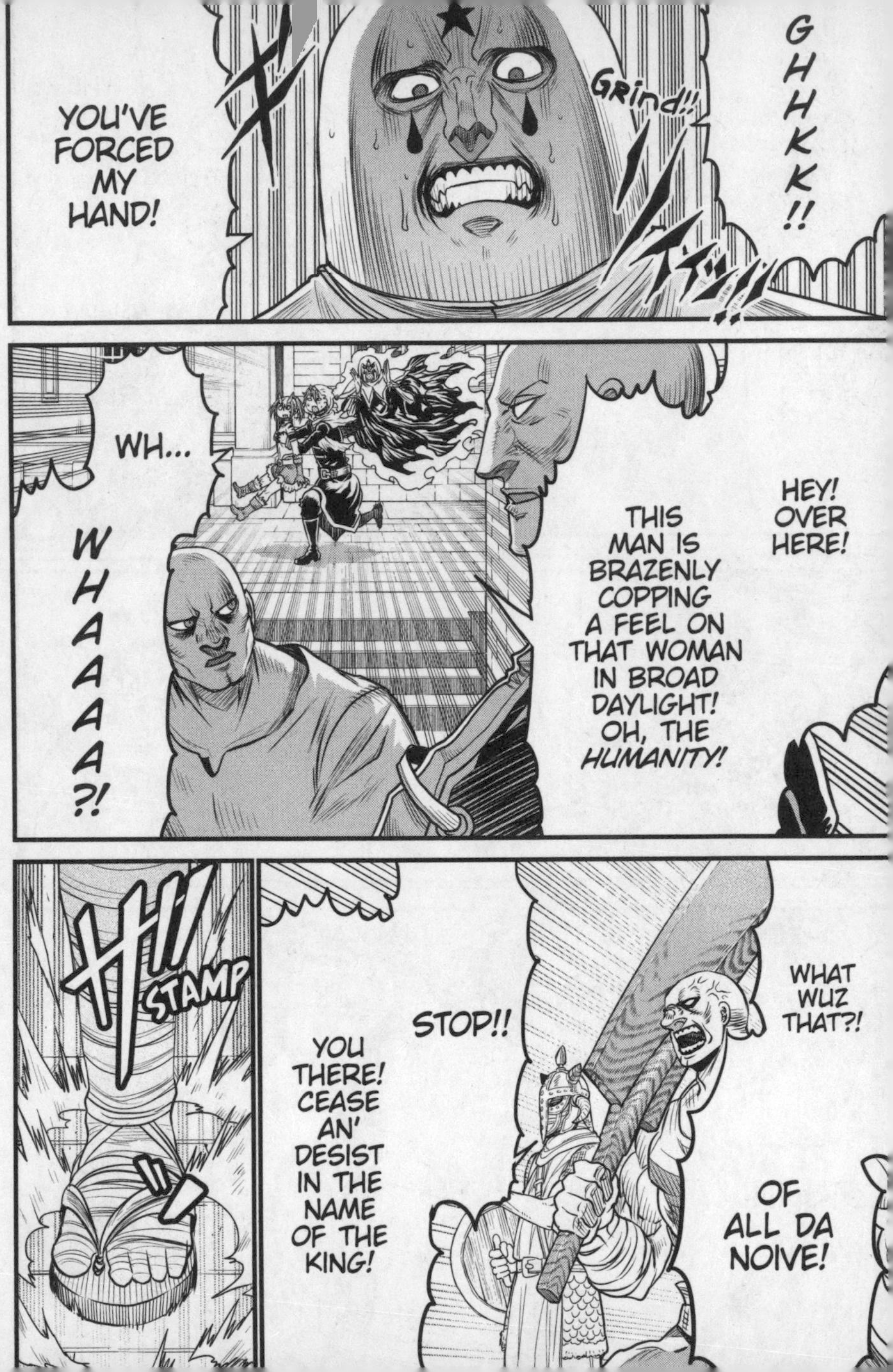
GHHKK!!
Grind!!
YOU'VE FORCED MY HAND!
HEY! OVER HERE!
THIS MAN IS BRAZENLY COPPING A FEEL ON THAT WOMAN IN BROAD DAYLIGHT! OH, THE HUMANITY!
WH...
WHAAAAAA?!
WHAT WUZ THAT?!
OF ALL DA NOIVE!
STOP!!
YOU THERE! CEASE AN' DESIST IN THE NAME OF THE KING!
STAMP

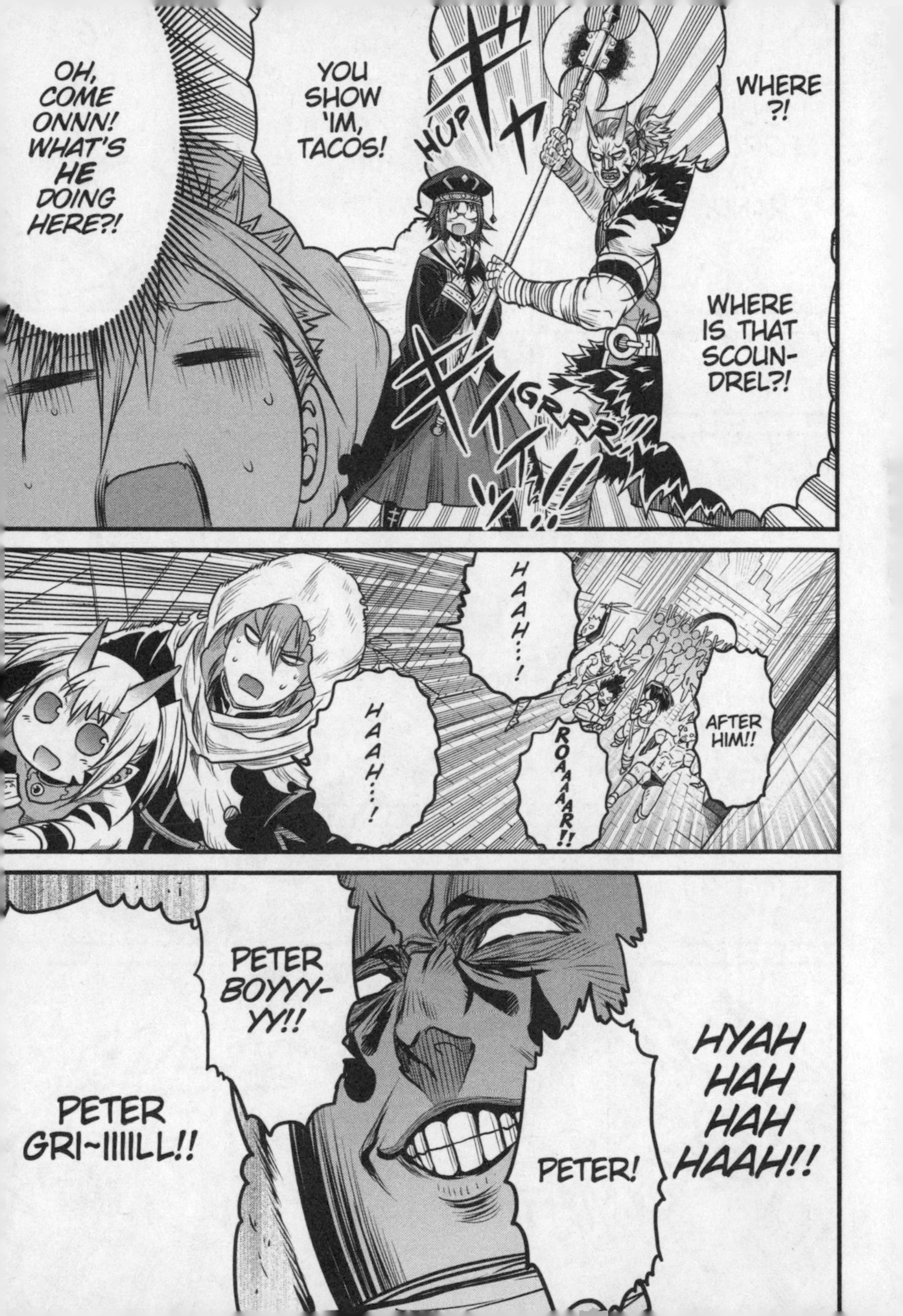
WHERE ?!
HUP
YOU SHOW 'IM, TACOS!
WHERE IS THAT SCOUN-DREL?!
GRRRR!!
OH, COME ONNN! WHAT'S HE DOING HERE?!
AFTER HIM!!
ROAAAAAAR!!
HAAAH...!
HAAAH...!
HYAH HAH HAH HAAH!!
PETER!
PETER BOYYYY-YY!!
PETER GRI~IIIILL!!

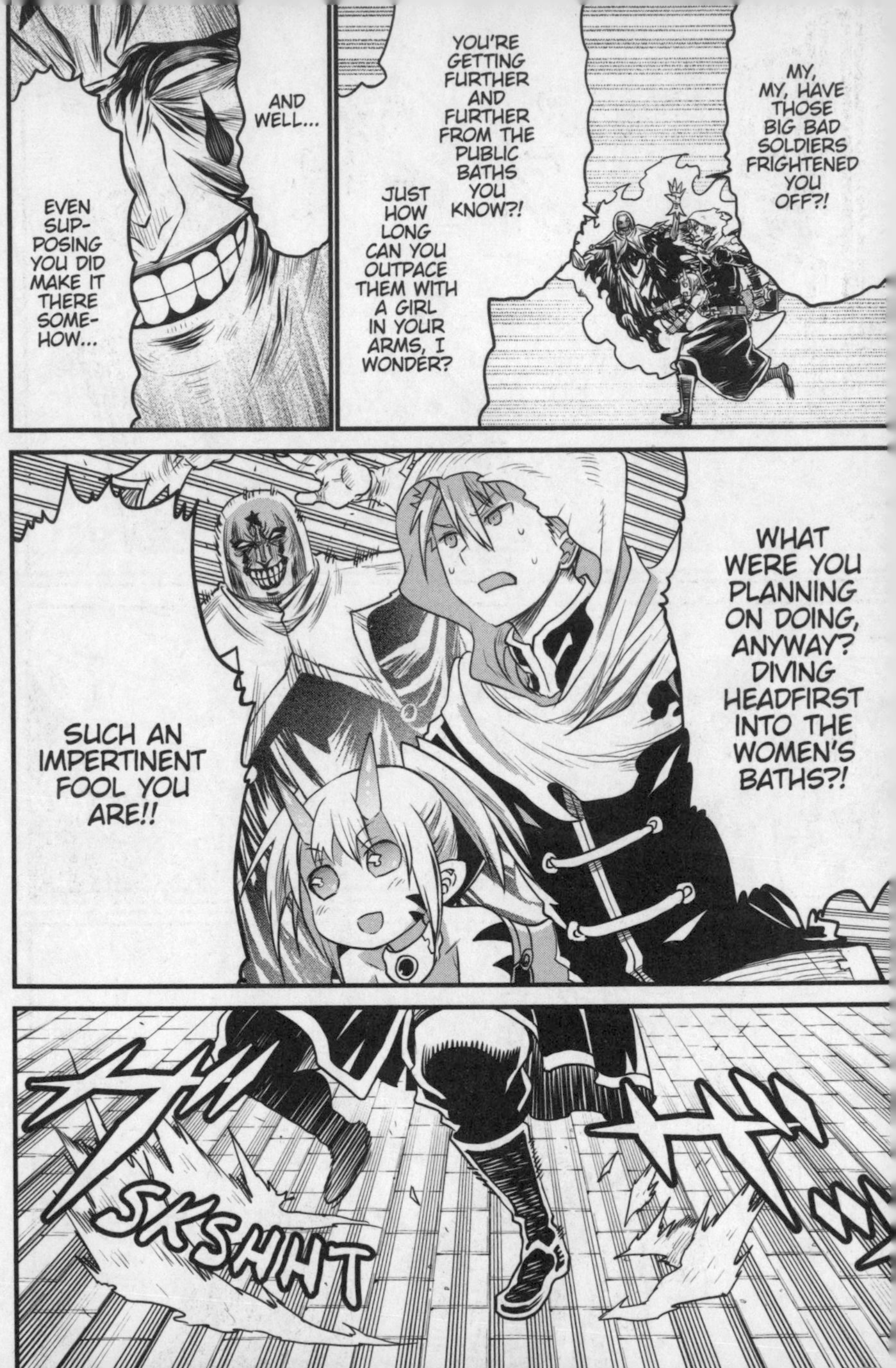
MY, MY, HAVE THOSE BIG BAD SOLDIERS FRIGHTENED YOU OFF?!
YOU'RE GETTING FURTHER AND FURTHER FROM THE PUBLIC BATHS YOU KNOW?!
JUST HOW LONG CAN YOU OUTPACE THEM WITH A GIRL IN YOUR ARMS, I WONDER?
AND WELL...
EVEN SUP-POSING YOU DID MAKE IT THERE SOME-HOW...
WHAT WERE YOU PLANNING ON DOING, ANYWAY? DIVING HEADFIRST INTO THE WOMEN'S BATHS?!
SUCH AN IMPERTINENT FOOL YOU ARE!!
SKSHHT

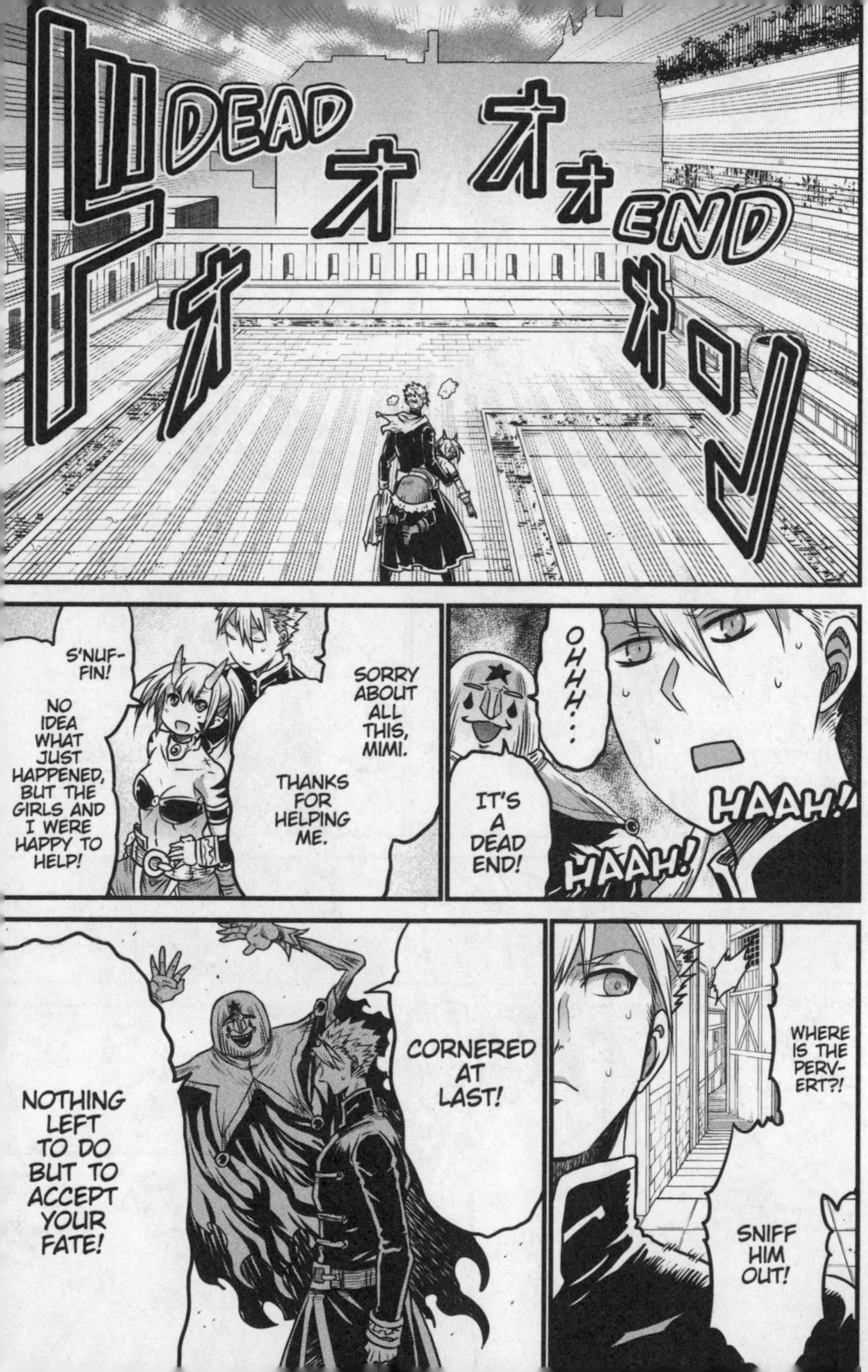
DEAD
END
OHHH...
IT'S A DEAD END!
HAAH!
HAAH!
SORRY ABOUT ALL THIS, MIMI.
THANKS FOR HELPING ME.
S'NUF-FIN!
NO IDEA WHAT JUST HAPPENED, BUT THE GIRLS AND I WERE HAPPY TO HELP!
WHERE IS THE PERV-ERT?!
SNIFF HIM OUT!
CORNERED AT LAST!
NOTHING LEFT TO DO BUT TO ACCEPT YOUR FATE!

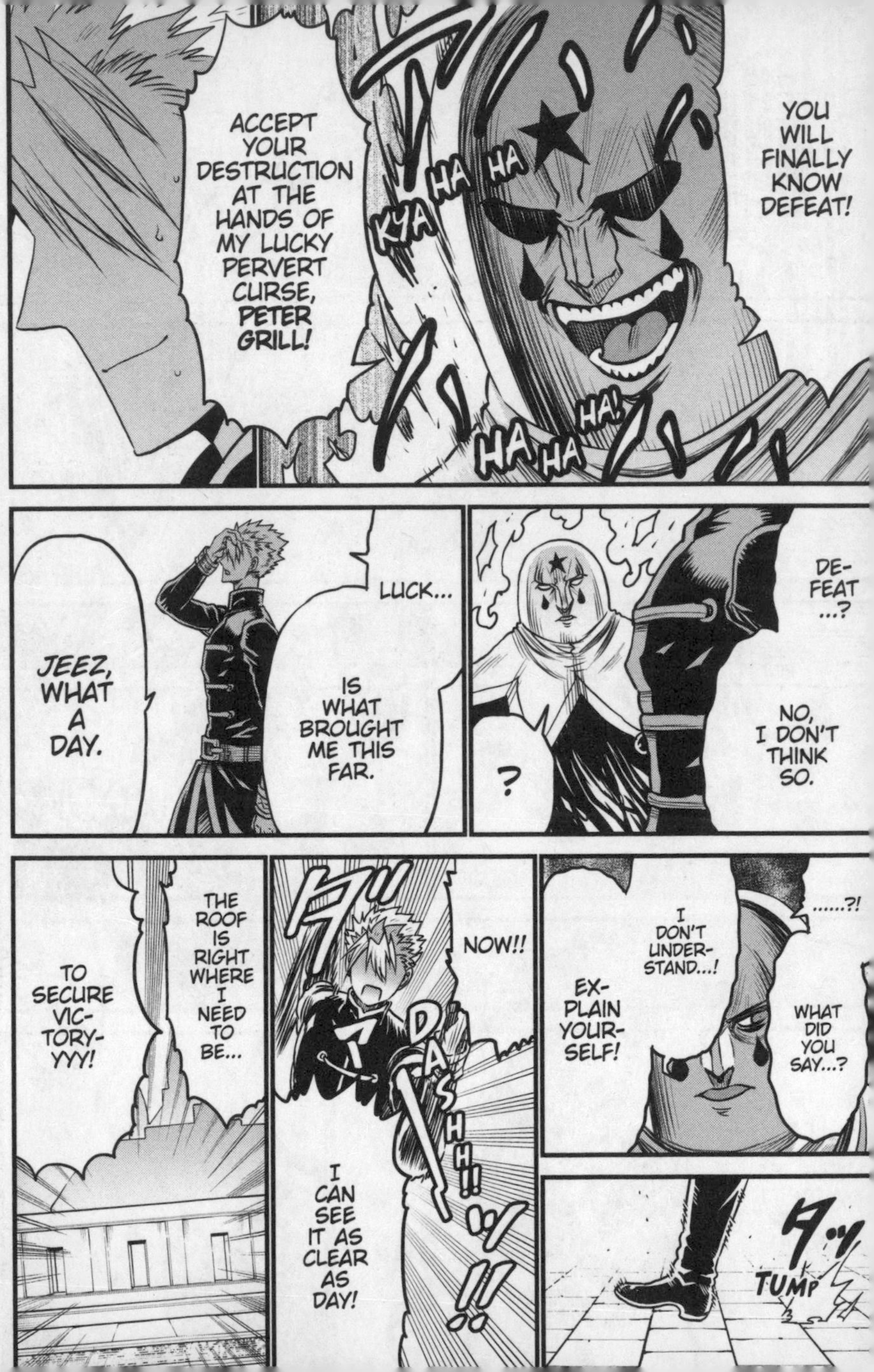
YOU WILL FINALLY KNOW DEFEAT!
KYA HA HA
ACCEPT YOUR DESTRUCTION AT THE HANDS OF MY LUCKY PERVERT CURSE, PETER GRILL!
HA HA HA HA!
DE-FEAT...?
NO, I DON'T THINK SO.
?
LUCK...
IS WHAT BROUGHT ME THIS FAR.
JEEZ, WHAT A DAY.
......?!
I DON'T UNDER-STAND...!
WHAT DID YOU SAY...?
EX-PLAIN YOUR-SELF!
TUMP
NOW!!
DASHH!!
I CAN SEE IT AS CLEAR AS DAY!
THE ROOF IS RIGHT WHERE I NEED TO BE...
TO SECURE VIC-TORY-YYY!

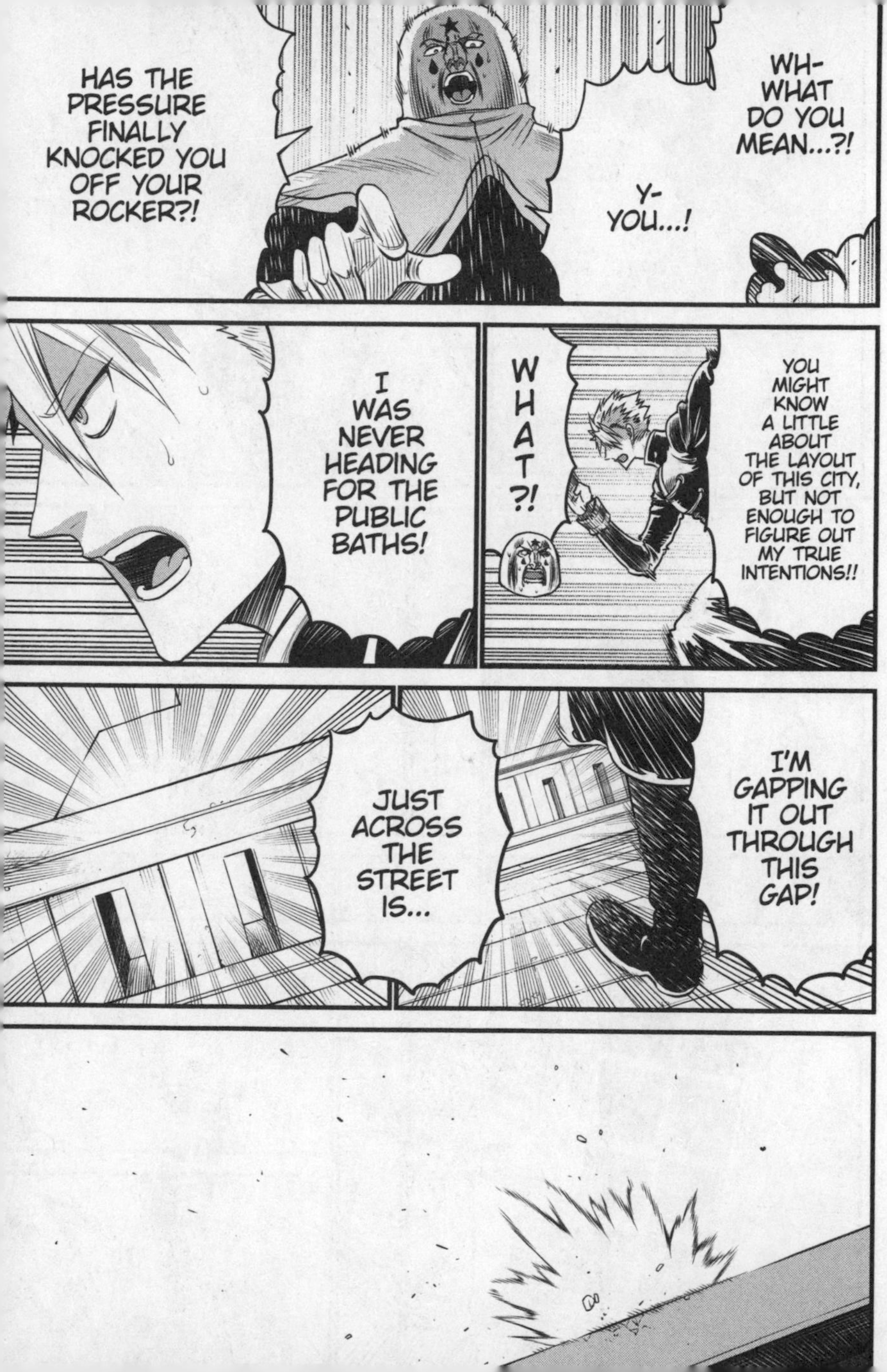
WH- WHAT DO YOU MEAN...?!
Y- YOU...!
HAS THE PRESSURE FINALLY KNOCKED YOU OFF YOUR ROCKER?!
YOU MIGHT KNOW A LITTLE ABOUT THE LAYOUT OF THIS CITY, BUT NOT ENOUGH TO FIGURE OUT MY TRUE INTENTIONS!!
WHAT?!
I WAS NEVER HEADING FOR THE PUBLIC BATHS!
I'M GAPPING IT OUT THROUGH THIS GAP!
JUST ACROSS THE STREET IS...

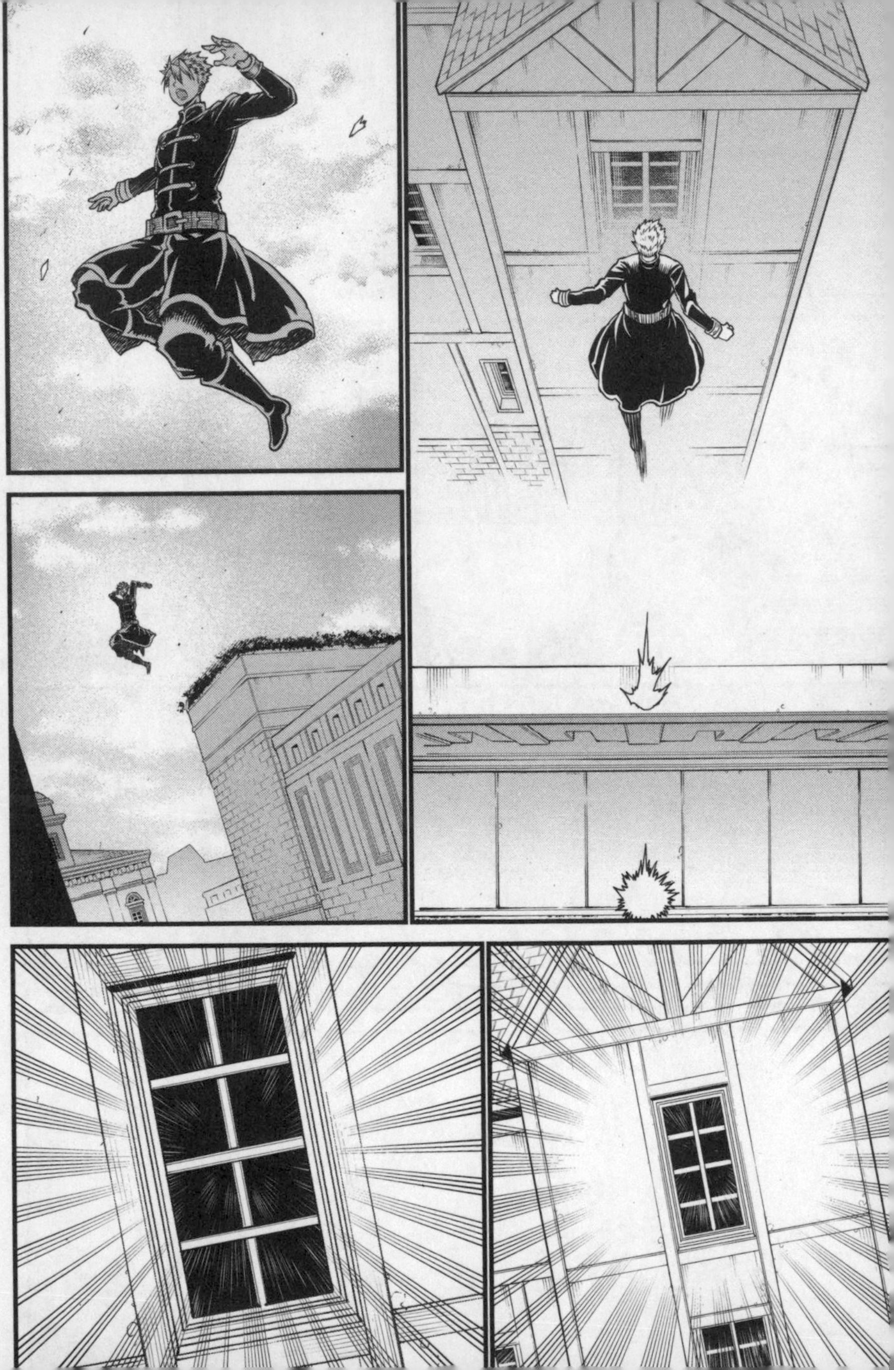

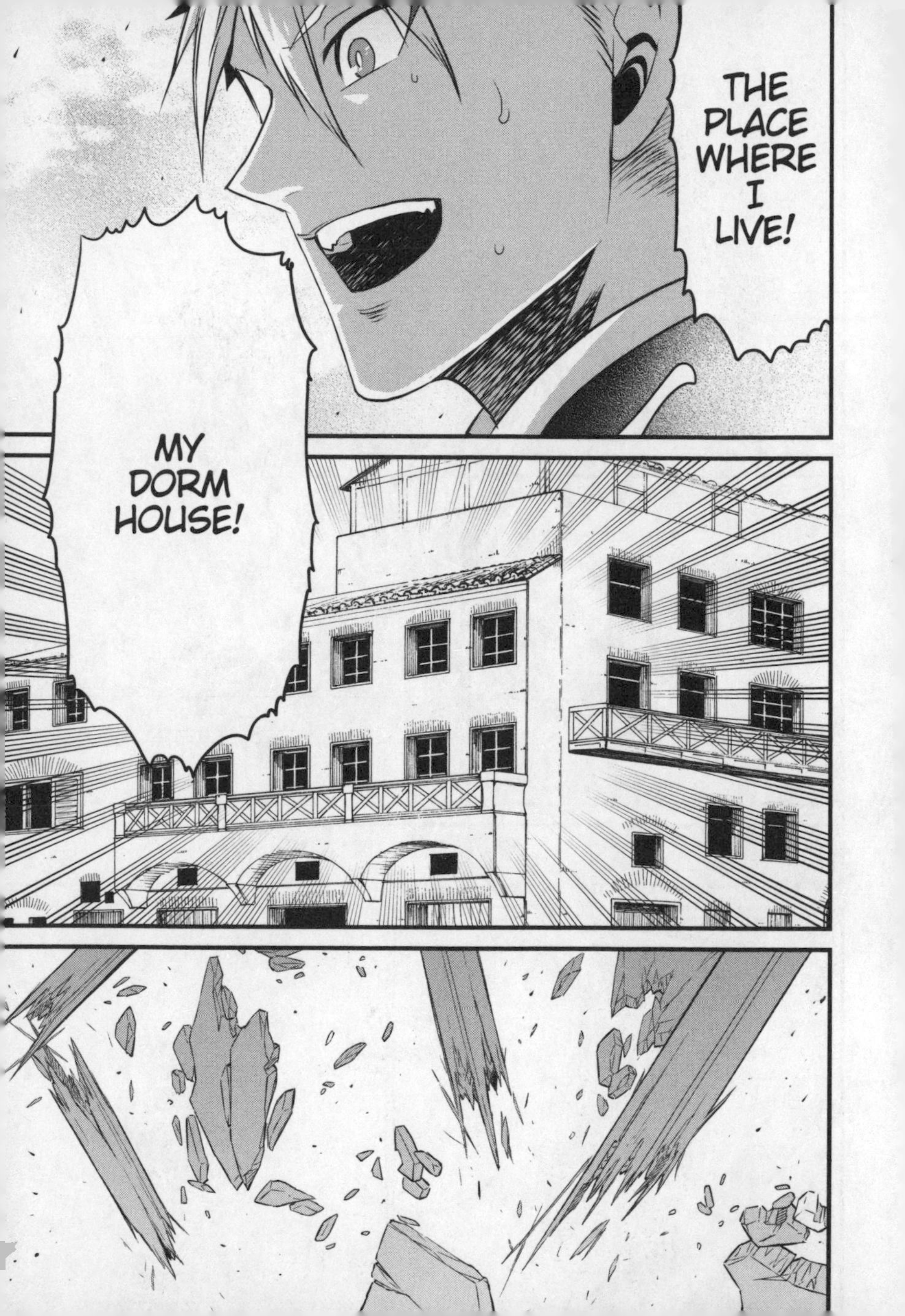
THE PLACE WHERE I LIVE!
MY DORM HOUSE!

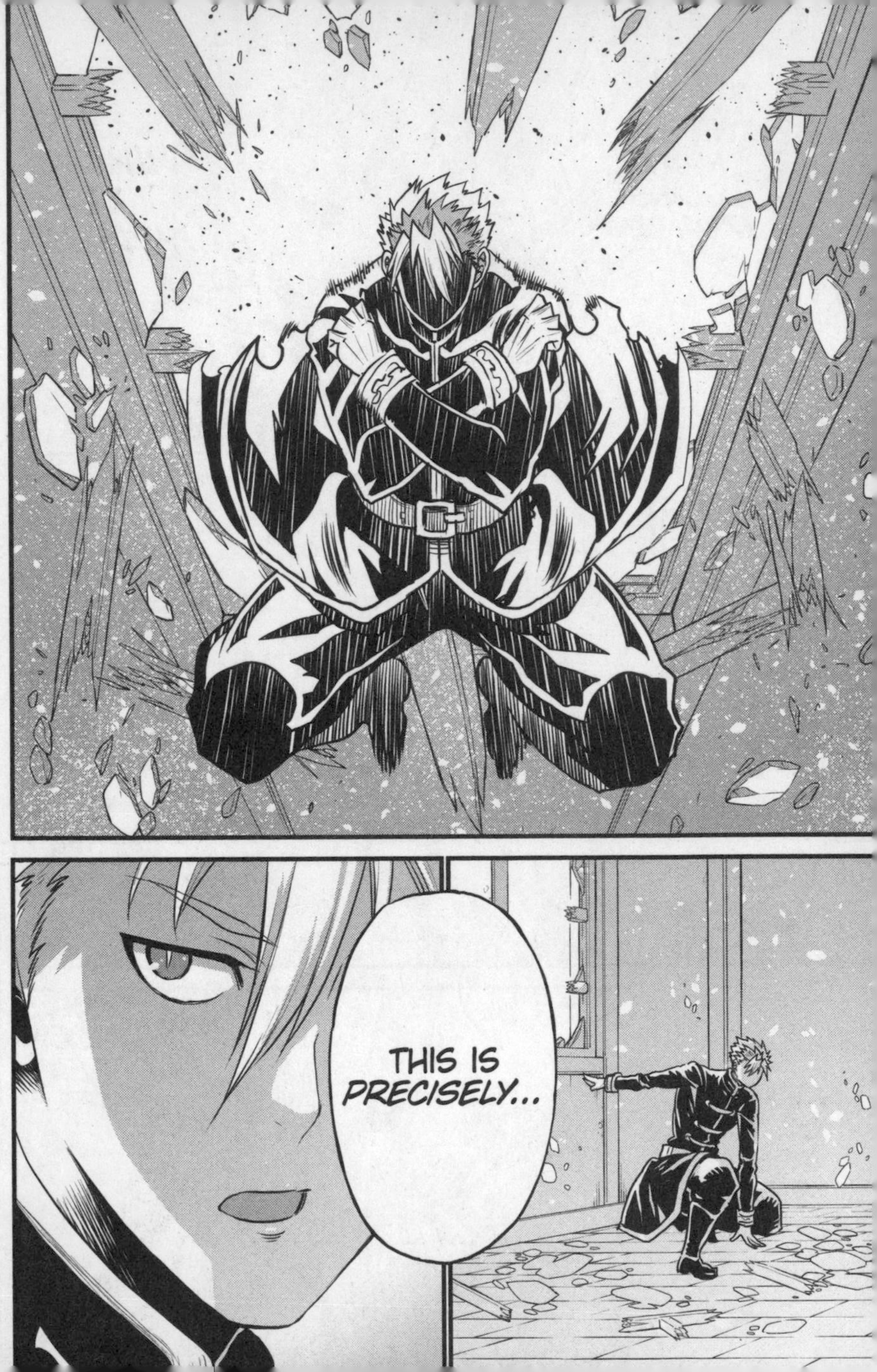
THIS IS PRECISELY...

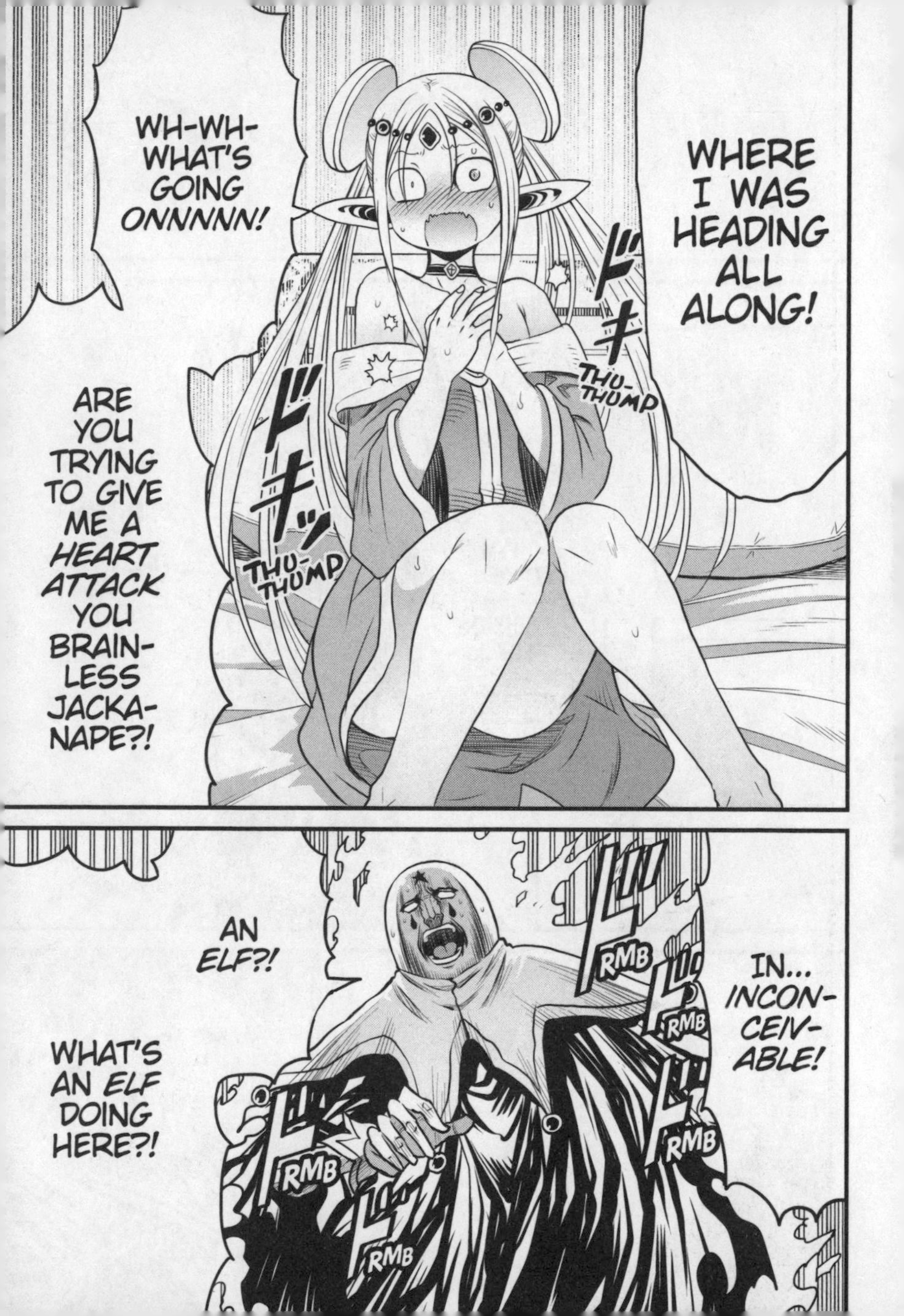
WHERE I WAS HEADING ALL ALONG!
WH-WH-WHAT'S GOING ONNNNN!
THU-THUMP
ARE YOU TRYING TO GIVE ME A HEART ATTACK YOU BRAINLESS JACKANAPE?!
THU-THUMP
IN... INCONCEIVABLE!
RMB
RMB
AN ELF?!
WHAT'S AN ELF DOING HERE?!
RMB
RMB
RMB

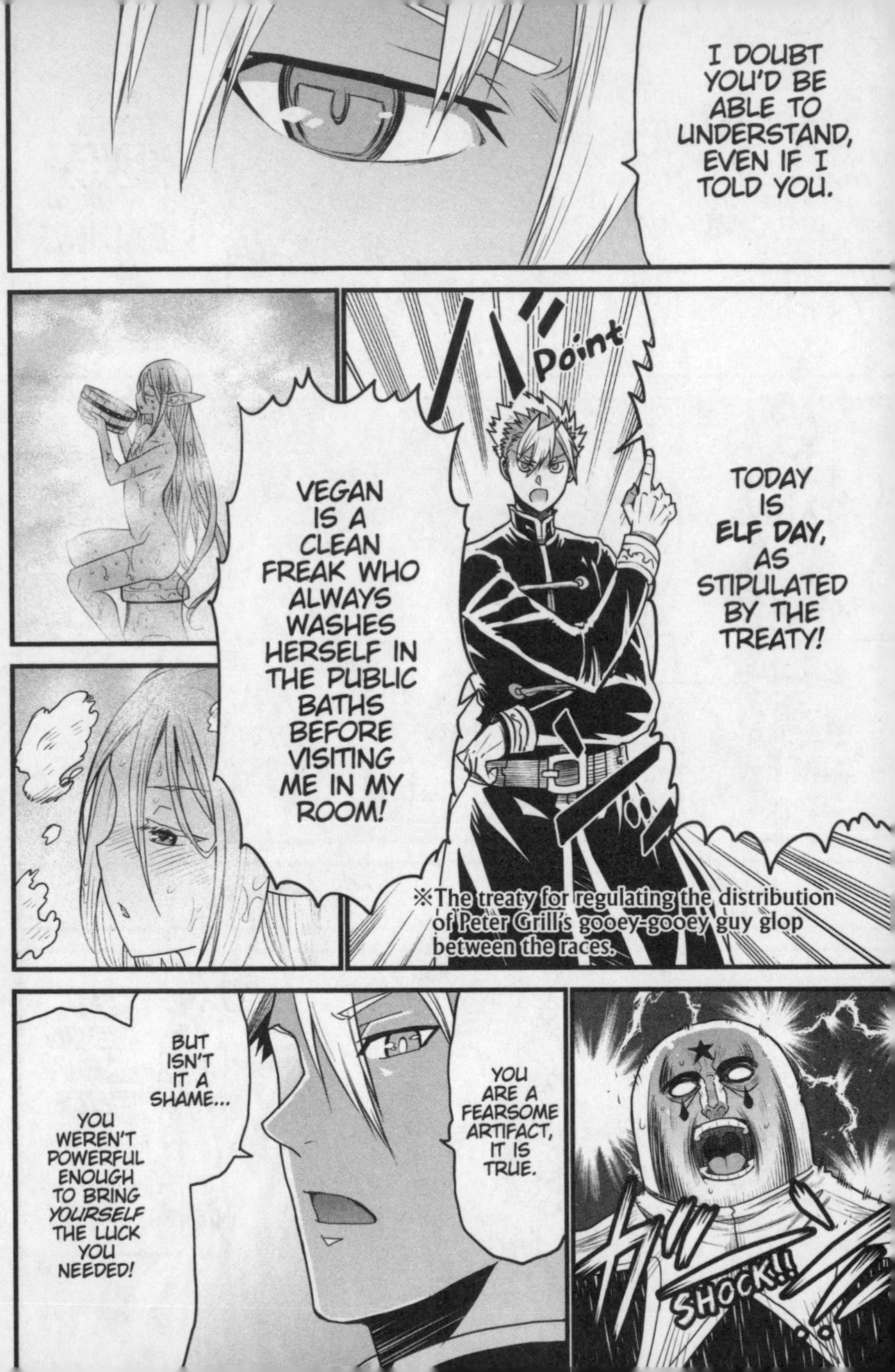
I DOUBT YOU'D BE ABLE TO UNDERSTAND, EVEN IF I TOLD YOU.
Point
TODAY IS ELF DAY, AS STIPULATED BY THE TREATY!
VEGAN IS A CLEAN FREAK WHO ALWAYS WASHES HERSELF IN THE PUBLIC BATHS BEFORE VISITING ME IN MY ROOM!
※The treaty for regulating the distribution of Peter Grill's gooey-gooey guy glop between the races.
SHOCK!!
YOU ARE A FEARSOME ARTIFACT, IT IS TRUE.
BUT ISN'T IT A SHAME...
YOU WEREN'T POWERFUL ENOUGH TO BRING *YOURSELF* THE LUCK YOU NEEDED!

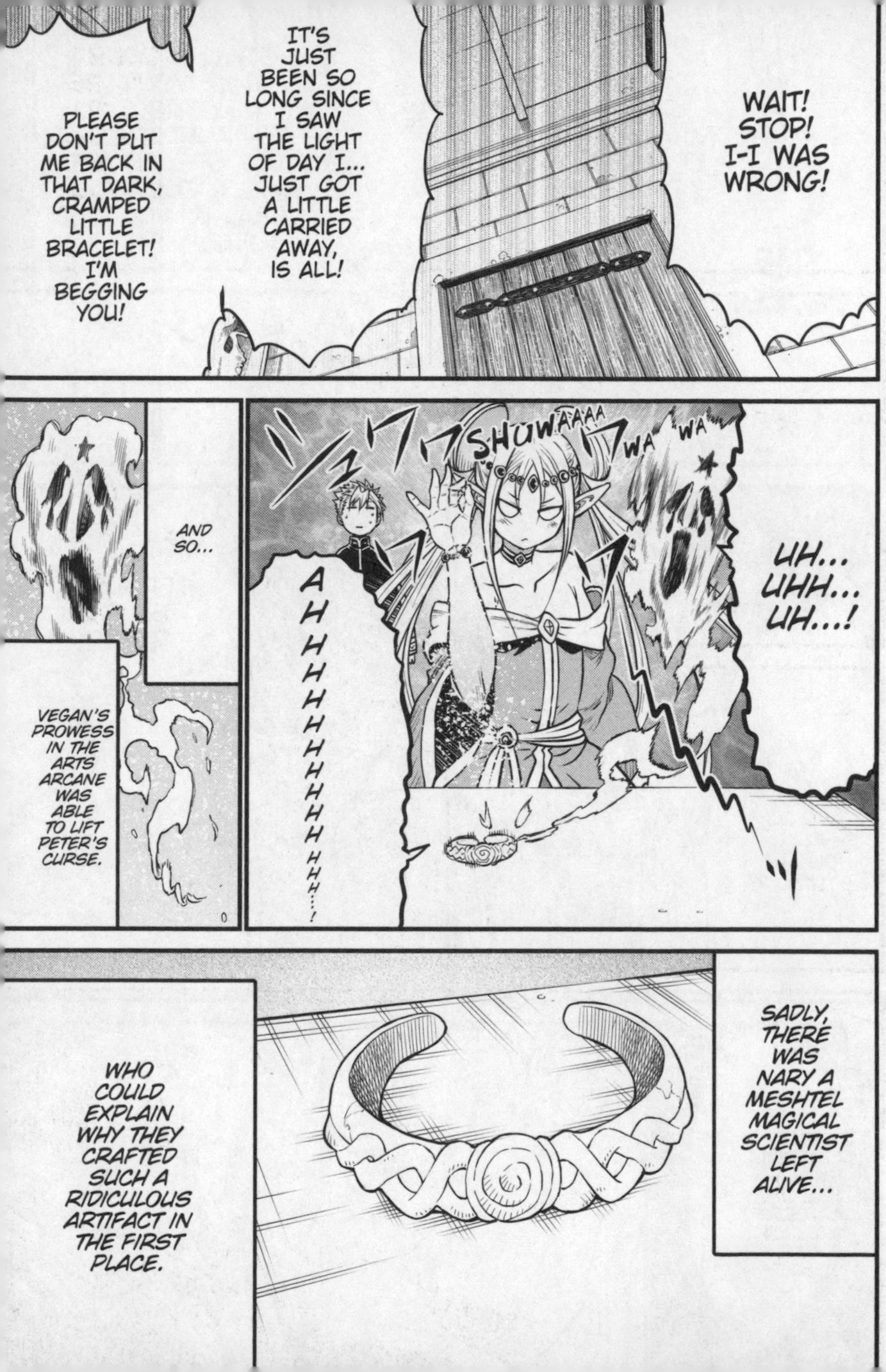
WAIT! STOP! I-I WAS WRONG!
IT'S JUST BEEN SO LONG SINCE I SAW THE LIGHT OF DAY I... JUST GOT A LITTLE CARRIED AWAY, IS ALL!
PLEASE DON'T PUT ME BACK IN THAT DARK, CRAMPED LITTLE BRACELET! I'M BEGGING YOU!
SHUWAAAA
WA WA
UH... UHH... UH...!
AHHHHHHHHHHHHHHH...!
AND SO...
VEGAN'S PROWESS IN THE ARTS ARCANE WAS ABLE TO LIFT PETER'S CURSE.
SADLY, THERE WAS NARY A MESHTEL MAGICAL SCIENTIST LEFT ALIVE...
WHO COULD EXPLAIN WHY THEY CRAFTED SUCH A RIDICULOUS ARTIFACT IN THE FIRST PLACE.

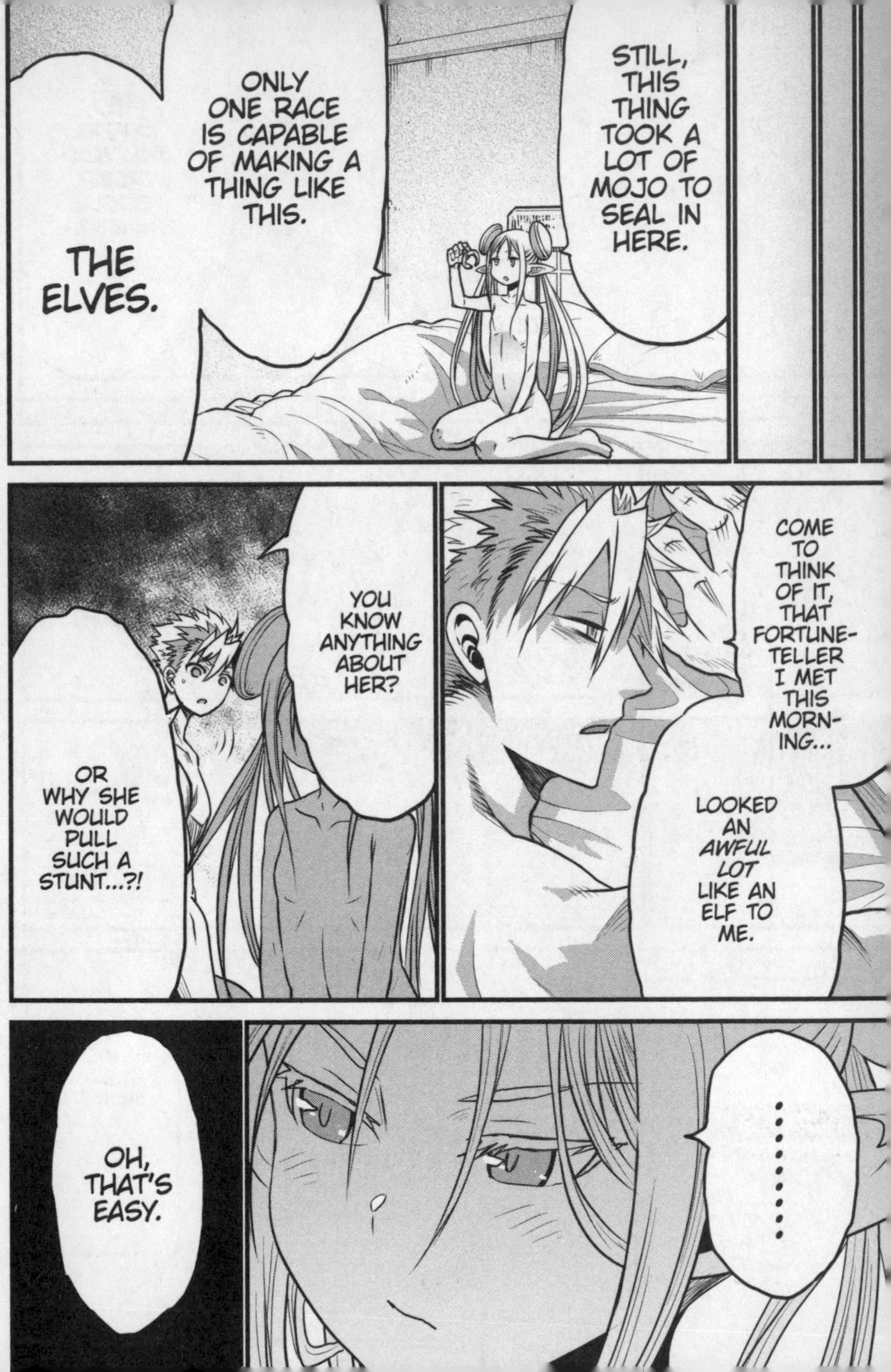
STILL, THIS THING TOOK A LOT OF MOJO TO SEAL IN HERE.
ONLY ONE RACE IS CAPABLE OF MAKING A THING LIKE THIS.
THE ELVES.
COME TO THINK OF IT, THAT FORTUNE-TELLER I MET THIS MORNING...
LOOKED AN *AWFUL LOT* LIKE AN ELF TO ME.
YOU KNOW ANYTHING ABOUT HER?
OR WHY SHE WOULD PULL SUCH A STUNT...?!
....
OH, THAT'S EASY.

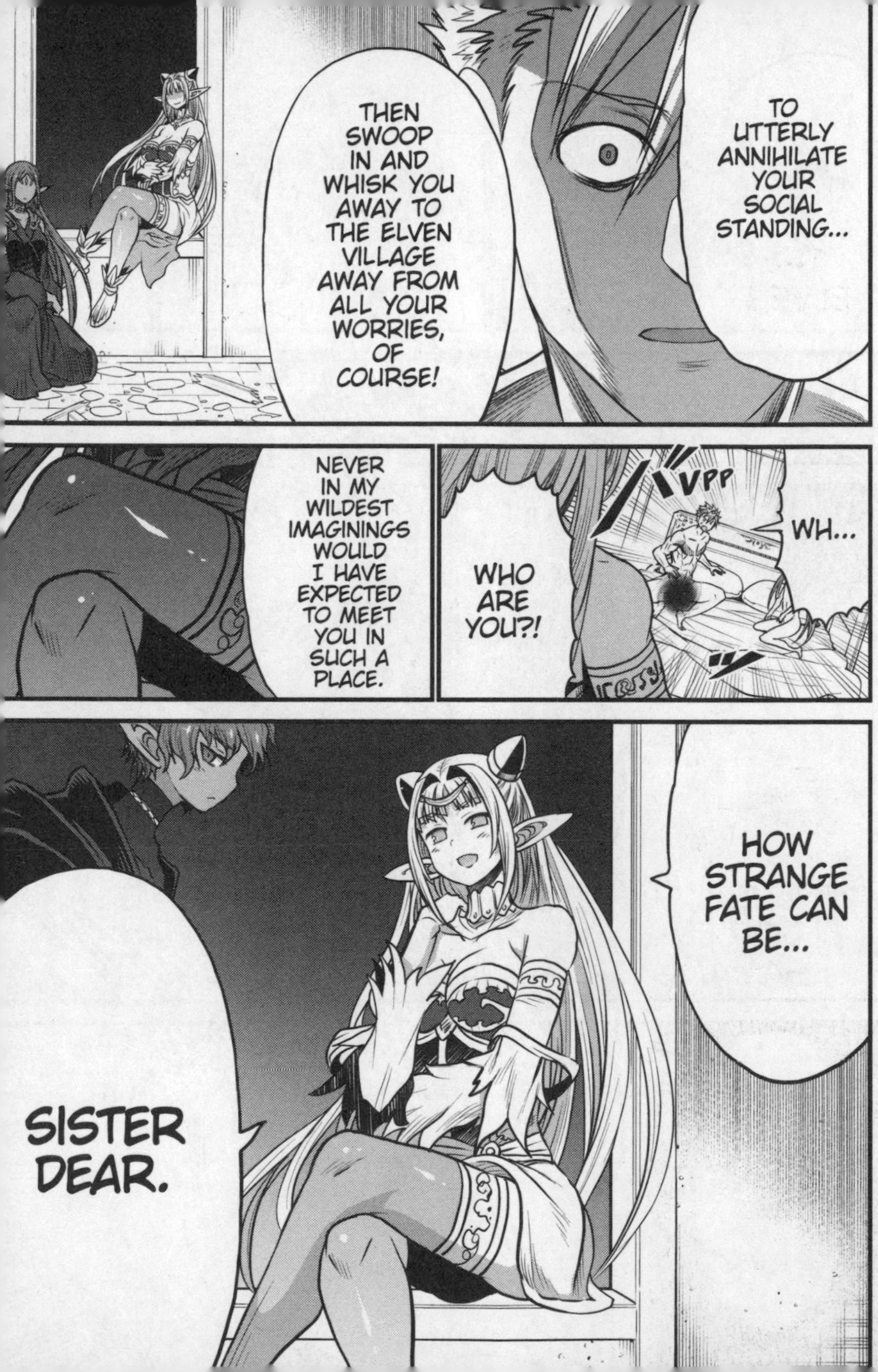
TO UTTERLY ANNIHILATE YOUR SOCIAL STANDING...
THEN SWOOP IN AND WHISK YOU AWAY TO THE ELVEN VILLAGE AWAY FROM ALL YOUR WORRIES, OF COURSE!
VPP
WH...
WHO ARE YOU?!
NEVER IN MY WILDEST IMAGININGS WOULD I HAVE EXPECTED TO MEET YOU IN SUCH A PLACE.
HOW STRANGE FATE CAN BE...
SISTER DEAR.

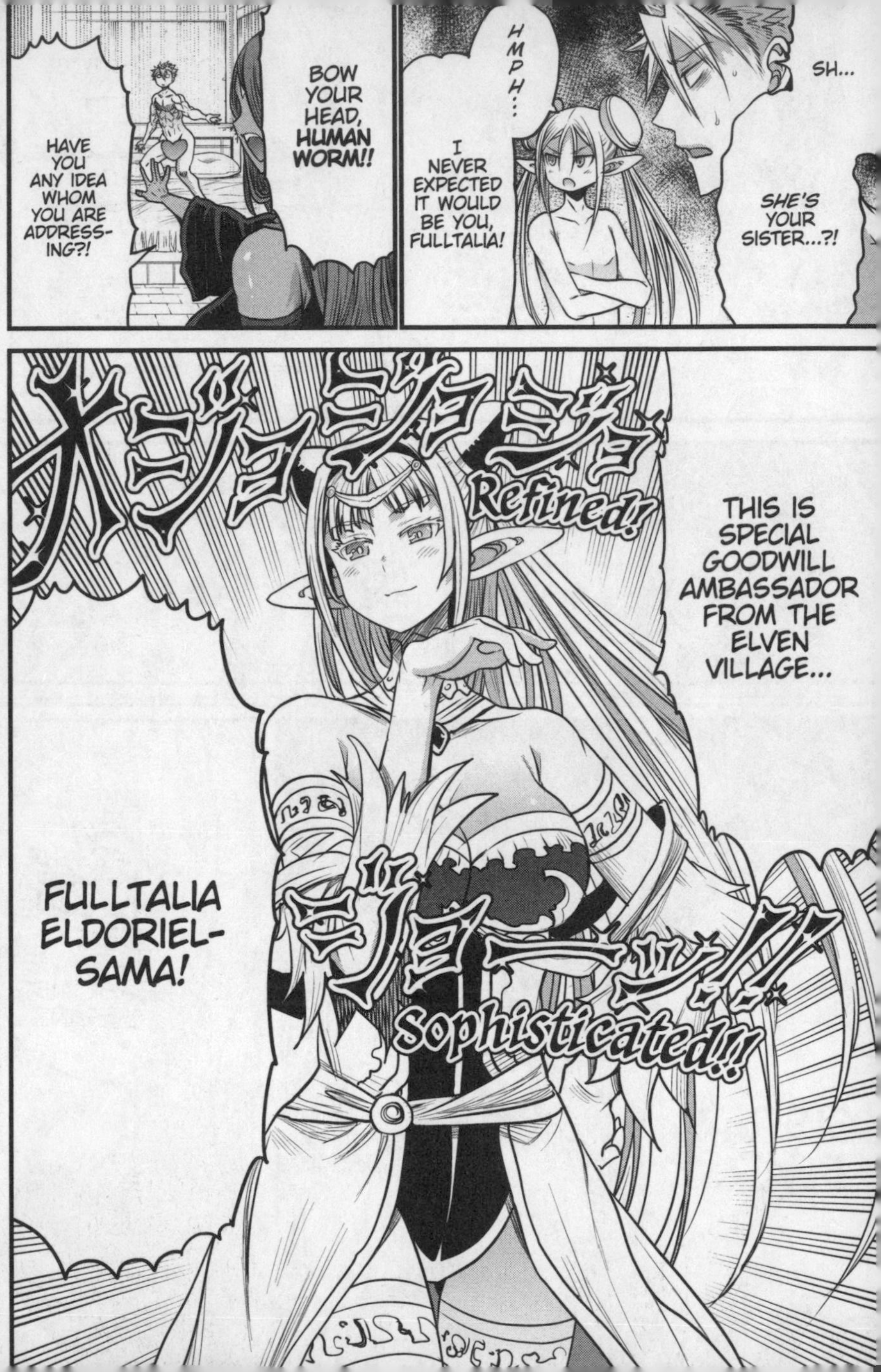
SH...
SHE'S YOUR SISTER...?!
HMPH...
I NEVER EXPECTED IT WOULD BE YOU, FULLTALIA!
BOW YOUR HEAD, HUMAN WORM!!
HAVE YOU ANY IDEA WHOM YOU ARE ADDRESSING?!
Refined!
THIS IS SPECIAL GOODWILL AMBASSADOR FROM THE ELVEN VILLAGE...
FULLTALIA ELDORIEL-SAMA!
Sophisticated!!

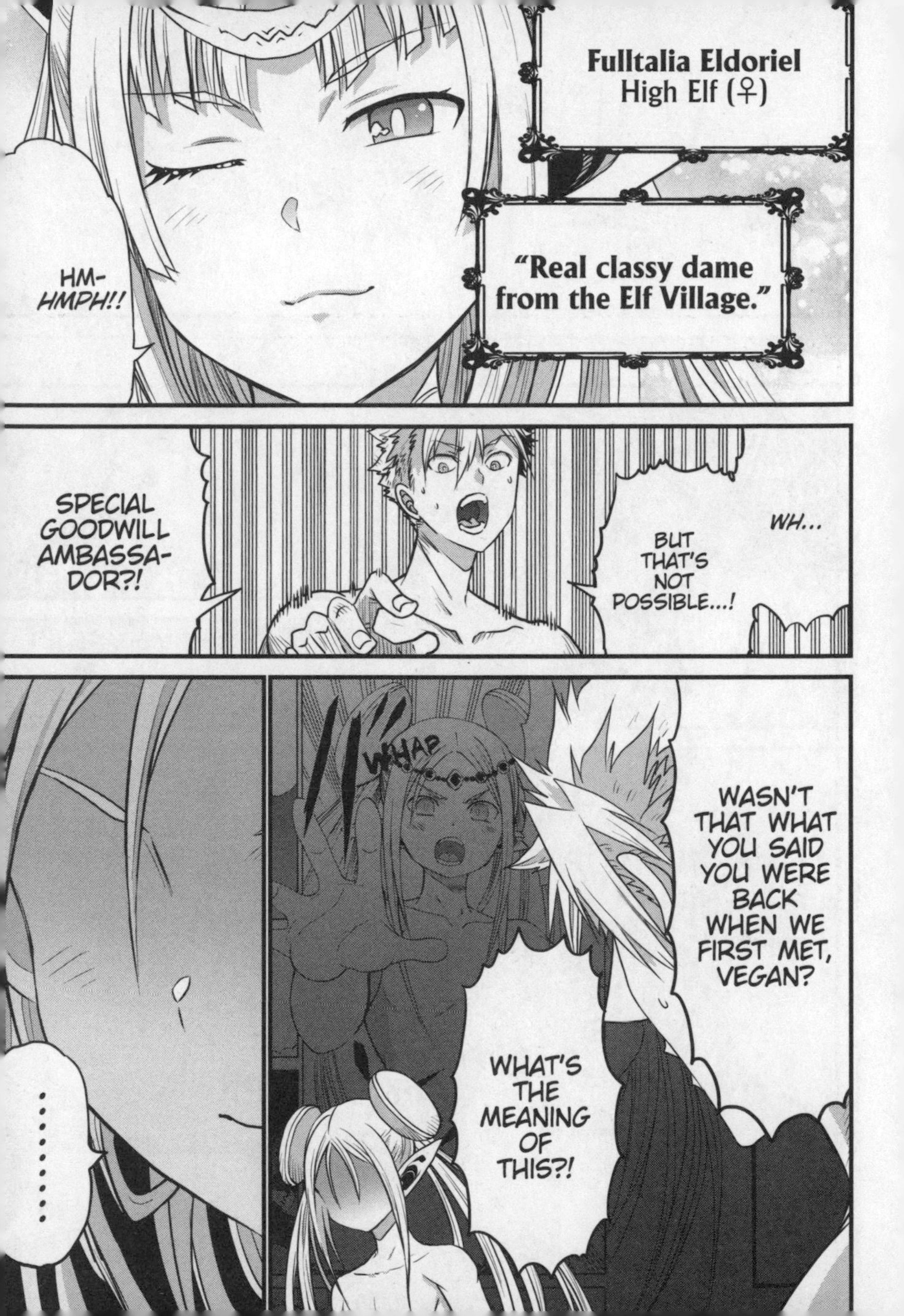
Fulltalia Eldoriel
High Elf (♀)
"Real classy dame from the Elf Village."
HM-HMPH!!
WH...
BUT THAT'S NOT POSSIBLE...!
SPECIAL GOODWILL AMBASSADOR?!
WHAP
WASN'T THAT WHAT YOU SAID YOU WERE BACK WHEN WE FIRST MET, VEGAN?
WHAT'S THE MEANING OF THIS?!
....

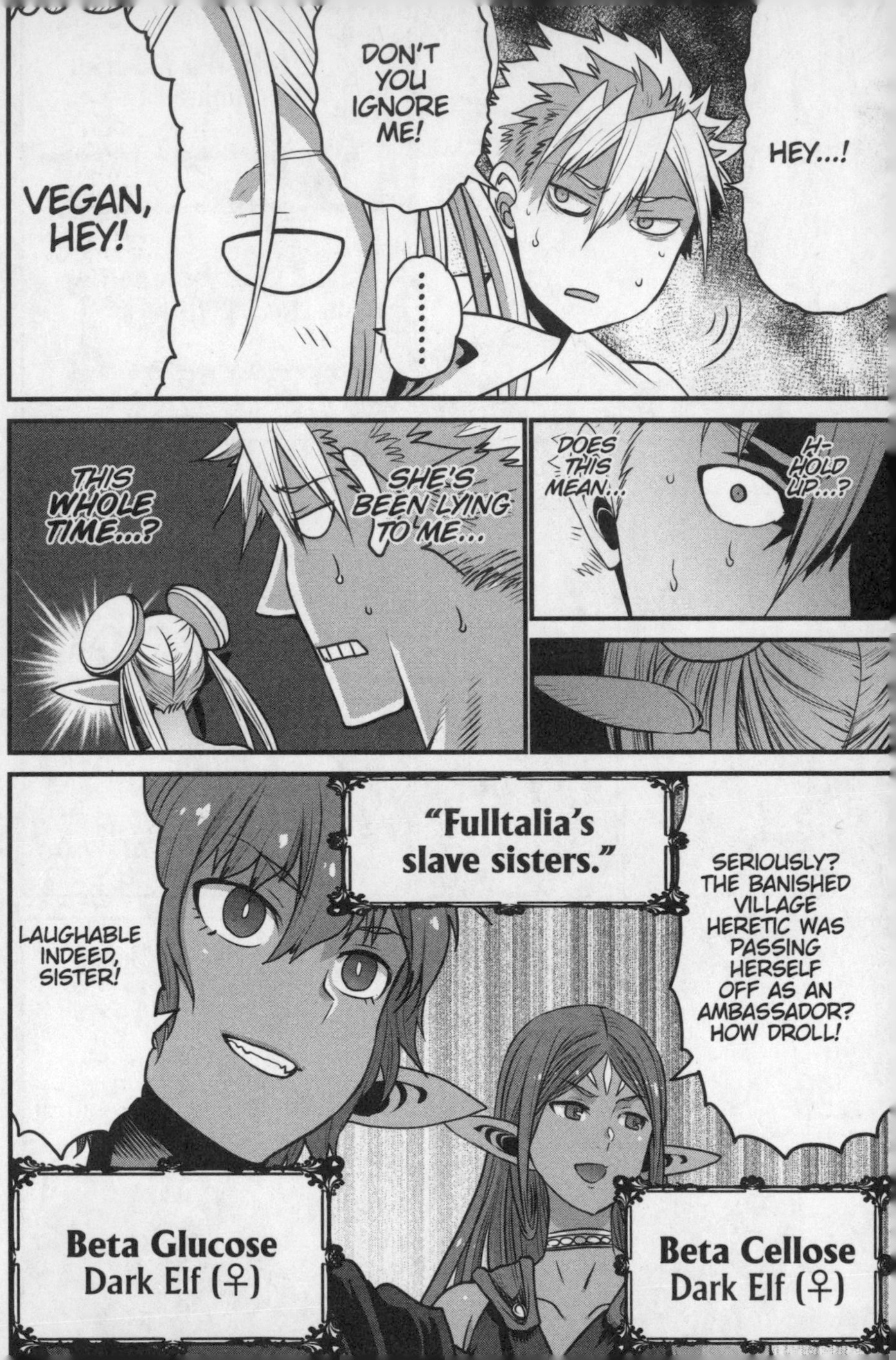
HEY...!
DON'T YOU IGNORE ME!
....
VEGAN, HEY!
H-HOLD UP...?
DOES THIS MEAN...
SHE'S BEEN LYING TO ME...
THIS WHOLE TIME...?
"Fulltalia's slave sisters."
SERIOUSLY? THE BANISHED VILLAGE HERETIC WAS PASSING HERSELF OFF AS AN AMBASSADOR? HOW DROLL!
LAUGHABLE INDEED, SISTER!
Beta Cellose Dark Elf (♀)
Beta Glucose Dark Elf (♀)

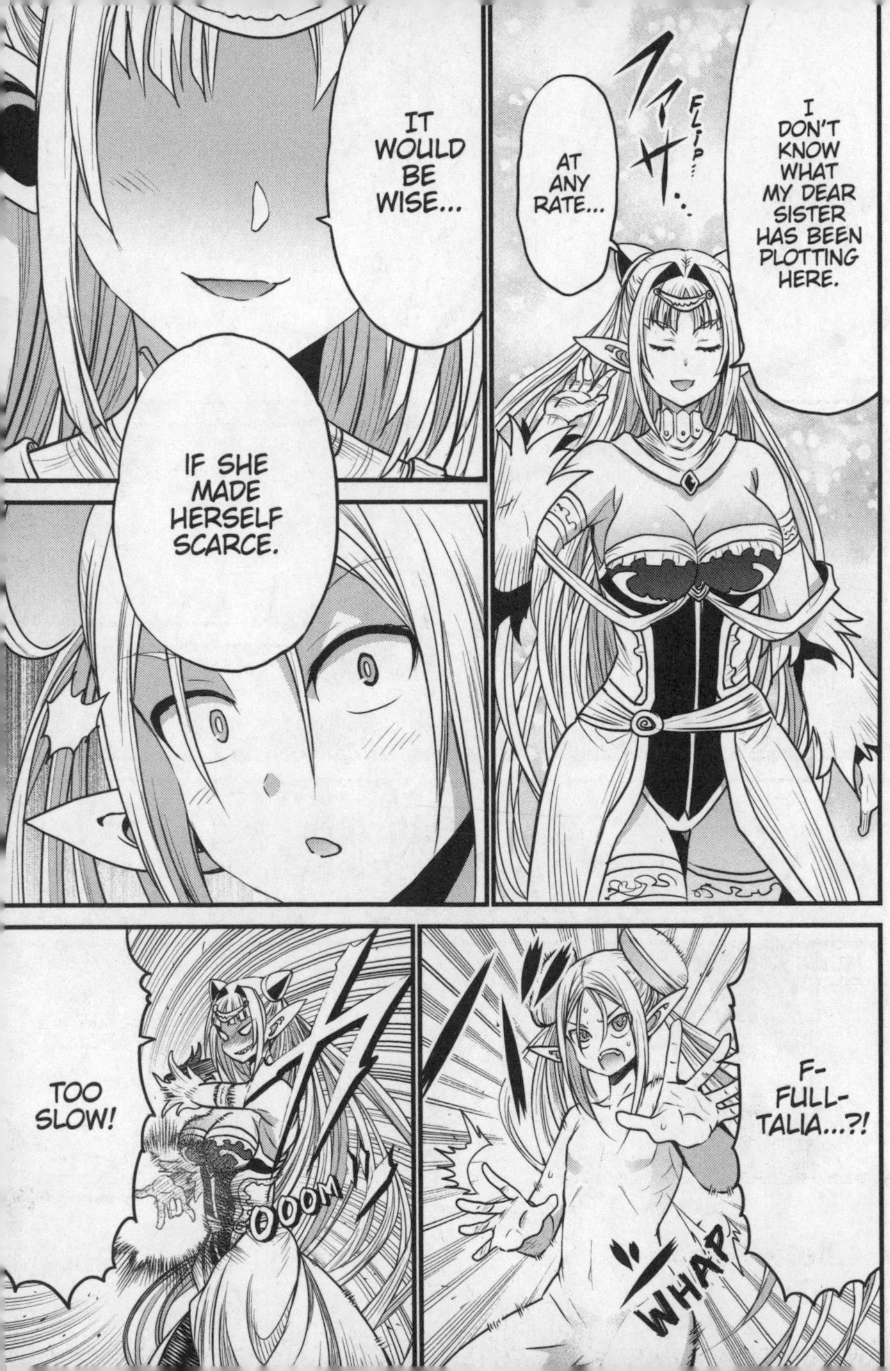
I DON'T KNOW WHAT MY DEAR SISTER HAS BEEN PLOTTING HERE.
FLIP...
AT ANY RATE...
IT WOULD BE WISE...
IF SHE MADE HERSELF SCARCE.
F-FULL-TALIA...?!
WHAP
TOO SLOW!
DOOM

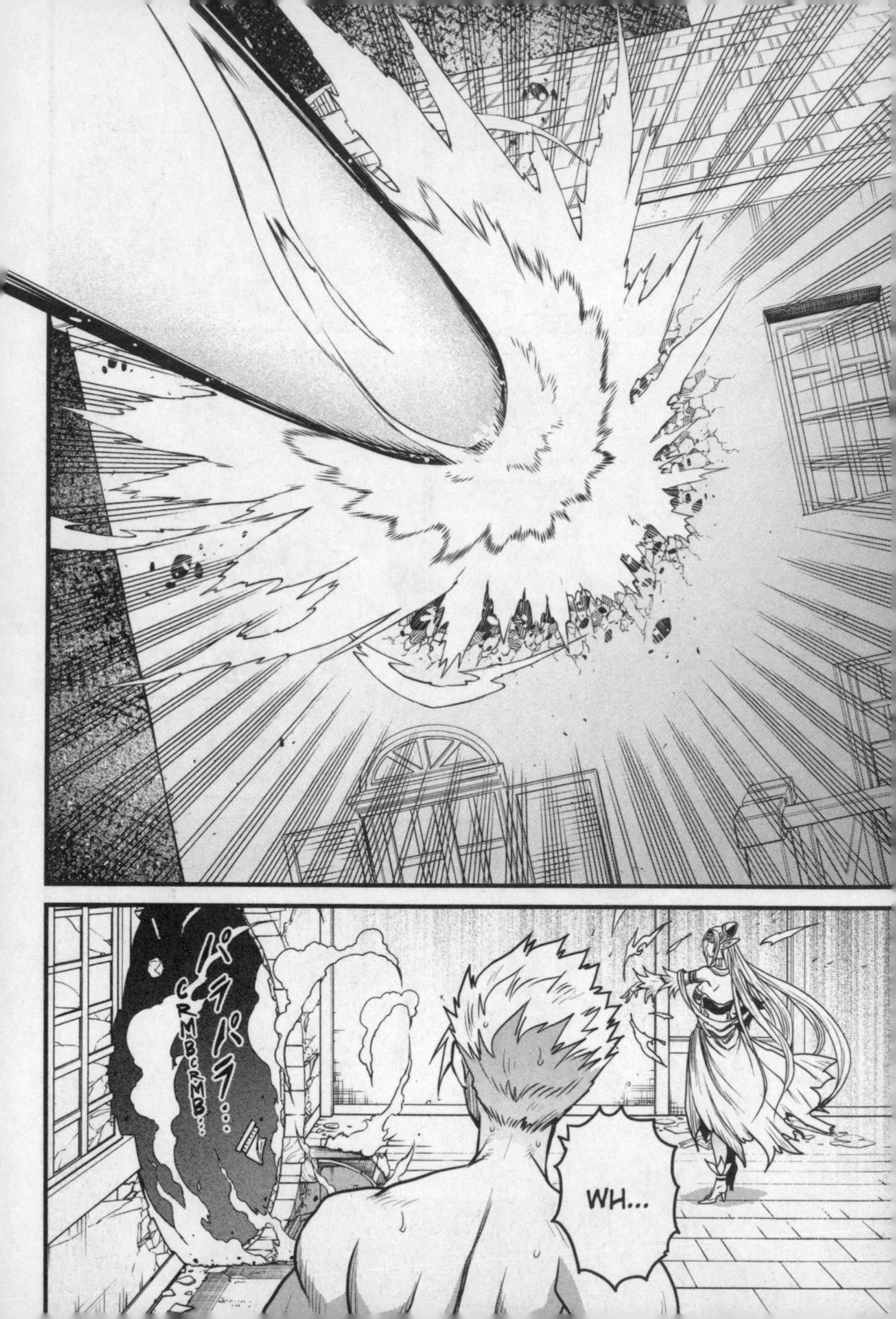
WH...
パラパラ…
CRMBCRMB...

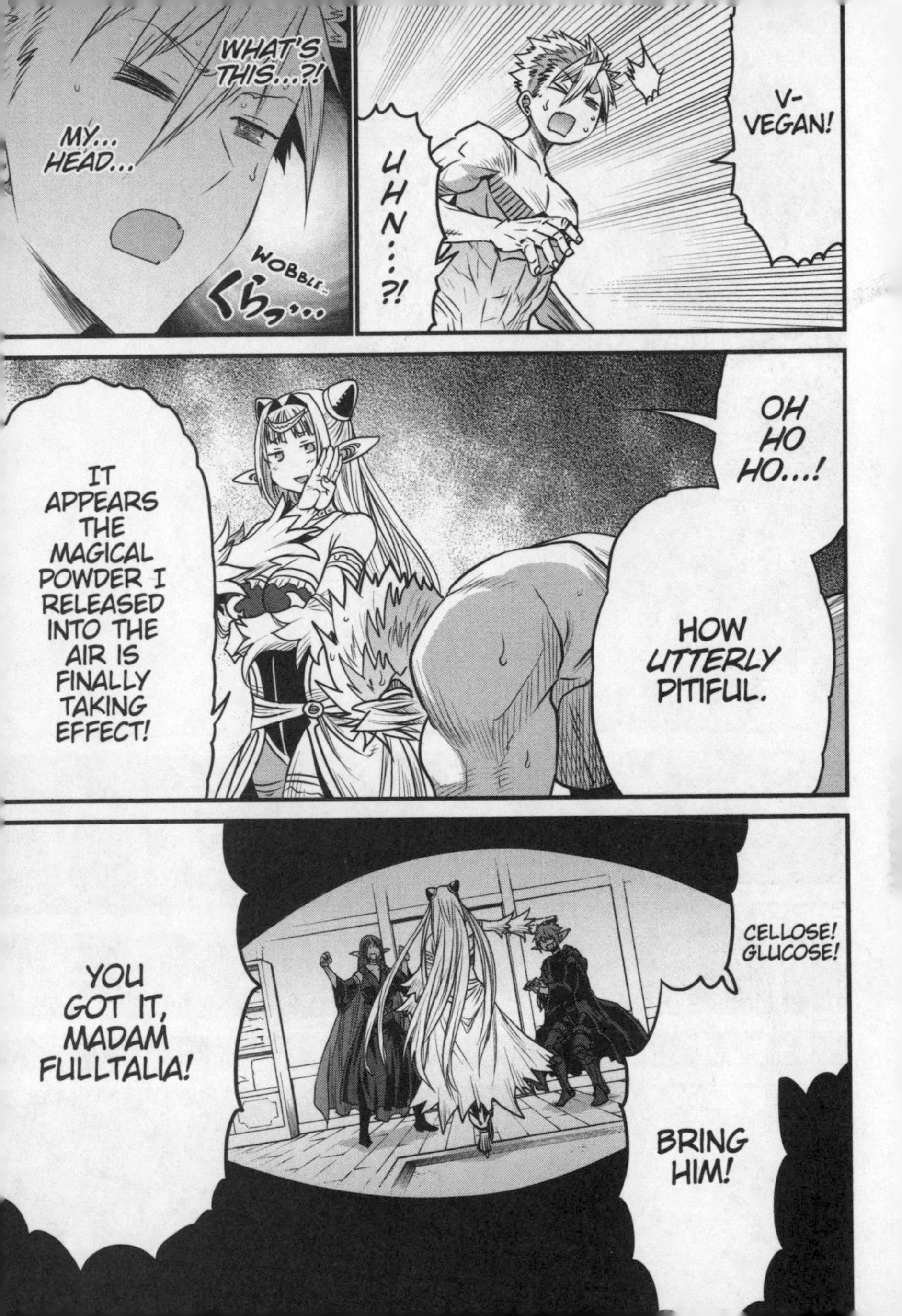
V- VEGAN!
UHN...?!
WHAT'S THIS...?!
MY... HEAD...
WOBBLE...
くらっ・・・
OH HO HO...!
HOW UTTERLY PITIFUL.
IT APPEARS THE MAGICAL POWDER I RELEASED INTO THE AIR IS FINALLY TAKING EFFECT!
CELLOSE! GLUCOSE!
BRING HIM!
YOU GOT IT, MADAM FULLTALIA!

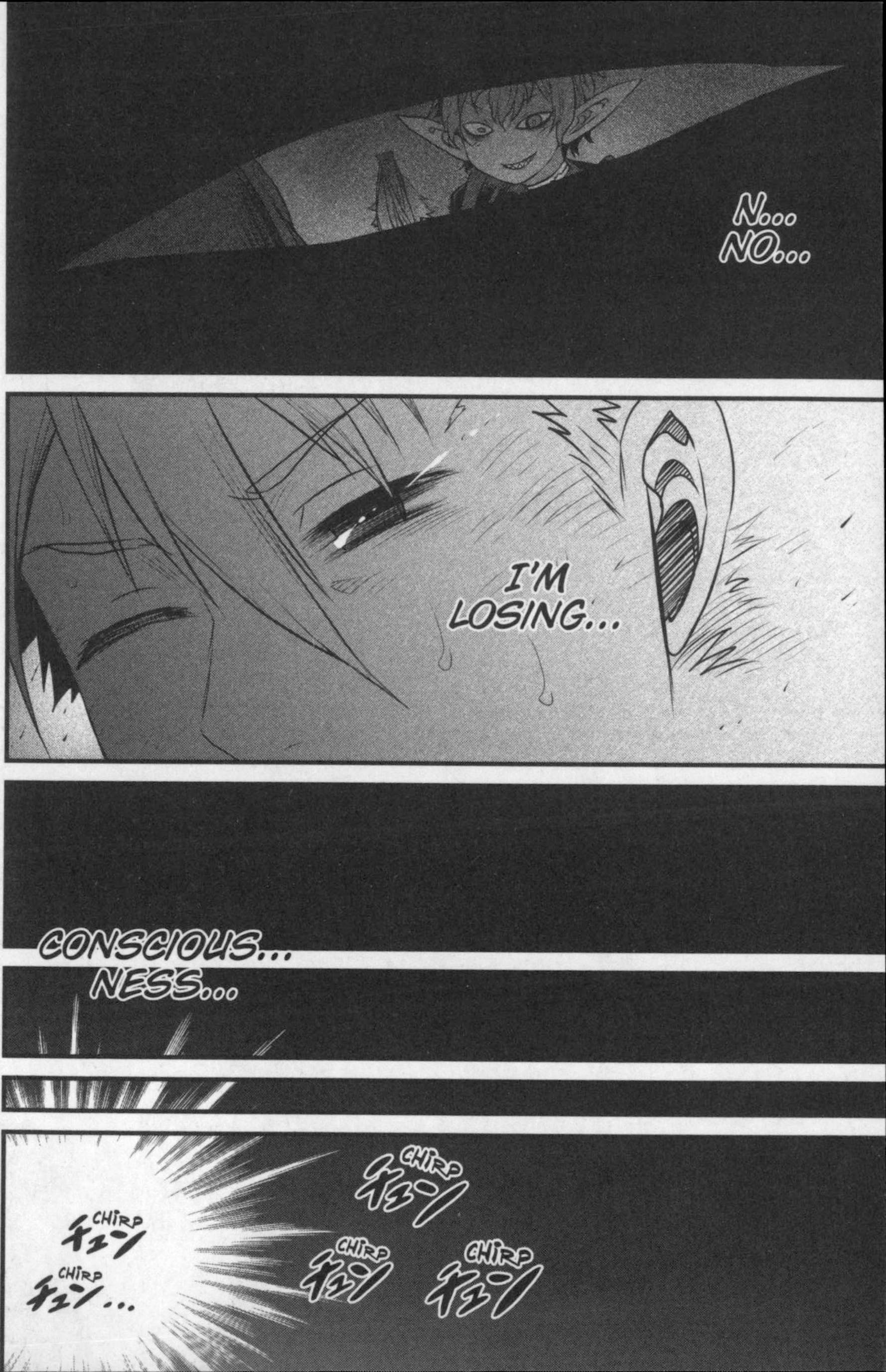
N...
NO...
I'M LOSING...
CONSCIOUS...
...NESS...
CHIRP
チュン
CHIRP
チュン
CHIRP
チュン
CHIRP
チュン
CHIRP
チュン...

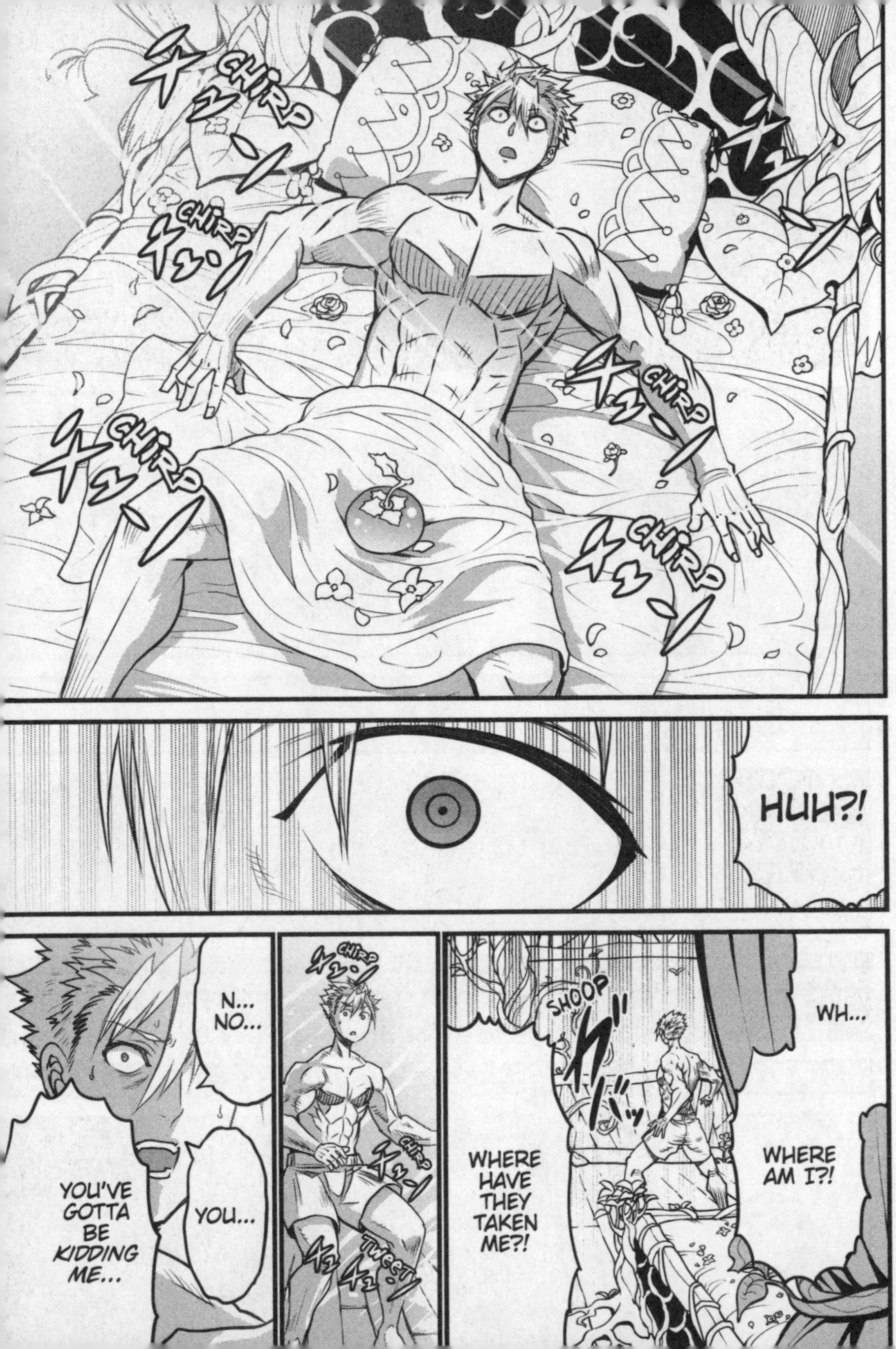
CHIRP
CHIRP
CHIRP
CHIRP
CHIRP
HUH?!
WH...
SHOOP
WHERE AM I?!
WHERE HAVE THEY TAKEN ME?!
CHIRP
CHIRP
TWEET
N... NO...
YOU...
YOU'VE GOTTA BE KIDDING ME...

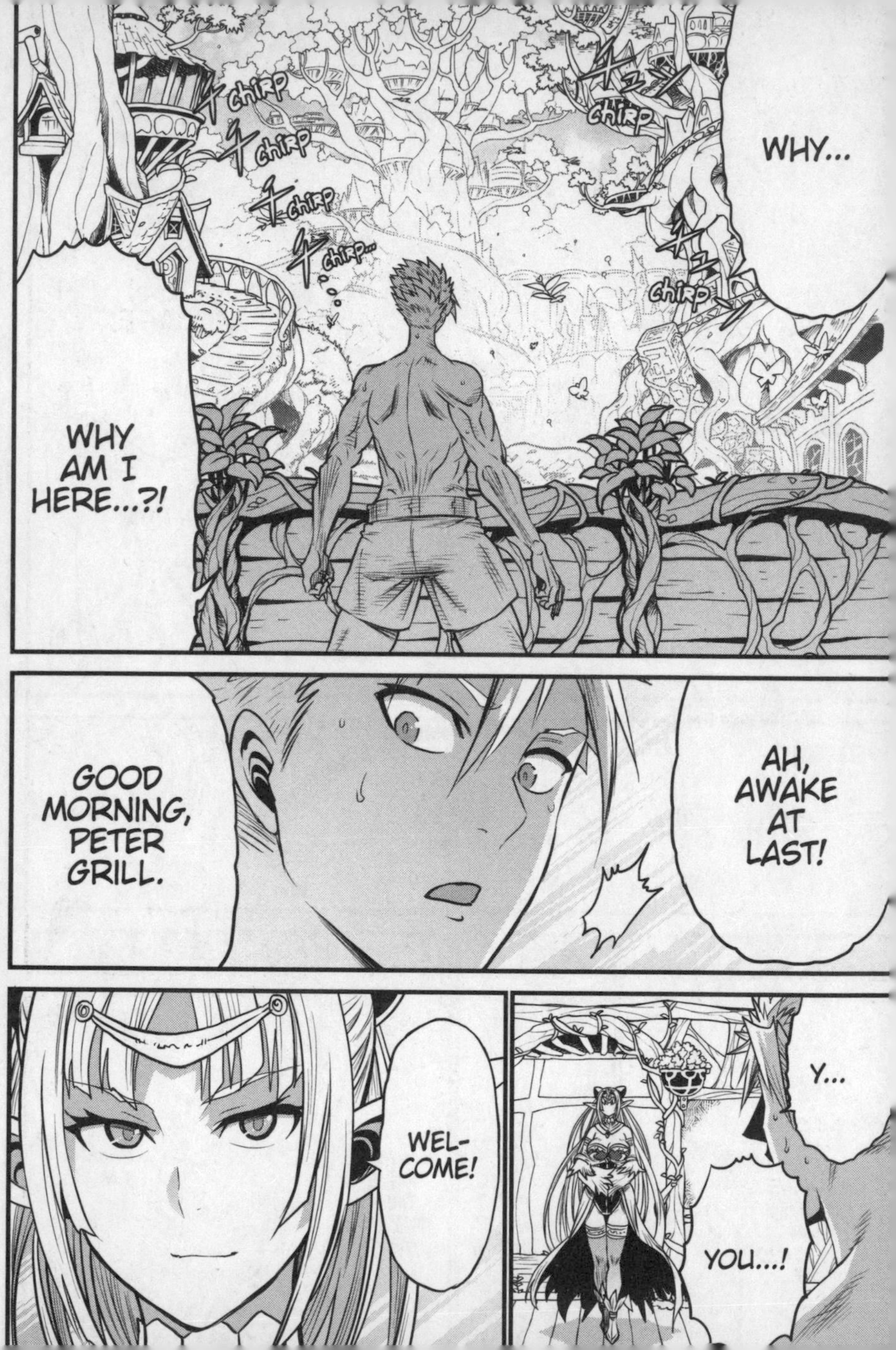
chirp
WHY...
chirp
chirp
chirp
chirp
chirp...
WHY AM I HERE...?!
AH, AWAKE AT LAST!
GOOD MORNING, PETER GRILL.
Y...
YOU...!
WEL-COME!

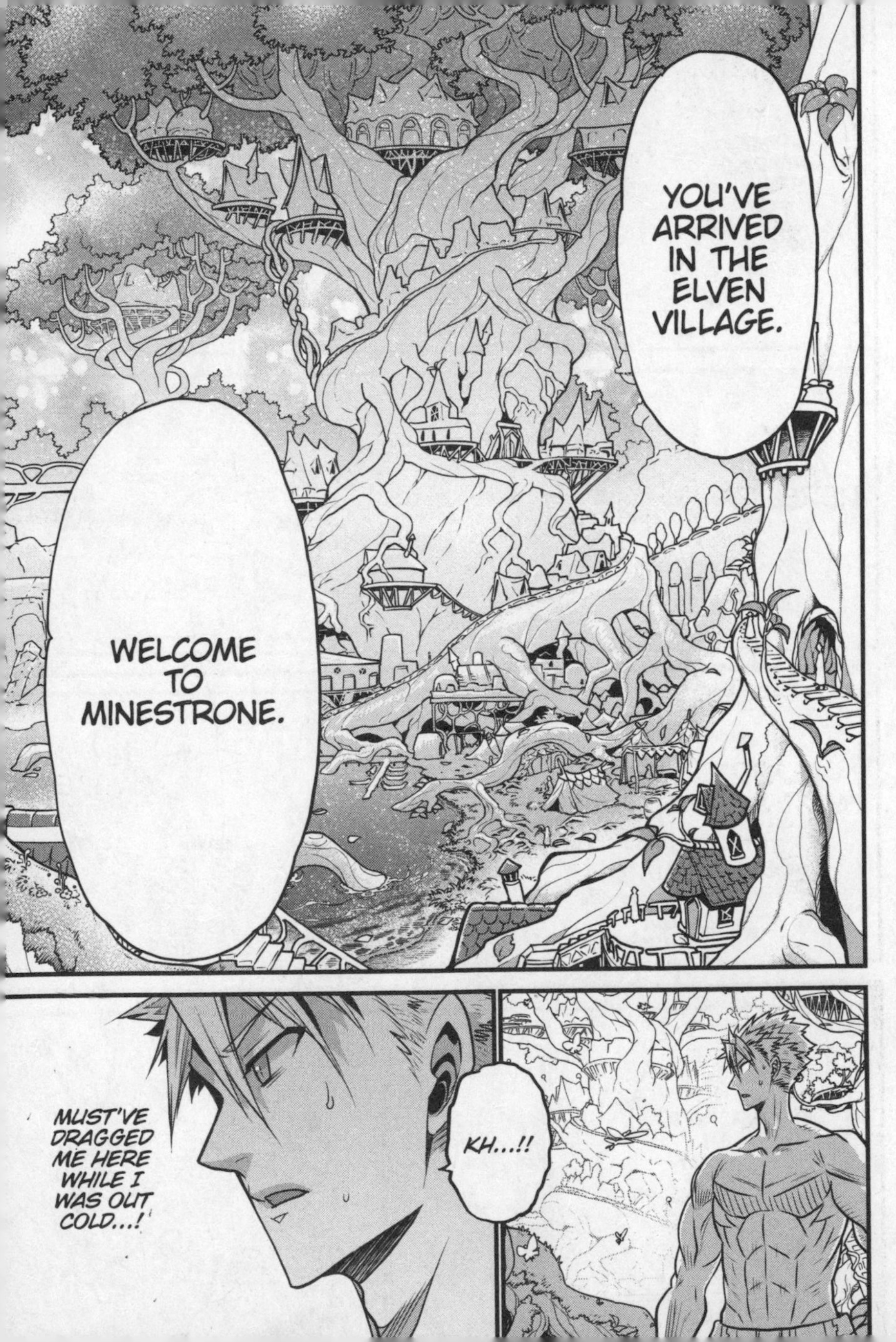
YOU'VE ARRIVED IN THE ELVEN VILLAGE.
WELCOME TO MINESTRONE.
KH...!!
MUST'VE DRAGGED ME HERE WHILE I WAS OUT COLD...!

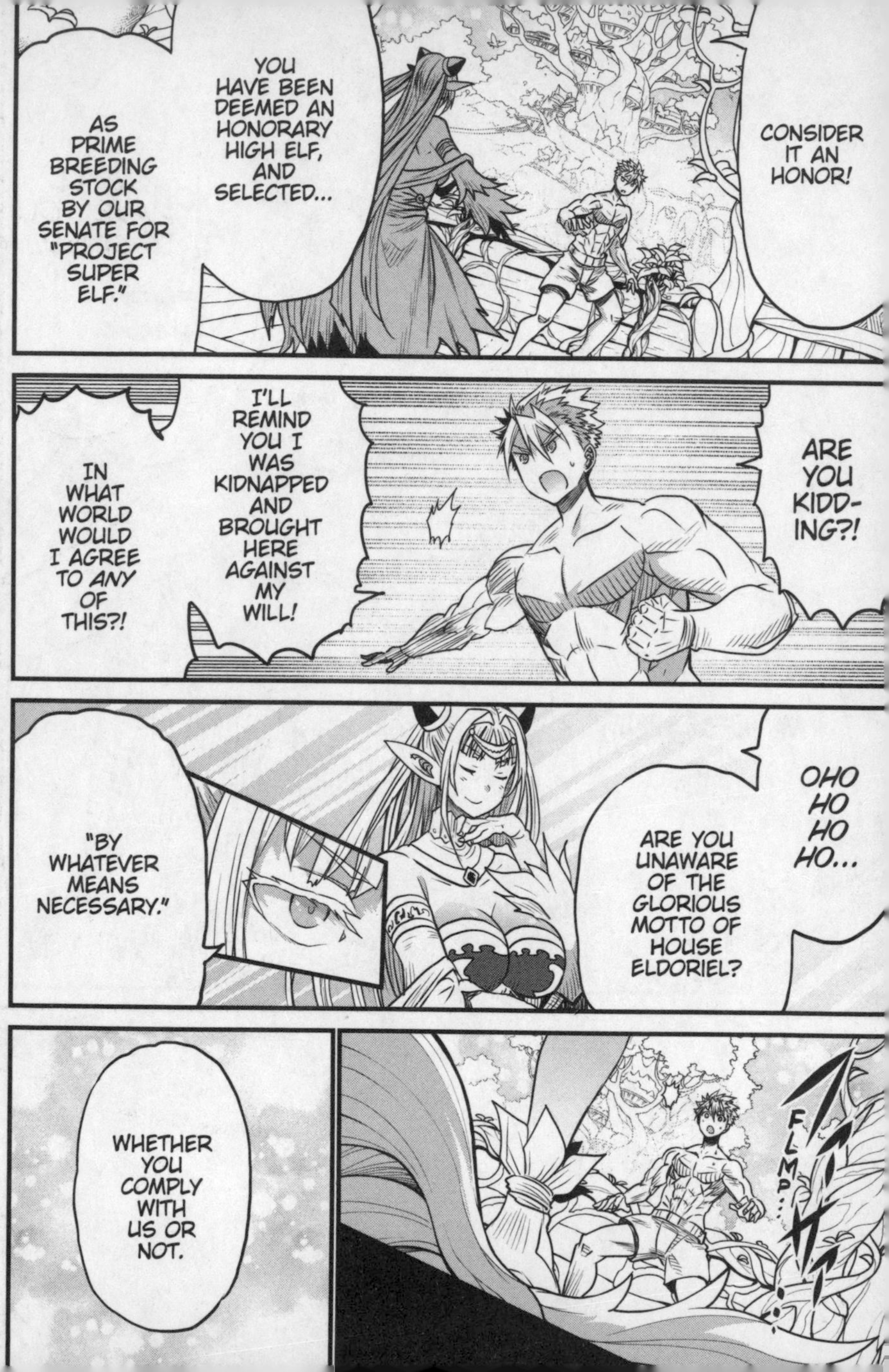
CONSIDER IT AN HONOR!
YOU HAVE BEEN DEEMED AN HONORARY HIGH ELF, AND SELECTED...
AS PRIME BREEDING STOCK BY OUR SENATE FOR "PROJECT SUPER ELF."
ARE YOU KIDD-ING?!
I'LL REMIND YOU I WAS KIDNAPPED AND BROUGHT HERE AGAINST MY WILL!
IN WHAT WORLD WOULD I AGREE TO *ANY* OF THIS?!
OHO HO HO HO...
ARE YOU UNAWARE OF THE GLORIOUS MOTTO OF HOUSE ELDORIEL?
"BY WHATEVER MEANS NECESSARY."
FLMP...
WHETHER YOU COMPLY WITH US OR NOT.

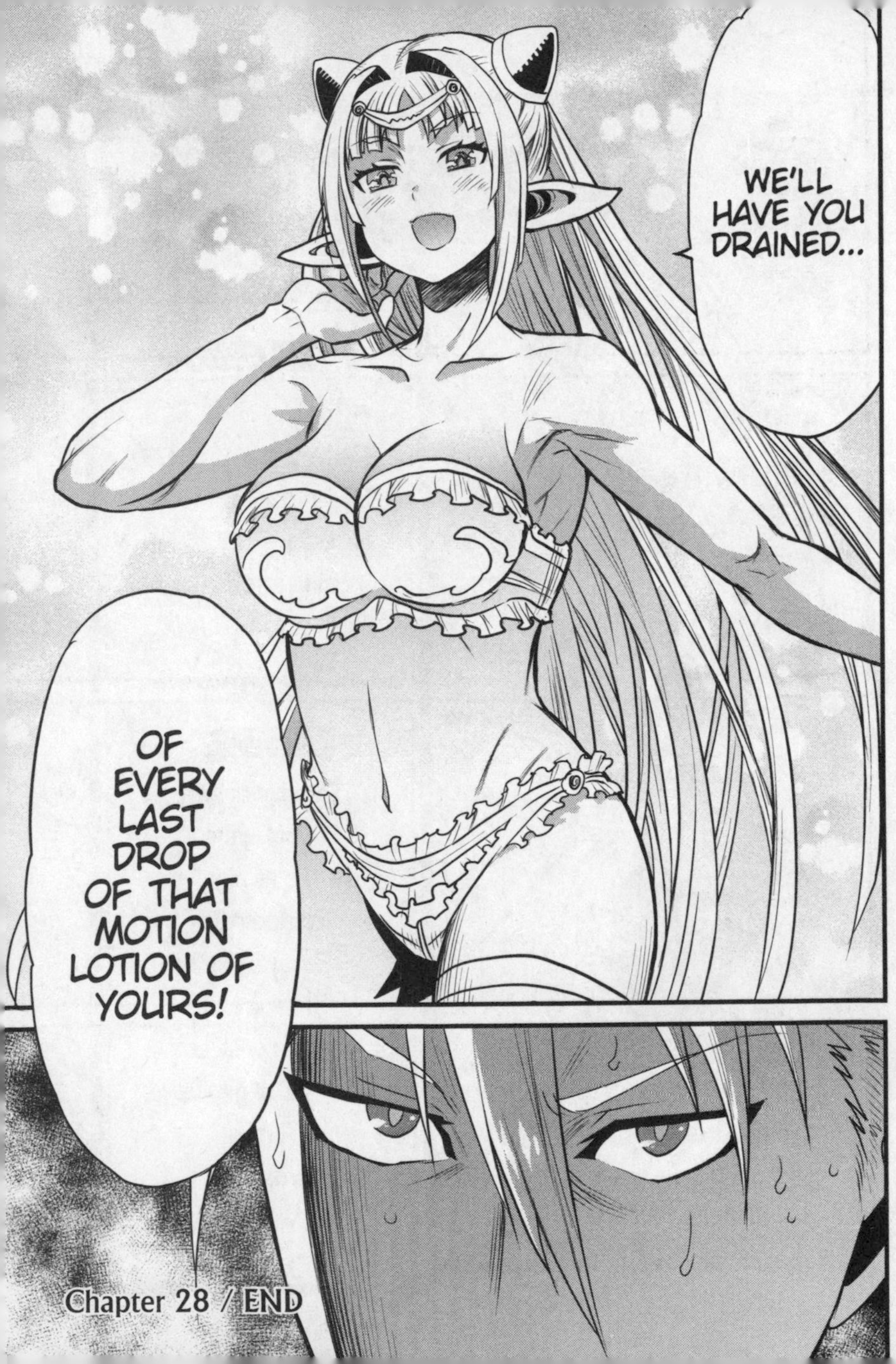
WE'LL HAVE YOU DRAINED...
OF EVERY LAST DROP OF THAT MOTION LOTION OF YOURS!
Chapter 28 / END

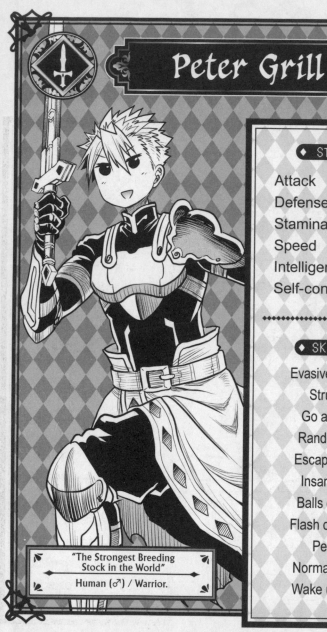

Peter Grill

"The Strongest Breeding Stock in the World"

Human (♂) / Warrior.

STATS

Attack	99
Defense	99
Stamina	99
Speed	99
Intelligence	7
Self-control	2

SKILLS

Evasive answer
Struggle
Go all night
Random flail
Escape death
Insane luck
Balls of steel
Flash of genius
Persist
Normal punch
Wake up early

Mimi Alpacas

◆ STATS ◆

Attack	75
Stamina	55
Speed	22
Intelligence	4
Teamwork	1
Shamelessness	99

◆ SKILLS ◆

Fast eater
Go all night
Horse riding master
Magic resistance
Expensive earplugs
Reckless charge
Deceive
Unconventional attack
Smash
Greatly inconvenient
Destroyer of objects

"Muscle-brain"

Ogre (♀) / Warrior

NEXT

An elf's issues become Peter's problem?! The "Unlucky Pervert" strikes again!

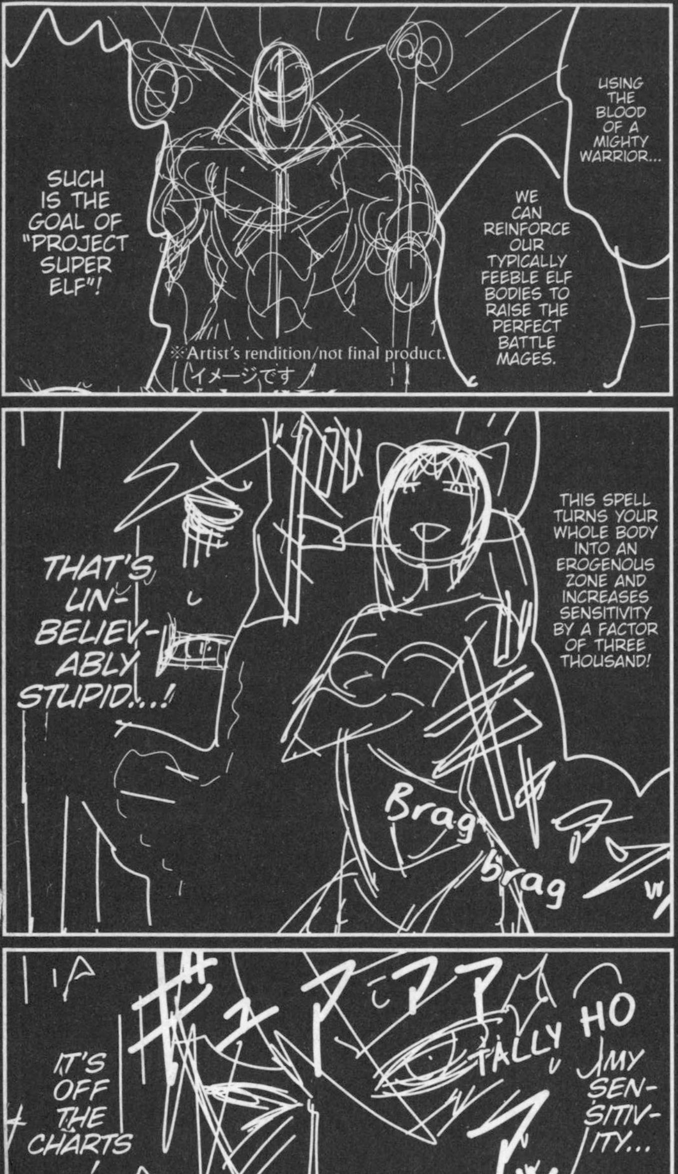
USING THE BLOOD OF A MIGHTY WARRIOR...
WE CAN REINFORCE OUR TYPICALLY FEEBLE ELF BODIES TO RAISE THE PERFECT BATTLE MAGES.
SUCH IS THE GOAL OF "PROJECT SUPER ELF"!
※Artist's rendition/not final product.
イメージです
THIS SPELL TURNS YOUR WHOLE BODY INTO AN EROGENOUS ZONE AND INCREASES SENSITIVITY BY A FACTOR OF THREE THOUSAND!
THAT'S UN-BELIEV-ABLY STUPID...!
Brag
brag
HO
TALLY
MY SEN-SITIV-ITY...
IT'S OFF THE CHARTS...!

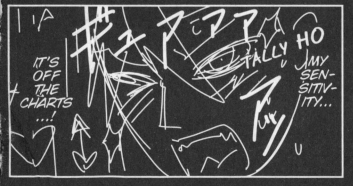

Sensitivity rising! Willpower falling!! Caught between a rock and a hard place, will Peter end up rock hard?

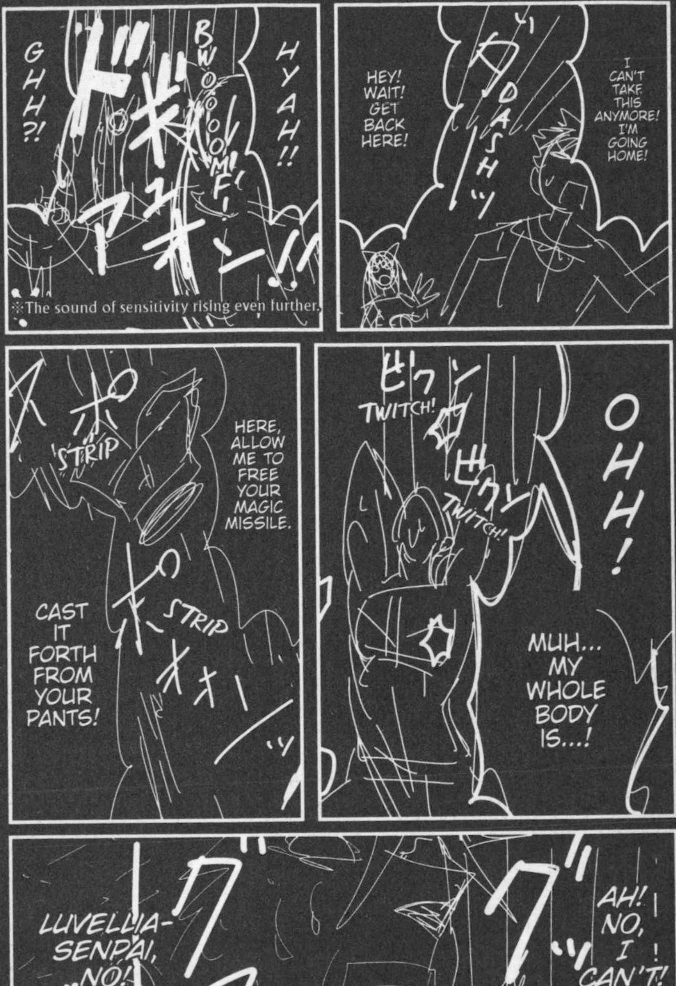
I CAN'T TAKE THIS ANYMORE! I'M GOING HOME!
DASH
HEY! WAIT! GET BACK HERE!
HYAAH!!
BWOOOOOMF!
GHHH?!
※The sound of sensitivity rising even further.
OHHH!
TWITCH!
TWITCH!
MUH... MY WHOLE BODY IS...!
HERE, ALLOW ME TO FREE YOUR MAGIC MISSILE.
STRIP
STRIP
CAST IT FORTH FROM YOUR PANTS!
AH! NO, I CAN'T!
waah!!
LUVELLIA-SENPAI, NO! DON'T DO IT, LUVELLIA-SENPAI!!!!!!

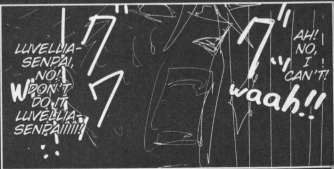

Peter Grill and the Philosopher's Time
Volume Seven—Coming soon!!!

SEVEN SEAS' GHOST SHIP PRESENTS

PETER GRILL
AND THE PHILOSOPHER'S TIME

story and art by DAISUKE HIYAMA   VOLUME 6

TRANSLATION
Ben Trethewey

ADAPTATION
David Lumsdon

LETTERING
Mo Harrison

COVER DESIGN
Nicky Lim

LOGO DESIGN
Kris Aubin

COPY EDITOR
Dawn Davis

EDITOR
Elise Kelsey

PREPRESS TECHNICIAN
Rhiannon Rasmussen-Silverstein

PRODUCTION MANAGER - GHOST SHIP
George Panella

PRODUCTION MANAGER
Lissa Pattillo

MANAGING EDITOR
Julie Davis

ASSOCIATE PUBLISHER
Adam Arnold

PUBLISHER
Jason DeAngelis

PETER GRILL AND THE PHILOSOPHER'S TIME VOL. 6
© Daisuke Hiyama 2017
All rights reserved.
First published in Japan in 2020 by Futabasha Publishers Ltd., Tokyo.
English version published by Seven Seas Entertainment.
Under license from Futabasha Publishers Ltd.

No portion of this book may be reproduced or transmitted in any form without written permission from the copyright holders. This is a work of fiction. Names, characters, places, and incidents are the products of the author's imagination or are used fictitiously. Any resemblance to actual events, locales, or persons, living or dead, is entirely coincidental. Any information or opinions expressed by the creators of this book belong to those individual creators and do not necessarily reflect the views of Seven Seas Entertainment or its employees.

Seven Seas press and purchase enquiries can be sent to Marketing Manager Lianne Sentar at press@gomanga.com. Information regarding the distribution and purchase of digital editions is available from Digital Manager CK Russell at digital@gomanga.com.

Seven Seas and the Seven Seas logo are trademarks of Seven Seas Entertainment. All rights reserved.

ISBN: 978-1-64827-356-8
Printed in Canada
First Printing: October 2021
10 9 8 7 6 5 4 3 2 1

▓▓▓▓ READING DIRECTIONS ▓▓▓▓

This book reads from *right to left*, Japanese style. If this is your first time reading manga, you start reading from the top right panel on each page and take it from there. If you get lost, just follow the numbered diagram here. It may seem backwards at first, but you'll get the hang of it! Have fun!!

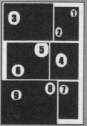